Landscape De

MW00800918

Architects, landscape architects and urban designers experiment with color and lighting effects in their daily professional practice. Over the past decade, there has been a reinvigorated discussion on color within architectural and cultural studies. Yet, scholarly enquiry within landscape architecture has been minimal despite its important role in landscape design.

This book posits that though color and lighting effects appear natural, fleeting, and difficult to comprehend, the sensory palette of built landscapes and gardens has been carefully constructed to shape our experience and evoke meaning and place character. *Landscape Design in Color: History, Theory, and Practice 1750 to Today* is an inquiry into the themes, theories, and debates on color and its impact on practice in Western landscape architecture over the past three centuries.

Divided into three key periods, each chapter in the book looks at the use of color in the written and built work of key prominent designers. The book investigates thematic juxtapositions such as: natural and artificial; color and line; design and draftsmanship; sensation and concept; imitation and translation; deception and display; and decoration and structure, and how these have appeared, faded, disappeared, and reappeared throughout the ages. Richly designed and illustrated in full color throughout, including color palettes, this book is a must-have resource for students, scholars, and design professionals in landscape architecture and its allied disciplines.

Mira Engler studied landscape architecture and architecture. She is an Emerita Professor of Landscape Architecture at Iowa State University. Her first book *Designing America's Waste Landscapes* and *Cut* explores societal and professional attitudes toward waste and the design of dumps and sewage grounds. Her second book *Cut and Paste Urban: Landscape: The Work of Gordon Cullen* explores image making in landscape and urban design in the postwar consumer culture era through the drawings and writing of Gordon Cullen, respectively. She currently studies immersive landscapes and virtual media culture.

Landscape Design in Color

History, Theory, and Practice 1750 to Today

Mira Engler

Routledge
Taylor & Francis Group

LONDON AND NEW YORK

Front & Back Covers. Photographic collage of Woburn Abbey gardens by Humphry Repton (back layer), Union Bank Plaza by Eckbo, Dean, Austin, Williams (middle layer), and Davis Garden by Martha Schwartz Partners (front layer). Photos: Mira Engler

First published 2023
by Routledge
4 Park Square, Milton Park, Abingdon, Oxon OX14 4RN

and by Routledge
605 Third Avenue, New York, NY 10158

Routledge is an imprint of the Taylor & Francis Group, an informa business

© 2023 Mira Engler

The right of Mira Engler to be identified as author of this work has been asserted in accordance with sections 77 and 78 of the Copyright, Designs and Patents Act 1988.

All rights reserved. No part of this book may be reprinted or reproduced or utilised in any form or by any electronic, mechanical, or other means, now known or hereafter invented, including photocopying and recording, or in any information storage or retrieval system, without permission in writing from the publishers.

Trademark notice: Product or corporate names may be trademarks or registered trademarks, and are used only for identification and explanation without intent to infringe.

British Library Cataloguing-in-Publication Data
A catalogue record for this book is available from the British Library

Library of Congress Cataloging-in-Publication Data
A catalog record has been requested for this book

ISBN: 9781138343955 (hbk)
ISBN: 9781138343962 (pbk)
ISBN: 9780429438790 (ebk)

DOI: 10.4324/9780429438790

Typeset in Perpetua and Helvetica Neue
by polytekton, Ames, Iowa, USA

Publisher's Note
This book has been prepared from camera-ready copy provided by the author.

To

My Blue Garden

My grandchildren Eden and Asher who fill my life with color

and

All those who chase away darkness and fill the world with light

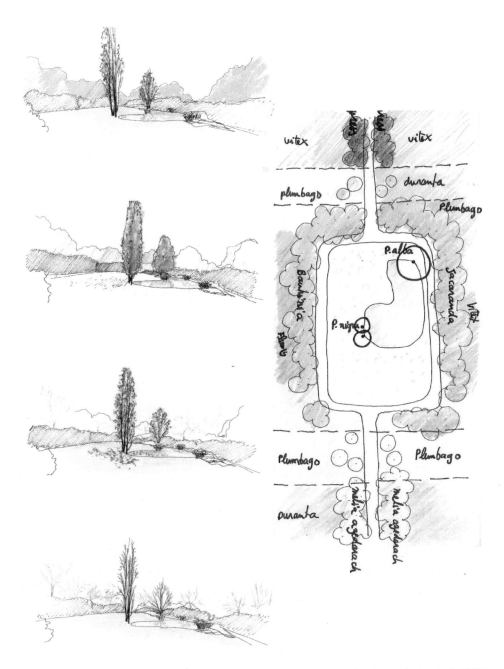

Mira Engler, "My Blue Garden," composite drawing, environmental autobiography, student project, 1977

Preface

M y scholarly interest in color first surfaced in a conversation with my doctoral advisor, Sylvia Lavin, a professor and architectural theorist at the University of California, Los Angeles. Her focus on color as an instrument of affect, one that announces a contemporary sensibility, or what she calls "presentness," informed my dissertation on the postwar work of the British architectural illustrator Gordon Cullen. Color was one of Cullen's representational devices to signal urban modernity. This small but meaningful exploration of color triggered a floodgate of ideas and made me conscious of the absence of color discourse in landscape architecture theory, even as color gained prominence in contemporary landscape and urban design practice, enhanced by digital representation programs and computer interfaces.

More deeply, I can trace my interest in color back to my neighborhood public park where I grew up in Holon, Israel. It was named "The Blue Garden" but we kids called it simply "the garden." Everything about it was designed with the color blue in mind. The amoeba-shaped fishpond at the center mirrored the blue skies, and all the surrounding trees and shrubs blossomed in blue and purple. I spent most of my out-of-school time playing there with neighborhood kids. We took over the lawns, benches, trees, bushes, and flowers for our games. I remember the clouds of purplish-bluish flower bundles and castanet-like fruits of the *Jacaranda mimosifolia* trees planted around the park's edges; the fragrant pink, purple, and white orchid-like flower of the *Bauhinia purpurea*; the purple flower clumps and minty smell of the leaves of *Buddleja* 'Lochinch,' the *Rosmarinus officinalis*, and the *Salvia leucantha*; the musky scent of the *Vitex agnus-castus*; the purplish flowers of the low-lying *Lantana montevidensis*; and the light blue flowers of the pervasive *Plumbago capensis* shrub. We carried the sticky flowers of the plumbago on our clothes and hair when we came out of our hiding places in the bushes during hide-and-seek.

It was only later, when I enrolled in landscape architecture at the Technion in Haifa that I learned about Zvi Miller, of Miller-Blume Landscape Architects, who designed the garden. Writing this book unraveled the trajectory that linked Miller's professional affinity to the one-color garden style, popular in the early 20th century in Europe, especially in England where he was educated. The style signaled a modernist bent that came on the heels of the late-career teachings of the British landscape gardener Gertrude Jekyll (see Chapter 3, "Special Coloring: One-Color Garden") and her modernist followers, such as Austrian architect Joseph M. Olbrich and his Garden of Colors (1904) (see Part II, "Modernism"). To my dismay, the name of my Blue Garden was changed in the 1970s to the Partisans' Garden, in honor of those who fought the Nazis in World War II. Its planting was replaced, ignoring the original blue. Yet for me this garden will always remain blue, an inspiration that planted a seed and nurtured my passion for color and gardens.

The five-year research for and writing of this book involved primary and secondary literature, archives, visits to featured gardens and landscapes, as well as interviews with the living designers. This would not have been possible without the support of several entities. I am indebted to the travel and research funding by the Landscape Architecture Department at Iowa State University (ISU). Further funding was provided by two university grants: ISU Small Grants provided course release, and an ISU Subvention Grant (a publication endowment of the ISU Foundation) contributed partial funding for editorial work, book design, and illustration copyright permission licenses. I have had the pleasure of working with landscape architecture graduate research assistants Mangtian Huang, Fan Lan, Asif Khan, and Seyedehmaryam Maddahzad, who assisted with library research and the beautiful color diagrams on the verso page opening of each chapter. I am grateful to my colleague Mikesch Muecke for his splendid book design. My sincere appreciation is extended to the exceptional work done on the manuscript by my editors Cameron Fletcher and Sue Cope. Finally, throughout the writing of this book I have had many conversations with and input by the journalist, editor, and my son Amir Efrati, for whom I am thankful.

Introduction

[I]maginative or creative drawing ... is usually the privilege of colourists. Pure draughtsmen are naturalists, endowed with one excellent sense; but their drawing is a rational exercise, whereas that of the colourists is a matter of feeling, an almost unconscious process.

Charles Baudelaire, "The Salon of 1846," 1846, 80

Color speaks to us in direct and emphatic ways. Some of our most powerful aesthetic experiences involve color and light. Color creates mood and evokes meaning, memory, and emotion. It is ever-changing and defies language; attempts to name and describe its physical properties and effects on viewers typically falter.[1] Yet this has not deterred numerous disciplines from studying it. Color has been explored in art, of course, as well as philosophy, science, optics, psychology, anthropology, social studies, architecture, even computer programming. In the past two decades, digital technologies have reinvigorated interest in color in architecture, urbanism, and art theory[2]—but landscape architects have largely remained silent on color, even though it is present in their works.

Landscape architectural history and theory on color may be scant because color is built into landscape and seems natural. It's impossible to think about working without it. Unlike in architecture or painting, color isn't something landscape architects add to the canvas or structure. Landscape color is especially difficult to grapple with because it constantly changes due to light and time, and because it is a surface issue in a profession that is preoccupied with using scientific processes to understand how landscapes operate beneath the surface. Color in gardening discourse in England peaked during the height of 18th century Romanticism but has since taken a back seat, mentioned only in passing.[3] Modern European experimental gardens in the 1920s and postmodern landscapes from the 1980s onward made bold statements with color and light, but it was overlooked by scholars. In today's digital world, as color—all-encompassing and brighter than ever— permeates urban, landscape, and architectural skins, discussing it is no longer avoidable.

Landscape design is an ideal discipline in which to explore color.[4] Landscape is first and foremost a visual field of effects. Color is inherent in nature and in landscape painting, the two primary sources of inspiration in early landscape gardening in 18th century England. Landscape architects have used color to attract, repel, camouflage, deceive, and otherwise affect emotions.

But even while embracing color, landscape design has had difficulty approaching it directly. The very question of what is meant by color in landscape architecture is nebulous. Most discussions about landscape color exclude the default color of nature: green, and sometimes also blue, brown, and other earthy hues. The discussions also muddle up the concepts of what is natural and artificial; for instance, they refer to bright red as an artificial color, when many blossoms are red, and, in contrary fashion, refer to artificially hybridized colored irises as natural.

The 19th century French poet and writer Charles Baudelaire's essay on color in painting, and by extension on nature and art, gives landscape designers two potent, conflicting color ruminations to wrestle with. As noted in the epigraph, Baudelaire aligns draftsmanship with reason and imitation, and art with imagination and feeling. In the hands of a draftsman-naturalist, color is used to imitate nature through a rational, emotionally sterile process, whereas the artist-colorist uses color creatively to interpret nature. "Drawing," Baudelaire wrote, "is a struggle between nature and the artist, and the better the artist understands nature's intentions, the easier will be his triumph over her."[5] Suspended between art and drafting, landscape design has always oscillated between nature and art. To study color in landscape architecture is to unravel the history of the discipline's reverence for nature (and science) on the one hand, and its affinity to art on the other.[6]

In the painter's approach to nature, Baudelaire recognized that color can be used to either hide perceived blemishes or to flaunt them. He opposed using color as a concealer type of make-up but welcomed using it to create visual effects or planned deception. Beaudelaire stated: "Make-up hides all blemishes bestowed by nature, rises above nature. But make-up itself is not for concealment. It should go on display."[7] Baudelaire would frown on landscape designers using color (i.e., plant, earth, and built materials) to make a built landscape look natural or hide undesirables and side with those who use color to emphasize human handiworks and flaunt or transform undesirables—like painting garbage cans in bright pink glitter, as Martha Schwartz did a century later. The acts of hiding human and nature's supposed imperfections and of making a designed landscape look natural have been integral to landscape design since its inception in 18th century England. Using Baudelaire's terms, then, are landscape architects draftsmen or colorists?

As I show in this book, viewing landscape architecture history through the lenses of both nature and art, and its practitioners as draftsmen or colorists, reveals a pendulum that has swung back and forth between the two, with varying inflections and gravitations. The acts of drafting and coloring, of making landscapes seem natural and artificial, are often conflated. And the distinction between concealment and deception remains a disciplinary impasse.

Landscape Design in Color explores landscape architecture's changing relationship with color over the past two and a half centuries in the West, beginning in late 18th century England through to 21st century Europe and North America, with a midway excursion to Brazil. I chronicle and weave together 12 distinct outlooks on landscape color design, lenses through which to understand broader landscape architectural disciplinary trends, associated design practices, and experiences. I examine color in the writings, representation, and built landscape of these 12 practitioners and others, and unravel the strategies and tactics they used to produce specific messages, effects, and experiences.

I argue that the history of color in landscape design is tied to three interrelated factors: (1) internal disciplinary traditions and ideas about art or culture and nature, (2) professional and cultural influences from outside the realm of landscape architecture, and (3) the media and technology with which color has been conceived, represented, and conveyed.

I discuss the first variable by bringing into focus several landscape disciplinary themes and debates, many of which are ongoing. A central and frequently discussed theme in landscape architecture is natural versus artificial as well as its corollary, color versus form (originally *colore* versus *disegno* in Italian). Other subthemes include sensation versus concept, imitation versus interpretation, deception versus display, decorative versus structural, affect versus code, and sentimental versus rational. Several of these themes have endured over the past two centuries; others have declined, disappeared, or reappeared. I also show how the 12 aesthetic color outlooks and practices have built on or opposed one another over the last two and a half centuries.

For external influences, I frame the history of color in landscape architecture as part of a larger picture, drawing links between landscape color design concepts and ideas and tastes about color in culture as well as in art and architecture at the time. Moreover, the discussion highlights the intermittent influences on landscape color design of philosophy, the natural and social sciences (physics, optics, botany, horticulture, chemistry, psychology, and phenomenology), and applied art and design (commercial art, fashion, interior design, and advertising).

A discussion about the third variable, media and technology, shows how premodern watercolor drawings, followed by modern gouache, postmodern mixed media collage, and today's e-collages or Photoshop have mirrored the color of built form over time. Throughout, advances in printing—premodern black line engraving, followed by aquatint and modern black-and-white photography—influenced color tastes and both reflected and shaped landscape color design. Other technological and industrial period developments, such as greenhouses for raising and acculturating plant imports and, later, modern, mass-produced, tinted construction material, followed by postmodern synthetic paint and transparent materials, and finally today's digital light color shaped the built landscape repertoire. I show, for instance, that prior to the 1900s, premodern landscape color hinged on the colors of plants. In modern times, landscape color largely relied on mineral and industrial material. Postmodern landscape design introduced colors of synthetic material, such as plastics and paint. And contemporary landscape color, influenced by digital technology, relies on a hybrid of physical and, increasingly, non-physical material such as sunlight and electric light.

For this book, I sourced primary texts and corroborated them with interpretive secondary texts, interviews with living designers, and my observations from visits to project sites. But I acknowledge several complications. The language of color has changed over time, which made it harder to compare the outlooks of practitioners from different periods; color nomenclature is largely media-based—spectrum color, printing color, pigment color, and computer color—which can be limiting, whereas landscape comprises infinite materials. In addition, the built landscapes and gardens of the past have either been modified or disappeared, and modern designers have left us only limited black-and-white documentation of their original garden form.

Each of the first eight chapters probes a landscape color design outlook by examining the written and built work of prominent authors or practitioners. Chapter 9 examines three contemporary approaches. The central themes of each theory are developed through a close study of exemplary built or proposed unbuilt works and their representations. The chapters are grouped into three periods: premodern (1750–1900), modern (1900–80), and postmodern and contemporary (1980–present). An introduction to each period explains the cultural, scientific, and technological developments that shaped landscape color discourse and trends during the era.

The introduction to the premodern chapters, Part I, "From Painting to Landscape," begins by examining the relationship between nature and art that coincided with the emergence of landscape painting in 16th century Italy. This new genre fostered the debate over color versus line, which became a permanent and central part of color discourse. The introduction proceeds to 18th century England, the birthplace of landscape gardening as a profession—distinct from both gardening and architecture that was modeled largely on landscape painting. The next three chapters cover the dominant color theories in English landscape gardening from the late 18th century through the turn of the 20th century by looking at Humphry Repton (1752–1818), John Claudius Loudon (1783–1843), William Robinson (1838–1935) and Gertrude Jekyll (1843–1932). (Robinson and Jekyll share a chapter because their color theories overlapped.) The three chapters rely heavily on these authors' writings as well as reviews of their work and my visits to their gardens in England.

The first chapter explains Repton's structural color theory, which privileged shades of green or the "color of verdure," as he called it. As a self-proclaimed landscape gardener, he anchored his position in the teachings of prominent art aestheticians and connoisseurs, even as he repeatedly insisted on the inapplicability of landscape painting aesthetics to landscape gardening. I demonstrate that despite Repton's rejection of landscape paintings as a model for landscape gardening, and his submission to nature as the prime colorist, the colors in his garden designs were calibrated to match those of landscape painting— earthy green and blue and golden hues, the "artist's favorite autumn colors," according to theorist Uvedale Price. Repton's color scheme eschewed fresh and bright blossom colors at least into the early 1800s—the latter part of his career. Green masses and voids were intended to propagate the experience of space and movement, as seen in the perspective drawings in his Red Books. To refine his watercolor palette and aquatint printing technique, as well as to demonstrate his fidelity to nature, Repton also relied on Newton's color theory and his own light experiments. The chapter highlights other influences on Repton's use of color, including nascent visual consumerism and social class distinctions. His practice of concealing or camouflaging "landscape improvements," as landscape design was often called, and "undesirables" fostered the deception-versus-display debate.

The second chapter shows how Loudon and his contemporaries replaced Repton's structural color with a decorative approach. Loudon's ideas on color are rooted in empirical philosophy, the science of botany, the practice of horticulture, and changing suburban taste. Loudon's bias toward polychrome is linked to the introduction of colorful foreign plants in England and developments in greenhouse technology as well as in optics, chemistry, and the industrial production of color dyes. His gardenesque style, followed by his formal style, showed his personal interest in "color for all seasons" as well as the growing appetite for bright and lavish complimentary-contrast flower bed compositions, or bedding, which dominated Victorian era gardens. Loudon's decorative style married color and form, replacing Repton's structural color that eschewed color in favor of composition. Loudon embraced the new lithographic color printing technology to accommodate the growing visual consumer culture and its enthusiasm for color in publications.

The color theories of Robinson and Jekyll (Chapter 3), which marked the peak of color discourse in landscape design history, rejected Loudon's formal and gaudy flower bedding system in favor of color as impression, to produce harmony, a calming mood, and lovely pictures. They called on landscape architects to follow nature's own color compositions, which they prescribed as spectrum-adjacent harmonies. In their work, color transcended form. I draw links between Robinson's wild garden theory and the writings of John Ruskin, and between Jekyll's color theory and Impressionist and post-Impressionist paintings, notably those of J. M. W. Turner. Debates over color versus form and imitation versus interpretation of nature took a new turn. I examine the use of photography and flowering calendars in Jekyll's color design. The chapter closes with a discussion of Jekyll's special, one-color garden, which she helped popularize at the turn of the 20th century.

Part II, "From Material to Sensation," recounts how European modern art, commercial art, and modern architecture, in particular, influenced the color frameworks of early to mid 20th century landscape designers. I show that whereas post-Impressionism and Cubism freed color from objects, decoration, and meaning to become color field of effects, color in landscape architecture was confined to form and surface in the service of space or composition, akin to how it was used in architecture. At the same time, landscape color borrowed from the decorative arts—fashion, commercial art, advertising, and industrial design—in the service of consumer desire. Debates over decorative versus structural, design versus draftsmanship, and sensation versus concept permeated landscape discourse. They played out in the early modern garden color experiments of the Viennese Secessionists, notably Joseph Maria Olbrich's "Garden of Colors" at the garden exhibition in Darmstadt, Germany (1905) and Josef Hoffmann's garden for the Palais Stoclet in Brussels, Belgium (1905). Black-and-white photography, advances in color printing, and rational color systems in art and design also made an impact. The three succeeding chapters review the modern landscape color practices of Gabriel Guevrekian (1892–1970), Garret Eckbo (1910–2000), and Roberto Burle Marx (1909–94). Whereas Eckbo frequently published his views on color, those of Guevrekian could only be gleaned from short essays and written reviews of his work, and those of Burle Marx from his many lectures and interview transcripts and monographs.

In Chapter 4, I explore the color propositions of Guevrekian, an Armenian-born French architect who used both harmonic and clashing color combinations and lighting to shape the observer's perception of a garden's depth, motion, and time. His interest in psychology and early phenomenology aimed to change the viewer's psycho-physiological state. Guevrekian stunned the landscape architecture community with his "Garden of Water and Light" at the 1925 Art Deco Exposition in Paris. His innovative uses of landscape media—plants as pigments, and water, glass, and artificial light—greatly expanded the garden material color repertoire. He unequivocally took the artificial side in the natural versus artificial color debate. Guevrekian's color design was influenced by his peers—André Vera, Paul Vera, Robert Mallet-Stevens, and Le Corbusier—and collaborators, especially the artists Sonia and Robert Delaunay and their simultaneous (*simultané*) contrast theory. I highlight his mastery of marrying and introducing traditional and avant-garde sentiments into landscape design, freeing color from meaning, with flat and predominantly primary-color compositions.

The color ideas of American landscape architect Garrett Eckbo, described in the fifth chapter, represented a return to, and revision of, Repton's structural color. Working closely with architects to fashion a midcentury outdoor lifestyle in suburban gardens, Eckbo showed an indifference to pure colors, as opposed to landscape colors, and a preference for achromatic palettes in support of spatial perception. Eckbo articulated a theory that subjugated color to space and anchored it in a mix of sources and considerations, including modern art, natural sciences, regionalism, Gestalt psychology, and pragmatism. In response to mass production and the rising market for outdoor products, he promoted new synthetic and industrially tinted and reflective material in landscape design, introducing a glowing and sleek look. This led to debates on color in support of space versus form and on subjective versus objective perception.

Roberto Burle Marx, a Brazilian painter and landscape designer examined in Chapter 6, composed his gardens and urban landscapes as chromatic and light performances using an extensive range of bold and muted colors to create tonal contrasts throughout a composition. To understand his landscape color design, I consider his painterly affinities together with his passion for botany, ecology, music, and theater. Inspired by his country's politics, landscape and cultural mosaic, as well as plant forms and colors, Burle Marx paired color design with modern and regional art, universal and tropical, to create a bricolage of artificial plant and color ecologies. In his landscapes and gardens, patterns and colors unite to create an impression of both permanence and temporality. His approach highlights the dichotomy and reciprocity of painting versus landscape and pigment versus color light.

The introduction to Part III, "From Pigment to Affect," shows how Pop Art, Minimal Art, and Land Art stripped color of meaning and material, turning it into powerful affective experiences that influenced landscape designers from the 1970s onward. Large-scale art installations by Christo and Jeanne-Claude and by James Turrell, among others, created a new technological sublime that recalls Edmund Burke's 18th century aesthetic sublime category, denoting intense light, darkness, and color contrasts.[8] Their artworks drove landscape architects to experiment with color fields on the landscape scale, a scale they have mastered. The introduction then recounts the postmodern turn in architectural practice in the 1970s, in which architects introduced bright and playful color in buildings, urban landscapes, and parks—the latter a move that compelled landscape architects to follow suit. Postmodernism entered landscape architectural practice only a decade later, as evident in the discourse on the pages on *Landscape Architecture Magazine*, the preeminent professional landscape journal. Following the landscape architect Peter Walker and his collaborator, Martha Schwartz, a cadre of young practitioners unleashed bold explorations of color free of disciplinary strictures, projects using paint, plexiglass, lighting, and other materials. The three succeeding chapters highlight postmodern and contemporary landscape and installation color design practices by American Martha Schwartz (b. 1950), Dutch-born Petra Blaisse (b. 1955), Claude Cormier of Canada (b. 1960), Martin Rein-Cano of Germany (b. 1967), and the American Walter Hood (b. 1958). In the hands of these designers, vivid monochromes and polychrome palettes that correspond with the project message and context have been used to transform space, narrate, critique, protest, entertain, puzzle, and bring laughter.

For Martha Schwartz, the subject of Chapter 7, color was a device to transform, surprise, and dramatize places. She also used color to confront and spark conversation about established cultural and disciplinary concepts, particularly nature versus artifice. She shocked the profession with her 1980 Bagel Garden, which sparked a much-needed debate about landscapes and gardens. Schwartz has used bright, synthetic color and light and bold, luminous graphics to produce landscapes of glowing color effects. I link her work to Pop Art and popular culture and an economy built on giant corporate brands, as in the stark black, white, red, and green geometric courtyard and grid of golden frogs in a shallow pool facing a giant globe in Rio Shopping Center in Atlanta, Georgia.

Since the 1990s interior and landscape designer Petra Blaisse, founder of the Amsterdam firm Inside/Outside, has produced private and public theatrical and affective environments. Chapter 8 explores her focus on color, light, and time and her use of myriad illumination strategies using textiles, plants, and landscape materials. Vacillating between mediums and disciplines and between interior and exterior, Blaisse inscribes color itineraries in space and produces ephemeral and luminous atmospheres. I discuss how she uses surfaces to filter and shape light color, making it tactile and seductive. Having worked with well-known architects and designers for three decades, Inside/Outside's renown as a unique hybrid practice has more recently filtered and inspired the landscape architecture circle.

In Chapter 9, I examine three contemporary practices that engage color in the identity politics of gender, ethnicity, and race. Cormier, Rein-Cano, and Hood each have touched professional and cultural nerves with bold color gestures of scale, exploiting and shredding entrenched meanings, structures, and stereotypes. Their provocative work, sometimes occurring at events and festivals, is coupled with visual color games, narratives, puns, and ambiguities, among other tactics. With scale and scope, the works produce hypnotic color and light effects, aided by new synthetic materials and technologies. In these landscape architects' representations and built work, color is part of the interplay between the real, surreal, and hyperreal in a digital culture.

A brief postscript, "Color Prospects," forecasts color and light approaches for landscape design in the future.

Landscape Design in Color answers the following questions: How has color been used as an instrument to express sensibilities, values, and ideas? How have landscape architects transformed color to alter human perception and shape new experiences while coping with the landscape's immense scale and ever-changing light conditions? How have deep-seated disciplinary and cultural concepts shaped color trends and use? And how have external disciplinary fields and technological developments affected landscape color design? Ultimately, this book shows how contemporary landscape designers can use color to shape the physical world and the experience thereof.

Color diagrams, graphical maps made from drawings, and photographs of selected projects from each chapter appear on the opening page of each chapter. The pie charts show the hues of the corresponding image in proportion and relative proximity. They are based on a grid method, whereby the image is divided into equal size pixels in Adobe Photoshop or Illustrator. To describe colors in this book, I used the standard color charts of the dominant drawing or print media used during each of the time periods referenced in it: the Winsor & Newton (W&N) watercolor chart in premodern work; the W&N gouache chart in modern work; and the CMYK (Cyan, Magenta, Yellow, Black) printing color system in postmodern and contemporary work.

Notes

1 Color is subjectively experienced, but there is some universal agreement on its effects. It is objectively and quantitatively specifiable in terms of saturation (i.e., intensity) and tone (i.e., level of darkness and lightness of hue). *Hue* is used here interchangeably with *color*; *tint* is used here to refer to the shade of an artificial dye.

2 See, for example, recent collections of essays on architecture and urbanism: Doherty, *Urbanisms of Color*, 2010; in architecture: Cees, *The Colours of… Frank O. Gehry…*, 2015; in art theory: Temkin, *Color Chart: Reinventing Color, 1950–Today*, 2008; in social studies, a series of books on individual colors by Pastoureau, beginning with *Blue: The History of a Color*, 2017.

3 An exception is the vigorous discourse on color in the urban landscape that took place in Britain as part of the mid-20ᵗʰ century *Architectural Review's* townscape policy. See Engler, *Cut and Paste Urban Landscape: The Work of Gordon Cullen*, 2016.

4 *Landscape architecture* and *landscape design* are used interchangeably in this book. Garden design is a subset of landscape design.

5 Baudelaire, "Salon of 1846," [1846] 1972,79.

6 Architecture, too, has had its share of coping with the art-draftsman and nature-color questions. See Lavin, "What Color Is It Now?" 2004.

7 Baudelaire, "The Painter of Modern Life," [1863] 1972, 248.

8 Burke, *A Philosophical Enquiry into the Sublime and Beautiful*, [1757] 2008. Burke's sublime was supplanted by Uvedale Price's picturesque and its soothing and weak color contrasts that continued to dominate landscape design.

References

Baudelaire, Charles. "The Painter of Modern Life" [1863]. In *Baudelaire: Selected Writings on Art and Artists*, trans. by P. E. Charvet, 390–435. Harmondsworth: Penguin, 1972.

Baudelaire, Charles. "The Salon of 1846" [1846]. In *Baudelaire: Selected Writings on Art and Artists*, trans. by P. E. Charvet, 47–107. Harmondsworth: Penguin, 1972.

Burke, Edmund. *A Philosophical Enquiry into the Sublime and Beautiful* [1757]. London: Routledge, 2008.

Cees, W. de Jong, ed. *The Colours of… Frank O. Gehry, Jean Nouvel, Wang Shu ….* Basel: Birkhäuser Verlag GmbH, 2015.

Doherty, Gareth, ed. *New Geographies 3: Urbanisms of Color*. Boston: Harvard University Press, 2010.

Doherty, Gareth, ed. "Urbanisms of Color." In *New Geographies 3: Urbanisms of Color*, 2–7. Cambridge, MA: Harvard University Press, 2011.

Engler, Mira. *Cut and Paste Urban Landscape: The Work of Gordon Cullen*. New York: Routledge, 2016.

Lavin, Sylvia. "What Color Is It Now?" *Perspecta* 35 (2004): 99–111.

Pastoureau, Michel. *Blue: The History of a Color*. Princeton, NJ: Princeton University Press, 2017.

Temkin, Ann. *Color Chart: Reinventing Color, 1950–Today*. New York: The Museum of Modern Art, 2008.

I.1 Giorgione, "La Tempesta," 1508, Gallerie dell'Accademia, Venice

Part I
Pre-Modernism
From Painting to Landscape

The Landscape Painting Genre: Privileging Color over Line

The Italian Renaissance painters who were the first to make landscape a subject in and of itself, devoid of religious and moral overtones, did so by using paint brushes from the beginning—rather than starting with line drawings. The result was a new landscape painting genre whose green, brown, and gold palette evoked sensation rather than reason.[1] Their work sparked a fierce debate about whether imitation of nature, using precise color can be considered art. When country estate gardens were conceived as copies of 17th century landscape paintings (known simply as "landscapes") the nature versus art debate, which coincided with the debate about color versus line, permeated the landscape gardening discourse among art critics and connoisseurs in 18th century England. Remarkably, line and composition, rather than color, were decreed to be true art. Therefore, when the first professional landscape gardeners in 18th century England mimicked those earlier paintings and gardening acquired its status as a Western art discipline, they eschewed color in favor of composition.

Giorgione di Castelfranco of the Venetian school of painting is credited with producing the first landscape painting, "La Tempesta" (1508), to take landscape as its subject, and is also the first to be recognized for using color without first making line drawings of the subject (Figure I.1). He replaced Leonardo da Vinci's soft lines and shadow gradations with warm and cool tints.

Half a century after *La Tempesta*, Giorgio Vasari, author of the first comprehensive book on the theory of Renaissance artists, sculptors, and architects, referred to Giorgione's pieces as "the most pleasurable and realistic relief-like pictures of any time," appearing to be painted "directly from life," and he confidently stated that "his living forms were more exact than any other painter, not of Venice only, but of all other places."[2] Yet Vasari compared Giorgione and Titian, one of Giorgione's followers, unfavorably to Michelangelo and Raphael. Vasari agreed with Michelangelo's criticism of one of Titian's late paintings:

> [I]f this artist had been aided by *art and the knowledge of design, as he is by nature*, he would have produced works which none could surpass, especially in imitating life, since he has a fine genius, and a graceful animated manner [italics added].[3]

Vasari held that art relied on the rigor of line and form rather than on the ambivalence and sensation of color seen in the new landscape painting genre,[4] and that color muddled form and composition. "Concept does not manifest to the eye when attractive color takes precedent," he declared. "He who can draw need not rely on color alone to hide the lack of design as many Venetians do."[5] Vasari's criticism laid the foundation for two different schools of painting, involving the debate over nature versus art and its corollaries: color versus line and sensation versus concept.

Giorgione's successors in the 17th century, Claude Lorrain and Salvator Rosa, took advantage of the realism, illusion, and pleasure that color could provide, and their work became the basis for landscape discourse among English intellectuals who avidly collected and studied these masters. Still, when it came to designing gardens in the real world, they were to remain loyal to the line-composition concept and adhere to the limited favorite landscape color palette of the painter.

Two disciplines allied with painting, architecture and landscape gardening came out on different sides in the debate over color versus line. Architecture rejected color in favor of line and form, while landscape gardening selectively borrowed formal and spatial principles from architecture and compositional and color schemes from painting. Landscape gardening equated painting with nature. It appropriated color from painting, on the one hand, and deferred the role of colorist to nature, on the other.

The color affinities of the burgeoning landscape gardening profession were shaped not only by art discourse but also by the science of physics, the introduction of newly available colorful plants, and the popularization of the watercolor medium. Sir Isaac Newton's colored light spectrum discovery in the mid-17th century and his correlation between increments of colored light on the prismatic spectrum and musical chords or octaves made color easier for people to understand (see Figure 1.1). It provided a language to expound on color aesthetics and prompted discourse on harmonious color schemes—monochromatic, analogous, and complementary. Newton's work prompted painters and, later, landscape gardeners to make their own inquiry into the relationship between nature's light spectrum and pigments in pictorial representation.

Locally available botanical selections limited the color scheme of early landscape gardening. In England, for example, the natural colors of the visible landscape and indigenous plants were predominantly green, with little colorful flower variety. That changed when flower imports made their way to English nurseries and were promoted in botanical journals in the 19th century.

Finally, the aesthetics of color were linked to drawing and print media. The growing significance of design drawings as the landscape gardener's primary ideation and projection tool, as well as a communication and entertainment device for those who commissioned their work, drew attention to the hues of the drawing itself. Watercolor became the landscape gardener's preferred medium on account of its translucent and nuanced color washes. Because effective color printing technology was still not available for most of the 18th century, and because "to the true connoisseur" color seemed "a distraction from the elegance and significance of the image," books were illustrated with line engravings and etchings.[6] This, in turn, promoted draftsmanship skills and promulgated an orthodox opinion in the art academies' growing preference for line drawing. Printmaking was therefore fundamentally associated with draftsmanship and correspondingly dissociated from color.

But the academies' preference for lines over color was rebuffed by the new architectural villa book genre of picturesque cottage and villa designs and travel guides that became popular in the late 18th century. Thanks to advances in color printing, especially mezzotint and aquatint, these genres depicted buildings in their landscape setting in color and propagated the new aesthetic of the picturesque.[7] The mezzotint displayed the tonal nuances and lucidity of watercolor, enabling the portrayal of textures and shadings in architecture, especially landscape elements of trees, shrubs, lawns, and rocks.[8] The popularity of the picturesque villa book with its realistic illustrations influenced color preferences in landscape drawings, but did not fully elevate color to the primacy still reserved for form and volume in landscape gardens.

The aquatint technique was just being perfected in England in 1763 when Horace Walpole, a defining figure in the development of picturesque gardens, identified lack of color to be "the capital deficiency of prints."[9] The first book to use colored aquatint plates and inaugurate the new architectural villa book was John Plaw's *Rural Architecture* (1785).[10] It prefigured a trend that increasingly replaced sophisticated theory with enticing and colorful images. It is therefore no surprise that at the turn of the 19th century, as landscape gardening matured and appeared in architectural books, it entered that medium in color. The desire of landscape gardeners to "sell" their design proposals and disseminate ideas through print media not only placed color in the context of printmaking and color printing but was conditioned by this technology, unless watercolor design drawings were directly bound and handed to the client, as Repton did.

Autumn Colors: The Painter's Favorite

Landscape gardeners in the 18th century also paid close attention to philosophical discourse among English intellectuals who sided with form over color when it came to perception. The empiricist philosopher John Locke, for instance, considered size, shape, texture, and motion to be the primary perceptual qualities of objects, and color to be a secondary, unstable side effect along with sound and taste.[11] This attitude persisted well into the 19th century, when science and rational thinking led to the now widely held belief that, in fact, our perception of form depends on the colors we see.[12]

Nevertheless, in keeping with the empirical philosophical tradition of enlightenment, the 18th century gave rise to an important theory involving landscape color: that it can help generate specific emotions. Philosopher Edmund Burke's *A Philosophical Enquiry into the Sublime and Beautiful* (1757) linked color and light directly to human physiology and sensation. He distinguished between two primary aesthetic responses to objects and landscapes: beautiful, which was akin to love and invoked pleasure and desire, and sublime, which was akin to terror and produced awe and astonishment. Both responses excited passion, yet each was triggered by different qualities and intensities of the visual source, including its color and light. The perception of beauty was generated by clean, smooth, and soft shapes of weak intensities and cheerful, soft colors—light green, blue, off-white, pink-red, and violet, "not of the strongest kind"—as well as their mixtures and gradations.[13] Conversely, the sensation of the sublime was produced by conditions of vastness, infinity, and by the opposite presence of intense light and darkness and their associated cloudy, dark, and gloomy black, brown, and purple colors.[14]

However, landscape gardeners didn't adopt Burke's beautiful and sublime ideas. Instead, they opted for a third category, the picturesque, developed by Uvedale Price, art

I.2 Claude Lorrain, "View of La Crescenza," 1648–50 (top), Metropolitan Museum, New York; Humphry Repton, view to the northeast toward the town of Hampstead, Red Book of Brandsbury, Middlesex, 1789 (bottom), Dumbarton Oaks Research Library

aesthetician who built on Burke's theory.[15] In his book *On the Picturesque, with an Essay on the Origin of Taste, and Much Original Matter* (1784), Price distilled Burke's beautiful and sublime to produce the desired effect of "picturesque beauty," leaving out the awe-ful quality of the sublime. Breadth, vastness, glaring and jarring light and deep shadows, darkness, and saturated colors did not belong in the picturesque,[16] whose character distinguished itself by its tameness relative to the sublime and its roughness and agitation relative to the beautiful. It even displayed occasional neglect, decay, deformities, and irregular lines. Ultimately, the picturesque encapsulated a scene worth painting.

Price considered colors to "have the power of exciting emotions," yet, he relegated them to a secondary role in landscape gardening, inferior to form and composition. His instruction on light and color began with an explanatory statement that showed his position vis-à-vis color and form: "I have said little of the superior variety and effect of light and shade …, as they of course must follow variety of forms and of masses, and intricacy of disposition."[17] Form, mass, and the experience of movement underlay his garden design principles; light, shadow, and color were subservient. In fact, partial concealment and warm and soft colors were desirable:

> A cottage of a quiet colour half concealed among trees, with its bit of garden, its pales and orchard, is one of the most tranquil and soothing of all rural objects, when the sun strikes upon it, a number of lively picturesque circumstances, one of the most cheerful; but if cleared round, and whitened, its modest retired character is gone, and is succeeded by a perpetual glare.[18]

Price did, however, appreciate landscape effects involving water: "Of all the effects in landscape, the most brilliant and captivating was produced by water." He highlighted its properties of the "mirror which gives a peculiar freshness and tenderness to the colours it reflects."[19] The interface of water and light and the mirroring of the sky and trees at the water's edge became objects of fascination in color and light discourse at the time.[20] (The sublime ideas espoused by Burke, meanwhile, didn't resurface until the late 20th century.)

Price deepened his influence over color in landscape gardening by dictating what he said were the most suitable colors for picturesque: mellow and earthy autumn tones, which he referred to as being from the painter's favorite season. Conversely, bright colors of fresh spring blossoms "are not those which are best adapted to painting," because, Price contended, they destroy the richness of variety and gradation of distance; they produce glare and spottiness, ruining the harmony of a picture, "whether in nature or imitation."[21] Price distinguished between color that supports composition and structure and color that is merely ornamental. Judging the colors of Claude Lorrain and Peter Paul Rubens "more fresh" and therefore inferior to the Venetian school of painting, Price countered Vasari:

> [i]t has often struck me, that the whole system of Venetian coloring, particularly, that of Giorgione and Titian, was formed upon the tints of autumn, whenever their pictures have that golden hue, which gives them such superiority over all others.[22]

Price's preference for foliage color impacted the late 18th century generation of landscape designers—notably Humphry Repton, who positioned himself as an authority on gardening taste in the 1790s (Figure I.2). He wholeheartedly agreed with the notion of the painter's favorite season because deciduous plants that produced autumn colors and evergreens accentuated solid masses and scenic composition over the merely ornamental color of flowering plants. Yet Repton also tussled publicly with Price because he positioned the profession of landscape gardening between art and gardening, picture and spatial experience, as a profession that must cater for both aesthetics and practicalities. [23]

Repton became the first writer to enter the discourse on color in gardening literature and to prolifically use color in his drawings and publications. As an accomplished artist and watercolorist by the time he began his gardening career in his 40s, he was well aware of the effects of color and light. His landscape garden was essentially a garden of composition— form and volume—in which unstable and temporary color effects were barred lest they destroy the basic organization.

Notes

[1] Gombrich, *Norm and Form: Studies in the Art of the Renaissance*, [1966] 1971, 107–21.

[2] Vasari, *Lives of the Most Eminent Painters, Sculptors, and Architects*, [1563] 1896, 396–9.

[3] Ibid., 395.

[4] The opposition between color and form/line in Western history possibly began in Ancient Greece with Aristotle. See Batchelor, *Chromophobia*, 2000, 80.

[5] Vasari, *Lives*, 247.

[6] Lambert, *The Image Multiplied*, 1987, 87. Etching and engraving are both methods of line drawing.

[7] Powers, "The Architectural Book," 2002. Mezzotint and aquatint can render tones and delicate gradations from light to shade. Mezzotint was invented in 1640 in Germany and perfected and widely used in England in the mid-18th century. Aquatint, invented in the 1650s and perfected in the 1760s, was another tonal method devised primarily to reproduce flat washes of watercolor marks made with roulettes and tints of a ruling machine or by hand. For a discussion on the techniques and their history, see Prideaux, *Aquatint Engraving*, 1909.

[8] Archer, *The Literature of British Domestic Architecture*, 1985, 23, 30–1.

[9] Lambert, *The Image Multiplied*, 1987, 87.

[10] Archer, *The Literature*, 1985, 30–1.

[11] Locke, *An Essay Concerning Human Understanding*, [1690] 1753, 110.

[12] For further discussion, see Elliott, *Victorian Gardens*, 1986, 48.

[13] Burke, *A Philosophical Enquiry into the Sublime and Beautiful*, [1757] 2008, 116.

[14] Ibid., 79–80. Burke's theory met with opposition from those who considered perception to be associative and subjective rather than object-related or objective. For Burke, the aesthetic response was universal and visceral, in contrast to associative aesthetic theories, which conditioned the response on cultural associations and personal memories.

[15] The word *picturesque*, meaning literally "in the manner of a picture; fit to be made into a picture," was used as early as 1703 (*Oxford English Dictionary*).

[16] Price, *On the Picturesque*, 1784, 124–5.

[17] Ibid., 72.

[18] Ibid., 132.

[19] Ibid., 213.

[20] Price's theory was corroborated by other picturesque theories of English garden art advocated by the aestheticians Horace Walpole and Thomas Whately and the architect William Chambers, who promoted subtle gradations of color and especially variegated greens, using as his model the Chinese garden that predominantly displayed green variations.

[21] Ibid., 138–9.

[22] Ibid., 141.

[23] Repton first expressed his positions vis-à-vis Price in a retaliatory letter published in the appendix of his first book. Repton, *Sketches and Hints on Landscape Gardening*, [1793] 1907, 71.

References

Archer, John. *The Literature of British Domestic Architecture 1715–1842*. Cambridge, MA: MIT Press, 1985.

Batchelor, David. *Chromophobia*. London: Reaktion Books, 2000.

Burke, Edmund. *A Philosophical Enquiry into the Sublime and Beautiful* [1757]. London: Routledge, 2008.

Chambers, William. *A Dissertation on Oriental Gardening*, 2nd ed. London: W. Griffin, 1773.

Elliott, Brent. *Victorian Gardens*. London: Butler & Tanner Ltd., 1986.

Gombrich, E. H. *Norm and Form: Studies in the Art of the Renaissance* [1966]. London: Phaidon, 1971.

Lambert, Susan. *The Image Multiplied: Five Centuries of Printed Reproductions of Paintings and Drawings*. London: Trefoil Publications, 1987.

Locke, John. *An Essay Concerning Human Understanding: In Four Books*, Vol. I [1690], 15th ed., London: printed by Robert Taylor, 1753.

Powers, Alan. "The Architectural Book: Image and Accident." In *This Is Not Architecture: Media Constructions*, ed. by Kester Rattenbury, 157–73. London: Routledge, 2002.

Price, Uvedale. *On the Picturesque, with an Essay on the Origin of Taste, and Much Original Matter* [1784], ed. by Thomas Dick Lauder. Edinburgh: Caldwell, Lloyd, 1842.

Prideaux, S. T. *Aquatint Engraving: A Chapter in the History of Book Illustration*. London: Duckworth & Co., 1909.

Repton, Humphry. *Sketches and Hints on Landscape Gardening* [1793]. In *The Art of Landscape Gardening*, 1–62. Boston: Mifflin and Co., 1907.

Vasari, Giorgio. *Lives of the Most Eminent Painters, Sculptors, and Architects* [1563], trans. by Mrs. Jonathan Foster. New York: C. Scribner's Sons, 1896.

Walpole, Horace. "The History of the Modern Taste in Gardening" [1771]. In *Anecdotes of Painting in England*, Vol. 4, 2nd ed., 247–316. London: J. Dodsley, 1982.

Whately, Thomas. *Observations on Modern Gardening*. London: T. Payne, 1770.

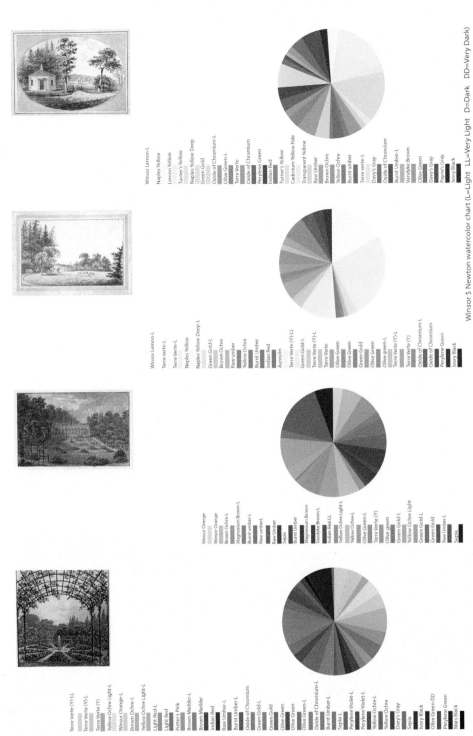

1.0 Diagrams, color analysis of Humphry Repton's watercolor drawings from the *Red Book of Brandsbury*, 1789 (upper two), and from the *Report Concerning the Gardens of Ashridge*, 1813 (lower two). Rendered by Fan Lan and Asif Khan

(Unless noted otherwise, drawings in Chapter 1 are by Humphry Repton.)

1

Structural Color
Uniform Verdure,
Humphry Repton (1752–1818)

The chief beauty of a park consists in uniform verdure; undulating lines contrasting with each other in variety of forms; trees so grouped as to produce light and shade to display the varied surface of the ground; and an undivided range of pasture. ... The farm, on the contrary, is for ever changing the colour of its surface in motley and discordant hue; it is subdivided by straight lines of fences.

Humphry Repton, *Theory and Practice*, 1803, 137

Autumn is the favourite season of study for landscape painters, when all nature verges towards decay, when the foliage changes its vivid green to brown and orange, and the lawns put on their russet hue. But the tints and verdant colouring of spring and summer will have superior charms to those who delight in the perfection of nature, without, perhaps, ever considering whether they are adapted to the painter's landscape.

Humphry Repton, *Theory and Practice*, 1803, 149

Art aestheticians and connoisseurs engaged in extensive discourse about color throughout the 18th century, but there was no source of advice for a gardener to manage color in the garden. Humphry Repton was the first landscape gardener to write about color theory in a manner that was intelligible to amateur and professional gardeners alike.[1] As evident in the first epigraph above, he followed the principles of beauty of art aestheticians, whereby the undulating lines and uniform verdure of a landscape park lay in stark contrast to the unsightly straight lines and discordant hues of a farm. As he noted in the second epigraph, however, the painters' favorite autumn colors varied greatly from those of laypersons, whose natural attraction was to the verdant colors of summer and spring and with whom he sympathized.[2] The two positions constitute a color dilemma that plagued Repton throughout his career: a preference for "cultured" picturesque color aesthetics, on the one hand, and its rebuke in favor of empirical observations and subjective penchants, on the other. Repton ended up applying both selectively to his drawings and designs.

Repton was both art- and business-minded and acutely aware of color. Initially a textile merchant who sketched the surrounding countryside and sold local landowners watercolor views of their estates, he quit the textile business and turned his attention to his primary source of income, producing paintings, theater set designs, and even trying his hand as a playwright and critic. In 1788, at the age of 37, he decided "to render [his] leisure profitable" and become a professional "landscape gardener."[3]

Repton's savvy entrepreneurship enabled him to reconcile highbrow and lowbrow tastes and opposing ideologies—between art theoreticians and gardening professionals, and between elite landed gentry and laypersons and middle-class suburbanites.[4] He deemed

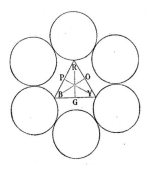

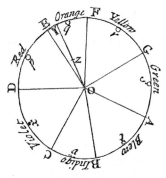

1.1 Humphry Repton, interpretation of Isaac Newton's theory showing primary and compound colors, from *Theory and Practice*, 1803 (top); Isaac Newton, color chart, from *Opticks*, 1704 (bottom)

landscape gardening "a happy medium between nature and art" and therefore a vocation subject to judgments beyond painterly principles. He worked to free himself from the grip of picturesque canons, though with mixed results. Repton's main contribution to landscape design color theory was the distinctions he drew between painting and landscape gardening, which enabled him to develop a color theory unique to landscape gardening, albeit not totally independent of painting. The color principles he devised left space for gardeners to enjoy their own stylistic and color whims.

Repton built few gardens, unlike his predecessors William Kent (1685–1748) and Capability Brown (1716–83). His mark on the history of landscape architecture hinged on his professional writings and inventive drawings. He laid out the foundation of the landscape gardening profession (the predecessor of landscape architecture) by articulating its principles and working modes and by devising a system of landscape representation. He participated in the aesthetic discourse of the time and disseminated his ideas widely: he produced more than 400 design proposals (half of which were compiled into bound books known as "Red Books") and published five books on landscape gardening theory and practice.

Repton's interest in color developed over time. His first book, *Sketches and Hints on Landscape Gardening* (1793), articulates the difference between landscape paintings and landscape gardening, but does not explicitly discuss color except in a section on the light effects of water.[5] A lengthy discussion on the color of artifacts and buildings appears a decade later in his second book, *Observations on the Theory and Practice of Landscape Gardening* (1803). He dedicates the final chapter, "Concerning Colour," to the color theories of physicist Isaac Newton (1642–1727 and mathematics and philosophy professor Isaac Milner (1750–1820), with extensive explanatory notations (Figure 1.1).[6] In Repton's last book, *Fragments on the Theory and Practice of Landscape Gardening* (1816), one chapter is devoted to the effects of color contrasts and another to coloring.[7] The latter details his experiments with the progression of the early morning light spectrum and their application to watercolor rendering (Figure 1.2).[8] *Fragments* also references his late-career shift in interest to more diverse garden styles and brighter color schemes, as exemplified in Ashridge Gardens (discussed below). I focus here on Repton's early to mid-career through the early 19th century, when the work of a new landscape gardening taste authority, John Claudius (J. C.) Loudon, began (Chapter 2).

Repton's color design propositions were directly linked to the medium with which he worked, from landscapes to artifacts, drawings, and bound books, known as Red Books. To each he assigned different color concepts. For landscapes, he combined painterly aesthetic color principles with empirical observations of nature, using color to establish composition, shape space and movement, and camouflage "undesirables." His "structural color" theory placed color in the service of the visual composition and the garden's spatial organization or structure and choreographed movement.[9] At the same time, he assigned nature the role of colorist, and in doing so freed himself to interpret nature's color, often through the eye of a landscape painter. For artifacts and buildings, he relied on aesthetic color principles pertaining to ornaments and on social color codes. He distinguished the flower garden from a landscape park and placed the former in the category of artifice, with color as ornament in flower beds and trellis vines. For drawings, he joined the "painter's favorite" greens and autumn color palette with lessons learned from physical and optical sciences and verified through his own experiments, and then subjected them to expediency, economy, and marketing.[10] In bound books and print media, his color design

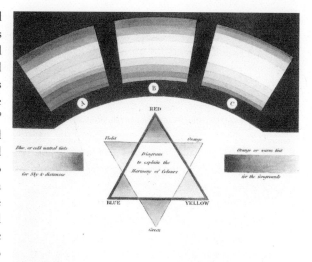

1.2 Aquatint, record of tint scales from experiments with prism and perspectives showing early morning light before and after sunrise, page spread, *Fragments on the Theory and Practice of Landscape Gardening*, 1816. Getty Research Institute, Los Angeles

was a direct function of printing techniques, paper availability, and production cost while using color to codify and brand (i.e., the Red Books).

Landscapes: Nature the Colorist

Repton was active in the pivotal 1790s debate over the degree to which landscape painting served as a basis for landscape gardening, challenging the establishment. English garden aesthetic authorities on the picturesque, Uvedale Price (1747–1829) among others, contended that the aesthetic of landscape paintings was the proper pictorial model for garden design and the experience of landscape, whereas Repton also pinned garden design aesthetics on more subjective impressions, the idea of landscape as a three-dimensional living space, with the practical factors of comfort, privacy, and shade. He posited the essential difference between the landscape painter and the landscape gardener to be "that a dwelling-house is an object of comfort and convenience, for the purposes of habitation, and not merely the frame to a landscape, or the foreground to a rural picture."[11] Furthermore, in contrast to painting, a landscape was experienced through a sequence of ever-changing views along a prescribed line of movement and the effects of water and lighting conditions.

Repton found grounds to differ with and confront Price and the "painter's favorite" golden autumn scheme. In his polemic, "Pictures may imitate Nature—but Nature is not to copy Pictures," he explained his position:

> The best painters in landscape have studied in Italy or France, where the verdure of England is unknown: hence arises the habit acquired by the connoisseur of admiring brown tints and arid foregrounds in the pictures of Claude and Poussin, and from this cause he prefers the bistre sketches to the green paintings of Gainsborough.[12]

The golden, brown, and red shades of Giorgione and Titian and their successors, Claude and Poussin, echoed the local color of their respective terrains, not the verdant English landscape. Adherence to local pigments inherent in the material world was unimportant in the aesthetic judgment of art connoisseurs but important to Repton's "nature as colorist" taste.[13] It also conformed to his interrelated concepts of "character" and "situation"— character being the genius loci, and situation the conditions of the project site and its views. Color was relevant not only geographically but also for different people. Those who cared little about a painter's favorite colors could simply delight in the perfection of nature: pure and vivid color during spring and summer. Hence, painting, place, culture, and perception all had roles in shaping Repton's landscape color aesthetics.

The aesthetic principles of paintings handed down by Price nonetheless guided Repton's landscape color: the primacy of composition and form over color. Color was subsidiary and dependent on the general rules of composition as the organizing design features, of which the first principle was unity.[14] The rules of the "painter's favorite" chromatic scheme have been summarized as:

> [t]he use of areas of uniform colour for broad effect, the subordination of individual colours to a prevailing tone, the separation of warm from cold colour, the darkening of the foreground and lightening of the distance to give greater definition to the principal objects."[15]

Accordingly, garden color design was to display earthy, harmonious color gradations and avoid patchy and contrasting tones (Figure 1.0).

The subordination of color to composition is explicit in Repton's work; choice of color applied only to artifacts.[16] In landscape, unity of composition was the prime principle, and green, a nature-given color, the unifying and principal color of landscape design. Green shades shaped the spatial composition and camouflaged nonconforming elements. As Repton put it, "The chief beauty of a park consists in uniform verdure."[17] Blue and light reflections in bodies of water were welcome special effects (Figure 1.3). When a color other than green or blue was involved, it was to be used only "so far as it relates to certain artificial objects."[18] In practical terms, to increase unity and minimize visual interference in the composition implied using a limited palette of plant varieties and avoiding flowers and flowering trees and shrubs. A limited tree palette secured some variety of green tones, textures, and forms; Repton preferred elms and oaks with occasional accents of single trees such as willows and maples.

Penchants for green and blue were also embedded in the popular pictorial and poetic genres of the time. The growing popularity of green in the late 18th century has been linked to Romanticism and a renewed attraction to nature. The green of the plant world and nature became glorified as a source of peace and contemplation away from the upheavals of society.[19] Repton occasionally ended his texts with a poem that reflected these sentiments (see the section on the Brandsbury Red Book below). His Romantic palette included greens (verdure) and the blues of sky and water—themes of dreams and infinity, celebrated in paintings and poetry.

Consistent with his principles, Repton compromised loyalty to the actual colors of a view by using artistic license to correct or embellish views he considered dull. For example, he contended that the contrast between dark green woods and a light green lawn did not "satisfy the eye" and required additional color variety to

1.3 "Water at Wentworth, Yorkshire," views with and without flap, *Observations on the Theory and Practice of Landscape Gardening*, 1803. By kind permission of Leeds Libraries

soften the contrast. He introduced elements such as rocks, water, benches, gravel roads, and garden structures to enrich the color composition with yellow, reddish-brown, and off-white.[20] He even considered the merit of animals grazing in the fore- and middle ground to animate a scene, provide a sense of scale, and enhance the chromatic palette. Still, color and light or shade were to interfere as little as possible in the experience of enjoying the spatial landscape composition,

> its masses and voids as they were perceived by the mobile observer and the views he paused to examine. The presence of light and shade, whether in a landscape or a picture was to be broad and unbroken, lest the eye will be distracted by the flutter of the scene.[21]

Broken shade or tint and uneven coloration implied a discontinuous occurrence. Repton paid close attention to the changing effects of daylight on objects, space, and distance, and concluded that natural objects such as woods, trees, lawn, water, and distant mountains appear best when the sun is behind them, and artificial objects such as houses, bridges, roads, boats, arable fields, and distant villages are seen best when the sun shines fully on them.

The reflective, animated, and changing light qualities of water fascinated Repton. He had a special interest in the reflection of trees and sky on water, and applied his observations to the design of bank slopes. The brilliant and cheerful effect produced by the reflection of the sky on a water surface as seen from a house became a central

1.4 Welbeck Abbey, Nottinghamshire, main view from the back of the house. Photo: Mira Engler, 2018

element in his work (Figure 1.4). In some cases, he included a cascade or stream, and even confronted Capability Brown for turning any running river into a stagnant lake.[22]

Understanding color perception was crucial for landscape "improvement," as landscape gardening was often called. Repton studied the mechanics of the eye's vision and sensitivity to brightness in, among other sources, Joseph Priestley's book on the history of optics (1772), and drew on this knowledge to shape landscape composition—alter topography, define spatial expanse, orient viewpoint, create focal points, locate tree groups, and provide shade.[23] He also used optics to manipulate perception and produce spatial illusion, deception, and camouflage. The capacity of color to disguise and deceive was integral to cosmetic landscape improvement procedures. The natural materials of earth, plants, and water were the artist's "paint" in the gardener's hand, used to control experience and stimulate emotion. In Tatum Park, for instance, Repton applied the principles of foreshortening in the linear perspective and receding colors across distances or the "aerial perspective" to deceive the viewer into believing that two water bodies at different distances are connected.

The principle of deception, especially of hiding the art of landscape and displaying the artificial as natural, was integral to landscape gardening. Repton accepted Price's argument that "Perfect imitation so skillfully as to pass for nature itself, would certainly be acknowledged as the highest attainment of art."[24] Indeed, mimicry of nature was an active ideological and aesthetic act of deception. Repton too equated concealment of the art of gardening (i.e., camouflage) with deception,[25] writing:

> [I]t is the business of taste in every polite art to avail itself of stratagems, by which the imagination may be deceived: and thus, also in Landscape Gardening, many things may be deemed deceptions, by which *we try to conceal the agency of art*. We plant the hills to make deceptions where they appear higher; we sink the fences necessary to make the lawns appear larger; we open the banks of a brook to make it appear a river, or stop its current to make an expanse of water: and we disguise terminations to give appearance of continuity; nor is the imagination so fastidious as to reject well supported deceptions, even after the want of reality is discovered [italics added].[26]

The skilled use of topography, form, and color was a requisite for the creation of the desired picturesque beauty through concealment, of which the central objects were the "boundary," to clear and extend the view, a concept known as "borrowed landscape"; "situation," to "fix"

24

incongruent topography or tree grouping that interfered with the visual composition; and "utility," to hide functional elements.

Camouflage operations required designers to act as colorists, masking "undesirable" elements such as fences and utilitarian objects by using plant "screens" or artifacts of "proper" colors. For example, Repton maintained with reference to wooden fences or rails: "[I]t is hardly necessary to say that the less they are seen the better; and therefore, a dark, or, as it is called, an *invisible green*, for those intended to be concealed, is the proper colour" [italics added].[27] Generally, evidence of human industry, such as fences, and alteration of the landscape was eliminated or minimized (Figure 1.5). The kitchen garden, a place of labor and bright color, was either relocated to distant portions of the grounds, where it would not impinge on the main views from the house, or concealed with planting. But Repton clarified that

> [c]onvenience and comfort have occasionally misled modern improvers into the absurdity of not only banishing the appearance but the reality of all comfort and convenience to a distance; as I have frequently found in the bad choice of a spot for the kitchen-garden.[28]

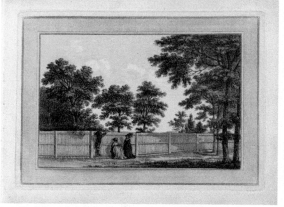

1.5 *Red Book of Brandsbury,* 1789, views to the south and distant hills with and without flaps, showing the paling fence in the foreground eliminated and the fence around a tree clump at the distance painted in "invisible green." Dumbarton Oaks Research Library

Repton reserved different color concepts and tactics for landscape and artifice. When it came to artifice, however, art was on display and so were colors.

Artifacts: Color as Ornament and Social Code

Colored artifacts differed from the landscape color. They introduced desirable contrast, made artistic statements, and signified social status. Proper coloring required knowledge of color theory, but not necessarily of the arts. Repton cautioned that "[i]mproper colouring may destroy the intended effect of the most correct design and render ridiculous what would otherwise be beautiful."[29] A successfully designed landscape should be unembellished and subdue bright colors; artifacts may be ornate and display color conspicuously, but with care not to offend the landscape (Figure 1.6). In Repton's words:

1.6 *Red Book of Brandsbury,* 1789, a garden seat (top) and view of the approach and gate lodge (bottom). Dumbarton Oaks Research Library

The perfection of landscape gardening depends on a concealment of those operations of art by which nature is embellished; but where buildings are introduced, art declares herself openly, and should, therefore, be very careful, lest she have cause to blush at her interference.[30]

In the artifice category, manufactured artwork and furniture were expected to display colors not found in nature or buildings. A manufactured bench or a stucco wall might be artificially colored, but it "must [be] … guided by certain general laws of nature,"[31] specifically Newton's theory of color harmony and discord.[32] Based on Newton and modifications presented in Milner's *Theory of Colours*, Repton concluded, "Harmony consists in distance and contrast, not in similitude or approximation."[33] Accordingly, colors next to each other on the color wheel were discordant, while complementary colors were harmonious. Thus, Repton claimed that for furniture, red and green, orange and blue, and purple and yellow were harmonious, and green and blue discordant. He contrasted this with nature, where adjacent green and blue are always pleasantly perceived. Repton considered color theories extremely useful to artists who endeavor to produce effects through contrast and harmony, but he did not promote color dogma—the laws were not universal truths, color effect was relative, and each situation was to be considered separately.

Unlike artifacts, painted buildings should be subdued and complement the overall color scheme of the landscape. They were integral to the production of picturesque landscape beauty, where color saturation and tonal contrasts were to be avoided or carefully controlled, in what Repton called "weak" contrast (Figure 1.7). The beauty of a composition was enhanced when the landscape did not present sharp contrasts, including those due to lighting.[34] Whitewashed buildings stood out in the landscape and created too strong a contrast with the surroundings and therefore "offended the eye," especially when the sun hit their walls. He suggested mixing lime-tinted paint with black or yellow to reduce

1.7 *Red Book of Brandsbury,* 1789, view of the house. Dumbarton Oaks Research Library

its brilliance and resemble more closely natural stone,[35] whose color was also encoded to signify high class, as white or yellowish-brown stone was thought to be an expensive material.[36] In contrast, a red house, even if built of Herefordshire red stone, was perceived to be made of cheap, common red bricks and therefore unattractive.[37] Similarly, the colors of sashes and window frames were chosen with propriety in mind:

> [I]n small cottages, they may be green, because it is a degree of ornament not incompatible with the circumstances of the persons supposed to inhabit them. … But in proportion as it approaches to a mansion, it should not derive its decoration from so insignificant an expedient as colour, and, therefore, to a gentleman's house the outside of the sashes should be white, whether they be of mahogany, of oak, or of deal. …[38]

Repton's prescription for painted oak sashes indicates that artifacts made of an expensive material were to display the color of the material used in their construction, unless their color compromised the sense of propriety and of the owner's status—the artist must be attentive to the integrity of the social scene. Thus Repton approved of camouflaging undesirables such as fences, but he disapproved of hiding or faking architectural material elements, such as painting a brick wall to look like stucco. Landscape camouflage concerned the integrity of the natural image, and was therefore a legitimate disguise for which color was functional and essential. Camouflaging buildings, on the other hand, was a sham, deemed decorative and superfluous.

An example of legitimate color intervention was the chimneys and roof of the manor house at Welbeck: in his rendering Repton painted the red brick chimneys white because

1.8 *Red Book of Welbeck Abbey*, 1790, views of the country house with and without flaps, showing the blue slate roof (top) replacing the red tile roof (middle); The Portland Collection, Harley Gallery, Welbeck Estate, Nottinghamshire/Bridgeman Images. Photograph of the same view in 2018 (bottom). Photo: Mira Engler

their original color next to the white stone house broke "the unity of effect" and destroyed "the magnificence of the most splendid composition."[39] His tableau also replaced the red tile roof with blue slate to indicate the owner's stature. In his 1790 Red Book for Welbeck Abbey, Repton's before-and-after perspective drawings show the original red tile roof compared to his proposed blue slate (Figure 1.8). As for gates and ornamental iron rails, Repton painted them with copper powder or gold dust on a green base to create a bronzed look, a material superior to lead that was commonly painted white or green.[40] The artist's choice of colors for building and structural elements thus implied material quality that, in turn, suggested the owner's corresponding social standing. Repton's color treatment of artifacts has been called an embrace of "social illusionism" aesthetics.[41]

To achieve drama with artifacts, contrasts depended on complementary hues rather than tonal contrasts. Conversely, in painting, as Repton argued, strong light and dark contrasts produce drama. In his drawings he displayed tonal contrast to produce dramatic scenes, demonstrating his color sensibility and marketing savvy.

Drawings: Color and Consumer Appeal

Repton used drawing to design, communicate, and sell his work in the nascent visual consumer culture of the late 18th century. His art mediated between real and imagined, present and proposed landscape, and was also a product in and of itself. Color was active in all these operations. The writing that accompanied the drawings was meaningful to landscape builders, and his drawings and written word both appealed to amateur and gardening professionals.

Repton was instrumental in uniting landscape painting and gardening, which elevated the latter to the status of the art of landscape gardening and made design drawings central to the new professional activity of the landscape gardener. In Repton's words: "The art [of gardening] can only be advanced and perfected by the united powers of the landscape painter and the practical gardener. The former must conceive *a plan*, which the latter may be able to execute [italics added]."[42] He considered Capability Brown, who did not produce drawings, to be "a kitchen-gardener who acquired good taste through his contacts with his patrons, …[but] could not design, himself."[43] Still, Repton's landscape sketches neither intended to achieve the high art of painting nor conformed to the aesthetics of the art connoisseur. His watercolors were uniformly executed and lacked the expressive and atmospheric quality of the landscape painter. They displayed polite or amateur art to be used by the landscape "improver" rather than a painter.[44] Referring to his sketches as working tools to distinguish from landscape painting, he highlighted his favorite colors:

> The slight and often gaudy sketches by which I have found it necessary to elucidate my opinions are the strongest proofs that I do not profess to be a landscape painter, but to represent the scenes of nature in her various *hues of blue sky, purple mountains, green trees*, etc., which are often disgusting to the eye of a connoisseur in painting [italics added].[45]

Color in his watercolors was restrained and coordinated to create an attractive harmony without undermining the integrity of the spatial design or structure of the garden. Greens and blues dominated landscape scenes because they coincided with Repton's deference to and romanticism of nature.

Repton sketched outdoors on site. He began with pencil or brown or black ink outlines to delineate foreground objects, added human figures for scale, filled in the middle- and background, and finally introduced light and shade effects. These on-site, rough sketches were then completed in his studio with wet brush color washes. Darker tints, followed by lighter tints, and final details were added to enliven the foreground. Hand-colored with the help of studio assistants, Repton's watercolors expressed the translucency and wide-ranging tonal gradation of the medium. All landscape hues were tinted to look earthy, never pure. Repton used dark olive and slate green mixed with browns for trees, pale greens for grass, light blue-gray and jade green for the sky and water features, and off-white for clouds. Garden paths introduced goldenrod yellow and khaki contrasts to the compositions. Expediency and uniformity were requisites of Repton's business-minded production: the appeal of his drawings to both upper-class and bourgeois clients was calibrated to sell.[46]

Repton invented a landscape design representation that would appeal to a broad audience. He borrowed and mixed drawing and color techniques from high- and low-brow art and from diverse genres: villa books, picturesque travel manuals, and theater scenic set design. His proposals displayed picturesque compositional rules of asymmetry, a spectator eye-level position, hidden features, horizontal strips of undulating terrain, and an illuminated horizon leading the eye to the distance. He often introduced abbey or castle ruins to add to the scenic "consequence" or meaning, and side trees as view-framing devices (a convention known as "coulisse" in theater jargon) (see Figure I.2). Unlike architectural plans and elevations, Repton used perspectives that placed the viewer at the center, at eye level with the landscape, thus making his design proposals more accessible to laypersons. On occasion, maps were used to help orient a client to the view of the site. Repton's invention of the flap, or "slide" in his vernacular, displayed views of a proposed landscape improvement in a comparative "before and after" pairing: an overlaid flap could be lifted to show how the scene would appear when the work was completed. The flap was a device borrowed from scenic set design.[47]

Repton was aware of the newly acquired status of illustrators and the growing commercialization of landscape in the burgeoning visual culture. The representational elements of illusion, surprise, and magic served as marketing tactics to instill a desire for a design product, especially through "scenic illusionism."[48] Not unlike the criticism leveled against Giorgione—for using colors as "trickery"—Repton's colorful perspectives and flap-lifting "trick" were considered seductive, distasteful, and even immoral among contemporary art collectors, aestheticians, and professional rivals.[49] His adversaries argued that he manipulated proposed designs by presenting an unrealistically more cheerful scene to demonstrate the supposed superiority of the proposed improvement. He was accused of using fictitious harmonious color schemes, including water reflections and washes of orange tint (the complement to blue), to increase visual appeal and promote consumer desire. In his defense, Repton cited Edmund Burke (echoing Baudelaire): "A true artist should put a generous deceit on the spectators and effect the noblest designs by easy methods. ... No work of art can be great but as it deceives; to be otherwise is the prerogative of nature only."[50] Repton described his approach in fabricating the position of an observer's gaze and exaggerating color harmony in his sketches for Barton Park in Sussex (1798) in a similar fashion: "I have taken a painter's license in the warmth of the foreground, to preserve that degree of keeping in a picture which in Nature is done without such artificial management."[51]

Repton used his experiments with the light spectrum to verify and adjust the Old Masters' tints he applied to his drawings and prints. He used what he learned from testing

the laws of optics to create drawings as close
to nature as possible. For example, he studied
the manifestations of color under different
atmospheric conditions and at different times
of the day and seasons. In one experiment, he
registered light through a prism on a white
paper fastened to a black cloth and systematically
observed the changes of hues as the cool tints of
early daylight were succeeded by warm tints (see
Figure 1.2). He recorded the succession of color
from the neutral tints of brown and gray before
sunrise to the bright rainbow colors of full sun,
noting the aerial perspective and color variations
between distant and near objects, as he had
observed in Old Masters' paintings.[52] He brought
these observations to his watercolors, applying
warm washes in the foreground and cool and blue
tints to backgrounds to emulate natural effects
and strengthen the depth of aerial perspectives.

Among his experiments with color and light,
Repton discovered that shadows are not simply
black and used indigo or purple instead.[53] Yet
he limited contrast to produce soft picturesque
beauty and to avoid breaking up the landscape
composition, by creating a relatively uniform
and subtle gradation scheme, with color glazing

SUNSHINE AFTER RAIN

1.9 Aquatint, "Sunshine after Rain," *Fragments on the Theory and Practice of Landscape Gardening,* 1816. Yale Center for British Art, Paul Mellon Collection

intended to soothe and unify the whole. Occasional sequential views depicting extreme
or abrupt changes from an enclosed to an open scene were carefully handled to avoid the
"shock of the sublime" by keeping the intensity of the light quality constant.

In his chapter "Concerning Contrasts," Repton discussed four kinds of tonal contrasts he
observed in nature: transparency versus opacity of foliage; gaudy coloring versus relaxing
white flowers or a mass of dark and light foliage; fine versus coarse texture of flower colors;
and the contrast of small and large flower size. In the analysis of his drawing "Sunshine after
Rain", he elaborated on the topic, advocating for "weak" contrast:

> [T]hough we may admire the stately and aspiring character of the hollyhock and
> larkspur among flowers, with the cedar and cypress among trees, yet if we turn to
> the opposite side, we shall confess the justice of Mr. Burke's remarks, that *a certain
> degree of weakness* is not incompatible with beauty; and that in vegetables, as in the
> human form, the apparent need of support increases the interest we feel in what
> is graceful or beautiful [italics added].[54]

Repton clearly appreciated picturesque beauty, but he ceded the creation of awesome and
sublime effects to nature, reasoning that he could neither create nor represent such drama
(Figure 1.9). The bright and contrasting colors of red, blue, and purple as well as black and white
entered the composition only as artifacts and, especially, people's clothing. Like architectural

color codes, clothing tints represented the social status of the wearer; brighter colors denoted higher status. Water and sky elements are the most expressive parts of Repton's drawings, projecting atmospheric and temporal conditions to create different moods. The primary effect of water was that of a mirror, reflecting surrounding trees and clouds and refracting and animating colored forms. Repton brightened the lower part of the sky to accentuate the landscape skyline and to draw the viewer's gaze to the horizon. He often animated the sky with stylized clouds—white and fluffy to create a serene and cozy atmosphere, gray and heavy to foster a stormy, unsettling mood.

Repton's Red Books and five commercial books involved careful product design considerations. Color, dependent on the printing process and available technology, was used to convey status and brand. It was functional as well as business and culture coded.

1.10 Typical Red Book cover of the early period in light brown calfskin (Scrivelsby, Lincolnshire) 1790 (top); typical Red Book cover from May 1793 onward in Morocco red (Welbeck Abbey), 1793 (middle); one of three types of marbled paper, Type II: English spot (Brandsbury), 1789 (bottom)

Red Books: Status and Brand

Like his drawings, Repton's books both borrowed product design from existing genres and were original products. The practice of packaging architectural design proposals in loose folios for patrons was established, but Repton was the first to do so for landscape gardening. He bound his drawings and packaged his proposal as a book, which became an educational device, a marketing tool, and an item of visual curiosity considered "more creative than any other architecture representation of the period."[55] It enabled patrons to comprehend and imagine proposed landscape improvements, learn to appreciate and judge landscape scenes, and use the book for "living room coffee table" conversation and to flaunt their esteemed consultant, the landscape gardening taste authority of the time.

Repton dubbed his bound products "Red Books" after he began using "Morocco red" dyed goatskin in 1793 (Figure 1.10); until then, the books were bound with light brown calfskin. The Morocco red was used for branding, to form identity and recognition. It was a fashionable aristocratic book cover color at the time, and the cover's gold floral frame decoration befitted this status, while elaborate marbled-paper were used as endpapers inside the cover.[56]

Written and packaged as visual performances for patrons, the books were free of technical jargon and excessive detail; they were descriptive, engaging, and entertaining. The manuscript pages and drawings were alternatingly arranged and carefully sequenced to produce an intelligible and engaging reading experience, emulating the experience of strolling through the proposed gardens. All pages were line-framed to reinforce the picturesque nature of the project—a line-frame for the manuscript page, and triple or double rectangular frames for the drawings. The inner golden-beige band, chosen to best display the image, was framed with dark and light gray bands. In the garden, physical framing devices such as gates and trees produced similar effects. The framing also recalled watercolor mounts used in exhibitions and collectors' portfolios at the time, giving each page the status of a mountable artwork.[57] Oval frames, a convention derived from a Claude glass used by painters, contained vignettes of built features such as gates or benches.

Whereas the costly customized and handmade Red Books featured an abundance of original hand-colored drawings, commercially produced print books were sparing in their use of illustrations and color, in part due to ineffective printing technology and in part due to the expense. The 250 copies of *Sketches and Hints* sold initially for an exorbitant 2½ guineas apiece. When a new edition was to be published 12 years later, Repton pledged to reduce costs by avoiding expensive engravings, and thus reach a wider and more diverse audience.[58] When possible, he used the new aquatint technique, in which engravings were overlaid with watercolor washes. For his plates, he used a two-step process: an initial engraved print with neutral brown and gray tints that were then hand-glazed with rainbow watercolors.[59] He was known to work closely with and give specific instructions to printers and colorists. In *Fragments* he shared these laborious instructions:

> The Plates to be printed in a bluish-grey ink (this is the neutral tint for the light and shade of the Landscape); the colourer to wash in the sky with blue or violet, etc. according to each sketch; also going over the distances with the same colour; then wash the foregrounds and middle distances with red, orange, or yellow, copying the drawings; and when dry, wash over with blue, to produce the greens in the middle distances: this being done as a dead colouring, a few touches with the hand of the master, and a harmonizing tint to soften the whole, will produce all the effect expected from a coloured print.[60]

Later and posthumous editions of Repton's work included few color plates, drawing on the newly invented color engraving printing process or intaglio that used three plates, each dyed with one of the three primaries—red, yellow, and blue—to produce all the colors in the spectrum. The color engraving technique affected color aesthetics, as green lost its status in the color hierarchy to blue. In both color production and in painting, green was no longer a basic or primary color, but a mixture of blue and yellow.[61] Intaglio also signaled an end to the color-versus-line drawing debate that ensued in the fledgling phase of color printing. It was replaced by a debate on color versus form.

* * *

The small number of projects that Repton built, and the changes made since the time of their construction, make the Red Books the best source to study Repton's approach to color. The shift in color aesthetic over the three decades of his practice is most evident in two works that anchor his early and late career: the earliest surviving *Red Book for Brandsbury* (1789) and the *Report Concerning the Gardens of Ashridge* (1813).

1.11 *Red Book of Brandsbury*, 1789, view from the main lawn southeast toward London. Dumbarton Oaks Research Library

The Red Book for Brandsbury, Hon. Lady Salusbury, Middlesex, March 1789; planting completed in 1790

Repton's first Red Book, for Brandsbury, became the template for his future Red Books and is therefore a valuable reference. Among other landscape improvement projects, Repton used Brandsbury to demonstrate key design principles articulated in his first book, *Sketches and Hints*.[62]

The brown calfskin-bound manuscript opens with an introductory letter to the owner, Lady Salusbury, and proceeds to analyze the site and its topography and visual assets and deficiencies. The core of the book is a description of the proposed experience using a planned tour, an itinerary with scenes from the garden to the surroundings, and from the house toward the garden. Two maps, one coded with the letters A–K, enable the reader to follow the described tour and locate corresponding views on the map. The book's 11 drawings—two plans, six perspectives that include before-and-after slides, and three vignettes—illustrate the design intentions described in the 19 folios. Their placement corresponds to the narrative. The book ends with four pages entitled "Deviations" in which special, built garden features are addressed, including garden seats, shade, water, and apple trees. The design illustrations focus on three directional "good" views toward London, Hampstead, and the nearby hill (the framing of the distant city view is a longstanding tradition dating to villa design in Ancient Rome and Renaissance Italy).

Brandsbury's landscape garden exemplifies the picturesque aesthetic color principles that Repton endorsed early in his career. Color words are absent in the description except for Repton's favorites, "green" and "verdure," to describe the plantings. Nor is there any

1.12 *Red Book of Brandsbury,* 1789, views with and without flaps of the yard west of the house.
Dumbarton Oaks Research Library

mention of light quality or contrast. As the sketches demonstrate, Repton did not choose watercolor tints to produce realism but rather to illustrate the main principles of his design: the scenic and spatial structure of the garden. Throughout the composition he kept to a limited color palette, contrasts, and shading range, as seen in Figure 1.11. Nature-coded green is the unifying agent of the illustration: light green for the grass and darker greens for the trees. The blue sky and its reflection in the pond balance the mostly two-color composition of green and blue. Tones and details gradually diminish to build up the aerial perspective of depth, with increasing blue washes added to the middle and background. The foreground shows washes of red-orange-yellow fall tints to enliven the palette, and fades toward the middle ground. The golden path, its end hidden by a bush thicket, stands out in the color scheme and animates the image with its line-of-beauty curvature, leading the viewer's eye through to the depth of the prospect. Its color is echoed in the inner frame of the picture. The eye also glides over the smooth bends of grassy terrain to the bright skyline and white clouds just above the silhouette of London on the horizon. The green, blue, and golden-yellow frame the distant city. And the low fences that protect the new tree clumps from grazing stock, painted in "invisible green," are (hardly) seen around the tree clump in the middle ground.

In Repton's letter to Lady Salusbury, he articulated the key gardening principle in terms of "concea[ling] the defects and displaying the beauties of nature." The perspective in Figure 1.12 is positioned and framed to conceal the enclosure surrounding one of these defects, the colorful working kitchen garden, just to the right of the orchard on the right side of the picture. As Repton instructed: "the principal apartment looks at present to the southeast

35

into the kitchen-garden, this I propose to remove, and have allowed about an acre for it …
this garden may be either paled, or walled …."

The before-and-after perspective illustrates the merit of removing the fence and
transforming the grand view. The gridded orchard, as the proposed view shows, was
also removed and replaced with more casual oak and elm groupings. The geometric
water feature was refigured into the picturesque curvilinear shape in the proposed
view, while the properly designed bank slopes and surrounding planting were reflected
on the water surface.

If the perspective views exude a serene pastoral mood, the three oval-framed
vignettes of built structures in the garden, the white-washed garden lodge, gate,
and seat set against a dark thicket of greenery generate excitement through tonal
contrast (see Figure 1.6). Repton designed artifacts to produce a forceful impact on
the observer, and used color-coded wooden artifices to denote the owner's status. To
weaken the deflection of the glare of full sun off the lodge walls, its paint was toned
to a darker, off-white shade, preserving the desirable weak contrast in the landscape.
Because Repton considered comfort near a residence an important factor in design,
he placed large trees in the foreground, even though they interrupt the view, for wind
protection in the winter and shade in the summer. Vivid colors could be used in a
composition to depict clothing, as with the three people climbing the fence to admire
the view (see Figure 1.5). Otherwise gaudy colors did not belong in the ideal view.
On the flap of the proposed open view, Repton replaced the people with cows in the
middle ground.

Repton often quoted a poem to close the text, as he did in the Brandsbury Red Book,
which featured a selection from *The English Garden: A Poem – Book the First* (1772) by William
Mason. It begins with a reference to cheerful colors in the foreground and proceeds to
greens in reference to the broad views of the surrounding landscape park:

> enrich with all the hues
> That flowers, that shrubs, that trees can yield, the sides
> Of that fair path from whence our sight is led
> Gradual to view, the whole. Where'er thou wind'st
> That path, take heed between the scene and eye,
>   To vary and to mix *thy chosen greens* [italics added].

The Gardens of Ashridge, Earl of Bridgewater, Hertfordshire, 1813, created in the 1820s

The *Report Concerning the Gardens of Ashridge* was one of Repton's last and favorite works
and serves as a counterpart to Brandsbury, although very different.[63] At Ashridge,
Repton was able to adhere to picturesque rule in the landscape park and, at the same time,
to free himself to experiment with flower color in the garden. In his last book, *Fragments*, he
devoted a chapter to Ashridge, where he wrote:

> the youngest favourite; the child of my age and declining powers: when no
> longer able to undertake the more extensive plans of *Landscape*, I was glad to
> contract my views within the narrow circle of the *Garden*, independent of its
> accompaniment of distant scenery.[64]

The Ashridge design marked a conceptual shift in landscape gardening, as Repton distinguished between *garden* as a work of art, a site of comfort and activity, and *landscape* as the scenery of nature. The latter was to abide by picturesque terms, whereas the garden was an artifice deserving of special treatment:

> [I]t was therefore to be wished, that the exterior of a garden should be made to assimilate with Park Scenery, or the Landscape of Nature, the interior may then he laid out with *all the variety, contrast, and even whim*, that can produce pleasing objects to the eye, however ill adapted as studies for a picture [italics added].[65]

1.13 *Report Concerning the Gardens of Ashridge*, Hertfordshire, 1813, views with and without overlay toward the park from the house terrace. Getty Research Institute, Los Angeles

Repton now believed that bright color, variety, contrast, and whim were desirable in the garden. Although he made no mention of color and only a few comments about light in the text, lighting effects and brightly colored blossoms dominate his garden drawings.

The Ashridge report was not a Red Book but a large (450 × 330 mm, roughly 18" × 13") 23-page portfolio with 14 illustrations: an annotated watercolor map, two monochromatic drawings of black ink with gray or brown washes, and 11 colorful watercolor perspectives. The drawing folios follow the text, which consisted of a long letter to the Earl of Bridgewater, an introduction that focuses on the two distinct parts of the grounds, and remarks about water and invisible fences.

The landscape park, called the "ancient garden," is a three-acre open lawn to the east and south of the house with tree-lined straight walks and trimmed hedges. The garden, called the "pleasure ground," is set in an eight-acre wooded area to the west and comprises curvilinear walks and a series of 15 small, enclosed gardens, each distinct in character and style. The folios are structured as a captioned illustrated itinerary of the 15 gardens, not unlike the Red Book of Brandsbury but without the extensive text. Repton referred to the gardens as "episodes."

Of the 11 perspectives only 1 shows the landscape park as a typical, framed landscape format in watercolor with a flap illustrating before-and-after scenes (Figure 1.13). The color palette of the open landscape park displays the bowling green, using the same tints as at Brandsbury: green, blue, and goldenrod yellow, with touches of purple in the sky. The foreground, however, shows a new terrace adorned with a white stone balustrade and framed in a colorful flower border. The boundary fence in the middle ground was removed to create a seamless sweeping view of the countryside dotted with the light brown and

1.14 "Flower Stone Garden," *Report Concerning the Gardens of Ashridge,* 1813. Getty Research Institute, Los Angeles

off-white accents of deer and livestock. The existing grand lawn is animated with people playing cricket and walking dogs. The proposed "invisible fence," essentially Capability Brown's off-sight trench, known as a "ha-ha," was the preferred choice to replace the existing wire-fence and keep grazing animals off the park.[66]

In contrast, the ten interior perspectives of the enclosed gardens are of a completely different character and format—smaller, with a narrower span in both horizontal and vertical formats, and devoid of picture frames. They take on a new expression, distinct from the picturesque, boasting a wide range of color and tonal contrast: in the Ashridge gardens Repton experimented with new color arrangements, new rules, and new representations (see Figure 1.0). Each garden "room" was enclosed in dark woods or grown hedges, against which Repton displayed bright, colorful, seasonal flower beds and borders, and behind which he hid bare, out-of-season beds. Pergolas and trelliswork lifted color to a vertical dimension with flowering vines.

The various color schemes in the proposed gardens were gleaned from different garden models. As shown in Repton's watercolors, several rooms featured single-color flower beds in shapes reminiscent of the Tudor and Jacobean eras—squares, rectangles, ovals, teardrop shapes, and circles. The Monk's Garden's raised, geometric, single-color flower beds were in the medieval tradition; the Flower Store (Figure 1.14) and the Broad Sanctuary gardens' embroidered parterres were in the Baroque and medieval traditions, respectively; and the Flower Garden's and County Stone garden's entrance, and Souterrain rockery's circular beds of single or mixed color plants sunk in the lawn reflected a modern garden trend of the time. The Rosarium, patterned after a rose-window, stood out as a novelty garden, displaying one type of plant of uniform pink or reddish color with white accents (Figure 1.15). The effect of roses in the low beds covering most of the ground area, and the trellis vines framing the garden and entrance arches, produced intense color saturation. But it was a wishful color effect impossible to achieve with the limited variety of low and climbing roses available in the 1810s.[67] The proposed scene is depicted at sunset, when orange light to the west supplants the gray sky and a fountain in the middle is illuminated.

The display of water throughout the gardens was central to light effects and animation. Water was not only a prerequisite for sustaining the gardens (considering the water scarcity at the estate) but a source of pleasure. Repton made visible a variety of water uses for the gardens: a conduit in front of the conservatory, a jet d'eau in the rosary, drips in the grotto, and a drinking pool for animals in the park.[68] He emphasized both the "bright splash of water" in the fountains and the pleasure of seeing a working irrigation system.

There are few flowering shrubs and no flowering trees in the drawings. Yet Repton embraced exotic imports, and even created a special garden for American plants, among which the magnolia was notable. Hothouses in several gardens were used for cultivating out-of-season plants for seasonal flower displays, in support of the new colorful garden

1.15 "Rosarium," *Report Concerning the Gardens of Ashridge,* 1813. Getty Research Institute, Los Angeles (top). View of the rosarium looking toward the house in 2018 (bottom). Photo: Mira Engler

trend. Flowers planted in wire baskets sunk into the lawn, mostly containing one color, created a splatter of colorful patches in the sea of green grass.

For Repton, an ornamental garden transcended painterly depiction: "The open trellis fence, and the hoops on poles over which creeping and climbing plants are gracefully spread; give a richness to garden scenery that no painting can adequately represent."[69] Ashridge exemplifies the artificiality that Repton attributed to garden art in his late career, a concept that would be further developed in the 19th century.

* * *

The distinctions Repton made between paintings and landscapes and between landscapes and artifacts in texts and in drawings enabled him not only to devise different color concepts for each but also to distance himself from the picturesque painterly color scheme and introduce a more subjective approach to landscape gardening that catered to a broader audience. By consigning the role of landscape colorist to nature, he could steer landscape gardening toward a "structural color" theory focused on space making. At the same time, his nature-coded landscape color and his delegation of the colorist role to nature aligned landscape designers with the role of draftsman rather than artist-poet, in Baudelairean terms. In Repton's work, color remained secondary to form.

As his late work demonstrates, the shift to a new conception of color that took advantage of vibrant colors coincided with his idea that gardens are works of art rather than of nature. This shift was necessary for landscape gardeners to loosen the grip of and assert their independence from both nature and painterly aesthetic. Repton's successor, J. C. Loudon, who republished Repton's books in 1840 and boosted his legacy, continued to overturn the picturesque color canon, distance garden design from nature, and advance a distinctly artifactual color concept for Georgian and Victorian gardens. His elaborate, interlocking, geometric-shaped flower bedding positioned form and color as equal partners in the garden.

Notes

[1]   According to the horticulture historian Brent Elliott (1986), the gardener James Meader was the first to provide a plant list arranged by color under the title *The Painter's Guide* in 1779. See Elliott, *Victorian Gardens*, 1986, 48.

[2]   Repton, *The Theory and Practice of Landscape Gardening*, [1803] 1907, 137, 149.

[3]   Daniels, "Scenic Transformation and Landscape Improvement," 2008, 47.

[4]   For Repton's savvy business tendencies, see Engler, "Landscape Design and Consumer Culture," 2018, 1–4. Also see Hunt, "Sense and Sensibility in the Landscape Designs of Humphry Repton," 1992.

[5]   Repton, *Sketches and Hints on Landscape Gardening*, [1793] 1907, 60; Repton, *An Enquiry into the Changes of Taste in Landscape Gardening*, 1806.

6   Chapter XI, "Concerning Colour," and its many corresponding notes were based on the writings of personal acquaintances William Wilberforce and Milner. See Repton, *Theory and Practice*, [1803] 1907, note 47, pp. 245–50.

7   Chapter XII, "Concerning Colour" and Chapter XX, "Concerning Contrasts," in Repton, *Fragments*, [1816] 1982, 49–51; 97–101.

8   On Repton's drawing tints, see André Rogger, *Repton's Red Books*, 2007, 111.

9   Repton did not give a name to his color theory. The word "structural" is consistent with his attention to the structure of composition and garden space.

10 Pastoureau, *Green*, 2014, 190. The use of green on canvas was not perfected until the 1840s. The "painter's favorite" chromatic scheme may have had much to do with the unstable quality of the green pigment at the time, which turned into browns and blues.

11 Repton, *Sketches and Hints*, [1793] 1907, 56.

12 Repton, *Theory and Practice*, [1803] 1907, 149.

13 The frequent advice to "follow nature" was premised on the 18th century view that beauty was innate to the external world, objective, and independent of human will. Elliott, *Victorian Gardens*, 1986, 8.

14 Ibid., 33.

15 Elliott, *Victorian Gardens*, 1986, 48–9.

16 Repton, *Theory and Practice*, [1803] 1907, 217.

17 Ibid., 137.

18 Ibid.

19 Pastoureau, *Green*, 2014, 172.

20 Repton, *Sketches and Hints*, [1793] 1907, 41.

21 Ibid., 40. Repton borrowed the "broken color" concept from Price.

22 Repton, *Theory and Practice*, [1803] 1907, 100.

23 Ibid., 249.

24 Ibid., 218–19.

25 A distinction that Baudelaire would make a century later.

26 Repton, *An Enquiry*, 1806, 95; Repton made a similar statement in *Sketches and Hints*, [1793] 1907, 36.

27 Repton, *Theory and Practice*, [1803] 1907, 189.

28 Repton, *Sketches and Hints*, [1793] 1907, 43. An early drawing of bright colors in a garden, in circular flower beds in lawns, can be seen in Repton's sketch for Tewin Water, Hertfordshire (1799). It was to add "cheerfulness" to the scene. In the 1800s his perspectives increasingly displayed more vivid tints, with orange and yellow added to the washes. This coincided with the growing taste for geometric flower beds with bright colors near the house.

29 Repton, *Theory and Practice*, [1803] 1907, 186.

30 Repton, *Sketches and Hints*, [1793] 1907, 17.

31 Repton, *Theory and Practice*, [1803] 1907, 218.

32 Following Isaac Newton's 1666 discovery of the light spectrum and its measured increments, experiments to measure color using color charts, scales, laws, and norms were developed. In the early 18th century, most artists followed scientists in color classifications.

33 Repton, *Theory and Practice*, [1803] 1907, 186.

34 Repton, *Sketches and Hints*, [1793] 1907, 54.

35 Repton, *Theory and Practice*, [1803] 1907, 186.

36   Repton, *Sketches and Hints*, [1793] 1907, 54.

37   Repton, *Theory and Practice*, [1803] 1907, 186.

38   Ibid., 187.

39   Repton, *Sketches and Hints*, [1793] 1907, 16.

40   Repton, *Theory and Practice*, [1803] 1907, 189.

41   Elliott, *Victorian Gardens*, 1986, 23.

42   Ibid., 4.

43   Repton, *Sketches and Hints*, [1793] 1907, 4.

44   Rogger, *Red Books*, 2007, 108.

45   Repton, *Theory and Practice*, [1803] 1907, 149.

46   Engler, "Consumer Culture," 2018, 8–10.

47   Before-and-after tactics persist as a central technique in landscape architecture to this day and have become the quintessential advertising representation.

48   For a discussion of Repton's Red Book drawings, see Daniels, *Humphry Repton*, 1999.

49   Daniels, "Scenic Transformation," 2008, 48.

50   Repton, *Theory and Practice*, [1803] 1907, 167.

51   Rogger, *Red Books*, 2007, 170, 261.

52   Repton, *Fragments*, [1816] 1982, 49–51. Repton explained that "the intervening mass of vapour (called aerial perspective) takes away colour and blends it with the neutral tint."

53   The chemically produced natural colorant indigo was discovered at that time and began to be used in paintings and drawings.

54   Repton, *Fragments*, [1816] 1982, 97.

55   Powers, "Architectural Book," 2002, 166. Some landscape proposals were commissioned with no intention of executing them; instead, the Red Books were used for coffee table display and living room conversation. Repton also used the books to promote his business by inserting his professional card in the front cover of each book.

56   Rogger, *Red Books*, 2007, 67.

57   Ibid.

58   Repton, *Sketches and Hints*, [1793] 1907, iv.

59   Repton, *Fragments*, [1816] 1982, 51–2. Repton also discusses some of the improvements he instituted to make the operation less laborious and more cost-effective.

60   Ibid., 51.

61   Pastoureau, *Blue*, 2017. Color engraving was invented by Jakob Christoph Le Blon in the early 18th century and perfected late in the century.

62   For a reproduction of the Brandsbury Red Book, see Daniels, *The Red Books,* 1994.

63   Repton designed Ashridge with his son, John Adey Repton. It was executed by Sir Jeffry Wyatville.

64   Repton, *Fragments*, [1816] 1982, 137 [italics in original].

65   Ibid., 142.

66   Ibid., 147.

67   Rutherford, "Introduction," 2013, 14. The rosary was implemented in the 1820s, when rose varieties such as Portlands became available with repeated flowering qualities.

68   Repton, *Fragments*, [1816] 1982, 144–6.

69   Ibid, 147.

References

Daniels, Stephen, ed. *Humphry Repton: The Red Books for Brandsbury and Glemham Hall*. Washington: Dumbarton Oaks Research Library & Collection, 1994.

Daniels, Stephen. *Humphry Repton: Landscape Gardening and the Geography of Georgian England*. New Haven, CT: Yale University Press, 1999.

Daniels, Stephen. "Scenic Transformation and Landscape Improvement: Temporalities in the Garden Design of Humphrey Repton." In *Representing Landscape Architecture*, ed. by Marc Treib, 42–55. Trowbridge, Wiltshire: Cromwell Press, 2008.

Elliott, Brent. *Victorian Gardens*. London: Butler & Tanner Ltd., 1986.

Engler, Mira. "Landscape Design and Consumer Culture in the Work of Humphry Repton and Gordon Cullen: A Methodological Framework." *Architecture_MPS* 13, no. 1 (2018): 2. DOI: https://doi.org/10.14324/111.444.amps.2018v13i2.001

Hunt, John Dixon, ed. "Sense and Sensibility in the Landscape Designs of Humphry Repton." In *Gardens and the Picturesque*, 138–68. Cambridge, MA: MIT Press, 1992.

Mason, William. *The English Garden: A Poem. Book the First*. London: R. Horsfield and H. Dunoyer, 1772.

Pastoureau, Michel. *Green: The History of a Color*. Princeton, NJ: Princeton University Press, 2014.

Pastoureau, Michel. *Blue: The History of a Color*. Princeton, NJ: Princeton University Press, 2017.

Powers, Alan. "The Architectural Book: Image and Accident." In *This Is Not Architecture: Media Constructions*, ed. by Kester Rattenbury, 157–73. London: Routledge, 2002.

Priestley, Joseph. *The History and Present State of Discoveries Relating to Vision, Light, and Colours*. London: J. Johnson, 1772.

Repton, Humphry. *Plans, Sketches & Proposals for the Improvement of Her Ladyship's Villa Lately Purchased, Call'd Brandsbury at Wilsden, in Middlesex*. 1789. Available online from the library at Dumbarton Oaks, Washington, DC.

Repton, Humphry. *An Enquiry into the Changes of Taste in Landscape Gardening*. London: J. Taylor, 1806.

Repton, Humphry. *Sketches and Hints on Landscape Gardening* [1793]. In *The Art of Landscape Gardening*, ed. by John Nolen, 1–62. Boston: Mifflin and Company, 1907.

Repton, Humphry. *The Theory and Practice of Landscape Gardening* [1803]. In *The Art of Landscape Gardening*, ed. by John Nolen, 63–217. Boston: Mifflin and Company, 1907.

Repton, Humphry. *Fragments on the Theory and Practice of Landscape Gardening* [1816]. New York: Garland Publishing, 1982.

Rogger, André. *The Art of Humphry Repton's Red Books*. Abingdon: Routledge, 2007.

Rutherford, Sarah. "Introduction." In *The Gardens of Ashridge by Humphry Repton*, 11–15. Ashridge, Hertfordshire: Ashridge Trust/Getty Research Institute, 2013.

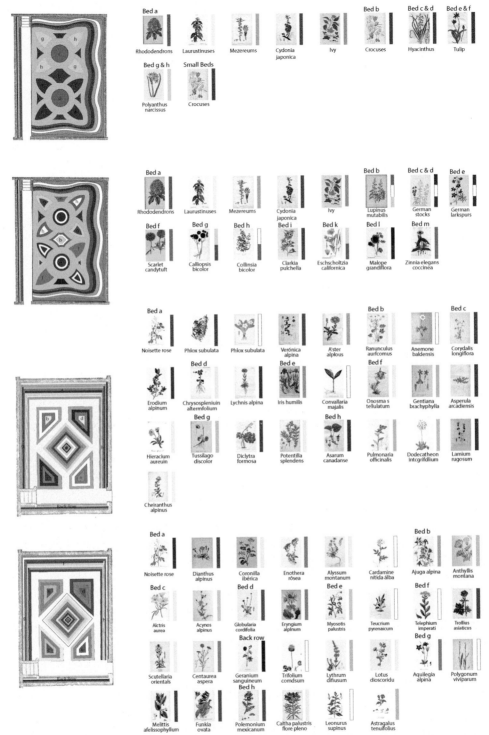

Bed a — Rhododendrons, Laurustinuses, Mezereums, Cydonia japonica, Ivy
Bed b — Crocuses
Bed c & d — Hyacinthus
Bed e & f — Tulip
Bed g & h — Polyanthus narcissus
Small Beds — Crocuses

Bed a — Rhododendrons, Laurustinuses, Mezereums, Cydonia japonica, Ivy
Bed b — Lupinus mutabilis
Bed c & d — German stocks
Bed e — German larkspurs
Bed f — Scarlet candytuft
Bed g — Calliopsis bicolor
Bed h — Collinsia bicolor
Bed i — Clarkia pulchella
Bed k — Eschscholtzia californica
Bed l — Malope grandiflora
Bed m — Zinnia elegans coccinea

Bed a — Noisette rose, Phlox subulata, Phlox subulata, Verónica alpina, A'ster alplous
Bed b — Ranunculus aurfcomus, Anemone baldensis
Bed c — Corydalis longiflora
Bed d — Erodium alpinum, Chrysospleniuin altermfolium, Lychnis alpina, Iris humilis
Bed e — Convallaria majalis
Bed f — Onosma s tellulatum, Gentiana brachyphylla, Asperula arcadiensis
Hieracium aureuin
Bed g — Tussilago discolor, Diclytra formosa, Potentilla splendens
Bed h — Asarum canadanse, Pulmonaria officinalis, Dodecatheon intcgrifdlium, Lamium rugosum
Cheiranthus alpinus

Bed a — Noisette rose, Dianthus alpinus, Coronilla ibérica, Enothera rósea, Alyssum montanum, Cardamine nitida álba
Bed b — Ajuga alpina, Anthyllis montana
Bed c — Alctris aurea, Acynos alpinus, Globularia cordifolia
Bed d — Eryngium alplnum, Myosotis palustris, Teucrium pyrenaicum
Bed e —
Bed f — Telephium imperati, Trollius asiaticus
Scutellaria orientals, Centaurea aspera, Geranium sanguineum
Back row — Trifolium comdsum, Lythrum difiusum, Lotus dioscoridu
Bed g — Aquilegia alpina, Polygonum viviparum
Bed h — Melittis afelissophyllum, Funkia ovata, Polemonium mexicanum, Caltha palustris flore pleno, Leonurus supinus, Astragalus tenuifolius

2.0 J. C. Loudon, 4th rate suburban garden designs, *Suburban Gardener and Villa Companion*, 1838. Planting schemes producing symmetrical masses of color in two seasons: bulbs from March to mid-May followed by annuals from mid-May to July (Upper two; figure 57, pp: 227–9) and planting color schemes of perennial varieties from February to May and June to August (lower two, figure 65, pp. 217–19). Colors are based on selection from proposed plant lists. Plant illustrations from various 19th century botanical magazines. Rendered by Fan Lan, Asif Khan, and Maryam Maddahzad

2

Artificial Color
Bright and Complementary,
J. C. Loudon (1783–1843)

The choice ... is deficient in evergreens, and in sorts which blossom and are in perfection early in spring, and late in autumn; for by attention to these there might be trees, shrubs and flowers, in blossom and luxuriance every month of the year, and particularly in winter. ... [S]uch a selection ought to be made, as that our squares might perpetually abound with flowers ... the most enchanting effects, and grateful fragrance.

J. C. Loudon, *Literary Journal*, 1803, col. 740

When John Claudius Loudon first arrived in London in 1803 at the age of 20, he was struck by the gloomy appearance of public squares and attributed this impression to the limited palette of mostly evergreen shrubs and trees, notably Scotch pines, yews, and spruce firs. His observation prompted him to publish a letter to the editor of the *Literary Journal*, entitled "Hints Respecting the Manner of Laying Out the Grounds of the Public Squares in London, to the Utmost Picturesque Advantage." He suggested replacing yews and firs with a mix of evergreen, deciduous, and ornamental trees, such as oriental and occidental plane trees, sycamores, and almonds.[1] In this very first publication, Loudon rejected Uvedale Price's and Humphry Repton's picturesque scheme of uniform verdure and autumn tints, calling instead for a larger plant palette and a year-round celebration of colorful blossom.

Loudon linked "the proper idea of what these urban squares would be, if they were judiciously decorated" and "congruously laid out" with a lack of knowledge about new plant varieties that were becoming available at the time.[2] With apt botanical knowledge, he averred, "there would be an everlasting variety that would at once interest and relieve the eye, and satisfy the mind."[3] In his view, the new requisite for good taste in gardening involved equal knowledge of botanical science and the art of landscape painting. But this approach to landscape gardening began to undermine the authority of 18th century pictorial aesthetics and the role of the painter and to raise the status of 19th century botanical science and the gardener.[4] The gradual detachment from painting has been associated with the emergence of a new perception of color and a desire for showy polychrome and complementary contrast in the garden (Figure 2.0).[5]

Loudon was a farmer, nurseryman, landscape gardener, and self-taught botanist and horticulturalist. His influence hinged on his prolific publications about landscape gardening and related subjects: 34 books, multiple articles, and four monthly periodicals between 1804 and 1843.[6] His literary genre of choice was the encyclopedia, in contrast to Repton's textual hints and fragments,[7] and the encyclopedias and gardening periodicals continued to shift landscape gardening discourse from scholarly and erudite readers to amateurs. These

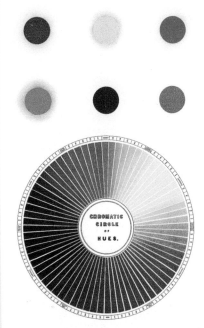

2.1 M. E. Chevreul, "Illustration of Simultaneous Contrast of Colors," plate I (top) and "Chromatic Circle of Hues," plate VI (bottom), *The Principles of Harmony and Contrast of Colors and Their Applications to the Arts*, 1854

publications were directed toward a growing audience of laypersons and professional landscape gardeners who lacked design skills and sought guidance on care for the exotic plants that were becoming available. The art of gardening turned toward science and horticultural practice, and garden color became the subject of a new aesthetics based on botanical specificity, new scientific color theories, and the nascent consumer culture.

Loudon's work was rooted in the expanding horticultural and technological worlds. Floriculture, which emerged in the 17th century as imports of plant varieties arrived in the British Isles from Europe, North America, South America, and the Indies, reached its peak during Loudon's life time. The influx of foreign plants and the greater variety of naturalized and hybridized plants were coupled with advances in greenhouse technology.[8] Society, too, radically changed with the sudden increase in middle-class suburbs with their small gardens. As a result, the landscape park was joined by colorful flower gardens and, by midcentury, color had established itself as the leading artistic gardening trend and discourse topic. The desired effect was showy displays of bright, complementary colors in geometric bedding patterns, each bed a solid color mass. In the color-versus-form debate, color would rise from an inferior position to the status of form by midcentury, and the two became interdependent. It was a major shift in garden color history, if not a revolution.

For Loudon, unlike Repton, color had little to do with spatial structure or pictorial composition; it was a statement of artistic expression and garden ornament. He extended Repton's late-life small flower gardens in large estate grounds to small and midsize suburban gardens and urban parks.

Loudon's landscape gardening approach changed over his four-decade career, following shifting, contemporaneous philosophical theories—from Archibald Alison to Antoine-Chrysostome Quatremère de Quincy—and scientific color theories—from Isaac Newton to Michel Eugène Chevreul (Figure 2.1). He never fully subscribed to the picturesque garden style, but for a brief period in the 1800s he endorsed a style based on direct observations of plant growth in nature, which he called the Natural Style. A decade later, the idea of gardens as distinctly artificial in form and color emerged. It persisted throughout his career in the two garden styles he promoted, gardenesque and formal, and became central to the Victorian garden color aesthetic.

Specimen: The Necessity of Observation ("Not All Greens Are the Same")

Loudon had an urge to assemble, typify, catalogue, and teach vast subjects, from farming to architecture, from interior design to botany, horticulture, and gardening. The wealth and market availability of foreign species from warmer climates, new plant hybrids that yielded brighter colors than the native flower varieties and herbaceous plants traditionally available, and the growing status of scientific knowledge all drove Loudon to classify the plant world.

His initial interest in color was an extension of his love of botany and plant classification. Most of his landscape color references concerned plants, with occasional mentions of color in walks and fences. He considered the selection, arrangement, and management of plants to be the most significant landscape gardening tasks. All other landscape materials came by default and "are commonly beyond our control."[9] This position made Loudon the father of planting design, a subfield of landscape design and the only one in which color has been consistently considered. His requisite for garden designers was the capacity to identify plant genera and species based on form and color, the chief identifiable characteristics of a flowering specimen.[10] Yet he recognized that while color was clearly the first characteristic to be observed, it was not an end in itself.[11]

Loudon introduced the use of botanical science in English landscape gardening, but it was not purely scientific (it has been characterized as a "soft science" mixed with art and prose).[12] He put greater emphasis on the visual than the scientific botanical classification in order to appeal to a wider audience. In so doing, he abandoned the Linnaean taxonomy based on the means of propagation and its vast number of unconnected images and facts, in favor of the natural system of Antoine Laurent de Jussieu (1748–1836), grouping plants according to natural similarities of form and other visual characteristics. His plant characterization was less abstract and thus more accessible to an untrained eye and was perceived as more harmonious in terms of plant form and color.[13] Loudon deemed Jussieu's plant taxonomy essential for the landscape gardener, who looks for "*a clear and distinct picture* of every individual species in his mind; that, whenever a tree is wanted, that kind may instantly present itself which is best fitted for his purpose" [italics added].[14] His choice of the word "picture" instead of "order," clearly favored visual over purely scientific classification.

Loudon's first book, *Observations on the Formation and Management of Useful and Ornamental Plantations* (1804), encapsulated the knowledge of plants in a list of 22 characteristics. Color, although a highly prominent plant feature, was listed fourth, after size, form, and texture. He subsequently addressed color across plant parts—flower petal, leaf, bark, and fruit—and seasonal change, classified as permanent color (all shades of green during the summer months) and accidental color (the reds and yellows of autumn or spring),[15] taking great care to name nuanced tints:

> Accidental colours are infinite in number, and each kind is liable to much variation. In autumn, however, it will generally be found that the wild-cherry assumes a bright red, the birch a deep red, the beech a brownish red, the scarlet oak a deep scarlet, the hornbeam a russet colour, the sugar maple a rich yellow, the oak a reddish yellow, the lime and ash a straw colour, the poplar black, the sycamore brown, &c.

Yet permanent color was indeed varied, and Loudon recognized these differences:

> Not all greens are the same. It may be thought by some, that the different tints of green in trees are too minute distinctions to be attended to; but reflection and experience shew that they are of material consequence in scenery.

47

Some permanent colors

> are of a dark green, as those of the horse-chestnut and the yew; some are of a
> light green, as those of the ash and the common laurel; some are of a blue green,
> as those of the Scotch fir and the bladder senna;

others display greens tinged or spotted with brown, yellow, red, or purple. Loudon attributed the reason many people consider trees to have no color but green (except in autumn) to a lack of careful observation and ignorance of the natural laws of Newton, referring to the plant light absorption principle. Green, he explained, is only one tree color and dominant for only a few weeks in midsummer when other colors are nearly absorbed; in autumn and spring, green tints "are merely weakened, not destroyed."

The exploding variety of color of new plant imports and a concern about botanical plant genus and species identification led Loudon to minute specificity of plant color characteristics. In his epic *Encyclopaedia of Plants* (1829), he listed 75 flower plant color variations and their abbreviations. This classification includes 12 distinct hues, such as red, yellow, white, and purple; more than 30 tint variations, such as russet, rosy, reddish, lemon-colored, citron, tan, and lilac; and some 20 tonal impressions, such as bright, dull, dingy, dark, and vivid; in addition to textural specificity, such as variegated, veiny, and spotted.[16]

The popularity of color in gardens and accompanying discourse also hinged on advances both in color systematization and print media technology. As a writer and publisher, Loudon understood the influence of both on discourse about color. Systematization improved the capacity of the print media to render appealing highly accurate botanical illustrations, both hand- and mechanically colored engravings and lithographs.[17] The availability of new botanical and horticulture periodicals with accurate plant illustrations was vital to both gardeners' education and consumer demand for color (Figure 2.2).

In his *Gardener's Magazine* (published from 1826 to 1844), Loudon was outspoken about the quality of other magazines' plates and the staggering cost involved.[18] Although colored images increasingly appeared in his magazines, from the 1830s on, to remain competitive, his thick books remained largely colorless to minimize cost.[19] With some textually labeled color names, the illustrations—whether on separate plates or integrated in the text—ranged from crude line wood engravings to elegant copperplate engravings of landscape scenery and scientifically accurate plant drawings, depending on the publication audience and cost.

Loudon's early notes on color in *Observations* (1804) were rooted in empirical science and accompanied by a deep interest in the capacity of colors to affect perception and elicit emotion. The picturesque aesthetic and reliance on nature as the only safe guides for gardening were replaced with reliance on empirical aesthetics and grounded in a new philosophical underpinning, the theory of association. Loudon aligned his ideas with the writing of the Scottish philosopher Archibald Alison (1757–1839), although he mentioned him by name only in the 1822 *Encyclopaedia of Gardening*.[20] Alison's association theory rejected the idea that the aesthetic response was universal and external, determined by objects or views. Instead, he posited that emotional responses to landscapes rely on associations in the observer's mind. Works of art and nature first signify material quality through form, color, smell, sound, and composition; emotions are then elicited through impressions generated in the mind in response to both the overall quality and its components. Material qualities thus affect the perception of beauty only through impressions or associations. Alison's theory, in

2.2 Title page (left) and hand-colored engravings of exotic plants from *The Botanical Register*, Vol. VI, 1820, plates 438, 446, 488 (top, left to right)

which nature was a matter of subjective observation and response, would lead to varied tastes.

Alison privileged form over color. He posited that most colors relate to "an established imagery in our minds, and are considered as expressive of many very pleasing and affecting qualities."[21]

Thus colors are not beautiful in themselves; rather, they evoke an association in the mind of the observer—and a perception of beauty may dissipate when the association fades. He divided color association into three categories: permanent, metaphorical, and accidental.[22] Permanent association derived from a recurrent and known colored object; for instance, green is associated with the color of the plants and new growth in spring, and consequently evokes the delight associated with that season after the muted colors and colder temperatures of winter. Metaphorical association stems from an analogy between certain colors and certain dispositions of mind—such as soft or strong, cheerful or solemn. Accidental association is formed through cultural or personal connotation; for instance, purple denotes dignity from its cultural association with kings' robes.

In *Observations*, Loudon's permanent color category aligned perfectly with Alison's. And although he did not explicitly embrace Alison's category of metaphorical association, he addressed it under the topics of plant "expression or character" and associated "train of emotions".[23] Considering the capacity of colors to elicit sensations of warmth and coolness, or strength and weakness, Loudon held that the way physical weight—heaviness or lightness—was expressed through form was analogous to the dark and light qualities of colors. For instance, he linked cheerfulness with the light and airy form of the ash, and melancholy with the cypress's dark green and narrow, rigid shape. He wrote about the solemn emotion evoked by the bowing branches and drooping spray of the yellow weeping willow, which "suits with scenes of solitude, and leads to meditation."[24] He also noted the emotions generated through cultural associations with plants; sorrowful emotions aligned with the use of cypresses and weeping willows in a cemetery. But he did not place this kind of association under Alison's accidental category.[25]

Throughout the 1820s, Loudon followed Alison's theory that "[o]f all material qualities, that which is most generally, and most naturally productive of the emotions of sublimity and beauty, is form."[26] He concurred that form was the highest order of aesthetics, both in artwork and in nature:

> [The sources of beauty] were conveyed to the senses by the different qualities of matter, forms, sounds, colors, smells, and motion; but form is the grand characteristic of matter, and constitutes in a great degree its essence to our senses. In our remarks, therefore, on the beauties of inventive art, we shall chiefly consider design, fitness, and utility, *in regard to form* [italics added].[27]

When form was implemented, according to Alison, pleasure derived its strength from the combination and interaction, or harmony, of colors: the color expression of trees and shrubs depended on the way certain colors were made dominant or subdued when perceived.[28] Loudon therefore named three types of color combinations—those that agree, disagree, and "destroy":

> The harmony of tints, in general, is derived from certain laws in optics, by which certain colours, as red and green, yellow and purple, blue and orange, agree with one another respectively; and certain other colours, as red and orange, yellow and green, blue and purple, disagree with each other respectively: and again, certain colours, as green, purple, and orange, when mixed together, destroy each other.[29]

This led Loudon to think that color and tonal contrasts were key elements for triggering the impression of beauty, giving a scene vividness:

> When weak colours that agree are placed adjoining, they support and give spirit to each other. A hawthorn hedge, among the green of pasture fields, has the same dull, green appearance; but when opposed to the brown of a ploughed field, it appears with peculiar spirit and force.[30]

To create a color display that had an impact, the principle of grouping similar species gained prominence. Alison wrote that "[t]he great difference in the colours of trees, requires attention in their composition into groups."[31] Groupings coincided with Loudon's endorsement of the Natural and Modern or Picturesque Styles, which used nature as a guide for plant grouping and compositions that produced the color masses seen in nature.[32] This affirmation, however, was short lived.

Loudon's extensive travels to gardens throughout Europe and America in the 1810s gave rise to his admiration for different garden styles and color ideas. These and other experiences ultimately led him to the artificial method or style. In his *Encyclopaedia of Gardening*, he discussed multiple design styles:

> The object of the natural method is to promote our knowledge of the vegetable kingdom by generalizing facts and ideas; the object of the *artificial method* is to facilitate the knowledge of plants as individual objects. The merits of the former method consist in the perfection with which plants are grouped together in natural families or orders, and these families grouped among themselves; the

merits of the latter consist in the perfection with which they are arranged according to certain marks by which their names may be discovered [italics added].[33]

The artificial method used botanical knowledge and new aesthetic principles as guides. It rendered the art of landscape gardening independent from nature and its visual impression. In the late 1820s, Loudon's work moved toward greater emphasis on artificiality. His close attention to plant qualities led to his preference for planting specimens in isolation, a practice he coined the Gardenesque Style in 1832.[34] It called for an optimal and full display of the features of individual species in an overall composition. The impression of form and color became inseparable in the garden.

2.3 Engravings, detail showing Gardenesque Style tree specimen on a slope (top left) and the 1840 opening ceremony of the Derby Arboretum designed by Loudon (top right). Photograph of the approximate view in 2018 (bottom). Photo: Mira Engler

Artifice: Color of Distinction

Unlike nature, where plants intermingle, Loudon explained that the main principle of the gardenesque was "*distinctness,* or the keeping of *every particular plant perfectly isolated*, and, though near to, yet never allowing it to touch, the adjoining plants [italics added]."[35] The main gardenesque principle thus rejected any arrangement that blended or risked obscuring plant features (Figure 2.3). As a botanist, Loudon believed that if each specimen was planted in relative isolation, its natural form could develop to perfection: each flower, shrub, or tree would prominently display its distinct features (e.g., form, texture, color) so that it could be readily contemplated by

2.4 Hendon Rectory, Middlesex, Gardenesque Style garden, front garden view, *The Gardener's Magazine* XIV, May 1838

an observer. Therefore, there were no dense, intermingled masses in a gardenesque plan, only single or lightly grouped same-species trees and shrubs (Figure 2.4). He hoped that, as a result, knowledge and appreciation of plants would increase.

Loudon's artificial concept for gardens continued to evolve and in the late 1830s he embraced the formal, or "ancient," garden, which emphasized the artificiality of human handiwork through geometric, brightly colored bed patterns. The Formal Style needed a new philosophical validation, and it was explicated in the aesthetic theory of the French architectural theorist Antoine-Chrysostome Quatremère de Quincy (1755–1849), who had advanced the "principle of distinction" as early as 1823, calling for all arts to be distinct from nature. Much like his contemporary, the French art critic Charles Baudelaire, Quatremère contended that all artists should strive to create a semblance of reality in their works, not copies. He further posited that an artist should never intend to deceive the beholder—a true work of art must openly acknowledge its artifice. Picturesque gardening, therefore, could not be considered fine art, as it was an imitation of nature and concealed its artifice in order to be mistaken for a work of nature.[36] Furthermore, theorized Quatremère, color harmonies in the landscape are always agreeable—nature avoids discordant or antagonist colors. Therefore true art should confuse and visually clash.[37] By extension, color harmony in art, including garden art, should be clearly distinct from that of nature.

From 1837 onward, Loudon promoted Quatremère's theory, which he deemed to be "the only satisfactory theory of gardening, as an art of imagination, that has yet appeared; and we freely acknowledge ourselves more indebted to it than to all the other works on landscape gardening, or the fine arts, put together."[38] He held that any garden that is considered art and provides artistic pleasure must satisfy the condition of artificiality, and so must contrast with nature and its surroundings in several ways:

> Simply, let foreign trees and shrubs, or such as are totally different from the trees in the given locality, be planted, instead of indigenous trees; let the same be done as to the water plants; the same as to the stones and gravel; the same as to the slopes of the turf; the same as to the outline of the water; and, as far as practicable, the same even as to the grasses composing the lawn.[39]

Having embraced Quatremère's principles, Loudon cautioned against his predecessors' use of deception through camouflage and called on his fellow gardeners to openly display their handiwork. Repton's "invisible green" for fences, which Loudon promoted early on, made way for new ideas. For example, he proposed a fence with a novel, "party-colours" painting scheme—parts of the fence were painted clearly to stand out, while other parts were painted indistinctly, barely visible—and "a proper gradation from bright to dull colours."[40] Generally, though, bright colors were reserved for flowers, whereas other garden artifacts such as pavements were to be indistinct and constructed of wood blocks or earth-colored stone.[41] Furthermore, wirework such as rims and basket handles, edgings, and props for climbers were to be of "colours subordinate to the plants which they enclose, protect, or sustain, and thus painted stone-color, dull white, or greyish black, and not with the common green, which competes with nature's green."[42]

Camouflage was different from visual manipulation. The latter was permissible and welcome, and relied heavily on color. Loudon, like Repton, advocated manipulating distance by using plants of darker or lighter hues—darker hues being perceived as closer than lighter ones.

In the formal garden color and form now became equal partners, the lingering Renaissance argument that color muddles form and composition dissolved. Art, previously aligned with the rigors of line and form, now embraced the merging of form and color. Gardens displayed artificiality through elaborately interlocking, solid-color bedding forms. These initially followed intricate parterre patterns characteristic of rococo ornamentation: acanthus, volutes, braces, half-moons, S-scrolls, and shell patterns; Loudon published bedding plans in rococo styles as early as 1828. His preference for simpler geometries, though, is visible in several projects, including his recommendation to replace elaborately shaped bedding with circular beds at the Hoole House garden in 1831 (discussed below) (Figure 2.5). The circle was especially favored because it was largely free of arbitrary associations. By midcentury horticultural opinion preferred simple shapes for flower beds, although architects still favored elaborate or fanciful designs.[43] Geometry and the classic axis of symmetry reappeared as important design elements, creating a balanced and mirrored impression. Often lateral parallel lines were added to give depth and lead the eye to distant views.

In addition to a taste for form and knowledge of individual plant color, the formal compositions of solid-colored plant or mineral surfaces that dominated midcentury gardens required an understanding of color interaction—how neighboring colors affect each other and are perceived—and of the color harmony principles of the ensemble.

Color Charts: Mixed-versus-Solid Debate

Loudon often noted the importance of color theory for gardeners. The 18th century systematization of color terms and the creation of color charts (for both light and pigment) by European scientists and naturalists enabled gardeners and artists to perceive and discuss tint variations, and greatly aided in the identification of botanical specimens, all of which benefited both artisans and scientists.[44] His 1820s explanations of the ways color behaves and is perceived relative to nearby or background color based on philosophical theories (i.e., Alison's theory) were further validated and systematized by science. By the 1840s he was directing gardeners to the color theory of Michel Eugène Chevreul (1786–1889), a French chemist and professor of physical science who was director of the dye works at the Gobelins Manufactory in Paris.

2.5 Hoole House, Cheshire, view of flower garden from the drawing room, showing a grid of circular baskets in the lawn replacing the original S-shaped flower beds upon Loudon's recommendation, *The Gardener's Magazine* XIV, May 1838

2.6 M. E. Chevreul, "Roses and their leaves on various colored ground," *The Principles of Harmony and Contrast of Colors and Their Applications to the Arts*, plate XV [1854] 1967

The basis of Chevreul's theory was the scientifically proven phenomenon he named the Law of Simultaneous Contrast of Colors (see Figure 2.1). In his book *The Principles of Harmony and Contrast of Colours and Their Applications to the Arts* (1855, originally published in French in 1939), Chevreul explained that the perception of color is relative and depends on the juxtaposition of neighboring colors, and he demonstrated how juxtaposed colors can enhance or diminish each other's intensity.[45] In a 60-page discussion he presented the optical results and modified effects of juxtaposed colors in theory as well as their applications to several art fields, including horticulture. Moreover, based on experiments in his own garden, Chevreul described the effects and harmonies of garden plant colors, both flowers and foliage (Figure 2.6). He specified desired effects and recommended plant varieties, combinations, spacing, and bed arrangements, noting the impact of bed forms on the overall impression. The book contains extensive and detailed lists of each plant genus and species' color while flowering and the month of bloom. It is no surprise that Chevreul's work influenced Loudon and his successors through to modern times.

Chevreul's theory prompted a new debate on the "abstract-versus-real experience" between those who were loyal to Chevreul and "purists" who maintained that his theory was too abstract and not based on real experience. The purists claimed that it was not applicable to gardening because the positions of colors and distances between them were much more important than their interactions. They also argued that Chevreul's theory ignored the relationship between the color of the flower bed ground and the mostly green background, which cancelled the effects of color pairs. This stance raised the status of ground color (be it grass or gravel), but did little to turn the gardening community against Chevreul's theory.[46] The architect Owen Jones (1809–74), a Chevreul adherent who was responsible for the color scheme used at the Crystal Palace at Sydenham, suggested that the number of tints and their combinations were a matter of degree and refined taste, best achieved by "the use of the primary colours on small surfaces and in small quantities balanced and supported by the secondary and tertiary colours in the larger masses."[47]

Knowledge of color perception and interaction enhanced gardeners' ability to control and manipulate form, space, outline, focal point, and the depth and breadth of a scenic composition. From the 1830s onward, new physiological responses to colors were introduced and considered by garden designers. Certain colors, such as blue, were perceived as "retiring"; others, like yellow, as "advancing"; yet others, such as red, as "intermediate." These observations helped designers base their groupings on the visual appearance of foreground and background; for instance, advancing color plants were placed in peripheral beds, and subdued color plants at the center, thus directing attention outward and increasing the apparent size of a garden. Similar principles had been proposed by 18th century picturesque landscape designers, but they now attained a new rationale.

Other optical phenomena relevant to gardening were introduced at that time. The Purkinje effect—colors are affected by light: red is seen as an advancing color in bright daylight, blue as an advancing color in declining light—became known and led to an awareness of particular varieties that were best seen at sunset. Darwin's phenomenon of the afterimage was also discussed in gardening circles; it involved the lingering perception of a color seen on a neutral background following an intense focus on its complementary color, like seeing orange after gazing at blue.

A new debate on mixed versus solid—"massing versus mixing"—color in flower beds became central to gardening discourse. Massing was the winner. While Loudon permitted color mixing in shrubberies and flower borders to accommodate diverse tastes, his preference for color massing in flower beds was evident in 1826 when, in one of the first articles on the topic in *Gardener's Magazine*, he described an illustrative experiment in a Dublin park.[48] A decade later, a flower garden with a coherent pattern of solid color was Loudon's favorite: a small public garden he designed in 1835, for an unnamed English town, incorporated shrubs and herbaceous flowers to create masses with a clear avoidance of mixture.[49] He wrote,

> A great improvement has been made in the planting of flower beds within the last twenty or thirty years. This consists in planting each bed with only one kind of flower, by which means a brilliant display of colour is produced.[50]

Loudon expounded on the brilliant effect of monochromatic plant cover, especially by newly available plants from warmer climates. New species—pelargonium, lobelia, petunia, verbena, *Calceolaria*, and *Salvia splendens*—gained favor on account of their brilliant hues and were intensively hybridized. One of Loudon's early arguments for massing was that in the wild nature scatters one type of plant profusely en masse,[51] although this analogy was later replaced with the contention that a flower garden was a work of art.

John Caie (1811–79), the head gardener at Bedford Lodge in Kensington, was one of the chief proponents of massing. In an 1838 account of his garden in *Gardener's Magazine*, he proposed that solid masses allow the eye to rest, instead of being continually agitated by small color juxtapositions, and that the first impression ought to be one of bold color.[52] By 1850 the bedding color range included six color groups: yellow, purple, scarlet, blue, pink, and white (Figure 2.7).[53] Clean, simple, and solid bed masses rather than mixed color beds became widespread in gardening communities.

The debate over color harmony (the color combination in a bedding garden) became a question of the proper balance and proportion of, for instance, green to gray, light to shade, warm to cool colors, breadth of bed to extent of open space, and height of plants to bed size. Caie's color principles called for contrasting colors, using those distant rather than adjacent on the rainbow spectrum: arrangements to be avoided were, for example, orange and reds and blue and lilacs, "but orange and purple, yellow and blue, blue and white, red and blue always contrast well and set off one another."[54] Beds of equal size called for colors of equal brightness, whereas differing sizes were to be balanced through the use of bright and subdued colors. Published bedding plans with plots numbered according to an

2.7 John Caie, "Color Scheme," *The Florist's Magazine*, 1841. RHS Lindley Collections

accompanying flower color plant list became the norm, accommodating a growing interest in design pattern books that were widely copied by gardeners. The principles of massing and color contrast were increasingly adopted by the gardening community throughout the 1840s, and by midcentury it was widely considered an error not to contrast colors.[55]

Solid color beds—one plant type per bed—created an impression of distinction, solidity, and vigor. Loudon's favorite color arrangement was adjacent beds of homogeneous colors—a bed of a compound color next to a bed of a primary color—purple flowers should have yellow flowers next to them, orange should be contrasted with blue, and green should be complemented by red.[56] He also favored the vivid effect created by placing complementary colors of similar brilliance next to one another, and was fascinated by the changing effects of colors under different daylight conditions.

Loudon provided multiple guides for planting color schemes relative to garden size and type. The application of color harmonies and effects to landscape gardening was coupled with attention to the continuous display of color. His garden design depended on carefully selecting and coordinating the placement and flowering time of plants.

Ornament: Color for Every Season

Loudon maintained a lifelong keen interest in continuous blooms in parks and gardens, especially gardens near and within full view of the house. The general effect was to be "gay" and of "brilliant glow."[57] His plant encyclopedias and magazine articles included calendars of flowering annuals, herbaceous perennials, shrubs, and trees, but it was "the changeable flower garden," planted with flowering annuals, that made spectacular displays. Tender plants were kept in pots and grown in a nursery or reserve ground, then planted in the soil as soon as they began to flower. When they showed symptoms of decay, they were removed and replaced by others of similar kind and from a similar source. Since the practice of planting flowers and shrubs in full bloom during the appropriate season flourished in the 1830s, it became possible for the gardener to alter the appearance of the garden every year, and eventually every season.

The availability of imports and the popularity of eye-catching color beds were made possible by the technological advances of the hothouse and greenhouse, which first came into use at the end of the 18th century. Loudon was fascinated by greenhouses and involved in the development of greenhouse technology, or what he called the "artificial climate enclosure" (Figure 2.8).[58] In 1816 he invented a curved glazing bar in wrought iron to facilitate construction of a dome or curvilinear structure that allowed more light to enter.

As technology developed and aesthetics improved, the greenhouse changed from a utilitarian structure for plant propagation and off-season storage, tucked away at the edge of the garden, to a fashionable glass conservatory attached to the residence to showcase blooming flowers as the owner's point of pride. The plant-filled glass room also served as an extension of the outdoor garden. Suffused with greenery and sunlight, it became an indoor garden—and another color design problem. Loudon described different modes of organizing potted plants in hothouses by mingling, grouping, or "being methodical." In the mingled mode, potted plants of various colors were arranged in a checkerboard pattern; in the grouping mode, one to three dozen potted plants of the same color succeeded each other in large irregular masses; and the methodical mode involved an arrangement based on genus and species. In greenhouses attached to living rooms he suggested only plants in bloom grouped together.[59]

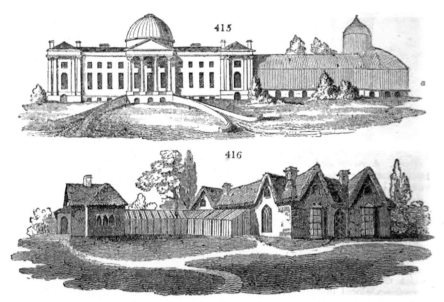

2.8 Ornamental conservatory for a mansion (top) and for an economical residence (bottom), *Encyclopaedia of Gardening*, 1822

The appetite for year-round color in the flower garden and the influx of new plants with vast color options led to an excess of colorful and incongruently mixed flower garden beds. Loudon warned landscape gardeners that it was more difficult to accomplish an intended effect with a mixture of colors and a large number of planting varieties. "Less is more," he cautioned, estimating the proper plant variety at 36: four flowering types for nine months, from February through October; anything above that number would result in blank spaces between blooming plants. Being frugal, he decried the gardening trend of choosing plants based on rarity and limited variety in favor of commonly available nursery flowers of "well-disposed colors and quantity."[60]

The lavish polychrome taste of the time called for a neutral background to effectively display color, and green served that purpose best. Loudon instructed gardeners to plant ivy on walls in small gardens and to use hedges and woods in large lots to create this effect. Similarly, manicured lawns, increasing in popularity, were a most effective background to colorful flower beds (Figure 2.9). Recounting the evolution of flower gardens, Loudon stressed the utility of the lawn:

> It is only lately that beds wholly planted with flowers have been introduced on lawns; and, though what are called flower-gardens (that is, assemblages of beds wholly devoted to flowers) were to be met with in first-rate places during the latter half of the eighteenth century, yet, during that period, the principal places where they were planted were in the shrubbery or in the borders of the kitchen-garden. With the commencement of the present century, the practice of forming flower-gardens has increased; and, within the last twenty years, that of forming beds exclusively devoted to flowers on grass lawns, either in groups among the scattered shrubs, or by themselves, here and there along the walks, has become general [italics added].[61]

2.9 Typical Victorian spring bedding, upper and lower terrace gardens at Bowood, Wiltshire, designed by Sir Robert Smirke, completed in 1818. RHS Lindley Collections

The polychrome garden set against green turf thus coincided with and became dependent on technological developments: first, the greenhouse that produced instant flowering color in the garden, and subsequently the lawn mower (Loudon first featured one in an 1832 issue of *Gardener's Magazine*).[62] The mechanical lawn mower not only reduced maintenance labor, it also removed two important gardening challenges: ornamental flower bed damage from grazing sheep and cows, and unsightly fences needed to keep grazers out. The aesthetics of colorful pattern arrangements around and within smoothly manicured lawns thrived without the need for fences.

The change in color taste from green to polychrome during Loudon's career coincided not only with botanical and technological developments but also with shifts in British social structure. A debate arose over the use of colors in the garden in relation to class.

Class Distinction: Color as Social Code

Initially, bedding filled with annual plants and arranged as bright blocks of color to be viewed in a downward gaze from the principal windows of a mansion served to emphasize the status of the owner and his command over hired labor and resources.[63] The labor-intensive gardens, which required extensive manual propagation of plants and hothouse management, necessitated a labor force and financial means reserved to the upper economic echelon.

> Accordingly, these bedding schemes were not only indicative of a particular way of using colour but … the structural representation of the hegemonies involved in their production, epitomizing the value of work well done at the same time as exemplifying the taste and refinement of the garden owner.[64]

By midcentury cheaper, larger, and higher-quality sheet-glass became available, greenhouses grew more affordable, and colorful, previously elite gardens filtered down to the middle class. The increase in commercially available and affordable colorful annuals and perennials between 1820 and 1850 also undercut the exclusivity of private greenhouses. As a result, bedding-out schemes expanded from the premises of the wealthy to the average suburbanite garden.

As a champion of the burgeoning middle class, Loudon's own experiments with glasshouse glazing, heating, and structure had helped democratize the greenhouse. Affordable greenhouses and commercially grown flowers permitted him to encourage even suburban small-lot owners to plant a flower garden for every season. And large estate owners could still maintain both a landscape park in the Picturesque Style and install several smaller garden rooms for specific seasonal blooms near the house and around the estate grounds.[65] With this in mind, Loudon drew up a hierarchy of gardens—first to fourth rate—based on lot size and economic status—simultaneously affirming and sidelining class distinctions, he provided garden design alternatives for large and small estates, country houses, and suburban residences with small lots.

But by midcentury color preferences shifted to maintain what has been called "the visuality of class distinction."[66] As the growing middle class increasingly subscribed to the elite tastes of bedding systems, the upper class returned to both old design styles that dominated the formal English gardens of the past and a new style and color taste propelled by late-century gardeners William Robinson and Gertrude Jekyll (see Chapter 3). This development gave rise to a color debate that equated bright colors with primitivism and uncultured taste, which led to the vogue of planting beds of mixed colors and an emphasis on displays of foliage.[67] Brightly contrasting color beds became the domain of middle- and lower-class gardens. Values embraced and encoded by the garden design profession through Victorian garden colors were echoed in the class hierarchies and reflected by color in the social environment.

* * *

The two exemplary gardens discussed here, those at Hendon Rectory and Hoole House, have been selected from Loudon's published descriptions of the hundreds of gardens that he admired. He did not design the Hendon garden and only consulted on the Hoole garden, but he repeatedly praised them, described them in detail, and provided meticulous illustrations.

The gardens at Hendon Rectory, in Middlesex, and Hoole House, near Chester, exemplify Loudon's gardenesque and formal garden principles, respectively, while combining several styles representative of Loudon's stylistic permissiveness. Both were written about in *Gardener's Magazine* in 1838 and reprinted posthumously in *Loudon's Villa Gardener* in 1850. The illustrations were colorless, and only a few specific references to color were included in the text. Instead, the publications listed the genus, species, and seasonal specification of each plant and the planting composition, all of which indicate the gardens' color concepts.

Hendon Rectory, Middlesex, the Rev. Theodore Williams, 1838

This garden represents the gardenesque aesthetic principles that Loudon endorsed midcareer. "Hendon Rectory is remarkable for its pine and fir trees grown in pots; and for the strictly gardenesque manner in which the greater number of the plants are cultivated, as well as for general high keeping," he wrote.[68] Located in Hendon, Middlesex, the four-acre property featured a pleasure garden surrounded by a grass field, pond, and irregular hedges of oaks and elms planted in the Gardenesque Style (Figure 2.10).[69] Loudon especially praised the choice and display of specimen trees and shrubs, most notably the rare collection of exotic conifers and fruit trees in tubs, boxes, vases, and pots. He was generally impressed by the cultivation, propagation, and maintenance techniques of the owner, the Reverend Theodore Williams, and his head gardener, and featured the garden as a way to uphold his mission of extending readers' botanical knowledge and plant care.

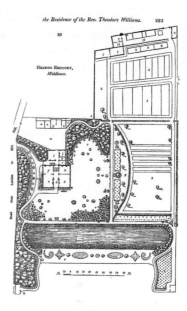

The essay focuses on the planting of distinct specimens in isolation, the primary gardenesque concept. Loudon highlighted the placement of carefully trimmed and positioned plants for optimal display of individual species features: "standing as they do a few inches apart from each other, the separate shape of each plant is seen by the spectator." Behind the house was a "gardenesque plantation, in which every tree and shrub is kept distinct, and every one trained into a symmetrical shape." And he touted and illustrated another guiding design principle: the role of the lawn in providing a neutral background to highlight individual specimens. He also noted two greenhouses: one principally devoted to conifers, the other to fuchsias and myrtles.

2.10 Hendon Rectory, plan, *The Gardener's Magazine* XIV, May 1838

The overall impression was that of an ornate, gay, colorful garden. Loudon's text and illustrations draw attention to garden ornaments and structures and to the perfect order and form of specimen plants. Garden décor—trelliswork with blooming vines, vases planted with colorful annuals, statuary, large pots, and boxes—add to the garden's ornate quality. A small rockery is placed among boxes of specimen firs, a collection of dahlias planted in rows, a row of dwarf hybrid rhododendrons, and roses "cut into symmetrical roundish forms." All installations stress particular effects and the seasonal change of individual species.

2.11 Hendon Rectory, side garden view, *The Gardener's Magazine* XIV, May 1838

Loudon described the garden from various viewpoints that are cued in a plan—four of them illustrated with perspectives—specifying plant names and the manner in which each is displayed and seen (Figure 2.11). For instance, point *u* on the plan is described as

> A point round which there is a constellation of rare and beautiful trees and shrubs in pots, besides various statuary and sculpturesque objects. Among the hardy trees are, Photinia harbagh and Pinus Pallasitana; and among the green-house plants, in pots and vases, are, oranges, myrtles, fuchsias, tree rhododendrons, &c.

The text is journalistic, and at times prescriptive, with professional commentary on the merits and broader applicability of the design and plant collection. Targeted at both professional and amateur gardeners, the essay is replete with plant names and maintenance instructions. The illustrations include a ground plan and four perspectives of the garden and one of the greenhouses, with legend labels of the garden parts and expanded descriptions of the four full-page perspective engravings, which show the fore- and middle ground, but no background. People, outdoor furniture, and ornaments occupy the foreground. Plant shapes are drawn precisely, foliage textures are distinctly rendered, shadows and shades are minimal. As such, the essay mostly highlights the organization of the garden and the forms and textures of the planting design.

Loudon ended the essay with a tinge of criticism of the impractical and labor-intensive nature of Hendon Rectory garden, specifically its use of expensive plants and the practice of keeping mature plants in pots, thus restricting full growth and the perfection they would have attained in their native habitat.

Hoole House, Lady Broughton, near Chester, Cheshire, 1838

The Hoole residence, an estate of over 20 acres near Chester was, Loudon claimed, "by far the most celebrated garden of the kind in that part of the country for the last ten years."[70] It combined a formal flower garden with an informal rockery and was surrounded by several specialized garden rooms, a grass field, pond, kitchen garden, and stable yard (Figure 2.12). During his 11 years of garden tours (1831–42), Loudon first visited Hoole House in 1831, at which time he provided some consultation to Lady Broughton. Deeply impressed by the garden, he revisited it in 1838 and featured it in *Gardener's Magazine* as part of the garden tour series in a column entitled "Notes on Gardens and Country Seats." The illustrations are colorless, but a list of more than 70 plants, with genus and species, sufficed to imply color for gardeners.

In 1838 the original S-shaped flower beds had been replaced with circular baskets upon Loudon's recommendation during his 1831 visit; he felt that the perfect geometry of the circular beds was superior to the S shape as it produced a more complete contrast with the diverse and rugged rockwork, and that flowers in beds and baskets created colorful effects during every season. He urged that they be planted with mixed perennial and annual varieties to "keep up the colour until the frosts destroy them."[71] The beds were planted with spring, summer, and autumn bulbs, and any empty spaces were filled with greenhouse annuals, such as geraniums and verbenas. Loudon provided detailed specifications of the iron rod and wire baskets in terms of not only color but also size, spacing, and placement in the lawn. He suggested subdued colors for both pots and baskets so they would not compete with flower colors planted in them, and proposed yellow-stone paint for the baskets "to harmonise with the rocks and the veranda."

The relationship of the flower gardens to the house, conservatory, greenhouses, and surrounding garden are explicitly noted. The text focuses on indoor-outdoor visual relationships, describing the entrance, a plant-filled conservatory between the house and the front garden, and the veranda with its climbing vine latticework between the drawing-room window and the main flower garden at the back. The veranda also connected the two greenhouses: for camellias at one end, for geraniums at the

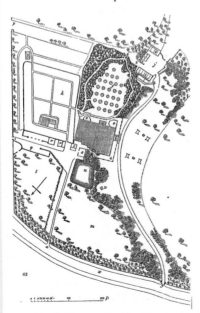

2.12 Hoole House, plan, *The Gardener's Magazine* XIV, May 1838

other. Loudon's passion for glasshouses is evident in the text and three detailed architectural drawings, including the camellia greenhouse and the front conservatory entrance.[72] Hoole House breached the division between house and garden as the greenhouses and (front) conservatory made the building's walls appear porous and the house was both flooded with light and invaded by greenery from the garden.

Loudon was particularly attracted to the rock garden's artistry, considering it "one of the most remarkable specimens of the kind in England."[73] He observed that its "striking effect … depends on the contrast between the smooth flat surface of the lawn, with the uniformity of the circular beds, and the great irregularity of the surrounding rockwork." The lawn and regimented grid of 27 circular flower baskets sunk in the lawn against the irregularity of the rugged rocks created the artifactual drama captured in two illustrations (Figure 2.13).

References to color were particularly detailed in the description of the rockery. The design of the rock work was conceived by Lady Broughton and modelled after the mountains of Savoy, representing "La Mer de Glace." Loudon was impressed by the rockery's uniqueness and distinction from the surrounding landscape, mingled creeping alpine plants, and technical construction. Enclosing one side of the main garden, the rockery featured red, gray, and white rocks and minerals. A barren, exposed peak of gray limestone and quartz rocks was lined with small fragments of white marble to look like snow, with a spar for the glacier peak.[74] To those who criticized the rockery feature in an otherwise flat landscape, Loudon countered that the incongruity of the rockwork with the surrounding landscape and the display of alpine plants created a powerful contrast that invited residents and visitors alike to appreciate it as a work of art.[75]

The feature perspectives were originally watercolor drawings done by a Mr. Pickering of Chester, and from them Loudon made small colorless engravings for his publication. The illustrations show people enjoying the garden, perhaps included to establish scale. Strong shades and shadows and white paint accents were applied to some rocks and shrubs to enhance contrast and extend the range of tones on the midtone journal paper. Despite the meticulous execution of the perspective illustrations, Loudon lamented the insufficiency of copper engravings to depict the strong impression of the rockwork.

* * *

Loudon's color outlook advanced an alternative position in the nature-versus-art debate. For him, a garden was

2.13 Hoole House, view of the rockwork, lawn, and camellia house seen from northeast corner of the garden (top), and elevation view of house, front entry conservatory (bottom), *The Gardener's Magazine* XIV, May 1838

a creation of human expression and thus its display artificial rather than natural. Gaudy garden colors followed stylistic garden shifts—from natural to gardenesque to formal—and demonstrated the gradual heightening of the garden's artifactual status. Inspired by horticulturalists, botanists, and the social aspirations of the suburban middle class, Loudon challenged traditional color ideals in the profession and reworked them in new ways. Color was rescued from its subsidiary position and made equal to form.

The supremacy of art over nature, the marriage of form and color, and the preference for year-round complimentary color beddings became signatures of the Victorian garden. Propelled by the teachings of William Robinson's wild garden and Gertrude Jekyll's impressionist garden, late 18th century color design would continue to redefine professional ideals about art, nature, and architecture, to undermine form relative to color, and to devise new color schemes. Newly conceived, color in the garden would advance closer to both nature and art, gain supremacy over form, and become an instrument of effects.

Notes

1. Loudon, "Hints Respecting the Manner of Laying Out the Grounds of the Public Squares in London, to the Utmost Picturesque Advantage," 1803.

2. Ibid., 740.

3. Ibid., 741. Loudon advocated the use of parks as botanical gardens to educate the public and professional gardeners about the new plants being introduced to Britain. His essay revealed a socially progressive bent and thrifty aesthetics due in part to the depression of the Napoleonic wars.

4. Loudon considered Repton to be lacking in plant knowledge and arrogant. He also criticized both William Kent and Capability Brown for not understanding plant material and the principles of nature. All subsequent well-known 19th century landscape gardeners had immense botanical skills. See Tait, "Return to Formality," 1980, 73.

5. Elliott, *Victorian Gardens*, 1986, 50.

6. For a complete biography of Loudon, see Simo, *Loudon and the Landscape*, 1988. For a complete list of Loudon's publications, see MacDougall, *John Claudius Loudon*, 1980, 127–9.

7. He wrote six massive encyclopedias with his wife, Jane Loudon: *An Encyclopaedia of Gardening*, 1822; *An Encyclopaedia of Agriculture*, 1825; *An Encyclopaedia of Plants*, 1829; *An Encyclopaedia of Cottage, Farm, and Villa Architecture and Furniture*, 1834; and two voluminous plant encyclopedias, *Arboretum et Fruticetum Britannicum*, 1838, and *An Encyclopaedia of Trees and Shrubs*, 1842. These were unprecedentedly comprehensive and furthered knowledge of landscape gardening, botany, and other subjects.

8. For a study of plant imports, see Taylor, "The Contribution from America to British Gardens in the Early Nineteenth Century," 1980.

9. Loudon, *Observations on the Formation and Management of Useful and Ornamental Plantations*, 1804, 28.

10. Loudon, *Encyclopaedia of Plants*, [1829] 1866, iii.

11. Loudon, *Observations*, 1804, 41.

12. Simo, *Loudon and the Landscape*, 1988, 167.

13. Loudon, *Encyclopaedia of Gardening*, 1822, 141–2.

14. Loudon, *Observations*, 1804, 36.

[15] Ibid., 42. The next several quotations (until marked otherwise) are also from Loudon's *Observations*, pp. 43, 61, 70–1.

[16] Loudon, *Encyclopaedia of Plants*, [1829] 1866, xix.

[17] Desmond, "Loudon and 19th-Century Horticulture Journalism," 1980, 94. With the gradual change to lithography in the 1840s, the standard process for reproducing plates was hand-colored copper line engraving.

[18] Ibid., 95.

[19] The vast compilation of imagery turned Loudon's books into copybooks, known as pattern books, which gained popularity among amateur and professional gardeners with limited design skills.

[20] Loudon, *Encyclopaedia of Gardening*, 1822, 1150–4. Also see Simo, *Loudon and the Landscape*, 169–70.

[21] Alison, *Principles of Taste*, [1790] 1821, 175.

[22] Ibid.

[23] Loudon, *Observations*, 1804, 59. Also see Loudon, *Encyclopaedia of Gardening*, 1822, 1153. For further discussion of Alison in Loudon's work, see Turner, "Loudon's Stylistic Development," 1982, 178.

[24] Loudon, *Observations*, 1804, 59.

[25] Ibid., 59–60.

[26] Alison, *Principles of Taste*, [1790] 1821, 185. One of Stewart's arguments was that the pleasure of color is one of the most simple and primitive sensations, and therefore the most inferior. The theory attributing color satisfaction to the primitive susceptibility of the mind originated in the 18th century works of William Hogarth.

[27] Loudon, *Encyclopaedia of Gardening*, 1822, 1151.

[28] Alison, *Principles of Taste*, [1790] 1821, 238–47, 72.

[29] Loudon, *Observations*, 1804, 69.

[30] Ibid. This principle led him to recommend using warm-tinted plants (not evergreens) in a landscape with a large body of water that is perceived as cool, and alternatively, cold-tinted plants near warm-looking buildings for a harmonious composition.

[31] Alison, *Principles of Taste*, [1790] 1821, 240. Alison noted the link between time of day and lighting and color perception.

[32] The color effects of drifts and intermingled grouping, which Loudon abandoned in favor of the gardenesque, were picked up by William Robinson and popularized in the 1870s.

[33] Loudon, *Encyclopaedia of Gardening*, 1822, 141–2.

[34] Turner, "Stylistic Development," 1982, 182.

[35] Loudon, *The Suburban Gardener and Villa Companion*, 1838, 216.

[36] Quatremère de Quincy, 1837, 170–1. Initially published in French in 1823; first translated into English in 1834.

[37] Ibid., 60.

[38] Loudon, *Suburban Gardener*, 1838, 139–40.

[39] Ibid., 138–9.

[40] Loudon, *Observations*, 1804, 156.

[41] Loudon, *Suburban Gardener*, 1838, 156.

[42] Ibid., 436.

[43] Elliott, *Victorian Gardens*, 1986, 44.

[44] Lowengard, *The Creation of Color*, 2006.

45   Chevreul, *The Principles of Harmony and Contrast*, [1839] 1855, 855.

46   Elliott, *Victorian Gardens*, 1986, 127.

47   Ibid.

48   Ibid., 50.

49   Loudon, "Public Garden for a Corporate Town," 1836.

50   Loudon, *Villa Gardener*, 1850, 174.

51   See Elliott, *Victorian Gardens*, 1986, 87.

52   John Caie, "Descriptive Notice of Bedford Lodge," 1838.

53   Elliott, *Victorian Gardens*, 1986, 88.

54   Ibid.

55   Ibid., 89.

56   Jane Loudon, "An Account of the Life and Writings," [1845] 1980, 15.

57   Loudon, *Encyclopaedia of Gardening*, 1822, 895–6.

58   Loudon's visionary schemes for climatic control and diverse environments were the subject of his book *Construction of Hothouses*, 1817, 49.

59   Loudon, *Encyclopaedia of Gardening*, 1822, 935.

60   Ibid., 904.

61   Loudon, *Villa Gardener*, 1850, 174.

62   The first lawn mower was patented by Edwin Budding in 1830, but its broad use and popularity were delayed until its mechanism was more fully developed in the 1860s.

63   Lear, "Colour in Gardens," 2012, 79.

64   Ibid.

65   Loudon, *Observations*, 1804, 263.

66   Lear, "Colour in Gardens," 2012, 80.

67   Elliott, *Victorian Gardens*, 1986, 127, 97.

68   Loudon, "Descriptive Notice of Hendon Rectory," 1838. Reprinted in Loudon, *Villa Gardener*, 1850, 560.

69   Loudon, *Suburban Gardener*, 1838, 481–2. The next several quotations are also from *Suburban Gardener*, pp. 482 and 485.

70   Loudon, "Hoole House," 1838, 353. Reprinted in Loudon, *Villa Gardener*, 1850, 315–23. Unless otherwise indicated, the quotations in this section are from "Hoole House."

71   Loudon, *Villa Gardener*, 1850, 317.

72   The architect Thomas Harrison of Chester did the original plans and elevations.

73   Loudon, *Villa Gardener*, 1850, 107.

74   Loudon, "Hoole House," 1838, 358.

75   Ibid., 362.

References

Alison, Archibald. *On the Nature and Principles of Taste* [1790]. Hartford, CT: George Goodwin & Sons, 1821.

Caie, John. "Descriptive Notice of Bedford Lodge." *Gardener's Magazine* IV (Sept. 1838): 401–11.

Chevreul, M. E. *The Principles of Harmony and Contrast of Colors and Their Applications to the Arts* [1839], 2nd ed., trans. by Charles Martel. London: Longman, Brown, Green, and Longmans, 1855.

Desmond, Ray. "Loudon and 19ᵗʰ-Century Horticulture Journalism." In *John Claudius Loudon and the Early Nineteenth Century in Great Britain*, ed. by Elisabeth B. MacDougall, 77–98. Washington: Dumbarton Oaks, 1980.

Elliott, Brent. *Victorian Gardens*. London: Butler & Tanner Ltd., 1986.

Lear, Beverley. "Colour in Gardens: A Question of Class or Gender?" In *Cultures of Colour: Visual, Material, Textual*, ed. by Chris Horrocks, 77–96. New York: Berghahn Books, 2012.

Loudon, Jane. "An Account of the Life and Writings" [1945]. In *John Claudius Loudon and the Early Nineteenth Century in Great Britain*, ed. by Elisabeth B. MacDougall, 9–43. Washington: Dumbarton Oaks, 1980.

Loudon, J. C. "Hints Respecting the Manner of Laying Out the Grounds of the Public Squares in London, to the Utmost Picturesque Advantage." *Literary Journal* 2, no. 12 (December 31, 1803): cols. 739–42.

Loudon, J. C. *Observations on the Formation and Management of Useful and Ornamental Plantations; on the Theory and Practice of Landscape Gardening; and on Gaining and Embanking Land from Rivers or the Sea*. Edinburgh: Archibald Constable & Co., 1804.

Loudon, J. C. *Remarks on the Construction of Hothouses*. London: J. Taylor, 1817.

Loudon, J. C. *An Encyclopaedia of Gardening Comprising the Theory and Practice of Horticulture, Floriculture, Arboriculture, and Landscape Gardening*. London: Longman, 1822.

Loudon, J. C. "Public Garden for a Corporate Town." *Gardener's Magazine* II (January 1836): 13–26.

Loudon, J. C. "Descriptive Notice of Hendon Rectory." *Gardener's Magazine* XIV, no. 98 (May 1838): 220–34.

Loudon, J. C. "Hoole House." *Gardener's Magazine* XIV, no. 105 (August 1838): 353–63.

Loudon, J. C. *The Suburban Gardener and Villa Companion*. London: H. Bohn, 1838.

Loudon, J. C. *Loudon's Villa Gardener: Comprising the Choice of a Suburban Villa Residence*, ed. by Jane Loudon. London: Wm. S. Orr & Co., 1850.

Loudon, J. C. *An Encyclopaedia of Plants*. [1829]. London: Longmans, Green & Co., 1866.

Lowengard, Sarah. *The Creation of Color in Eighteenth-Century Europe: Number, Order, Form*. New York: Columbia University Press, 2006. www.gutenberg-e.org/lowengard/A_Chap03.html

MacDougall, Elisabeth B. *John Claudius Loudon and the Early Nineteenth Century in Great Britain*. Washington, DC: Dumbarton Oaks, 1980.

Quatremère de Quincy, Antoine-Chrysostome. *An Essay on the Nature, the End, and the Means of Imitation in the Fine Arts*, trans. by J. C. Kent. London: Smith, Elder and Co., Corn Hill, 1837.

Simo, Melanie Louise. *Loudon and the Landscape: From Country Seat to Metropolis, 1783–1843*. New Haven, CT: Yale University Press, 1988.

Tait, A. A. "Loudon and the Return to Formality." In *John Claudius Loudon and the Early Nineteenth Century in Great Britain*, ed. by Elisabeth B. MacDougall, 59–76. Washington, DC: Dumbarton Oaks, 1980.

Taylor, George. "The Contribution from America to British Gardens in the Early Nineteenth Century." In *John Claudius Loudon and the Early Nineteenth Century in Great Britain*, ed. by Elisabeth B. MacDougall, 105–23. Washington, DC: Dumbarton Oaks, 1980.

Turner, T. H. D. "Loudon's Stylistic Development." *Journal of Garden History* 2, no. 2 (1982): 175–88.

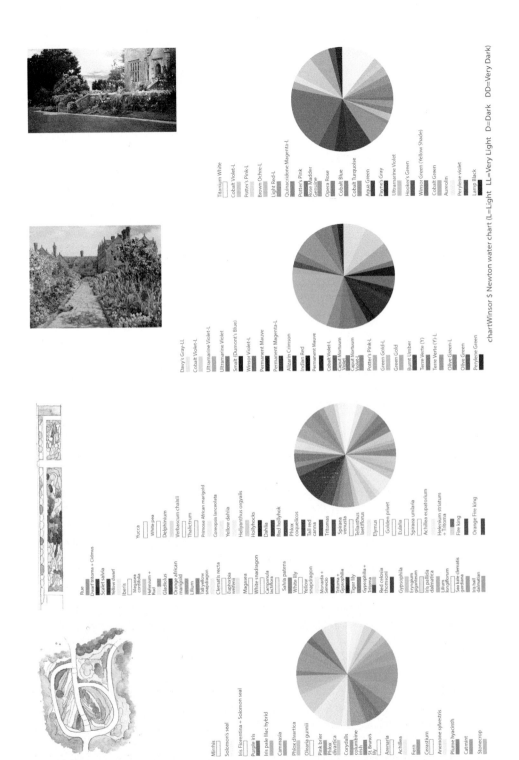

3.0 Diagrams, color analysis of paintings depicting William Robinson's south garden (top) and west garden (second from top) at Gravetye Manor, West Sussex, ca. 1900. Gertrude Jekyll's planting plan color schemes for the main hardy border (third from top) and the Secret Garden (bottom) at Munstead Wood, Surrey, ca. 1908. Rendered by Asif Khan

3

Graduated Harmony
Color as Impression,
William Robinson (1838–1935) and Gertrude
Jekyll (1843–1932)

Nature is a good colourist, and if we trust to her guidance, it is possible to be very good flower gardeners without considering laws of colour. We never find colour wrong in the wood, in the meadow, or on the mountain.

Gertrude Jekyll, *Colour in the Flower Garden*, 1883, 19

By the plans of grouping adopted[,] the colour difficulty vanished. There was good color in the beds without the geometric monotony of patterns. There was sufficient mass and[,] the things being good in themselves, a colour scheme was never considered. When it was studied by putting things which harmonized in the same bed, the plan was usually set aside by subsequent plantings and without apparent loss.

William Robinson, *Gravetye Manor: Or, Twenty Years' Work …*, 1911, 19

The idea that artifice was the only safe guide for gardening in the context of landscape design was replaced in the late 19th century with the concept of "cultivated wild," designs inspired by nature's "moods and ways."[1] William Robinson and Gertrude Jekyll blurred the boundaries between nature and art and repositioned landscape design closer to both. Their concepts of nature and art, differing from those of Repton and Loudon respectively, were reconceived in the vein of late 19th century Romanticism and a renewed attraction to nature. The highly contrasting and artifactual Victorian short-term color beds were replaced with long-term displays of changing effects: subtle foliage variations and spectrum-adjacent color sequences of soft color transitions (Figure 3.0). The transition in aesthetic taste from bold to restrained and delicate colors reflected a growing preference for neutrality and comforting places away from the upheavals of society, as well as a desire to maintain a class distinction from lower social tiers, which were associated with the bright and more contrasting colors.[2]

The late 19th century color preferences of Robinson and Jekyll, who together developed a theory for the new taste in landscape design, were complementary. Robinson spent little time writing on matters of color; not that he did not care about color—he clearly did— but he let others do the writing on the topic. He noted in his diary that the use of color in Victorian bedding-out gardens was a debatable subject at a time when a limited variety of plants were planted in solid-color pattern beds: "The color question only forces itself when confined to the exclusive use of a few plants which produce showy and formal effects. In such cases it is important to make the display as inoffensive as possible."[3] But with the vast increase in plant and color palettes new tonal gradation opportunities arose, and the early debate about mixed-versus-solid was no longer relevant. More deeply, as noted in this chapter's epigraph, Robinson believed that there was no need to defend the use of color if one followed nature's grouping effects, following the theories of the social and architectural critic John Ruskin.[4] Both he and Jekyll were devotees of Ruskin's moral stance on nature[5]—among other things, Ruskin believed that the principal role of the artist was to be true to nature—yet their romantic outlook was also tinged with pictorialism.

The early issues of Robinson's magazine, *The Garden* (published 1872–1927), featured only four pieces on matters of color, but the topic featured more prominently in his publications after 1881. Essays included commentary on the aesthetics of color in his own garden, largely focusing on the surrounding landscape of grassland and woodland. He was especially fond of foliage tints and the seasonal effects of large color massing. He deferred deeper discussions on flower garden color schemes to other authorities, notably Jekyll, who wrote about color aesthetics in Robinson's influential book, *The English Flower Garden* (1883), and magazines.[6]

Robinson was a journalist, horticulturalist, gardener, author of the seminal *Wild Garden* (1870) and 18 other books, and publisher of gardening journals.[7] Although he exerted authority on gardening through his publications, he designed few gardens. In contrast to Robinson, Jekyll was a painter, decorator, gardener, and author of hundreds of journal articles and a dozen books, including her most popular one, *Colour in the Flower Garden* (1908).[8] She designed more than 400 gardens between 1899 and 1937 and became the definitive authority on flower garden color. In the 1880s she practiced tapestry, embroidery, woodwork, and interior design. A decade later, her early interest in home decoration expanded to the garden, though this did not extend to the wider landscape (Figure 3.1).

The two met at the offices of *The Garden* in 1875 and became friends. They consulted and influenced each other's personal estate garden design, agreeing on key garden design principles and complementing each other's conceptual lens. As persons of private means, they used their estates—Jekyll's garden was in Munstead Wood in Surrey, and Robinson's in Gravetye Manor in West Sussex, 20 miles away—as experimental grounds, keeping strict records and reporting on their successes and failures.

The period in which Robinson and Jekyll worked, from the 1870s to around

3.1 Sketches of interior and garden décor, Gertrude Jekyll's scrapbook (undated). Gertrude Jekyll / RHS Lindley Collections

1910, marked the height of garden color discourse in Britain. The two crusaded against the Victorian bedding system, targeting the growing professional and amateur gardening audience in the waning phase of high Victorian gardens.[9] Together they offered a new take on color as effect. The best color effects followed three key principles: restraint and repose of foliage color, soft gradations of spectrally adjacent color harmony with intermittent neutral colors, and color combination sequencing in space and time. An indifference to form was implicit in these principles. Robinson and Jekyll advanced a radical shift in the debate over color versus form, advocating for the primacy of color over form.

Primacy of Color over Form

For the first time in the color-versus-form debate in landscape design, color was independent of and actually superior to form. The elimination of rigid bedding shapes elevated color and made it the primary focus of garden discourse. Robinson instructed:

> To get artistic effects in such a flower garden we must not … adopt the close pattern beds usual, because no system allows of a good effect from beds crowded on each other like tarts on a pastrycook's tray. … The contents of the beds and not the outlines are what we should *see*" [italics added].[10]

Freedom from the straitjacket bedding outline and a shift to "open beds" redirected the viewer's attention to the "content" of the beds, the plants themselves (Figure 3.2).

The alignment of art with the rigor of line and form was subverted under Robinson's influence. The logic that color, in contrast to line and form, puts itself beyond the reach of rational analysis and, instead, within the reach of emotion was a welcome change. The lingering Renaissance and 18th century picturesque idea that color muddled and was inferior to form and composition was abandoned and, in the works of Robinson and Jekyll, color was used to disrupt form. Nature reemerged as the prime model for artistic imitation, rooted in the nature-suffused ideology of Ruskin.

An examination of color in nature had led Ruskin to conclude that color is independent of form. In *The Seven Lamps of Architecture* (1849) he called for color in architecture to appear as it does in nature: in "simple masses" or "zones," as in rainbows, clouds, shells, and marble.[11] He based his theory on his study of nature's flora and fauna tints. Citing examples such as a zebra's stripes, he claimed that in nature, plant and animal colors never follow form or internal anatomy but are arranged using an entirely different system. It was a harmonic relational color system, whereby color repeated itself in both figure and ground. Following Ruskin, Robinson and Jekyll regarded color as nature-coded and treated it as independent of form.

However, Robinson's model for gardening and color was not raw nature. It was a "cultivated wild" exemplified by English cottage gardens.[12] His "wild garden" theory had little to do with wilderness, as in a garden sown haphazardly

"I wish it to be framed, as much as may be, to a naturall wildnesse."
LORD BACON.

3.2 William Robinson, engraving, frontispiece, *The Wild Garden*, 1870

3.3 Helen Allingham, watercolor, "A Cottage and Garden," Surrey, originally published in *Cottage Homes of England*, 1909. © British Library Board. All Rights Reserved / Bridgeman Images

or allowed to run wild. Instead, it involved planting a garden that accommodated the local conditions of soil, moisture, and orientation—and in which constant care and control were necessary. The "cultivated wild" was a garden ideology that played down the need to strictly emulate nature but at the same time held that conspicuous artifice was inappropriate. It was in keeping with a new picturesque modeled on the English cottage gardens of estate laborers, rather than Uvedale Price's 18th century landscape park. Robinson considered cottage gardens very picturesque, "little gardens with big effects and simple materials."[13] He maintained that a keen sense of picturesque beauty was a prerequisite of a true landscape gardener, as will be shown by the many descriptions of his estate garden, Gravetye (discussed below).

Both Robinson and Jekyll considered cottage gardens the prettiest of gardens, not least because of their informality (Figure 3.3).[14] A mix of fruit trees, colorful climber-covered walls, and herbaceous beds that had an informal appearance constituted the cottage garden, where nature seemed to have been allowed to take its course. In reality, it involved careful manual labor, though it was not overt. Expounding on their charm, Robinson wrote:

> It is the absence of pretentious "plan" in the cottage garden which lets the flowers tell their own tale; the simple walks going where they are wanted; flowers not set in patterns; the walls and porch alive with flowers. Can the gentleman's garden, too, be a picture? Certainly; and the greater the breadth and means the better the picture should be. But never if our formal 'decorative' style of design is kept to [italics added].[15]

Robinson's dislike of plan and form went beyond ideology. He was an avid art connoisseur, not an artist or designer. He refrained from drawing plans and used the word "form" only in reference to plant growth and leaf patterns. In response to a magazine editor's request to provide a plan for his own garden, he wrote, "Plans should be made on the ground to fit the place and not the place made to suit some plan out of a book … [that] any clerk can copy."[16] Robinson used the term "planning" to refer only to the layout of garden and flower beds, which should be free of borders with "no complication or crowding, no fanciful or angular beds."[17] The *Wild Garden* contained no plans, only perspectives and botanical drawings.

Jekyll, in contrast, drew many planting plans and garden layouts. Most illustrations in her books are plan views, showing beds filled with a patchwork of intermingled plant groupings (with botanical plant names). Flower borders were elongated rectangles, and the layout of each garden space displayed formal, often symmetrical bed arrangement. For these reasons she was often called a "formalist." Jekyll recognized the importance of drawings in planning a garden. Designers, she noted, make "drawing—by which is meant a right movement of line

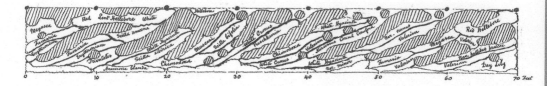

and form and group."[18] Nonetheless, she considered herself a gardener-painter: gardening was analogous to painting or, in her words, "living pictures," with plants as pigments, albeit ephemeral.[19] Color was her primary focus, which she defended on the grounds that form and proportion had already been covered by others, whereas color had been overlooked.[20] Neither form-based nor formless, her gardens were compositions in color. Yet most of her drawings lack color. The black, ink line planting plans display quick and decisive lines and handwritten common and botanical plant names and last-minute alterations (Figure 3.4).[21]

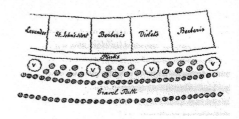

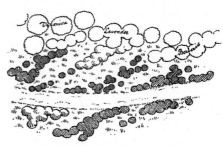

3.4 Gertrude Jekyll, planting plans for the Bank of Early Bulbs (top) and the wild Heath Garden before and after Jekyll's redesign (bottom), Munstead Wood, *Colour in the Flower Garden*, 1908

Jekyll's indifference to form should be understood in the context of artistic trends in the second half of the 19th century, specifically Impressionism and Neo-Impressionism, which eschewed form in favor of paint strokes and dots that become recognizable forms when seen as a whole. Thanks to less expensive and higher-quality pigments, painters such as Monet and Van Gogh were able to paint outside, not attempting to reproduce forms stylistically or accurately but suggesting them through color and light. This artistic trend, culminating in the works of Neo-Impressionists like Georges Seurat, also known as "pointillists," perfectly suited the garden context. Seurat's work involved small dots ("points") of spectral hues placed on a canvas instead of being mixed on a palette; the image was broken down to a basic level and executed on the canvas as mere dots of color. Pointillism also demonstrated how color perception results from the optics of different-colored brushstrokes seen in concert.[22]

Jekyll's art education at London's Kensington School of Art in the 1860s introduced her to this painting trend and guided her perception of the garden in terms of color effects done with floral pigments. From the works of Impressionist painters that she studied later at the National Gallery (now Tate Britain), she learned how to free color from form and make it the central unifying and animating element. The development of the camera, with its ability to record light effects, also played a critical role in the development of Impressionism and Neo-Impressionism or pointillism, and in Jekyll's works (see "Living Pictures, Flowering Calendar" below).[23] Another influence was her long-time watercolorist tutor and friend, English watercolorist Hercules Brabazon, who adopted the Romanticist J. M. W. Turner's approach to color in which a rich color mixture range and color transitions from cool to warm played across the pictures.[24]

To Jekyll, then, the garden appeared as myriad points of spectral hues that corresponded with light-deflecting leaves and blossoms (Figure 3.5). The garden's overall impression

3.5 Ghent hybrid azaleas mixed with common yellow azaleas massed at Munstead Wood, ca. 1990 (top). Photo: Martin Wood. Claude Monet, "Monet's Garden at Giverny," 1895 (bottom), ©Emil Bührle Collection (Long Term Loan at Kunsthaus Zurich). Photo: SIK-ISEA, Zurich (J.-P. Kuhn)

was produced by the orchestrated light-color ensemble: form was but the outcome of color-light compositions. Thus, when Jekyll referred to painting as a "true" model for gardening, she was not thinking about formal composition, as Repton did, but of color effect. Her affection for Impressionist painting earned her the title "impressionist gardener" or "pointillist gardener."[25]

Together, Jekyll and Robinson propelled a shift to chromatic dominance in landscape gardening. They recommended beds of open borders and simple geometry (square, rectangular) to diminish attention to form. They called for gardens in which plants could attain their natural growth capacity and display their natural form and "formless" color. Jekyll particularly admired gardens with creepers, twiners, and climbers.[26] Any gardening tradition that confined plant growth and shaped a garden into complex geometric forms was considered heresy. Robinson deplored the tradition of pleaching trees and the burgeoning revival of topiary as a distortion of beautiful natural forms. Instead, vertical structures such as latticework, arches, and pergolas were acceptable as support systems for training flowering vines to create displays of bursting color in semicontrolled forms, and to layer and mix colors.

Foliage Aesthetics:
The Return of Green

Jekyll and Robinson replaced the formal high Victorian garden bedding system with a garden of orchestrated color effects, where, Robinson wrote, "Repose and verdure are essential."[27] By "repose" he meant space for the graceful expression and beauty of plant groups without overcrowding and formality. "Verdure" meant greenness, a color that was refreshing, a calming daily necessity, and attractive to many people, especially in wintertime.[28] To that end, Robinson promoted foliage aesthetics: the appeal of leaf patterns and textures and of varied tints and shades of green. Now, however, green was neither used to support the structure and spatial quality of the garden nor to act as camouflage, as Repton did. Rather, it was embraced as a symbol of nature and a "relaxer" to other bright colors.[29] The calming psychological effect of green was higlighted by the German philosopher Johann Wolfgang von Goethe: "The eye experiences a distinctly grateful impression from [green] .... The beholder has neither the wish nor the power to imagine a state beyond it. Hence for rooms to live in constantly, the green colour is most generally selected."[30] Goethe's perception-based color theory, which suggested that color has a direct effect on the mind and feelings, resonated with Robinson and Jekyll, as it did with late 19th century Impressionists (Figure 3.6).

The affinity for green was also grounded in a moral ideology of nature, as nature and green acquired associations with health, hygiene, relaxation, and leisure. Ruskin's spiritual search for the essence of nature and for "honest" labor influenced Robinson, propelling him to the Alps in the 1860s in search of earthly paradise.[31] His two early books, *Alpine Flowers for Gardens* (1870) and *The Subtropical Garden; or Beauty of Form in the Flower Garden* (1871), promoted foliage aesthetics. Subtropical gardening introduced a desire for plants with large, graceful, or remarkable foliage or growing habit. It was a return to Loudon's gardenesque appreciation of plant form, but without the isolation of individual plants.[32] Leafy plants rather than flowers dominated the subtropical garden. Robinson went so far as to propose that if half the bedding plants used in a garden were foliage plants without distinct flowers, "it would not be out of proportion."[33] And the British gardener William Wildsmith (1838–90), a contributor to Robinson's *English Flower Garden,* endorsed bedding or parterres with the variegated foliage of dwarf and subtropical succulents:

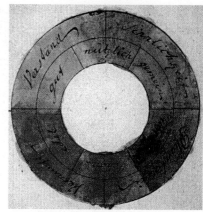

3.6 Johann Wolfgang von Goethe, color chart, showing correspondence of color and emotions, *Theory of Colours,* [1810] 1840

> [T]hose who cannot have elaborate designs and variety in colour, may have an equivalent in graceful foliage and beautiful tinted shrubs of hues varying from deep green to bright yellow, and in habit tapering, weeping, or feathery, such as Yews, Yuccas, hardy Sedums, Saxifrages, and Veronicas, which may even be arranged in bedding-out form, the shrubs for centres and panels, and the dwarf hardy plants for massing and carpeting.[34]

Green ceased to be a default background color in gardens and warranted its own attention, in keeping with its prominence in Impressionism.[35] Painters' palettes grew lighter, tones became livelier and purer, and the range of greens was appreciated. Painters' manuals now included instructions on how to produce numerous green shades.

The revival of green prompted a debate in gardening magazines known as "greenist versus colourist," or "naturalist versus formalist." The two camps attached morality to color choice—and both used Ruskin's authority for their opposing arguments.[36] The greenists, hewing to the conventional alignment of bright color and vulgarity, accused the colorists of primitivism, claiming that Ruskin's call to imitate nature argued against the artificiality of the bedding system (Ruskin did note that bright colors were traditionally associated with a sensuous or primitive response and lower-class taste). The colorists defended love of color, claiming that Ruskin drew the connection between pure color and profound, noble thought, not barbarism, and referenced nature's bright color plant patches. Indeed, Ruskin proclaimed that all the great epochs of architecture, from the Egyptian and Greek, had used highly colorful decoration on their buildings.[37]

Robinson's foliage aesthetics relied on ideology, psychology, and practicality. For the latter, he explained that, for example, a combination of hardy variegated plants, such as Japanese honeysuckle, periwinkle, ivies, sedums, and saxifrages, was "better than any to be had from flowering plants alone, as they stand all weathers without injury."[38] His preference for both native, hardy plants and naturalized exotics in the garden (the two horticultural traditions are best encapsulated in *The Wild Garden*, which was widely used during the 1870s and early 1880s) sidelined greenhouses. In fact, contrary to Loudon, Robinson advocated the abolition of greenhouses, considering them wasteful:

> Glass-houses are useful and charming helps for many purposes, but we may have noble flower gardens without them. ... Therefore one great source of expense may be saved, and the numerous glass-houses in our gardens may be turned to better use.[39]

Indeed, Robinson believed that a garden, especially in the wider landscape, should be left to care for itself. "The owner might go away for ten years and find it more beautiful than ever on his return," he wrote.[40]

His affection for green and natural growth was also evident in his attention to grassy fields and meadows, which he often called lawns. The value of the lawn as a constant and continuous green carpet appealed to him. "A simple lawn is the happiest thing in a garden," he wrote, "flowers may come and leaves go, but lawns go on forever."[41] He enjoyed lawns both on flat terraces and on undulating broader expanses. The grass sheltered and then set off seasonal flowers and bulbs in natural groups or fringe colonies. He frowned on mowing grass—aside from the benefit of saving labor, the owner could enjoy "a world of lovely flowers that will blossom and perfect their growth before the grass has to be mown" and harvested for hay.[42]

For all her love of color, Jekyll made a special place for green in the garden, noting its artistic and psychological merits. She reminded her readers of the artful and graceful leaf forms, and the visual relief that abundant verdure provides amid masses of brilliant blossoms. Green foliage was a mediator between bright contrasting colors and, as such, a relaxing agent for the human eye. Referring her ideal model, nature, she wrote: "Where mountain and meadow plants of one kind produce a sea of colour at one season, there is intermingled a spray of pointed grass and leaves, which tone down the colour masses."[43] Evergreens, for example, both provide respite from the glare of brilliant color and heighten the beauty of color. Green between flowers is more intense at close range than at a distance and its tone varies with the angle of sight, so Jekyll calibrated the amount of green and tonal composition accordingly. She even showcased a green room in her one-color garden series (see "Special Coloring: One-Color Gardens" below). She endorsed subtropical beds mixed with other plant types (not as a standalone garden), as the graceful leaves of subtropical plants helped relieve the monotony of texture as well as the visual saturation of color.

Beyond ideological connotations and psychological impacts, Jekyll and Robinson considered green a color of its own merit in an orchestrated chromatic palette and for pattern in both flower gardens and open landscape. They favored informal intergrouping of spectrally adjacent colors over solid blocks of color or casual mixing. Again, nature served as guide.

Intergrouping: Spectrally Adjacent Harmony

In his introduction to *The English Flower Garden*, Robinson expressed disdain for those who ignored nature's patterns and introduced artistic invention, "the bringing of the 'personality' of the artist into the work."[44] The garden should group and mass as nature does (Figure 3.7). His favorite plant groupings combined "nature's way" with the "picturesque way." For him, the picturesque was defined simply as a scene worth painting, and it was mostly irregular, to distinguish it from the Formal Style. He echoed this definition in describing his garden at Gravetye:

Plants carefully grouped in picturesque ways are far more beautiful and interesting than if set out in the common mixed way. Almost everything was planted in groups, varying the sizes and shapes, holding some apart and some 'together' by 'turfing' plants beneath and spaces of repose around, letting other groups merge one into another, suitable plants intermingling. This destroyed all set pattern to such an extent that it was impossible for the eye to take in the arrangement or contents of any single bed from one standpoint.[45]

He applied large color massing to open grassland and woodland, and smaller-scale grouping to the flower garden to link open landscape and flower garden. Jekyll agreed with the massing approach, following nature's way. She used the term "drift" to describe her preferred long, blob-shaped plant clusters in flower borders:

3.7 Photograph, "South Lawn, April View," Gravetye Manor, Sussex, *Home Landscapes*, 1920, plate III (top). Engraving based on photograph, "Garden of One Flower: Primrose Garden in Surrey," *The English Flower Garden*, 1900 ed. (bottom)

[I]n all flower borders it is better to plant in long rather than block-shaped patches. It not only has a more pictorial effect, but a thin long planting does not leave an unsightly empty space when the flowers are done and the leaves have perhaps died down. The word 'drift' conveniently describes the shape I have in mind and I commonly use it in speaking of these long-shaped plantings.[46]

On an aesthetic level, overlapping drifts carried a natural connotation of form associated with involuntary, aimless movement or gently conveyed by a current of air or water. Jekyll adjusted groups in size or breadth according to visual perception, using a foreshortening effect—the impression one has of seeing the breadth of each color mass in a flower border from end to end.[47] Accordingly, groups at a distance should be enlarged, and close-by groups contracted to maintain a unified impression. The informal, commingled, elongated drift, which may have echoed the repetitive brushstrokes that she used in her early paintings and others she admired, persisted in her work.

Jekyll poetically referred to nature as a colorist (as in this chapter's epigraph), recalling Repton's language. Their ideas of nature's colors, however, differed as each saw nature through the art lens of their time: Repton's was that of 17th century landscape painting, and Jekyll's was that of late 19th century Impressionist painting. For her, nature was creative and unpredictable, a source for the study of the production of effects and emotions. Nature was a "subtle chemist" with many surprises in store, she wrote in *Wood and Garden*:[48]

those of us who feel and understand in this way do not exactly attempt to imitate Nature in our gardens, but try to become well acquainted with her moods and

> ways, and then discriminate in our borrowing, and so interpret her methods as best we may to the making of our garden pictures [italics added].[49]

Jekyll's metaphor of nature as a chemist, concocting tint mixtures and creating dynamic impressions, legitimized her experiments with and interpretations of the chromatic scheme and arrangement.

Both Robinson and Jekyll adored large color effects, although Robinson was vague about specific color combinations and deferred to Jekyll. In *The English Flower Garden*, an anthology of practices by multiple authors, he published several, sometimes conflicting, planting arrangement and color options, yielding different color effects for different garden types.[50] Jekyll's contribution to the book endorsed unevenly distributed recurring colors in interlocking groups for beds and borders with chromatic principles: "One of the most important points in the arrangement of a garden is the placing of the flowers with regard to their colour-effect, and it is one which has been greatly neglected."[51]

Notwithstanding—or perhaps because of—her early training at art school, Jekyll often dismissed art and decorative color theories as inappropriate for plants. And she disagreed with the French chemist Chevreul's simultaneous color contrast theory, which became popular in midcentury, which stated that complementary contrasts were always satisfactory. Instead, she designed color schemes for specific effects: "There should be large effects, each well studied and well placed, varying in different portions of the garden scheme."[52]

Jekyll's spectrally adjacent color palette (colors that harmonize with those nearest to them in the spectrum) and the lessons she took from painting served as a foundation for her own experiments (see Munstead Wood discussion below). She was greatly influenced by the strategic paint application of Impressionist painters, especially soft color transitions and repetitive color brushstrokes that echoed in different parts of the canvas and produced vibratory effects. Jekyll applied these effects to garden design, and instead of uniform hue progression preferred an interrupted sequence.[53] Her color theory promoted a tonal structure of soft transitions between spectrally adjacent hues separated by neutral colors.[54] Following Goethe's theory about colorless space next to every hue in order to evoke the complementary hue,[55] she prescribed grays, silver, and white variations as visual "breaks" that allowed the eye to experience fluctuations and to relax between intense color patches and achieve a harmonic perfection. She described the sequential scheme in her famous summer herbaceous borders:

> [It began] with strong blues, light and dark, grouped with white and pale yellow, passing on to pink, then to rose color, crimson, and the strongest scarlet, leading to orange and bright yellow. A paler yellow followed by white would mediate between the warm colors and the lilacs and purples, and a colder white would combine them pleasantly with low-growing plants with cool-colored leaves.[56]

The cool colors at both ends enhanced the brilliant warmth of the middle; as the eye became saturated with reds, the grays and blues relaxed it. The sequence—a progression from cool to warm to cool hues—also echoed Turner's favorite scale of colors[57] (Figure 3.8).

Jekyll's most important rule was to avoid sharp contrast: "By all means have our colours in a brilliant blaze, but never in a discordant glare."[58] Plants with flowers of related color (for instance, reds and oranges or purples and pinks) should be grouped in one garden bed or area, and the colors should follow each other throughout the blooming season. To

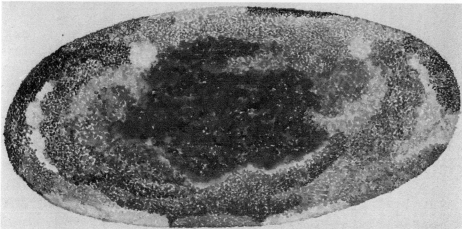

3.8 J. M. W. Turner, "The Fighting Temeraire," 1838 (top). National Gallery, London. Monica Epstein, painting of a planting plan by Gertrude Jekyll for Lady Alice Stanley's garden at Coworth Park, 1909, *Colour Schemes for the Flower Garden*, 1982 ed. (bottom). The color sequence found in many of Jekyll's flower beds is based on Turner. Photo: Kenneth Scowen

preserve the color scheme, plants that bloom in similar colors during different months were to be grouped together. She also prescribed combinations of warm- and cool-colored plants for specific sun and shade conditions: warm-colored blooms arranged in a progression of scarlet, crimson, pink, orange, yellow, and warm white were especially suited to sunny places, whereas cool colors such as purple and lilac went well together and complimented the cooler whites and gray foliage in shady places (Figure 3.9). Other guidance pertained to softening bright colors. For instance, bright white flowers were to be used sparsely and in

3.9 Gertrude Jekyll, autochromes, "Iris and Lupine Border" (top), "September Garden" (middle), and "Red Section of the Hardy Flower Border" (bottom), Munstead Wood, ca. 1912. Country Life Picture Library. Photo: Herbert Cowleywood

combination with softer whites; blue was best when positioned near warm whites and pale yellows or in an isolated flower group among rich dark foliage. Color and textural contrasts were to be used only in small, strategic plantings as accents to enliven color patches: a touch of contrasting color such as crystal lilies in a bed of dominant dark red, a spike of gladiolus in a soft cloud of *Gypsophila*, or a mass of orange lilies against blue gentians.[59]

Jekyll's lifelong goals were to train people to see and name colors as well as to be sensitized to color combinations. Consequently, she emphasized the importance of "[putting] color into words." In *Wood and Garden,* she devoted a chapter to common errors in naming colors and offered ways to avoid them, and she cautioned against the indiscriminate use of related color words, such as purple, violet, mauve, lilac, and lavender.[60] She rejected fanciful and incomprehensible names in favor of reference to texture or the senses to describe colors, as illustrated in her description of a Marie Legraye lilac in February: "The colour has a deliciously tender warmth of white, and as the truss is not over-full, there is room for a delicate play of warm half-light within its recesses."[61]

Beyond color vocabulary, Jekyll addressed the most challenging traits of living plants in color garden design: seasonal change and flowering calendar.

Living Pictures, Flowering Calendar

One of Jekyll's well-known passages compared gardening to painting a picture with living plants instead of paint:

> Should it not be remembered that in setting a garden we are painting a picture—a picture of hundreds of feet or yards instead of so many inches, painted with living flowers and seen by open daylight,—so that to paint it rightly is a debt we owe to the beauty of the flowers and to the light of the sun.[62]

Creating color harmonies with living material requires extensive botanical knowledge, including plants' color attributes and flowering calendar. Jekyll studied the changing combinations of flowering colors over the months as well as under various light and shade conditions. While Loudon had produced guides and plant lists based on seasonal blossoms, and Chevreul dedicated a section of his color theory to the monthly display of pleasing color harmonies and corresponding plants, Jekyll's calendar guide used prose and commentary instead of lists and charts in describing her Munstead Wood experiment.

Her garden consisted of various rooms and walks, each designed to display the best color effects during a specific month and season: one spring garden room showcased drifts of tulips, *Aubrieta* and *Arabis*, climbing *Epimedium*, and peonies; another, early bulbs with *Scilla*, white crocuses, and white hyacinths, among others; an August garden featured different varieties of asters; and an October display of Michaelmas daisies was offset by a gray border (Figure 3.10). Jekyll cautioned against attempts to represent all the seasons in one flower border. Instead, she celebrated microseasons in the garden by creating moments of harmonious crescendos, highlighting particular recurring landscape events (her increasing nearsightedness may have been a factor in the sequencing that affected her views and perception of space as well as her placement of cues, or "incidents," such as distinct rocks).[63]

The chapters in her books are similarly organized according to growing months and seasons. *Wood and Garden* reads like a diary with observations of the garden over the annual monthly calendar, describing the best-looking color harmonies of each month in various

3.10 George Samuel Elgood, "Michaelmas Daisies at Munstead Wood," undated. Private Collection © Look and Learn/Bridgeman Images

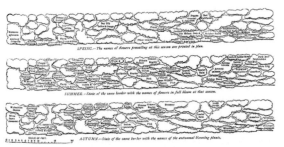

3.11 Gertrude Jekyll, planting plans of a portion of the main border at Munstead Wood in three seasons, *Colour in the Flower Garden*, 1908

garden plots. It also served as a practical reference for the amateur gardener's preparatory monthly gardening work; for example, the "May Garden" chapter focuses on rhododendrons and azaleas, the June chapter on the rose garden. *Colour in the Flower Garden*, on the other hand, is written as a series of seasonal and monthly itineraries of Munstead garden's walks, rooms, and main flower borders, focusing on the flowering months from March through September (Figure 3.11).

Temporal orchestration to ensure a persistence of color schemes across time and seasons required a large variety of plants, all of which had to bloom in close sequence and space. In *Wood and Garden* Jekyll proposed specific species for each color and temporal succession. In other publications, she addressed garden seasons that are generally considered colorless, although she believed that winter color could be cheerful and beautiful.

For winter she recommended grouping the colored bark of winter-hardy trees and shrubs such as red dogwood and scarlet willow with purple-barked trees, followed by the American black willow, and ending with "the comforting winter green" of junipers, heath, and fir. She appreciated the juniper's rugged bark stems with pale-green growths that had the silvery quality of lichen, and described the conifer with the same rich language and color nuances as the colorful rose:

> [I]ts tenderly mysterious beauty of colouring is by no means the least; a colouring as delicately subtle in its own way as that of cloud or mist, or haze in warm, wet wood land. It has very little of positive green; a suspicion of warm colour in the shadowy hollows, and a blue-grey bloom of the tenderest quality imaginable on the outer masses of foliage.[64]

Woodland winter color, too, could be delightful on both clear and overcast days with evergreen shrubs in the foreground set against the gray and purple hues of deciduous woodland in the distance.[65]

The color effects produced by the interaction of plant color with seasonal and other effects of light and weather were enigmatic and wondrous to Jekyll. On summer days when light quality produced an extraordinarily beautiful effect, she noted: "I have never been able to find out how the light on these occasions differs from that of ordinary, fine summer days, but, when these days come, I know them and am filled with gladness."[66]

Jekyll's focus on the flowering calendar and lighting effects happened to coincide with a new technology: the camera. The mechanical eye not only enabled people to freeze moments and preserve them as images but also made change visible for the first time. When Jekyll became interested in photography in 1885, it became a potent tool to record her garden experiments. Black-and-white prints, in addition to her annotated dairies, filled heavy albums. The pictures she took—of botanical species, planting beds, garden architecture, cottage gardens, and other built elements—enabled her to carry out close examinations and to share what she discovered widely. The camera lens and the photographic frame became Jekyll's allies and influenced her approach to garden design.[67]

Photographs, unlike drawings and engravings, enabled reliable documentation and accuracy. They also came closer to the spectator's viewpoint, projected an apparent objectivity, and brought unprecedented realism to garden representation. The fidelity of photographs popularized in print media at the turn of the century aligned with Jekyll's empirical tendencies, and her deteriorating eyesight made the camera an essential extension of her visual capacity and creative work. Her photographs taken with a large-format camera let her both see the garden in its entirety, something her nearsightedness prevented her from doing with the naked eye, and produce "images of work in progress to be examined, perhaps with the aid of a magnifying glass, in her study where she kept her photo-notebooks for frequent reference."[68]

3.12 Gertrude Jekyll, "September Border," vews in opposite directions, photographs from personal albums, 1907–8. College of Environmental Design archives, University of California, Berkeley

Jekyll mastered the entire photographic process, from taking the pictures to developing the film to printing, and experimented at all stages. Many different views of the same subject were taken in linear succession to show movement, days, and seasons, allowing her to see lighting and seasonal change. The way in which she placed photographs in albums also shows in some cases the sequencing of shots in a photo session—sequences that resembled the viewer's experience.[69] The photo-notebooks, more than any other available record, shed light on Jekyll's awareness of time in the garden (Figure 3.12). They also dominated her publications.

Black-and-white photography replaced black-and-white and color lithography as a vehicle for representing and disseminating new ideas in landscape design at the turn of the century. Although Jekyll's subject was color, her photographic illustrations made her publications colorless. The illustrations for *Wood and Garden*, her first book, were mostly black-and-white photographs of her garden, with a small number of wood engravings based on her photography. In the preface she apologized: "Some of them, owing to my want of technical ability as a photographer, were very weak, and have only been rendered available by the skill of the reproducer, for whose careful work my thanks are due."[70] However, watercolorists such as Helen Allingham left a colorful record of Jekyll's garden (see Figure 3.18).

Color photography entered Jekyll's late publications and reprints of early books in the 1920s. She also contributed several of her photographs for reproduction in wood engraving for Robinson's magazines, *The Garden* and *Gardening Illustrated*, and all new editions of *The English Flower Garden*.

Robinson, whose primary interest was writing and editing, restricted most of his book illustrations to colorless wood engravings. The first edition of *The Wild Garden* (1870) included only one frontispiece illustration (see Figure 3.2). Subsequent editions were chiefly illustrated with numerous engravings by two of his favorite artists: Alfred Parsons (1847–1920), a garden designer and regular illustrator for Robinson's books and magazines, and Henry G. Moon (1857–1905), a noted landscape and botanical painter. Robinson preferred Moon's graceful, naturalistic flower drawings and subtle colorings over the more stylized renderings appearing in the publications of competitors.[71] Moon's sketches frequently appeared in *The Garden* (1880–1905), and in 1901 he was invited to paint Gravetye "from the landscape painter's point of view" over a year-long period.[72] Black-and-white photography was used only in Robinson's late publications; he may have preferred the old-fashioned, grain-textured quality of engravings over newly realistic prints for aesthetic reasons as well as economy—photographic printing at that time was costly.

Special Coloring: One-Color Gardens

The "special coloring gardens" Jekyll introduced in 1908 pointed to a new sensibility in garden design: one-color immersion, although she was not the first to propose a one-color garden space. As garish bedding out came under attack by young gardeners of the 1860s and 1870s, the gardener and writer James Shirley Hibberd (1825–90), one of the old system's defenders, proposed to avoid contrast with one-color dominance using a dominant color plus green and varying its tones throughout the garden; he called this plan "nature's method," reminiscent of natural massing effects (here again nature was used in support of opposing positions).[73]

The one-color garden offered abstraction and, at the same time, sensory intensification through color immersion. Unlike the one-color bed seen as a pattern on the ground, the one-color garden space was an embracing experience of totality. Jekyll found one-color garden design interesting, opening out "a whole new range of garden delights" for artists who have an eye for color and welcome the challenge,[74] but she decried purists who planted one-color gardens simply for the sake of naming them after a color.

She preferred a one-color garden room as part of a sequence of different one-color spaces, as in, for example, five single-color rooms—orange, gray, gold, blue, and green—each surrounded by an evergreen holly hedge. The color sequence alternated between bright and neutral and between warm and cool to produce fluctuations in intensity to rest the eye (Figure 3.13). The shade and solidity of deep greens in one room offered rest and refreshed the eye and mind, readying the viewer to enjoy the next color-saturated garden. One room consisted primarily of gray or whitish foliage plants, with white, lilac, purple, and pink flower accents (Jekyll endorsed the addition of a few plants of different colors to strengthen the dominant color of a one-color room). The gold garden was bright and cheerful year-round, and its position at the center was "according to natural colour-law, for the enjoyment of the compartments on either side."[75] Also,

> after the grey plants, the Gold garden looks extremely bright and sunny. A few minutes suffice to fill the eye with Ute yellow influence, and then we pass to the Blue Garden, where there is another delight shock of eye-pleasure.[76]

The plan and the beds in each room were formal, geometric, and symmetrical, yet the viewer's perception of the one-color garden was that it was formless—the color-saturated effect filled the space, transcended any particular form, and positioned the garden design squarely as artifice. The one-color garden became fashionable at the turn of the century and forecasted the early modern garden design experiments of the 1910s and 1920s, to which the next chapter is devoted.[77]

3.13 Vita Sackville-West, the white garden and yellow-orange garden, following Jekyll's Special Coloring Garden model, Sissinghurst Castle, Kent, 2018 (top). Photo: Mira Engler. Gertrude Jekyll, general plan of the "Special Colour Garden" (middle) and planting plans of the orange and blue rooms (bottom), *Colour in the Flower Garden*, 1908.

* * *

The two private gardens described below were designed by Robinson and Jekyll respectively and demonstrate the application of their color concepts. The discussion is based on their books about these gardens, with images selected from photographic illustrations in these books as well as archival documentation, artwork depicting the gardens, and recent photographs by the author.[78]

Gravetye Manor, William Robinson, West Sussex, 1885–1935

Gravetye Manor, Robinson's home and garden, was a lifelong project where he put the theory presented in *The Wild Garden* (1970) to work. He acquired the estate—with more than 1000 acres of heathland, moorland, woodland, wetland, and fields that expand into the rolling countryside of Sussex, and a dilapidated Tudor manor—in July 1885.[79] Around the light brown and beige limestone house, crowned by a dark brown slate roof and red brick chimneys, Robinson created a series of garden zones where he tested the adaptation of plant communities to each site;[80] locating plants so they could "be at home" and thrive was a prerequisite for a joyful garden. Color was an important factor in plant variety and grouping choices in support of picturesque compositions, the key to the garden's beauty. More than in his other writing, his preoccupation with color is evident in his writings on Gravetye's gardens.

Gravetye Manor, unquestionably the best example of a Robinsonian garden, was the object of several of his books latterly.[81] *Gravetye Manor: Or, Twenty Years' Work Round an Old Manor House* (1911) is a straightforward diary of progress, observations, and lessons from the garden from 1885 through 1908.[82] *Home Landscapes* (1914) is both descriptive and didactic, its goal was to demonstrate the superior value and beauty of his wild garden theory compared with the Formal Style, which dominated garden design in the early 20th century. The narrative describes the transformation of the site from its original to its photographed condition, including planting design decisions: what trees and shrubs were cleared, thinned, encouraged, or added.

Home Landscapes, with 32 full-page black-and-white photographic plates featuring views of the estate's woods, lake, orchard, heath, and meadow zones (excluding the flower gardens near the house), reads like a photo album with expanded captions. The first plates in the book are a southeast view from the heath bank above Robinson's house, followed by a south view from the flower garden to the sloping south lawn or alpine meadow with the lake just below (Figure 3.14). Directly linked with the views from the house, these two scenes are among the most picturesque and are featured in different seasons. The photos were by George Champion (1891–1979), "who gave untiring care at various seasons to get true effects."[83] The resulting landscape "effect," based on composition and color, is emphasized in each view. Garden zones guided the book's chapter organization with associated seasonal colors; as Robinson explained, "We have to think of the trees and shrubs that give us even more reward in telling in the landscape throughout the year by their form and fine colour."[84]

Robinson designed his garden to be viewed as a series of "paintable" picturesque landscapes: "the key is to form a good picture, flowers are secondary," to create:

> a garden so true and right in its results as to form a picture that the artist would be charmed to study, we may call it an artistic garden, as a short way to saying that it is about as good as it may be, taking everything into account.[85]

And the Gravetye gardens were indeed captured in paintings that he commissioned from several artist friends: Moon, William Edward Norton (1843–1916), and the watercolorist Beatrice Parsons (1870–1955).[86]

Robinson took great joy in each garden—the bright yellow heath, pink and purple azaleas, and white yuccas—as well as the scrubland's large spring effects of the golden glow of yellow furze and yellowish brooms, the meadow's variegated alpine grasses, and the hillside grasses' billowing wildflowers and spring bulbs (see Figure 3.7). The rolling grasses provided a desirable green turf most of the year, and masses of spring wildflowers introduced bright color effects in the spring. Of the colors of the early spring flowers he wrote: "The Grape Hyacinths give one of the prettiest effects in grass, and seen near Daffodils often give lovely colour in April."[87] Perhaps of all the blue flowers in early spring, the most effective "are the Anemones, particularly the azure blue one called Robinsoni, which grows freely in any kind of soil."[88] Many of the Alpine leaves and flowers in the turf ripened before the grasses were cut for hay, a key principle for a wild appearance and low maintenance, avoiding "the labour of digging up the flower garden twice a year for any more artificial scheme of spring gardening."[89]

Robinson planted thousands of star narcissus bulb varieties (100,000 in 1897 alone) in groups and colonies along the driveways, in the orchard, on grassy slopes, and around

3.14 Gravetye Manor, "View of House from Heath Garden," plate I (top left) and "View across Terrace Walk from West Garden," plate II (bottom left), *Home Landscapes*, published by John Murray, 1920 Photos: George Champion. The same views in 2018 (right). Photos: Mira Engler

one of the lakes.[90] He enjoyed the variety of colors of water lilies, reeds, and willows and the white and red willow varieties along the banks of the lower lake that anchored the picturesque view south from the house in the summer.[91] In the winter, the reeds still looked good and the willows remained graceful, "some varying in colour every month in the year."[92] He focused on color in the wider landscape gardens, especially the woods, in part because Jekyll covered color only in the flower garden. Beyond the woods, trees and shrubs were grouped instead of dotted across the landscape.

In *Home Landscapes* (1914), Robinson devoted a chapter to woodland color, where he advocated mixing groups of native and naturalized deciduous and evergreen trees to maintain green colors through the winter, and the planting of evergreens in bare woods areas. He decried the artificial color and variegation effects of hybridized species such as the white maple, "which have nothing to do with true colour" (i.e., local or

LITTLE SOUTH GARDEN IN CARNATION TIME

3.15 Gravetye Manor, "Little South Garden in Carnation Time," ca. 1890 (top). Royal Horticulture Society, Lindsey Library. Alfred Parsons, oil painting of the same view, ca. 1900 (bottom). Courtesy of Gravetye Manor

native color).[93] He then turned to the undergrowth, where color effects can be integral to the woodland—dogwoods, viburnum, and hazel; bracken, briars, and wild roses, "often very good in colour"; foxgloves and clematis for pink and purple; and colonies of naturalized bulbs, primrose, and rhododendron to produce spectacular masses.[94]

Close to the house, in the flower gardens "[m]uch trouble is taken with 'schemes of colour.'"[95] With a more formal layout of simple geometric beds and border rambles, Gravetye's two flower gardens to the west and south of the house were filled with Robinson's favorite flowers for both experimentation and pleasure. The smaller, south garden, adjacent to an entrance door, was planted with tea and China roses against the house, along with beds of carnations (Figure 3.15).[96] The larger, west garden (originally a lawn) was an experimental ground of roses, carnations, starworts, and pansies in beds around a central lawn—Robinson loved pansies in particular for their "self-colored" capacity. This garden was laid out on a flat rectangular terrace supported by a tall retaining wall of brownish-gray stone, like the house, and opened out directly from the west door of the house.

In 1886 Robinson replaced the lawn with nearly 30 beds and footpaths to make working and planting more convenient. By 1895 the garden brimmed with showy climbing tea roses, overshadowing the lower plants. He delighted in training climbers, notably clematis and roses, over the house and terrace walls, preferring a single plant on a structure to accentuate the color and contrast it with the wall.[97]

Increasingly, beds took on an ornamental status, with colors chosen to complement the gray stone of the manor house and the old, well-worn York walkway pavers and edging stones; Robinson preferred stone to brick for path endurance and ease of maintenance. He consulted with Jekyll on color combinations, and the main flower borders along the walks and retaining walls reflected her penchant for chromatic sequencing and intermingled grouping. Certain bed schemes followed cool color palettes of purple, pink, silver, and pale white, while others took on warm color palettes of red, crimson, orange, yellow, and white. The spectral transitions from cool to warm to cool groups, with intervening neutral colors (grays, greens, and pale varieties), were reserved for large, long borders. The west flower garden was documented in its heyday and featured in *Country Life* magazine around 1912 (Figure 3.16). The article emphasized the garden's simple but rich effect created by the perennials' color and height differences, and the minimal labor involved in maintenance.[98]

Other garden rooms showcased distinct colors. The lengthy flat terrace lawn above the west garden was aptly named "the bowling green," and the east garden comprised pink, purple, and white rhododendrons, magnolias, and other ornamental trees and shrubs. Robinson wrote little about the one-acre, oval-shaped, walled kitchen garden, but he lavished as much care on it as on any of his ornamental gardens.[99] Located above the heath and azalea bank on a south-facing slope, it provided food as well as flowers for floral arrangements.

Munstead Wood, Gertrude Jekyll, Surrey, 1883–1932

The 15-acre Munstead Wood, where Jekyll created her garden and lived from 1883 until her death in 1932, is a testimonial to her color theory. The wooded plantation and early flower plots around the "cottage at the end of the woods" (also known as "the hut," where she lived early on) preceded the formal gardens around her Bargate stone house, which was designed by the Arts and Crafts architect Edwin Lutyens (1869–1944) and built in 1897.[100] Unlike Gravetye's hillside location and views of the larger landscape, Munstead is a relatively flat, low terrain of mostly heath and moorland, enclosed by woodland and bordered by lanes and other properties.[101]

Jekyll designed the wooded plantation to have two broad avenues, multiple curvy walks lined with bulbs, and understory shrubs in long drifts.[102] She created almost two dozen gardens around the house and in the woods, each enclosed by hedging (Figure 3.17). In these garden rooms she experimented with flower color schemes during specific one- to two-month flowering seasons. She wrote:

3.16 Gravetye Manor, rendered plan of the west garden in 1912 (top left); three views of the west garden looking east toward the house: photograph published in *Country Life* in 1912 (top right). Country Life Picture Library. Beatrice Parsons, watercolor (middle), courtesy of Gravetye Manor; photograph in 2018 (bottom). Photo: Mira Engler

> As my garden falls naturally into various portions, distinct enough from each other to allow of separate treatment, I have found it well to devote one space at a time, sometimes mainly, sometimes entirely, to the flowers of one season of the year.[103]

89

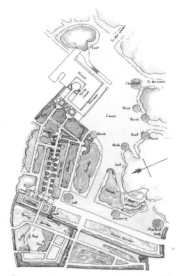

3.17 Munstead Wood, plan, from *The Gardens of Gertrude Jekyll*, 1992, by Richard Bisgrove. Rendered by Liz Pepperell

Each of the six lanes she designed in the woods also had their own character.

Munstead Wood was Jekyll's "grand teacher" and the subject of many of her publications,[104] which, in lyrical and expressive style, exude color as much as the garden itself. They include her own photographs, first in black and white and later color, chronicling the garden's progression through the seasons and years. In addition to color, the texts are replete with fragrance, tactile, and thermal descriptions to evoke the full range of sensations. She began each chapter by setting out the seasonal cycle and atmosphere of the day—light quality, wind, and temperature—before turning to the garden scene. The texts avoid botanical designations in Latin; instead, plant names are accessible and descriptive. Color words intersperse every sentence and scene.

Munstead Wood was designed with an eye to pictorial beauty, as a series of "framed pictures." In *Wood and Garden* Jekyll wrote:

> I am strongly for treating garden and wooded ground in a pictorial way, mainly with large effects, and in the second place with lesser beautiful incidents, and for so arranging plants and trees and grassy spaces that they look happy and at home, and make no parade of conscious effort. … Each room in the garden makes a distinctly framed picture [italics added].[105]

The gardens were sequenced, succeeding one another as in a film montage. Jekyll described the scenes from the perspective of a viewer standing still and in motion. For instance, she wrote of sitting on a birch bench and admiring the nut walk scene, her gaze moving from one plant and color to the next—from pink hydrangeas to green box trees, and then to pale blue hydrangeas in the shade, dark green yews, and native birch trees.[106] Clipped yews, walls, and garden arches distinguished between garden rooms (see Figure 3.12). Jekyll noted the role of changing light and color in enhancing the sequential experience.

The pergola at the end of a sunny path provided cool shade and summer breezes. Jekyll described entering it from the colorful and sunny summer border room:

> It seems wonderfully dark at first, this gallery of cool greenery, passing into it with one's eyes full of light and colour, …; but on going into it, and sitting down on one of its broad, low benches, one finds that it is a pleasant, subdued light, just right to read by.[107]

Jekyll's books, based on the color calendar, were written to provide lessons in color harmonies during specific months and seasons. The first chapter of *Wood and Garden*, "January," features the woodland tints of stems and barks; "February" focuses on colored leaves, moss, and the effects of snow; and "March" turns to the border colors of early bulbs at the wood's edge. In "April," woodland spring flowers—notably, a river of daffodils—take center stage. The colorful primrose garden was featured in "April" and "May." In "May" Jekyll provided instructions for grouping arrangements for color transitions from lawn to copse (she excluded azaleas because of their "incongruous" color). Rhododendrons in full bloom at the edge of a copse served as a lesson in color grouping, which she classified into:

> six classes of easy harmonies: 1. crimsons inclining to scarlet or blood-colour grouped with dark claret-colour and true pink; 2. light scarlet rose colours inclining to salmon; 3. rose colours inclining to amaranth; 4. amaranths or magenta-crimsons; 5. crimson or amaranth-purples; and 6. cool clear purples of the typical ponticum class, both dark and light, grouped with lilac-whites, such as Album elegans and Album grandiflorum.[108]

The "June" garden featured roses. In "July," the delphiniums, yuccas, carnations, and lilies were at their prime. The "August" garden celebrated the China aster. Other garden plantings were assigned to the remaining months through December.

The largest herbaceous summer border—200 feet long and 14 feet wide—was the highlight of Munstead and the subject of four chapters in *Colour in the Flower Garden* (Figure 3.18). Jekyll commented in the opening pages that "To plant and maintain a flower-border, *with a good scheme for colour*, is by no means the easy thing that is commonly supposed."[109] She described the color progression down the length of the border and the choice of flowers that provided and maintained their effects through the four months of its prime, June through September. The border was sheltered from the north by a solid sandstone wall about 11 feet high and mostly obscured by three-foot-wide evergreen shrubs, which helped bring out the color of the flowering plants in front. The juxtaposition of color and every detail of the view were calculated to be enjoyed both from a stationary vantage point at either end and while moving along the border path.

Cool-colored groupings at both ends set off the warm colors at the center (Figure 3.19). Colors spanning almost the entire spectrum were distributed linearly in gradations and with chromatic separation, each color displayed partly in distinct masses and partly intergrouped. The east end began with violet, purple, and plants of gray and glaucous foliage, moved to warm colors (yellows, oranges, and reds) at the center, and then again through pale pink and pale yellow to the cool graduated tints of gray-blue and pure blue at the other end. Jekyll was humble in her attempt to explain the color succession:

> I do not know whether it is by individual preference, or in obedience to some colour-law that I can instinctively feel but cannot pretend even to understand, and much less to explain, but in practice I always find more satisfaction and facility in treating the warm colours (reds and yellows) in graduated harmonies, culminating into gorgeousness, and the cool ones in contrasts. ...[110]

Jekyll's photographs of flower borders were often taken from an end vantage point that emphasized the border's linear and richly layered quality and demonstrated the foreshortening of perspective; they rarely showed elevation.[111] Oblique views also offered the advantage of obscuring gaps in the plantings caused by insect or weather damage; but, most importantly, "the overlapping condenses the volume of planes and makes their scintillating colors seem even more saturated."[112]

3.18 Munstead Wood, main flower border, planting plan, *Colour in the Flower Garden,* 1908 ed. (left) and watercolor by Asif Khan (middle). Gertrude Jekyll, photograph, "End of Flower Border," late 1890s. College of Environmental Design archives, University of California, Berkeley (top right). Helen Allingham, watercolor, 1900. Godalming Museum (bottom right)

* * *

The period from the 1870s to 1910 was the pinnacle of English landscape gardening color discourse. William Robinson, among the era's most vocal horticulturists and a proponent of native and naturalized hardy plants, kindled interest in foliage color and in large masses of color effects in grasslands and woodlands. Gertrude Jekyll made color and light the primary concerns of a garden, popularized color intergrouping or drifts in herbaceous flower beds and borders, and drew attention to color sequences in space and time.

3.19 Munstead Wood, photographic panorama of the main flower border, 2018. Photo: Mira Engler

Together, Robinson and Jekyll persuasively set forth alternatives to both the bedding out garden promoted by Loudon and his contemporaries, and the formal garden, or the "architect's garden" in Robinson's terms, and its avid advocate Sir Reginald Blomfield (1856–1942). Blomfield's book *The Formal Garden in England* (1892) would propel the renewal of historical European garden design models, in which color was confined to formal flower beds and clipped hedges.

The post-Victorian gardening appetite for spectrum-adjacent harmony and formlessness revived the debate on nature versus art and the meanings of these mostly incompatible concepts. If color affirmed the artistic and unnatural character of the Victorian garden, Robinson's color outlook showcased the garden's naturalness and pictorial aesthetics. Jekyll, with her painterly eye and affinity for Impressionism, allied color with both nature and art, shifting the use of color from artifact and decoration to color as impression.

Subsequent 20th century modern garden theories rejected Jekyll's spectrally adjacent color model and nature-coded design. Aided by new materials and technologies, the garden returned as artifact, where form supplanted color and spatial structure announced its primacy.

Notes

[1] Jekyll, *Wood and Garden*, [1899] 1904, 197.

[2] Lear, "Colour in Gardens," 2012, 80.

[3] Robinson, "Gravetye Manor: Tree and Garden Book I," 1885–1892, WRO/1/01.

[4] Robinson, *The English Flower Garden*, 1883, 192.

[5] Ruskin began his career writing for Loudon's *Architectural Magazine*.

[6] Jekyll's first essay on color was "Colour in the Flower Garden," 1883, 192–7. Jekyll was the first woman to rise to a recognized status in gardening.

[7] Robinson, *The Wild Garden*, 1870.

[8] Jekyll, *Colour in the Flower Garden*, 1908. The book was reprinted in 1911 under the title *Colour Schemes for the Flower Garden*.

[9] Jekyll appealed to nonprofessionals, particularly middle-class women, through her books and regular column in *The Garden*.

[10] Robinson, *English Flower Garden*, 1883, 31.

[11] Ruskin, *The Seven Lamps of Architecture*, [1849] 1984, 132–3.

[12] The turn to vernacular cottage gardens mirrored the philosophy of the contemporaneous Arts and Crafts movement in architecture. See Elliott, *Victorian Gardens*, 1986, 236–41.

[13] Robinson, *English Flower Garden*, 1883, 9.

[14] Ibid., 22. Jekyll, *Wood and Garden*, [1899] 1904, 4.

[15] Ibid., 9.

[16] Robinson, "The Flower Garden at Gravetye Manor," 1912, 409.

[17] Robinson, *English Flower Garden*, 1883, 31.

[18] Jekyll, *Colour in the Flower Garden*, 1908, 138–39.

[19] In a letter to Hercules Brabazon (December 13, 1889), she referred to her gardening work as "doing living pictures with land and trees and flowers!"

[20] Jekyll, *Colour in the Flower Garden*, 1908, 138.

[21] Bisgrove, *The Gardens of Gertrude Jekyll*, 1992, 6.

[22] Gage, *Color and Meaning*, 1999, 209, 219.

[23] Tunnard, *Gardens in the Modern Landscape*, 1948, 37.

[24] Tankard and Wood, *Gertrude Jekyll at Munstead Wood*, 1996, 27.

[25] Wood, *The Unknown Gertrude Jekyll*, 2006, 68–73.

[26] Jekyll, *Garden Ornament*, 1918, 269.

[27] Robinson, *English Flower Garden*, 1883, 31.

[28] Robinson, *Wild Garden*, 1870, 193.

[29] Ibid., 192.

[30] Goethe, *Theory of Colours*, 1840, 316.

[31] See Allan, *William Robinson*, 1982, 80, 183, 115.

[32] Elliott, *Victorian Gardens*, 1986, 152–4.

[33] Robinson, *English Flower Garden*, 1883, 205. As an alternative to foliage, his own alpine rock garden created a natural-looking setting for dwarf succulents and other alpines to grow close together as intermittent groundcover patches.

[34] Wildsmith, "Summer-Bedding Gardening," 1883, 168.

[35] Pastoureau, *Green: The History of a Color*, 2014, 191.

[36] Elliott, *Victorian Gardens*, 1986, 148–9.

[37] Ibid., 123, 185.

[38] Robinson, *English Flower Garden*, 1883, 205.

[39] Ibid., 199. Despite his criticism of Loudon, Robinson dedicated the first issue of *The Garden* (June 1872) to him. Robinson did agree with Loudon that gardeners needed to know plants, but distinguished between botany, which was Loudon's lens, and horticulture, his own lens. In botany, he wrote, "all plants are of equal value," as in a museum or botanical garden, whereas in horticulture one must exercise judgment to create beauty. Robinson, *The Virgin's Bower*, 1912, preface.

[40] Robinson, *Wild Garden*, 1870, 16.

[41] Robinson, *English Flower Garden*, 1883, 6.

[42] Ibid., 47.

[43] Ibid., 143.

[44] Ibid., 3.

[45] Robinson, *Gravetye Manor*, 1911, 20–1.

[46] Jekyll, *Colour in the Flower Garden*, 1908, 24.

[47] Jekyll, "Colour in the Flower Garden," 1883, 193–4.

[48] Jekyll, *Wood and Garden*, [1889] 1904, 3.

[49] Ibid., 197.

50 For instance, Robinson reluctantly added "summer bedding" in later editions, merely "for completeness."

51 Jekyll, "Colour in the Flower Garden," 1883, 193.

52 Ibid., 193.

53 Elliott, *Victorian Gardens*, 1986, 206–8.

54 Jekyll did not mention Goethe's color theory but echoes several of his principles, including the eye's search for a colorless spot next to each hue. See Goethe, *Goethe's Theory of Colours*, 1840, 317.

55 Goethe, *Theory of Colours*, 1840, 316.

56 Ibid., 194.

57 Turner, "Preface," in *Colour Schemes for the Flower Garden*, 1982, 9–11.

58 Jekyll, "Colour in the Flower Garden," 1883, 196.

59 Jekyll, "Colour in the Flower Garden," 1908, 195.

60 Jekyll, *Wood and Garden*, [1889] 1904, 227.

61 Ibid., 23.

62 Jekyll, "Colour in the Flower Garden," 1908, 193. Gardening and watercolor painting were Jekyll's penchant all along, especially when her eyesight began failing in 1892. She left some 2000 drawings; many are in the archive of the College of Environmental Design at the University of California, Berkeley.

63 Tankard and Van Valkenburgh, *Gertrude Jekyll*, 1988, 16.

64 Jekyll, *Wood and Garden*, [1899] 1904, 30.

65 Jekyll, *Colour in the Flower Garden*, 1908, 136–7.

66 Ibid., 121.

67 Tunnard, *Modern Landscape*, 1948, 37.

68 Tankard and Wood, *Gertrude Jekyll*, 1996, 13.

69 Ibid., 6; Tankard and Van Valkenburgh, *Gertrude Jekyll*, 1988, 10.

70 Jekyll, *Wood and Garden*, [1899] 1904, v.

71 Messingham, *A Century of Gardeners*, 1982, 24.

72 Robinson, *Gravetye Manor*, 1911, 68.

73 Elliott, *Victorian Gardens*, 1986, 151, note 12.

74 Jekyll, *Colour in the Flower Garden*, 1908, 89.

75 Ibid., 91

76 Ibid., 102–3.

77 Jekyll's one-color garden concept influenced the private designs of Lawrence Johnston's Hidcote Manor and Vita Sackville-West's Sissinghurst Castle.

78 The author of this book visited the two estates in July 2018 and reviewed several photo albums with photographs taken by Robinson of Gravetye, in the private possession of Mrs. Susan Herbert, at West Hoathly, Sussex, on July 21, 2018.

79 In 1889 the estate consisted of 1100 acres. It has expanded since.

80 Robinson, *Gravetye Manor*, 1911, 14.

81 Today the estate is privately owned and operated as a luxury hotel. While the gardens are well maintained and still reflect the spirit of Robinson's theory, they have been adapted to their new leisurely function.

82 The book is an abstract from Robinson's diary, entitled "Gravetye Manor, Tree and Garden Book and Building Record," currently in the Lindsey Library, London.

83 Robinson, *Home Landscapes*, 1914, vii.

[84] Ibid., 8–10.

[85] Robinson, *Gravetye Manor*, 1911, 34; Robinson, *The Garden Beautiful*, 1907, 20.

[86] Moon and Norton painted the garden from spring through winter, capturing the narcissi and crocuses in the lawn, woodland lanes, and autumnal harvesting scenes, and in 1891 they exhibited nearly 70 paintings in an exhibition titled "A Story of the Year Round an Old Country House in Woodland, Field, and Garden" at Stephen T. Gooden Gallery in London. See Tankard and Wood, *Gertrude Jekyll*, 1996, 25.

[87] Robinson, *Home Landscapes*, 1914, 52.

[88] Robinson, *Gravetye Manor*, 1911, 138. The blue anemone was named after William Robinson.

[89] Robinson, *Home Landscapes*, 1914, 7.

[90] Ibid., see plates III, XX, and XXI.

[91] Ibid., see plates VIII–X.

[92] Ibid., 52.

[93] Ibid., 54.

[94] Robinson, *Garden Beautiful*, 1907, 123–4.

[95] Robinson, *Gravetye Manor*, 1911, 142.

[96] The south terrace garden was redesigned by J. Tate in 1898.

[97] Robinson, *Virgin's Bower*, 1912, 105.

[98] Robinson, "The Flower Garden," 1912, 409–11.

[99] Winterrowd, "Robinson's Legacy," 1995, 24.

[100] Jekyll collaborated with Lutyens for four decades.

[101] Today the property is in private hands, but open for small tours. Although several of the gardens changed or were neglected, a handful are still worth a visit.

[102] Jekyll, *Wood and Garden*, [1899] 1904, 15.

[103] Jekyll, *Colour in the Flower Garden*, 1908, v.

[104] Jekyll, *Wood and Garden*, [1899] 1904, 6.

[105] Ibid., 2.

[106] Jekyll, *Colour in the Flower Garden*, 1908, 124.

[107] Jekyll, *Wood and Garden*, [1899] 1904, 213.

[108] Ibid., 66–7.

[109] Jekyll, *Colour in the Flower Garden*, 1908, v [italics in original].

[110] Jekyll, *Wood and Garden*, [1899] 1904, 206.

[111] Tankard and Van Valkenburgh, *Gertrude Jekyll*, 1988, 15–16.

[112] Ibid.

References

Allan, Mea. *William Robinson, 1838–1935: Father of the English Flower Garden*. London: Faber and Faber, 1982.

Bisgrove, Richard. *The Gardens of Gertrude Jekyll*. London: Little, Brown & Co., 1992.

Blomfield, Reginald. *The Formal Garden in England* [1892]. London: Macmillan and Co., 1901.

Elliott, Brent. *Victorian Gardens*. London: Butler & Tanner Ltd., 1986.

Gage, John. *Color and Meaning: Art, Science, and Symbolism*. Berkeley: University of California Press, 1999.

Goethe, Johann Wolfgang von. *Goethe's Theory of Colours*. London: J. Murray, 1840.

Jekyll, Gertrude. "Colour in the Flower Garden." In *The English Flower Garden*, ed. by William Robinson, 192–7. London: John Murray, 1883.

Jekyll, Gertrude. *Wood and Garden: Notes and Thoughts, Practical and Critical, of a Working Amateur* [1899]. London: Longmans, Green & Co., 1904.

Jekyll, Gertrude. *Colour in the Flower Garden*. London: "Country Life," Ltd., and George Newnes, Ltd., 1908.

Jekyll, Gertrude. *Garden Ornament*. London: Country Life, 1918.

Lear, Beverley. "Colour in Gardens: A Question of Class or Gender?" In *Cultures of Colour: Visual, Material, Textual*, ed. by Chris Horrocks, 77–96. New York: Berghahn Books, 2012.

Messingham, Betty. *A Century of Gardeners*. London: Faber and Faber, 1982.

Pastoureau, Michel. *Green: The History of a Color*. Princeton, NJ: Princeton University Press, 2014.

Robinson, William. *Alpine Flowers for Gardens*. London: J. Murray, 1870.

Robinson, William. *The Wild Garden*. London: J. Murray, 1870.

Robinson, William. *The Subtropical Garden; or Beauty of Form in the Flower Garden*. London: John Murray, 1871.

Robinson, William. *The English Flower Garden*. London: John Murray, 1883.

Robinson, William. "Gravetye Manor: Tree and Garden Book and Building Record (Vol. I, 1885–1892; Vol. II, 1893–1911)", unpublished manuscripts, Lindley Library, London, WRO/1/01.

Robinson, William. *The Garden Beautiful: Home Woods and Home Landscape*. London: J. Murray, 1907.

Robinson, William. *Gravetye Manor: or Twenty Years' Work Round an Old Manor House*. London: J. Murray, 1911.

Robinson, William. "The Flower Garden at Gravetye Manor." *Country Life* (September 28, 1912): 409.

Robinson, William. *The Virgin's Bower: Clematis, Climbing Kinds and Their Culture at Gravetye Manor*. London: J. Murray, 1912.

Robinson, William. *Home Landscapes*. London: John Murray, 1914.

Ruskin, John. *The Seven Lamps of Architecture* [1849]. New York: Farrar, Straus & Giroux, 1984.

Tankard, Judith B., and Michael R. Van Valkenburgh. *Gertrude Jekyll: A Vision of Garden and Wood*. New York: Harry N. Abrams, Inc., 1988.

Tankard, Judith B., and Martin A. Wood. *Gertrude Jekyll at Munstead Wood: Writing, Horticulture, Photography, Homebuilding*. Gloucestershire: Sutton Publishing; New York: Sagapress, 1996.

Tunnard, Christopher. *Gardens in the Modern Landscape*. London: The Architectural Press, 1948.

Turner, T. H. D. "Preface." In *Colour Schemes for the Flower Garden*, by Gertrude Jekyll, 8–15. Woodbridge, Suffolk: Antique Collector's Club, 1982.

Wildsmith, W. "Summer-Bedding Gardening." In *The English Flower Garden*, 166–77. London: John Murray, 1883.

Winterrowd, Wayne. "Robinson's Legacy." *Horticulture* (Aug.–Sept. 1995): 24–5.

Wood, Martin, ed. *The Unknown Gertrude Jekyll*. London: Frances Lincoln, 2006.

II.1 Theo van Doesburg and Cornelis van Eesteren, axonometry, gouache on lithograph, "Contra-Construction Project," 1923. © Museum of Modern Art/Licensed by SCALA/Art Resource, New York

Part II
Modernism
From Material to Sensation

Primary Colors Versus White

Premodern landscape color theories largely followed the art world and horticulture. Modern landscape architecture, while not fully detached from art influences, also veered toward architecture and nodded to the science of ecology and the social sciences of perception and psychology. Thanks to these late 19th century sciences, early 20th century artists freed color from object and meaning, allowing it to become a subject of exploration on its own, first in Impressionist and then Cubist art. Theories of how color is perceived and impacts sensation dominated art discourse at the time, leading to the rise of both abstraction and the elevation of primary colors, as painters used flatter tones and deemed red, yellow, and blue as superior to other colors.[1] Green lost its status as the emblem and moral connotation of nature, and so was avoided in art. In architecture, color theories focused on how color impacts the perception of space and form; color schemes (and everything else) of the past were cast aside.

For modern landscape designers, ditching green, the default landscape color, was neither desirable nor possible. Yet the profession's retreat from horticulture, and its move closer to architecture, led to the use of new materials and building techniques: plants were offset by colored minerals and synthetically stained or tinted modular structural materials. Unlike architecture, landscape architecture did not wholly abandon color traditions, rather, it modernized them. The industrial materials had a flattening effect on landscapes, but designers tempered that by incorporating the concept of regional identity (local plants, different angles of sunlight).

Landscape architecture's modern conception of color therefore should be understood, in part, through key preceding figures and discourses in art and architecture. In the late 1890s, Paul Gauguin declared that there is no true color: because it constantly changes with light in nature and on the canvas, color can only claim to imitate nature. He called for the rejection of gradations and harmonies and the use of pure and flat color to interpret nature in an abstract manner.[2] Freed from nature, the modern expression of color aligned with the modern properties of space, time, and motion. Fellow artist Paul Cézanne, considered the forefather of Cubism, forged a new color consciousness of space through the use of colored planes of receding and advancing values to suggest volume. By giving color and tone planar form, he replaced the illusionistic space of one-point perspective with pure spatial properties of color. His work greatly influenced the De Stijl movement and, ultimately, architecture.

Two decades later, the Russian painter Kazimir Malevich and his Dutch counterpart, Piet Mondrian, further developed this modern sensibility by plunging into pure primary colors. Working with basic geometric forms and planes in primary colors, together with white, black, and gray, Malevich ensured that color emerged from the pictorial mix as an independent entity, free from any aesthetic consideration of beauty, experience, or mood.[3] Mondrian, likewise, called for freeing color from individuality and associated subjective sensation, to enable it to express itself as the "only the serene emotion of the universal."[4] He equated modernism with universality and posited that color becomes pure light and is governed by relationships with nearby colors only. Furthermore, "[b]ecause colour appears as pure, planar and separate, the new plastic *directly expresses expansion*, that is, directly expresses the basis of spatial appearance."[5] Mondrian's use of a white field, on which rectangular planes of primary color floated in a defined network, had a major influence on modern architecture trends in the following decades. It offered a way for color and architecture to coexist.

Malevich's and Mondrian's use of the primary colors combined with black and white was the prevailing scheme in the teachings of the Dutch De Stijl and German Bauhaus schools of architecture. The De Stijl architect Theo van Doesburg's search for a coherent relationship between color and space solidified the role of color in support of space. Decorative color could hide construction, and van Doesburg extended Mondrian's scheme from a flat field into architectural space, where color emerged as a plane rather than form and was thus integral to spatial structure (Figure II.1).[6] Van Doesburg clashed with Le Corbusier (then known as C. E. Jeanneret), who criticized the De Stijl approach, claiming that because the intrinsic property of color is to advance or retreat in space, color interfered with the perception of volume.[7] The debate between the two positions came to a head after the 1923 De Stijl exhibition in Paris, led by van Doesburg and Mondrian.[8] Le Corbusier rejected pure color in favor of whiteness (although he occasionally used earthy or "solid colors") and reaffirmed the primacy of architectural form, reclaiming and positioning it as the superior property of architecture; everything else was subordinate.

The architectural attack on color was matched by one on decoration. In a 1908 essay, "Ornament and Crime," the Viennese architect Adolf Loos denounced contemporary ornate trends, including Neoclassical, Art Nouveau, and the German Werkbund, dismissing ornament and color as degenerative and unnecessary in modern architecture—in fact, when it came to volume or space, color was a destructive agent.[9]

The debate over color in architecture during the first half of the 20th century evolved into two camps: those who preferred whiteness and the intrinsic color of industrial material and those who preferred the use of the three primary colors plus the nonchromatic palette of white, gray, and black.[10] White gained the upper hand and came to dominate modern architecture: "whiteness was a rhetorical crusade that elevated the rule of line and rationality above color, and the muddiness and emotions it may generate."[11] White was clean, clear, and apt for ornament-free modern architecture.

Modern architectural color aesthetics can only be understood in the context of developments in building technology and materials. Increased standardization and mass production injected architecture with an expansive range of new materials. Machine aesthetics created a sleek and modern look through synthetic color and material light effects. Exposed steel construction and glass walls, signatures of architectural modernism, led to a well-lit house and indoor-outdoor convergence. With glass walls, daylight and landscape could enter the building, conferring a healthy and bright atmosphere. New emerging aesthetics, linked to the integration of interior and landscape in the growing suburbs, supported the elimination of color and embellishment indoors and outdoors. Architects expanded their territorial practice to garden design, while landscape architects increasingly aligned with architecture and art. Garden design came to be recognized as an art in and of itself. Garden color designers fell into the two familiar architectural camps: those that eschewed bright color and preferred the intrinsic palettes of verdure and industrial material, and those that preferred the use of bright monochromatic palettes, primarily resonating the three primary colors. The first group broke all ties with color's past; the second modernized color traditions.

Early Modernist Color Forays in European Gardens

During the first two decades of the 20th century, landscape architecture remained largely indebted to the canon of the Parisian École des Beaux-Arts and its associated neoclassical gardening models, heralded by the architect Reginald Blomfield. In fact, early modern gardens were designed by architects rather than landscape architects. William Robinson pejoratively called Blomfield's formal garden an "architect's garden," implying a lack of interest in (or knowledge of) plants and a focus instead on space. In England, early efforts to advance the garden to the modern age were rather feeble. Blomfield's garden model, largely based on Italian Renaissance models, was justifiably perceived by contemporary critics as backward-looking. His rejection of nature and emphasis on form and space were insufficient to make the leap into the new century.[12]

The first genuine modern garden experiments in Europe began in Vienna (Europe's prewar artistic and intellectual avant-garde center), Germany, and Belgium and matured in France—countries where abstract art trumped the Romantic and Beaux-Arts canons. In Darmstadt, Germany, the Viennese Secessionist architect Joseph Maria Olbrich showcased a series of garden rooms, each in one primary color, while in Brussels his compatriot Josef Hoffmann scarcely used color in the Stoclet Palace garden. As early as the first decade of the 20th century, Olbrich joined architectural critics and designers in Vienna who began envisioning new concepts of garden design that counteracted nature and broke with past models to elevate garden design to the status of the plastic arts. They named the practice "garden art." Olbrich boasted that gardens had joined the world of artifacts and edifices as a new art form that propelled "new possibilities and new ideas."[13]

In Darmstadt, Olbrich found an experimental ground, a place free from the struggle between emergent modernism and backward-looking tradition. For the city's 1905 Building Exhibition, he created the Garden of Colors, featuring bold forms and minimalist use of the three primary colors plus green. Surrounded by walls and sunk into the ground, the octagonal garden had four rooms, each filled with plants of red, blue, yellow, or green (in the vein of Jekyll's later one-color garden concept but not as a linear sequence). The watercolor postcard prints of the yellow and blue gardens vibrate (Figure II.2).[14] Planted in defined bed contours the blue, yellow, and red flowers were allowed, to some degree, to proliferate and grow into each other's domain; the abstraction of a single dominant color field and, at the same time, the freedom of colors to mix at the edges yielded a singular experiment in color. In this way

II.2 Joseph Maria Olbrich, Garden of Colors, postcards, "The Red Garden," (top) "The Yellow Garden," (middle) and "The Blue Garden," (bottom) Darmstadt Building Exhibition, Germany, 1905. Institut Mathildenhöhe, Darmstadt Municipal Art Collection, photo: Gregor Schuster

the Garden of Colors merged two color tendencies: Modernist and Impressionist. Against this rich chromatic palette, a strong green architectonic framework was created by clipped hedges and vine-covered arched pergolas. Built elements, such as yellow and red sphere-crowned posts in the blue garden, completed the primary color triad in each room.

In remarks on his garden at the German garden art conference that year, Olbrich attributed a wondrous efficacy to color: "The miracle of light that emanates from the flowers impels us in new ways: new ways to a new rhythm. New values appear in the wide field of garden art and between the large forces that surround."[15] He cited the principles of the emerging modern garden, among which the rejection of nature, formal simplicity, and tight relationship with the house were central. He touched on the physiopsychological dimension of color and light:

> Peace and unity will govern everything that composes the house and garden. … The light, this multicolor miracle, will bring that unity and peace which the people long for. And with the light and vivid colors fairy tale will return to our house and garden.[16]

Also built in 1905, the garden at the Palais Stoclet in Brussels by Josef Hoffmann was equally celebrated at the time but took a very different color approach. It made a similar bold statement about the negation of nature, but with an austere achromatic palette. Considered an important innovation by the contemporary architect and critic Joseph August Lux, the Stoclet garden served as a garden art model that used plants for their space-making properties, rather than architectural elements, such as walls, spheres, and cubes.[17]

In his theory, Lux permitted the three primary colors to be used merely to enhance the human perception of space, depth, and time: "the blue reflects the distance, the yellow and the red morning sky and the evening."[18] The Stoclet garden worked in concert with the house to extend the interior space outdoors. A marble-floored garden terrace overlooked the central garden space, which was defined by a white pergola on each side, a white stone–clad pool and fountain column in the center, and peripheral topiary columns and clipped hedges (Figure II.3). The white pergolas and fountain contrasted with the dark foliage background. Roses along the pergolas were the only flowers allowed in a garden dominated by green, white, and black or gray.[19] Viewed from the residence's ground-floor brown, gold, and white-honey interiors, the garden seemed starkly abstract and sculptural. The Stoclet garden's highly architectonic, unadorned, and achromatic palette set competed with the Garden of Colors as a model for modern garden art in Europe and America.

A decade later, in France, modern garden theorist and designer J. C. N. Forestier, who masterminded the evolution of French garden design to its modern form, advanced the first landscape color theory of the period. He reiterated the idea of the garden as an extension of the house, the use of plants as green volumes and hedges, and, importantly, the role of color to project form. Embracing simple geometries and symmetry, he remarried color with form, thus countering the Jekyll-Robinson primacy of color. Color that appeared independent from form, he contended, might irritate the mind when "the eye cannot rest at any point or on a simple, plain surface."[20] However, although his gardens featured textures (and fragrance), they had minimal coloration. Not unlike Hoffmann, Forestier's color scheme relied on light and dark tones:

II.3 Josef Hoffmann, "Garden View from the Veranda," Stoclet Palace, Brussels, ca. 1914, from *Josef Hoffmann* by Giuliano Gresleri, 1985

> An abundance of flowers and colors in uniform or contrasting masses will not give the brilliance or the gaiety which one might expect. Beauty and joy are born not merely of profuse and violent colors, but of the brilliance and natural bloom of flowers brought out by distinct and sombre accents and gleaming whiteness and dark masses of a background.[21]

Forestier's minimal use of flowers, ideally two or three, created accents and tonal juxtaposition. He played with changing daylight, alternately illuminating and contrasting background planting masses with flower beds and built floors, walls, and water elements in the foreground. His rejection of flower color, however, did not extend to built elements, such as the colorful floor mosaics and ceramic tiles of Moorish gardens, with which he was enamored. This sentiment legitimized the inclusion of color traditions in modern gardens.

In search of modern expression in the first two decades of the new century, Olbrich, Hoffmann, and Forestier negotiated new roles for color in the garden, setting the stage for bold innovations in garden forms, materials, and color at the 1925 Paris International Exposition of Modern Industrial and Decorative Arts (known as the Art Deco Exposition). Reflecting the Art Deco sensibilities of architecture and design at the time, their garden art combined Cubist, Secessionist, and other styles with fine craftsmanship and a rich material palette and colors. Attention to the relationship between solids and voids, dimensions and proportion replaced ornamentation as the primary formal concern. The central axis of the garden that lingered from the Beaux-Arts gradually disappeared, and was replaced by straight lines and sharp angles. Color merged with form and built materials, and simple geometric patterns took the place of applied decoration.

The American landscape architect and critic Fletcher Steele, who visited the Art Deco Exposition in Paris, said it heralded a new era in landscape design, pointing to the pioneering color design in Gabriel Guevrekian's Garden of Water and Light.[22] In that work, color entered free of meaning and in flat, simple, dynamic compositions of monochromatic fields that projected depth and movement. In that way, color became a creative tool for the production of special effects and a desirable mood, and a rational tool in the service of architectural space.

Garden design drawings similarly underscored the new era. Forestier's books, which included colorless, meticulous line and textured volumes in plans and perspectives, gave way to watercolor and gouache axons by his successors throughout the 1930s. But there was a countervailing force that slowed down the color explosion in landscape design: Black-and-white photography, which dominated print media and impacted design in many forms: in architecture it helped sustain the image of modern architecture as white, in landscape design it countered and may have retarded color explorations.

Notes

1   Pastoureau. *Green: The History of a Color*, 2014, 181.

2   Gauguin, "Notes on Colour," [1896–1898] 2008, 44–45.

3   Malevich, "Non-Objective Art and Suprematism," [1919] 2008, 75.

4   Mondrian, "The New Plastic in Painting," [1917] 2008, 70. Plastic refers to techniques of modeling (creating volumes) in painting.

5   Ibid., 71.

6   Van Doesburg, "Space-Time and Colour," [1928] 2008, 87. Van Doesburg ultimately abandoned Mondrian's color scheme and aligned himself with Le Corbusier.

7   Le Corbusier and Ozenfant, "Purism," [1920] 2008, 72–4. As painter and founder of Purism, together with the painter Amédée Ozenfant, Le Corbusier advanced the Purist scheme of earthy "stable colors" or "local colors"—ochre yellow, reds, ultramarine blue, and white and black, which were essentially unmodern. However, in late 1924, Le Corbusier broke with Ozenfant and developed his own architectural color theory.

8   On the modern architectural color debate, see Wigley, *White Walls, Designer Dresses*, 1995, 233–8.

9   Loos, "Ornament and Crime," [1908] 1970. Art Nouveau followed the romantic tradition in harking back to nature as its primary formal source of organic forms. The German Werkbund, founded in 1907, integrated the arts and craft traditions with industrial mass production techniques.

10 See Kane, "Broken Colour in a Modern World," 2015, 14, 1–13, 6.

11 Ibid.

12 Blomfield, *The Formal Garden in England,* [1892] 1901, 4.

13 Olbrich was a founding member of the Vienna Secessionist group and the architect of its headquarters. His early architectural façades and interiors demonstrate a neoclassical style that influenced the oeuvre of the architects Josef Hoffmann and Peter Behrens, among others.

14 The garden diverged notably from the colors seen in the prints of his earlier architectural oeuvre in Vienna, featuring the Purist earthy, "stable," color palette of red-brown, dark blue, and gray or a warm middle tone, such as gold-yellow, pink, orange, or ochre. Olbrich, *Architecture: Complete*, 1988. The chromatic palette coincided with and was limited by the four-color, photo-type publishing techniques; Olbrich, Beil, and Stephan, *Joseph Maria Olbrich,* 2010.

15 Olbrich, "Garden of Colors," [1905] 1981, 15. Paper presented at the Conference der Farben Garten, XVII meeting of the Deutscher Gartenkünstler, Garden Exhibition in Darmstadt, 1905.

16 Ibid.

17 Lux, "The Beautiful Garden," 1909, 120.

18 Ibid.

19 Freytag, "Josef Hoffmann's Unknown Masterpiece," 2010.

20 Forestier, *Gardens: A Note-Book of Plans and Sketches,* [1920] 1924, 18.

21 Ibid., 17–18.

22 Steele, "New Pioneering in Garden Design," 1930.

References

Blomfield, Reginald. *The Formal Garden in England* [1892]. London: Macmillan and Co., 1901.

Forestier, J. C. N. *Gardens: A Note-Book of Plans and Sketches* [1920], trans. by Helen Morgenthau Fox. New York: Charles Scribner's Sons, 1924.

Freytag, Anette. "Josef Hoffmann's Unknown Masterpiece: The Garden of Stoclet House in Brussels (1905–1911)." *Studies in the History of Gardens & Designed Landscapes* 30, no. 4 (2010): 337–72.

Gauguin, Paul. "Notes on Colour" [1896–1898]. In *Colour, Documents of Contemporary Art*, ed. by David Batchelor, 44–45. Cambridge, MA: MIT Press, 2008.

Kane, Carolyn. "Broken Colour in a Modern World: Chromatic Failures in Purist Art and Architecture." *Journal of the International Colour Association* (2015). www.aic-colour-journal.org.

Le Corbusier, and Amédée Ozenfant. "Purism" [1920]. In *Colour, Documents of Contemporary Art*, ed. by David Batchelor, 82–3. Cambridge, MA: MIT Press, 2008.

Loos, Adolf. "Ornament and Crime [1908]." In *Programs and Manifestoes on Twentieth Century Architecture*, 19–24. Cambridge, MA: MIT Press, 1970.

Lux, Joseph August. "The Beautiful Garden." *Der Architekt* XV (1909): 120.

Malevich, Kazimir. "Non-Objective Art and Suprematism" [1919]. In *Colour, Documents of Contemporary Art*, ed. by David Batchelor, 75–6. Cambridge, MA: MIT Press, 2008.

Mondrian, Piet. "The New Plastic in Painting" [1917]. In *Colour, Documents of Contemporary Art*, ed. by David Batchelor, 72–4. Cambridge, MA: MIT Press, 2008.

Olbrich, Joseph M. *Architecture: Complete Reprint of the Original Plates of 1901–1914*. With Peter Haiko and Bernd Krimmel. London: Butterworth Architecture, 1988.

Olbrich, Joseph M. "Garden of Colors" [1905]. *Rassegna* 8 (October 1981): 15.

Olbrich, Joseph, Ralf Beil, and Regina Stephan. *Joseph Maria Olbrich, 1867–1908: Architect and Designer of Early Modernism*. Art to Hear series. Ostfildern, Germany: Hatje Cantz; Darmstadt, Germany: Mathildenhöhe Darmstadt, 2010.

Pastoureau, Michel. *Green: The History of a Color*. Princeton, NJ: Princeton University Press, 2014.

Steele, Fletcher. "New Pioneering in Garden Design." *Landscape Architecture* 20, no. 3 (April 1930): 159–77.

Van Doesburg, Theo. "Space-Time and Colour" [1928]. In *Colour, Documents of Contemporary Art,* ed. by David Batchelor, 84–87. Cambridge, MA: MIT Press, 2008.

Wigley, Mark. *White Walls, Designer Dresses: The Fashioning of Modern Architecture*. Cambridge, MA: MIT Press, 1995.

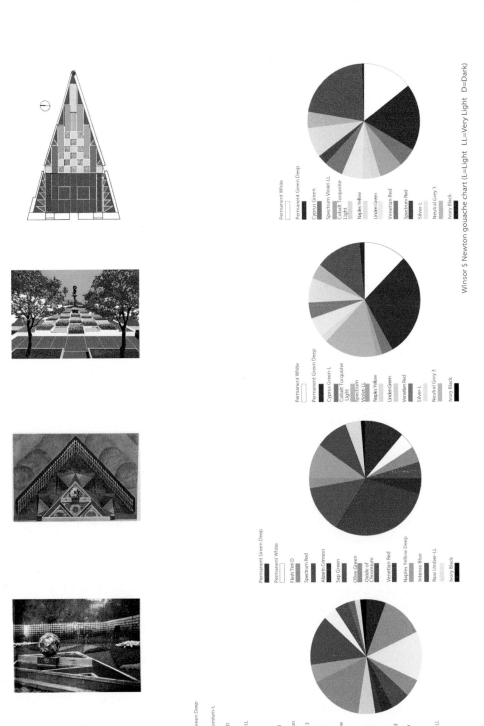

Winsor & Newton gouache chart (L=Light LL=Very Light D=Dark)

Permanent White
Permanent Green Deep
Cyprus Green
Spectrum Violet-LL
Cobalt Turquoise Light
Naples Yellow
Linden Green
Venetian Red
Spectrum Red
Silver-L
Neutral Grey 3
Ivory Black

Permanent White
Permanent Green Deep
Cyprus Green-L
Cobalt Turquoise Light
Spectrum Violet-LL
Naples Yellow
Linden Green
Venetian Red
Silver-L
Neutral Grey 3
Ivory Black

Permanent Green Deep
Permanent White
Flesh Tint-D
Spectrum Red
Alizarin Crimson
Sap Green
Olive Green
Oxide of Chromium
Venetian Red
Naples Yellow Deep
Intense Blue
Raw Umber-LL
Ivory Black

Permanent Green Deep
Oxide of Chromium-L
Olive Green-D
Naples yellow-LL
Flesh Tint-D
Spectrum Red
Alizarin Crimson
Neutral Grey 3
Orange Lake Deep
Naples Yellow Deep
Intense Blue
Zinc White
Venetian Red
Burnt Umber
Oxide of Chromium
Raw Umber-LL
Ivory Black

4.0 Diagrams, color analysis of plan, and perspective of the garden at Villa Noailles, Hyères, France, (upper two) and the Garden of Water and Light, Paris (lower two). Rendered by Asif Khan

(Unless noted otherwise, all drawings and photographs in Chapter 4 are by Gabriel Guevrekian.)

4

Material and Phenomenal Color
Simultaneous Contrast,
Gabriel Guevrekian (1900–70)

Another important factor is the color. Depending on the tone, it affects the human nervous system in very different ways. Experience and experimentation have shown that red stimulates, green calms, yellow increases the mood to work, and blue in stronger tones has a tranquilizing and 'neurasthenic' effect.

Gabriel Guevrekian, "Ein Landhaus in Neuilly," 1929, 298

The garden continues the plan of the house. Brick surfaces (grass, mosaic and optical effect) have enlarged and enriched this rather small garden. The light, the colors, the material and especially the proportion between the pieces, which are essential and create around the individual an atmosphere of well-being, concerned me most.

Guevrekian, "Une Villa à Neuilly," 1929, 8

When the Garden of Water and Light (*Jardin d'Eau et de Lumière*) was featured in the July 1930 issue of the popular fashion magazine *Vogue*, it affirmed the garden's kinship with textile design and the decorative arts as well as its inclusion in the modern lifestyle and consumer market.[1] Designed by the Armenian-born French architect Gabriel Guevrekian (1892–1970) for the 1925 Paris International Exposition of Modern Industrial and Decorative Arts (the Art Deco Exposition), the small triangular-shaped garden could only be seen from outside the garden (Figure 4.1). Owing to its strikingly novel use of color and material, the Garden of Water and Light was the winner of the jurors' Grand Prix in the garden category. Although heavily criticized in conservative circles, the garden's color concept was showcased by the contemporary landscape architect and critic Fletcher Steele, who broadcasted to Americans the new trends of European gardens, and the garden was subsequently described as "the first experiment to elevate the aesthetic of garden design to the level of modern painting."[2]

The Garden of Water and Light's chromatic scheme blended modern art and consumer culture sensibilities with paradise garden[3] and architecture décor traditions from Guevrekian's native Persia. Guevrekian rejected the dichotomy between modern and historical and created a chromatic synthesis precedent in modern garden design. His color concepts aligned with those of André Vera (1881–1971), a garden designer whose writing dominated French landscape architecture circles in the 1920s.[4] Both men broke with nature, used formal geometry and modern industrial material, created highly controlled viewpoints, and conflated garden design with contemporary fashion and lifestyle. They drew inspiration from the new era of machines, air travel, commodity, and leisure that influenced architecture, the decorative arts, and the plastic arts.

4.1 Garden of Water and Light, Exposition of Modern Industrial and Decorative Arts, Paris, 1925. Photograph from Marrast, *Jardins*, plate 14 (top) and autochrome print, 1925 (bottom). Collection Archives de la Planète, Musée Albert-Kahn/Département des Hauts-de-Seine

In addition, Guevrekian's approach to color design reflected his multi-faceted career as an architect, planner, political persona, educator, and designer of interiors, furniture, and gardens.[5] He had studied architecture and trained with Josef Hoffmann, designer of the famed Stoclet garden, in Vienna. In 1923 he worked with the architect Robert Mallet-Stevens in Paris, Europe's post-World War I center of avant-garde art and architecture.

While Guevrekian's innovative garden design work was brief (1925–8), his legacy rests on the three small gardens he built in France: the Garden of Water and Light (1925), and the gardens at Villa Noailles in Hyères (1926) and Villa Heim in Neuilly (1927–8). His brief period of experimentation ended when he adopted the stance, held by the International Congress of Modern Architecture, that color was considered bourgeois and overly decorative.[6] Yet despite a mere handful of short essays and just two dozen published black-and-white photographs of the three gardens, his work has remained the icon of garden art of the period and influenced generations of landscape architects, reemerging as a subject of study for the past three decades.[7]

In contrast to other major European modern garden designers in the 1920s—André and Paul Véra, Tony Garnier, Albert Laprade, Mallet-Stevens, and Le Corbusier—whose work has been described as rational studies in green forms,[8] Guevrekian modernized garden tradition by extending the inquiry into color. He molded colors into optical effects to produce depth, rhythm, and motion and to stimulate a psychophysiological response.[9] He also deployed natural and artificial light to create special visual effects and evoke the dimension of time. His garden for the Heim Residence in Neuilly, outside Paris, used devices other than color to produce similar outcomes.

Simultaneous Contrast, Color in Motion

Despite the strong similarities between his gardens and contemporaneous paintings, Guevrekian did not equate them with either architecture or art. Nor were they gardens in the traditional sense. He maintained that painting, sculpture, music, and poetry were art, whereas architecture, other than a church or a monument with a profound idea or message, was functional and therefore not to be considered as art.[10] Of the Villa Noailles garden, he wrote:

> The whole is more architecture than a garden; a work of utmost profound composition and detail [that] with particular consideration of proportions and tone and nuances of colors have produced a piece of organized soil, that integrates itself in an harmonic way into nature [italics added].[11]

With its scarcity of plants and dominance of inert, built elements, the garden at Noailles, much like the exposition garden, was a negation of both architecture and the traditional idea of a garden. Lacking function and mostly limited to sight, it was an exercise in composition and color. In contrast to his mostly white, achromatic architecture, his garden and interior furnishing exuded color of both modern and traditional sensibilities.

As a member of the Parisian avant-garde art circle, for whom color became a primary field of exploration, Guevrekian's color position was linked to the short-lived art movement in Cubism called Orphism. Pioneered around 1912 by textile designer and artist Sonia Delaunay-Terk (1885–1979) and her husband, painter Robert Delaunay (1885–1941), among

4.2 Robert Delaunay, "Circular Forms, Sun" 1912/1913. Museum Folkwang Essen/ARTOTHEK

others, Orphism, came on the heels of the 19th century simultaneous contrast theory devised by the chemist Michel Chevreul[12] and its development in the work of Paul Cézanne, who was a forerunner to Cubism.[13] Cézanne defined painting as a matter of pure visibility: "[t]he eye was not made for thinking but for seeing in judging modern painting," calling this experience "coloring sensations."[14] Nonrepresentational color devoid of signification or meaning would speak directly to the senses rather than the intellect, as pure optics. Like Cézanne, Orphists used color to isolate, intensify, and challenge sight. Unlike the Cubists Pablo Picasso, Georges Braque, and Juan Gris, who replaced the one-point fixed perspective with multiple, successive viewpoints and bifurcated planes to create optical depth and movement, Orphists produced depth, rhythm, and motion through color. Even though he employed symmetry and Cubist faceted surfaces, Guevrekian, too, used color in the Orphist manner. He participated in the new sensation-versus-intellect debate in painting, which replaced the old color-versus-line and color-versus-form debate, and sided squarely with color as sensation.

Following the Delaunays, Guevrekian's search for an image to offset his garden's relatively flat composition and fixed viewing position from outside led him to Chevreul's simultaneous contrast, or simultaneity, which, as Robert Delaunay explained, "*by means of complementary and dissonant colours* gives volume direction. Color acts to create depth. Depth of colour replaces linear perspective [italics added]."[15] He used his new color palette to elicit "multiple rhythms" in "synchronic action" by arranging colors in ways that combined harmonious and dissonant effects in the viewer's eye[16] (Figure 4.2).

While harmony increases color unity and reduces contrast, and dissonance decreases color unity and increases contrast, together they activate the perception of "synchronic action," an effect described by the Delaunays as a clash that simultaneously relaxes and provoked the eye:

> This means that the eye can see simultaneously how red complements and harmonizes with an adjoining green while reacting disharmonically and noncomplementarily to a neighboring blue, to the intensified excitement of the eye. This blue at the same time complements and harmonizes with an orange elsewhere in the picture. Hence this color group contains tensing and relaxing sensations which in turn and simultaneously are disturbed and pacified by further colors.[17]

Robert Delaunay recognized an innate disposition of colors toward a rhythmic simultaneity, differentiated through speed impulses—slow, fast, and extra-fast vibrations—that create varying optical speeds, or "readings," that, in turn, suggest motion.

Guevrekian's Garden of Water and Light, likewise, combined harmonic and disharmonic color combinations (Figure 4.0). Its radiant and rhythmic simultaneous color mosaic of plants, water, concrete, and glass created a spatial and dynamic optical experience, also seen in his gouache drawing done a year earlier (Figure 4.3). Three different sets of visual effects, rhythms, and speeds were at play in the garden. The color scheme consisted of red-crimson, blue, and white concentric circles painted by Robert Delaunay at the bottom of four triangular central pools whose concrete walls were also painted red, blue, and white, evoking the French flag and patriotism.[18] Four pairs of blue and yellow-ochre triangular flower beds framed by green grass and red-crimson triangular flower beds surrounded the pools.[19] Creating a low fence, horizontal rows of small triangular glass plates of top-to-bottom graduated tints—from white to pink to crimson to dark green—were suspended on wires that lined the two legs of the isosceles triangle-shaped plot. The complementary contrast in the paired red-crimson and green, contrasts in the pairing of yellow and blue and red and blue, and the graduated tonality of the pinks and green in the fence played out synchronically the interaction of contrasting effects of harmony, discord, and resonance, respectively. The eye was excited by the complementarities, agitated by the near complementarities, and soothed by the graduated spectral tonality.

Guevrekian's color system, similar to that of the Delaunays', was devoid of references to nature, defied perspective, and produced depth and multiple rhythms, or readings, through color contrasts—an instantaneous, immediate impact with the yellow-ochre and blue beds, a lesser impact through the harmonious contrast of the crimson bed and green grass, a slower, dissonant effect in the blue, red, and white pools, and the slowest reading (developing over time) of the red to green glass-tiered fence. Photographs taken at the fair show that the two middle red begonia beds were replaced at one point with white flowers, perhaps to increase the color range and contrast (see Figure 4.1). Guevrekian sought to create a picture that always looked new, that created itself repeatedly in a constant renewal of identity.

Not surprisingly, the garden's repetitive pattern and colors echoed Sonia Delaunay's textile design displayed in the window of her faux boutique, *Simultané*, at the same exposition—a boutique that Guevrekian designed. The pattern also recurred in the clothing of two models in front of Mallet-Stevens' exposition garden and on a specially painted Citroën B12 parked

4.3 "Jardin de Guéverkian," postcard, 1925. ©MAD, Paris (top). Gouache plan drawing, Marrast, *Jardins*, 1925, plate 15 (bottom)

4.4 Fashion models in front of the garden by Robert Mallet-Stevens wearing dresses made of "simultané fabrics" by Sonia Delaunay (left). Archives Famille Delaunay; photo: René Herbst. Boutique Simultanée, designed by Guevrekian, featuring Delaunay's simultané fabrics (right), Exposition of Modern Industrial and Decorative Arts, Paris, 1925, from *Devantures, vitrines, installations de Magasins à l'Exposition Internationale des Arts Décoratifs*, plate 18. Courtesy of the University of Illinois at Urbana-Champaign Archives

in front of Mallet-Stevens' Tourism Pavilion[20] (Figure 4.4). Sonia Delaunay referred to her design as "living color" and applied it to mass-produced luxury commodities, where design was detached from a specific commodity and used in multiple products, from hats and dresses to furniture and dinner plates.[21] The Garden of Color and Light was an application of her art in garden space.

Guevrekian's interest in color optics extended the Orphists' painterly scope to the physiological and psychological response of the viewer in space, to color as a phenomenon. It was loosely based on phenomenology, which artists increasingly used to "arrest" the viewer and generate specific sensations of and reactions to art and space.

Phenomenology: The Psychology of Color

Predecessors of Guevrekian—Loudon and Jekyll, among others—had already remarked on visual perception and moods elicited through color effects based on observations and empirical studies. Guevrekian's contemporary, André Vera, basing his comments on Chevreul's theory, wrote at length about the effect of color on garden composition and mood. He focused on color compositions that strengthen "the architectural unity of the ground," using a restricted number of simple colors, rather "than a fairyland big show" and monochromatic planting beds.[22] And he favored warm color schemes that generated a cheerful atmosphere: "If you want the sun and the flowers to dispel your sorrows and provide you, by their radiance, a feeling of comfort and happiness, use for each flower bed only one color of choice among yellow, red, and orange." He elaborated:

Indeed, in pleasure gardens, private or public, except in the case of a green room specially equipped to spend the warmer afternoon and adorned with the intention of procuring a feeling of freshness, of a design in green boxwood surrounded of white Agératum on a background of blue Agératum, it is not an impression of coldness, sadness, or unhappiness that is important to produce; but it is joy that must be suggested, with varying intensity, depending on the property … you want to adorn.

Vera used the terms "warm" and "cool" both as color descriptors and as thermometers of feeling. Yellow and blue neatly fell into their respective categories, gray plants produced a calming effect, and a touch of white could be used to create a sudden burst of joy and to enhance the intensity of nearby colors.[23] Combinations of two variations of the same hue side by side or one enclosing the other "constitute a particular spectacle extremely gentle on the eyes and easily create a calm impression which can become serious and lead to reflection, to meditation."[24]

In his search for harmonic effects to generate pleasant feelings, André Vera's approach, like Jekyll's, was based on subjective impressions. Conversely, Guevrekian sought to understand color effects that influenced both spatial sensation and psychological responses based on objective, psychophysiological studies. In the late 1920s the scientific nature of color experience, rather than the Orphist principles, grounded his interest in color. In several essays he wrote in 1929, he observed that "Experience … shows that colors have a different effect on the nervous system, … red stimulates, green calms down, yellow increases the motivation for work, and blue has a tranquilizing and 'neurasthenic' effect."[25] He called for study of the effect of color on the nervous system: "A whole study is also to be done on appropriate coloring."[26]

Increasingly, Guevrekian's position reflected the new field of phenomenology, which "integrates a kind of (descriptive) psychology with a kind of logic to study subjective perception and mental activities in response to stimuli."[27] Considered more scientific than psychology, phenomenology drew the fields of architecture and landscape architecture into an inquiry about viewers' responses to space and lighting as well as to patterns, known as Gestalt theory.[28] In the 1930s responses were framed as cognitive phenomenal "logics," and consciousness and behavior were traced to specific spatial and optical stimulants. There is no clear evidence that Guevrekian devoted much time to the study of color phenomenology, but his search for modern grounding in garden color design landed him in a unique place that permitted the modern and the traditional, the universal and the cultural, to coexist. He, therefore, holds a salient position in garden design history.

Seeing garden art and architecture through a personal cultural lens, Guevrekian found no contradiction—in fact, surprising compatibility—between modern European expression and Armenian-Persian tradition. In the Persian tradition, as in modern psychology, colors had commonly understood effects. But Persian psychological effects of color went together with symbolism, whereas modernism voided signification. Guevrekian managed to reconcile the two, masterfully integrating Persian color references in his gardens while making them sufficiently ambiguous and implicit to not control or condition the experience.

Modernized Tradition: Polychromatic Mosaic

Avant-garde European architecture discovered the allure of age-old décor found in North African and Middle Eastern art and craft and integrated it in 1920s and 1930s architecture.[29] References to the Persian paradise garden and its North African-Spanish strain, were echoed in gardens in southern France in the early 20th century.

Jean-Claude Nicolas Forestier (1861–1930), landscape designer and authority on European gardening, called for joining the formality of 17th century French garden tradition with the simplicity and colorful mosaic tile walls of Moorish gardens in Spain, which originated in ancient Persia.[30] As supervisor of the garden section at the 1925 Art Deco Exposition, he commissioned Guevrekian to design a garden that was "conceived in a modern spirit with some elements of Persian décor."[31] Guevrekian collaborated with the Delaunays to do so, and Forestier considered the outcome a success.

Several elements were key in marrying modern and Persian sensibilities in Guevrekian's gardens both at the exposition and at Villa Noailles, commissioned in its vein. The gardens' geometric layouts echoed patterns of both Art Deco and the Persian paradise garden. Their repetitive nature and color field treatment tapped both *simultané* fabrics and Islamic Persian principles seen in carpets, wall tiles, and stained-glass windows. Importantly, their intense chromatic scheme complied with both modern European and medieval Persian art.

The layout of the ancient Persian paradise garden, commonly crisscrossed by water channels emanating from a central pool, represented the four rivers of the Biblical-Quranic

4.5 Garden of Water and Light, montage of mirrored garden plan revealing four-quartered division, based on George Dodds, "Freedom from the Garden," 2002 (left). Garden carpet, early 18th century (right). Metropolitan Museum of Art, New York

paradise. Known as *charbagh*, meaning fourfold garden in Persian, gardens divided by two perpendicular paths with a water feature at the cross point were a common design on prayer carpets in the 17th century Persian Safavid dynasty and were perpetuated throughout the ancient Western world. The triangular garden at the exposition, conceived as half of a paradise garden, obscured its origin to the common observer (however, it has been suggested that Guevrekian chose the form because of the site's form and spatial limitations).[32] The central esplanade of the exposition grounds

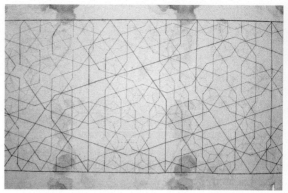

4.6 The Topkapi Scroll, drawing showing a star-and-polygon pattern of a sophisticated girih. Topkapi Palace Museum

served as a virtual cutting-line along the triangle base of Guevrekian's paradise garden. The four-quarter division was revealed in a mirror effect doubling the garden into a complete *charbagh* at the base of the triangle and along the viewing path (Figure 4.5). The tiered, four-part pools took their rightful place at the center as in a typical Safavid garden.[33] Guevrekian very effectively maximized the small triangular lot to construct his creation without producing an overt facsimile of a Persian paradise garden.

The Garden of Water and Light resonated with the garden style advanced by Guevrekian's contemporaries André and Paul Vera, Pierre-Émile Legrain, and Jean-Charles Moreux, among others, but diverged from theirs in several ways. Whereas they used asymmetry, plants to create volume and space, and a simplified knot pattern of the traditional *parterre de broderie*, Guevrekian kept both the central axis and symmetry (following the bilateral symmetry of Persian gardens), used plants as pigments and textures, and turned for inspiration to the *girih*, interlocking geometric patterns of Islamic tile mosaics that adorned Persian courtyard gardens, pavilions, and interior walls and ceilings. *Girih* comes from a Persian word for "knot" and thus bears some relationship to other ancient and Western medieval knot garden patterns. But the geometric *girih* and its counterpart, the floral arabesque (both of which developed out of the Muslim prohibition on figurative art and advances in geometry and mathematics), represented a new form of decoration comprising colorful interlocking modules. The tessellated *girih*'s polygons are closely fitted together in a repeated pattern without gaps or overlaps. Intersecting and continuous lines and the use of the circle were fundamental to *girih* and its capacity to expand infinitely[34] (Figure 4.6). The Garden of Water and Light's rotational symmetry, triangular module repetition, and octagonal outlines, making diamond or bowtie shapes, resonate with *girih* principles perfectly.[35]

The colors of the garden were those of the Persian favorite flower, the rose, in five colors—white, yellow, red, Spanish rose, and poppy red—and their combinations.[36] Bright cobalt blue tiles lined the pools and water channels, and pebbles and other stones in varied patterns and textures were embedded in paved areas. This basic color palette—yellow, red, blue, and white, with a touch of pink—is also found in 15th century medieval Persian paintings and miniatures. The colors also resembled those of *girih* mosaic and glazed tile pigments extensively used in Islamic-Moorish architecture in Spain from the 12th century onward; the tiles commonly comprise five colors—tin white, cobalt blue, copper green, iron amber, and manganese brown—all obtained from high-lead glazes.[37] Together, the

117

4.7 Orsi windows, Tekyeh Moaven al-Molk, Kermanshah-Iran
Kermanshah, Iran, 1903. Photo: Mohammad Ghomeishi

patterns produced the dazzling colors that Guevrekian sought for his garden.

Color and design similarities can be drawn between the *girih* and Islamic stained-glass windows known as *orsi*. The windows filter natural lighting and manipulate direct sun to project constantly changing and moving color patterns of light into the interior, creating an environment of comfort along with certain psychological effects and a dynamic and spiritual atmosphere (Figure 4.7).[38] Colors were selected based on symbolism, the desired psychological effect, and the intended emotional response. In Persia, blue, denoting eternity, tradition, and values, represents peace, truth, trust, surrender, and sacrifice; red, the life force in all forms, represents desire and passion and points to ambition and success; and yellow represents happiness, expansion, and exhilaration.[39] The most common colors in *orsi* glass are cobalt blue, yellow, red, and green, with additional light through transparent glass. This color scheme is also found in the Garden of Color and Lights.

Guevrekian selected plants for their uniform texture, monochromatic pigments, and prolonged blossoms. He used mowed grass and dwarf cultivars and ground covers to produce color "en masse," like paint pigments, contrasting green grass with red-crimson Begonia "Flamboyant" and yellow-ochre pyrethrum with blue *Ageratum houstonianum*.[40]

In general, though, horticulture became of lesser importance in the modern garden, merely "one of a series of materials, like colored gravel and marble, of which the different parts of the pattern are composed."[41] Ready-made and mass-produced building materials and minerals made gardens quick to construct, instantly colorful, and permanent. At the same time, new devices for special effects were being introduced to further rattle the status of horticulture.

Permanence: Minerals and Special Light Effects

Constructed in only 10 days in April and May (like its counterparts in the exposition), the Garden of Water and Light lasted the duration of the exposition (and was then dismantled). The very short time available for construction necessitated ready-made components. Architectural elements, such as fences and pergolas, replaced the vertical dimension of mature plants. To maintain color throughout the exhibition, in addition to long-flowering plants, designers used pavers, tiles, gravel, masonry, and reinforced concrete. With their low maintenance and expedient construction, these materials were soon adopted for use in private gardens. And as concrete walls began to replace traditional stone and wood walls, the garden became integrated with architecture.

Guevrekian constructed his gardens to be permanent and mostly visual. As in the Persian paradise gardens, his gardens were not a place to stroll but rather to sit, reflect, and entertain. Movement was visual, not physical. In addition to the illusory motion produced by the *simultané* color scheme in the Garden of Water and Light, actual movement was integrated in the reflections and motion of water and light (Figure 4.8). Sunlight speckles on water rippled during the day, and artificial light projected from a central rotation sphere at night ricocheted on the vertical fence, pulsating on glass panes and creating an effervescent effect in the garden. The reflections lent the garden an elusive and mutable affective quality.

The capacity to reflect, deflect, and magnify light in a garden has been explored for centuries. Planes of still water were used to unite earth and sky in 17th-century French gardens and to reflect surrounding landscapes in 18th-

4.8 Garden of Water and Light, photograph, detail of pool and fountain, from *Bâtiments et jardins,* 1925, by Michel Roux-Spitz

century England. Broken glass and mirrors were used in wall and ceiling mosaics in medieval Persia and Moorish Spain, as well as picturesque grottoes in England. The introduction of water and mirrors in modern gardens, however, went beyond the reflection of light to manipulate space, distort reality, alter perception. It followed the early Cubist technique of fragmentation to introduce movement and the fourth dimension of time into a two-dimensional medium. Broken surfaces, compression of foreground into background, and multiple simultaneous viewpoints characteristic of Cubism were actualized in the modern garden with tilted planes and glass and mirrors.[42]

Beyond its actual as well as elusive reflection—a mirror effect doubling the garden into a complete *charbagh*—the Garden of Water and Light employed tilted surfaces, compressed space, water surface, glass, and a new element: electric light. Electricity introduced a dimension of time into the garden, both activating the fountain and illuminating the decorative globe. A water jet (issued intermittently from a small pylon) fed the upper basin, which drained through sets of three pipes to the lower basins. At dark, the illuminated revolving faceted glass sphere created optical vibration[43] as it projected luminous images on the pools below, and the flickering basin ripples and iridescent colored glass on the two-sided diaphanous fence created a mesmerizing nighttime effect. The composition of the white and gray glass panes of the sphere was reminiscent of Robert Delaunay's series of sun and moon paintings. The sphere was also likened to symbols of the life-giver moon and the moon tree atop the mountain sky in early Mesopotamian culture, which fed paradise garden waters nocturnally.[44]

Guevrekian's electric device did not rival the extravagant water fountains of colorfully changing lights in other gardens but used electricity in a novel way that did not draw attention away from the rest of the garden but rather amplified the whole.[45] The electrically wired fountain and globe exuded energy and introduced programmed effects of light, time, and movement in the garden.

The artificially lit sphere in the Garden of Water and Light was hailed as the first time electric light made its appearance as an important element of the future garden, an utterly unconventional element with which landscape architects would have to come to grips.[46] Its introduction in Paris, "the City of Light," was an apt statement of modernity.

Photography: Gardens in Black and White

Despite their permanent materials, several of Guevrekian's gardens were short-lived. But their legacy was perpetuated by black-and-white photographs. Photography not only preserved the memory of gardens; it shaped the public's image of modern gardens. For both modern architecture and modern landscape architecture, black-and-white photography was the preferred medium of representation, notwithstanding its color limitations.

The efficacy of photography in the late 19th century coincided, counterintuitively, with a radical break from realism in modern art representation. Like art, architectural representation broke ranks with Beaux-Arts realism and began emphasizing abstract planes, spaces, and volumes. In the early 20th century architecture and landscape design representation featured highly textured line drawings—perspective, bird's-eye view, and plan—but were soon rivaled by a popular new drawing technique: axonometry, which revealed design in ways that the eye could not otherwise see, offering new viewpoints and expressions. Guevrekian's gouache drawing for the exposition garden is an example of axon[47] (see Figure 4.3). He used a "straight-up" or 90° axonometry to convey the symmetry, balance, and spatial ambiguity of the garden,[48] whereas the more common axonometric projection, using oblique 45° and 30° angles, favored asymmetry and imbalance of unequal parts, and conveyed accurate measurements, structure, and volume.

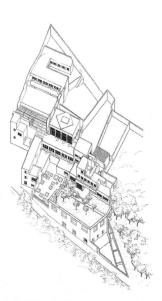

Guevrekian found the "straight-up" axonometric technique the most suitable for the exposition garden because of its capacity to simultaneously flatten the garden and register its frontally compressed depth. (For similar reasons, Paul Vera, Moreux, and Legrain also used the technique for some of their gardens, often with a touch of colored pencil or watercolor.) Importantly, the technique also resonated with Guevrekian's intention to elicit an emotional impact through the ambiguity of the half paradise garden with its reflective lens at the centerline. In Purist painting, too, paraline composition (axonometry) with exaggerated frontality and figure-ground reversals was

4.9 Villa Noailles, Hyères, axonometric drawing, *Mallet-Stevens: La Villa Noailles*, 1990 (top). Black-and-white photographs taken in 1928 from the lower salon (bottom left), from the lawn terrace roof garden (bottom middle), and from the vertex of the triangle below the sculpture (bottom right). Courtesy of the University of Illinois at Urbana-Champaign Archives. Photos: Thérèse Bonney

used to transmit a resonance that had a calculated but ambiguous emotional impact.[49] Set against a gray graphite background margin, Guevrekian's colorful gouache axon exuded the garden's desired ambiguity and chromatic impact. This was complemented by black-and-white photographs taken from the roof, balcony, and garden tip (Figure 4.9).

Advances in black-and-white photographic printing and the manufacture of affordable cameras in the 1920s enabled designers to accurately record and produce carefully framed depictions of their completed projects. The three gardens Guevrekian built in Paris, Hyères, and Neuilly were each designed to be seen from a specific, limited number of viewpoints that were readily captured in photographs. These photographic portrayals both reflected the tendencies and sustained the theoretical discourse on modern architectural space that took place in a growing number of illustrated magazines. Devoid of people and taken from an elevated position and from outside the garden, the photographs focused attention on architectural space and composition, rather than pictorial aesthetics. This portrayal has determined the way people look at and continue to design modern gardens even now.

Guevrekian's predecessors used photography to a somewhat limited extent. William Robinson used black-and-white photographs as the basis for his black line engraving in his books, Gertrude Jekyll used them to document the progression of her garden and to illustrate her publications. Modern landscape photography, however, developed as a creative act of framing and timing that brought new understanding and appreciation to the landscape.[50] The philosopher Walter Benjamin made this point succinctly when he wrote: "Evidently a different nature opens itself to the camera than opens to the naked eye—if only because an unconsciously penetrated space is substituted for a space consciously explored."[51] Thus, the photograph has never been a neutral representation, always subjectively framed by personal bias and artistic trend, among other factors.

Although color photography was available in the 1920s, gardens were by and large photographed and published in black and white, and not merely because of economy and available print technology. It was a purposeful decision to depict modern architectural interiors in pristine desolation, deserted of people and often furniture or other signs of human occupation. Their "removal … created an absence of significance, which, in turn, supported an intended understanding of the spatial organization. When a place is emptied out and familiarity disappears, an atmosphere that intrigues and appeals does emerge."[52] Color was also considered to interfere with the perception of composition and space.

Black-and-white photographs aimed to provide the optimal view of Guevrekian's gardens' space, composition, and atmosphere. Photographs of the Garden of Water and Light show it obliquely from the corner of the triangular plot to counter the garden's symmetry and flatness. And two black-and-white photographs in the exposition catalogue are taken from a similar angle but at different eye-level positions and distances to highlight certain details and effects.[53]

Black-and-white photography eliminates not only the deflection of attention away from space and composition but also the impact of changes in lighting throughout the day. Tints in cloudy or "neutral" daylight vary greatly in the soft morning, bright midday, and late afternoon light. Black-and-white photography can be timed precisely to bring out certain light-induced landscape atmospheres. Thus the reduction of a full-blown, polychromatic, in-person experience to a static, two-dimensional, black-and-white image can increase the understanding of and sensitivity to space. It is unclear, however, how it has affected color in

121

garden design. In 1942 the architectural critic Geoffrey Baker lamented the pervasiveness of black-and-white photography:

> The spread of modern architecture has been hastened by the perfection, during this century, of the half-tone system of reproducing black-and-white photographs. Unfortunately garden design depends so much upon color for effect, even for the modulation of form, that the wide spread of modern garden design may depend upon the perfection of some low-cost method of reproducing color pictures.[54]

Baker concluded that the black-and-white medium led to regression in garden and landscape color exploration. This assertion is difficult to ascertain. Guevrekian himself abandoned novel color explorations in the 1930s, perhaps because of his involvement with and position as general secretary (1928–32) of the International Congress of Modern Architecture (CIAM), although he continued to make written references to color psychology.[55] The garden he designed at Villa Heim lacked the contrasts of previous gardens but, as I demonstrate below, its effects on the viewer were largely consistent with the first two gardens.

* * *

The private gardens at Villa Noailles in Hyères and Villa Heim in Neuilly-sur-Seine were extensively photographed and featured in magazines and in a handful of essays by Guevrekian. The garden at Villa Noailles became a modernist icon soon after its completion.

The discussion that follows is based on original drawings, models, and black-and-white photographs of the projects from Guevrekian's archive at the University of Illinois at Urbana-Champaign, supplemented by first- and second-hand writings and commentary on the gardens.

Villa Noailles Garden, Vicomte Charles de Noailles, Hyères, France, 1926

Soon after he saw the Garden of Water and Light, the art connoisseur Vicomte Charles de Noailles commissioned Guevrekian to design a small, 120-square-meter garden for his villa near Hyères in Provence. The modernist villa was designed by the architect Mallet-Stevens and several renowned collaborators.[56]

Completed in 1926, the 120-square-meter, elongated isosceles triangle plot, one of three gardens at the villa, located in the southeast corner of the lot, rose toward a convergence point of upper and lower roads that flanked the site. It was entered from facing openings in the two side walls and from the lower salon of the villa. Guevrekian created an enclosed courtyard to isolate the garden and sharply contrast it with the surrounding landscape. At the same time, he left the triangular tip of the garden wide open with views toward the Mediterranean Sea. Inside the garden, a striking color scheme formed a faceted, bas-relief tableau equally reminiscent of a Persian carpet, a *simultané* fabric pattern, and De Stijl aesthetics. Special light effects, electricity, and reflections were abundant.

Unlike Guevrekian's garden in Paris, the garden in Hyères was designed to be entered, though it offered limited physical engagement and few olfactory or tactile experiences. A peripheral looping path was implied by a sequence of yellow-, blue-, gray-, and red-tiled rectangular tiered platforms leading to the view at the raised tip of the garden. But the garden primarily stimulated the sense of sight through its brilliant color composition, best seen from a static, elevated position rather than by moving through the space.

It was a symbiosis of modern and traditional elements. Like a walled Persian garden, it was a contemplative space and structured as a carpet to be viewed from above. Designed as a half-carpet, as in the exposition garden, it doubled into a complete *charbagh* when "mirrored" at the base of the triangle (Figure 4.10). Two zigzag terraced beds edging the forecourt partially framed the carpet and were reminiscent of the scalloped glass framing fence at the exposition. Like a cloister garden (the property was originally the site of a convent) it was designed to elicit a calm and protected atmosphere. Like a *simultané* fabric pattern it produced a sense of both depth and visual motion. And like the work of the Dutch architect and De Stijl founder Theo van Doesburg, who designed the lower "chamber des fleurs" from which the garden was entered, it was limited to flat primary and neutral colors.

Architectural critics at the time appreciated the allusion to both Persian carpets depicting the garden of paradise and modern French sensibility: "An interplay of gaily

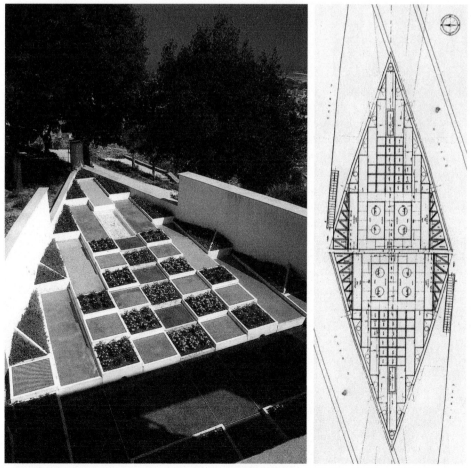

4.10 Villa Noailles, view from the lawn terrace, restored, 1991 (left). Photo: Marc Treib. Montage of "mirrored" garden plan revealing four-quartered division, plan excerpted from André Lurçat, *Jardins et Cottages* (January 1927) (right)

123

4.11 Villa Noailles, details documented after restoration. Façade reflection (left). Photo: Jacqueline Salmon. Paving and planting checkerboard (right). Photo: Julian Weyer

colored surfaces, inspired by oriental carpets, is twinned with a geometry that gratifies the French impulse for order and clarity."[57] Another wrote:

> Persia is justly famous for the eternity of her tiled and basined gardens, and it is delightful to see how saliently M. Guevrekian has blended certain of the more architectural elements of traditional Oriental design with the austere precepts of avant-garde modernism.[58]

As in the exposition garden, colored floor planes formed a geometric pattern that Guevrekian described as a "mosaic work from different colored porcelain designed [in] a sequence of the colors yellow, blue, grey, red."[59] The center of the mosaic was a checkboard pattern of alternating mauve porcelain platforms and yellow tulip beds. Edge planters along the garden's white walls were recurring triangular raised beds in pyramidal volumes, planted with groundcovers of two hues, blue-green and olive green, to heighten the subtlety of the relief.[60] The lower forecourt area at the base of the triangular garden was paved in dark gray, shaded by two Chinese orange trees planted in two square lawn pads. It was flanked by rectangular red tulip beds and the zigzag terraced beds.

The whitewashed walls and tan stucco villa façade sharply contrasted with the brightly colored garden and surrounding brown hills, green native pines and olive trees, and deep blue sea in the distance. The tilted and slightly extruded and depressed planes brought depth and motion to the garden. So did the chromatic scheme of harmonic, dissonant, and simultaneous contrasts, created by reds and greens, yellows and blues, and mauves and yellows, recalling the spectral effect of the glass fence of pink and green gradations of the garden in Paris. White and dark gray set the extremes of the tonality range, and light gray provided needed relief from the intense color saturation and contrast. All the geometric parts of the garden were framed with white cement, as if the entire garden were carefully traced with lines.[61]

Built with cement walls and porcelain pavers, bulb flowers, and pruning-tolerant plants, the instant, permanent garden left little scope for change. In early spring, colors and textures shimmered as the yellow and red tulips bloomed and floated on their long stems to form a separate plane that cast shadows on adjacent tiles. But the short lifecycle of the tulips left the beds green until they were completely empty by late fall, and the tulips produced no scent (in the floral history of the French garden the tulip has been characterized as a "useless flower").[62]

As in the Paris creation, though, special light and temporal effects entered the Noailles garden through reflection, rotation, electricity, and illumination (Figure 4.11). Reflection was both explicit and implicit. Glazed tiles, the glossy leaves of the orange trees, and a rotating bronze statue by the artist Jacques Lipchitz with a mirrorlike water basin below all shimmered with differing intensities. In contrast, the planting surfaces appeared darker in tone and rougher in texture.

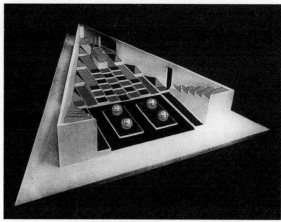

4.12 Villa Noailles, garden model, 1926, *Les Arts de la Maison*, Autumn 1926. © RMN, Médiathèque de l'architecture et du patrimoine. Photo: Thérèse Bonney

Looking from the villa, the sunken pool reflected the sculpture and sky above; from the other direction, it mirrored the building façade.

The illusionary movement created by the color and composition was complemented by the physical movement of the six-foot-high bronze sculpture, *La Joie de Vivre*, which was electrically rotated every four minutes because it was not possible to walk round it and see it from all sides.[63] Electrical movement thus replaced human movement around the sculpture. Illuminated at night, the rotating sculpture in the Noailles garden has been compared to the rotating globe in the exposition garden.[64]

Other special effects, elements of reflection in the paradise garden theme, were not completed based on the original model that Guevrekian exhibited at the 1927 Salon d'Automne in Paris and the construction drawing in *Jardins et Cottages* (Figure 4.12).[65] The model showed two pairs of reflective chromed globes in the lower forecourt, intended as reflecting devices in which the colors of the garden merged harmoniously; they were replaced by two dwarf orange trees during construction. The globes were to have been made of stained-glass similar to the globe at the Paris garden, internally illuminated, and placed on a pair of rectangular raised platforms colored green in the model. The forecourt's reflective glass floor, resembling a still water surface, would have been spectacularly illuminated by four glowing spheres at night and become a powerful tableau lit by the morning sun, reflecting dancing lights on the white walls. The intended unearthly associations of the garden and the four globes might, again, have symbolized Persian moon trees, and the water basin on the uppermost yellow platform (replenished by the red pylon water fountain from behind) might have suggested solar association and captured lunar reflection.[66]

Despite the vivid color scheme of the Noailles garden, it was primarily documented in black-and-white photography by Thérèse Bonney. In 1929, the famed Dada artist Ray featured the garden in a surrealist film of Villa Noailles, *Les Mystères du Château du Dé*. A handful of iconic photographs and stills of the garden succeeded in capturing Guevrekian's desired spatial composition and atmosphere.[67] The garden was designed as "framed pictures" seen from three primary viewpoints: the lower salon and drawing room entry, the wall opening of the lawn terrace roof above the salon, and the opposite point at the apex of the triangle. From all three places the garden could be seen in its entirety, but the experience from each was completely different (see Figure 4.9).

The garden view from below was on the central axis, framed by the orange trees and focused on the vanishing point of the converging checkerboard perspective lines anchored by the statue.[68] At midday, the sun aligned with the central axis and created a blinding effect, dissolving the enclosing white walls and thrusting the garden into infinity. The statue, in a sun halo above the yellow terrace and pool, magnified the ethereal atmosphere.

The second, most iconic photograph of this garden, looking down from the lawn roof terrace and through the left wall opening, was taken by Ray (published by André Lurçat in *Terrasses et Jardins*). It shows the garden contained within the white walls, surrounded by the landscape and with the sea on the horizon (this elevated view resembles the photograph of the model exhibited at the Salon d'Automne). With little distortion, this view presents both the sum of the garden parts and their distinct tonal and compositional relationships.[69]

The third photograph, taken from the opposite direction looking down from the sculpture, sets the garden against the backdrop of the villa, like a theater set molded in optical distortions—the floor seems flattened and the space compressed, the converging walls look parallel, and the triangular space is indiscernible.

Many color photographs taken since the reconstruction of the garden in the 1990s show a garden in immensely different and fleeting chromatic palettes, even from the same viewpoint. With the shifting direction of the sun and shadows cast by the walls, the garden colors constantly change, making any study elusive.

Villa Heim Garden, Jacques Heim, Neuilly-sur-Seine, France, 1927–8

In contrast to the gardens in Paris and Hyères, both of which followed specific client demands, the garden at Villa Heim was a product of Guevrekian's own creative and aesthetic inclinations. The famous fashion designer Jacques Heim, whose pavilion at the 1925 Art Deco fair was designed by Guevrekian, commissioned him to design his urban family residence in Neuilly-sur-Seine, which borders Paris. The comprehensive design work extended to the details of the interior, the furniture, and the garden (Figure 4.13).[70]

The chromatic scheme of the house and multiterrace gardens was bland and radically different from Guevrekian's gardens in Paris and Hyères. Yet despite the predominant whites, beiges, browns, and greens, Guevrekian produced pleasing psychological effects for the inhabitants. He wrote:

> My main concern in this house was the light, the colors, the material and especially the good relationship of the individual spaces to each other; these are the really important things, and only if they are well resolved will they create a comfortable environment.[71]

Thus, while the spatial scope and color scheme diverged from the previous two gardens, the optical and psychophysiological outcomes were somewhat similar.

The garden aligned with modern garden concepts adopted by other contemporary architects, notably Le Corbusier.[72] Among these concepts were convergence of indoor-outdoor living, emphasis on material and space, roof gardens with built planters—and minimal plant and color palettes. Color, unless inherent in material, was considered a threat to spatial design. Greens and neutral colors—white and gray—dominated. Guevrekian introduced color by using diverse paving material with inherent color and texture to create patterns, depth, movement, and optical interest. He abandoned his association with the Delaunays' and *girih* color aesthetics, and his interest in color, light, and tradition took on different forms.

The Heim residence and outdoor spaces opened on to an 18th century wooded park at the back. Conceiving of a seamless extension of the house floors, Guevrekian created a terraced garden of four descending levels. The exterior interlocking planes mirrored the interior division, whose proportions were derived from the subdivision of the golden rectangle. The roof and four levels of terrace gardens were reminiscent of another Middle Eastern ancient garden typology, the hanging garden of Babylon. Of the main roof garden by the games room, he wrote: "All means (grass, pergolas, flower boxes) have been used to make it a real hanging garden" (Figure 4.14).[73]

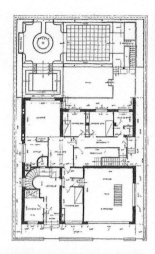

Guevrekian did not plant trees. Each terrace room was defined by narrowly built edge planters of boxwood hedges and flowers, at times in two tiers and pruned into simple geometric shapes. The flowering shrubs in the edge planters at each level were likely (but unsuccessfully) intended to produce the impression of a hanging garden and soften the austere building walls. Plants were not selected for their color but for their volumetric qualities, except for one roof garden which featured a lawn, planting borders, flower containers, and climbers—delicate vine roses were trained against the side wall and over a pergola of metal pipe, and the border contained variegated leaf plants.

4.13 Villa Heim, Neuilly-sur-Seine, plan of the ground level and garden, 1927, *L'Architecte*, 1929 (top). View down from the upper terrace, 1928 (bottom). Courtesy of the University of Illinois at Urbana-Champaign Archives

The exterior spaces comprised nine "rooms": three spaces surrounded a glass sunroom on the roof; two terraces extended the third- and second-floor living spaces; and four tiered rooms on paved platforms made up the lowest, ground-level garden. Laid out as a *charbagh*, the lower garden retained the paradise garden typology (Figure 4.15). The platforms, separated by a few steps, successively spiraled down, ending in a sunken garden

4.14 Villa Heim, "Roof Garden." Courtesy of the University of Illinois Archives

4.15 Villa Heim, the lower garden looking east, *L'Illustration*, 28, 1932. Courtesy of the University of Illinois at Urbana-Champaign Archives

by the servants' quarters. The surfaces alternated between brick pavers and grass. In the largest garden room at the far corner on the ground level was a two-tiered circular fountain at the center (fed from an elevated tank). Another tiered, half-circle fountain was built on the second-floor terrace against the wall. The water circulation and colored tiles lining both fountains were clearly of Persian garden origin.

As with Guevrekian's other projects, only black-and-white photographic documentation is available, making it difficult to study the color scheme. Two original axon drawings of the villa suggest early intentions that were not realized in the built project (Figure 4.16). In the axons, the stucco building façade is light beige; most of the exterior spaces are paved with light cream-colored pavers; and three spaces, one on the roof and two in the lower garden, show a dark green grass surface. All the built edge planters contain volumetric green shrubs that function as screens and walls. In one of the drawings, the lower fountain terrace appears to be paved in light turquoise tiles, in line with Persian gardens. Guevrekian effectively used the axonometry to capture spatial relationships, interpenetration of indoor and outdoor spaces, and a seamless flow between house and garden. The technique also accentuated the cascading terraces in a view from the roof, as the complex was meant to be seen—a perfectly self-contained world of in- and outdoor spaces.

In contrast with the axon drawings, the black-and-white photographs of the built garden show the use of the different materials and textures and provide clues to the colors. They display a range of tonal and textural subtleties in paving material distinct to each room. The range of tonality extends from the bright white building walls to the dark lawns and evergreen shrubs. A closer look at the photographs reveals close attention to form and tone: light, possibly gray, square terrazzo tiles or precast pavers on the roof and third-floor balcony; light, possibly brown, precast concrete pavers divided by light-colored bricks into squares on the second floor; and dark-colored bricks laid in two different floor patterns in the lower garden; the brick paving shifts in herringbone directions and from herringbone to basket-weave patterns. Based on Guevrekian's axonometric drawings and other accounts, the play between the pink and blue of the glazed pool tiles brought a touch of color; the only color contrast, of blue benches and rose bushes, was in the roof garden.[74] Finally, much like the Noailles garden, all the exterior garden terrace compartments seem to have been outlined in white.

The photographs also display the geometric richness of the terraced gardens and their complex, dynamic flow. In lieu of color, the platforms' depth and movement were accomplished with diverse textures of pavers, brick, grass, and mosaic surfaces. Unlike the Paris and Hyères gardens, the observer in Neuilly was placed inside the spaces and meant to view the terrace-garden from the roof and balconies above. But like the previous gardens, the staggered, faceted composition of the floor planes created an interlocking square and

4.16 Villa Heim, axonometric drawings, 1927. Courtesy of the University of Illinois at Urbana-Champaign Archives

rectangle pattern (Figure 4.17). The Neuilly project thus demonstrated a shift from an actual bas-relief pattern to an optical one, seen slightly differently from each level and angle. The perceived movement of garden spaces at Villa Heim was enabled by the treatment of each platform and by an observer's movement through the elevated viewpoints.

Limited seasonal change and the presence of very few blooming plants made the Neuilly terrace-garden mostly permanent and austere. Efforts to achieve special effects and the "sought after optical effects, [that] enlarged and enriched this rather small garden," may have been ineffective.[75] However, although this project's colors and light effects were the least conspicuous among Guevrekian's gardens, and neither the effects of electric light nor color are discernible from the photographs, he apparently appreciated its subtlety, remarking on its light, color optics, and psychology:

> Flat red gemstone, lawn and mosaic give the bounded garden expansion, and enrichment. ... The electric light, the most tremendous discovery of our time, is still poorly understood. This unshaped light, applied by those who know, provides the strongest impressions; it is full of nuances, one can make rooms appear smaller, or wider, or higher, one can replace daylight with it. ... Another important aspect is color, it influences, depending on its tone, the human nervous system in many different ways. Through experience and experiments, it has been proven, that red is stimulating, green is calming, yellow enhances the working mood, while blue in its stronger hues, is causing sleepiness and exhausting conditions.[76]

* * *

Guevrekian's brief garden practice went beyond an interrogation of the act of seeing to produce a revolution in landscape color design. As he turned away from garden

129

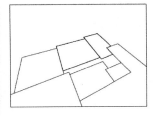
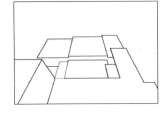

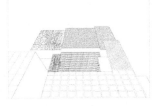

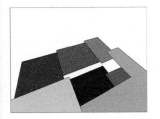
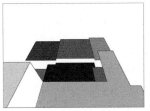

4.17 Analytical diagrams, two views to the garden from the roof showing the staggered and faceted compositions of the floor planes. Rendered by Asif Khan

design to other arenas, the legacy of his early gardens, primarily their spatial and compositional arrangement, was perpetuated. The garden designer A. E. Powell built a garden near Bristol inspired by that of Villa Noailles; although it was criticized as a pale imitation[77] it was featured, together with Villa Heim, in the first US exhibition of landscape architecture, at the San Francisco Museum of Modern Art in 1937 and in Christopher Tunnard's landmark *Gardens in the Modern Landscape* (1938).[78]

Gabriel Guevrekian's gardens have been cited as the first to make a dramatic break with formal garden traditions.[79] He used color to free landscape architects from the representational color fixation and imitation of nature, made color central to the modern garden, and emphasized the perception of color by the spectator. Furthermore, by associating color with modern fashion and lifestyle and mixing it with architectural color traditions, he modernized color in garden design. Yet, except in the work of Roberto Burle Marx, who advanced color exploration in the modern landscape in both small gardens and large urban parks and public spaces, color design inquiry in Western landscape architecture did not blossom. It went into hibernation for the next four decades.

Notes

[1] Guevrekian's gardens were featured in numerous style magazines of the period. For links to his textile design, see Khosravi, "The Multiple Lives of Gabriel Guevrekian," 2015, 54. Garden design had strong links to French Baroque fashion and textile design; 17th century gardens featured *parterres de broderie*, which emulated the embroidered and dyed patterns of the French nobility's clothing and the ceiling tiles in their houses.

[2] Wesley, "Gabriel Guevrekian and the Cubist Garden," 1981, 15; Steele, "New Pioneering in Garden Design," 1930.

[3] A traditional paradise garden in Iran is typically enclosed and square or rectangular in shape with four quartered division and a fountain in the center. It is further discussed in the section on "Modernized Tradition, Polychromatic Mosaic."

[4] Vera's two early books, *Le Nouveau Jardin* (1912) and *Les Jardins à l'Exposition* (1919), made extensive references to color. His later books covered the broad topics of the modern city and modern life.

[5] Khosravi, "The Multiple Lives," 2015. In 1933 Guevrekian moved back to Iran, but the gardens he created there, all in Tehran, did not display any innovations. In 1948 he immigrated to the United States and taught at universities in California, Ohio, and Illinois.

[6] Dodds, "Freedom from the Garden," 2002, 198.

[7] In addition to several short articles about Villa Noailles and Villa Heim, Guevrekian published two photographic portfolios: *Bâtiments industriels* (1931) and *Hotels and Sanatoria* (1930).

[8] Imbert, *The Modernist Garden in France*, 1993, 151.

[9] Guévrékian, "Ein Landhaus in Neuilly," 1929, 298; Guevrekian, "Une Villa à Neuilly," 1929, 8.

[10] Guévrékian, "Propos de Guévrékian sur l'Art Moderne," 1929.

[11] Guévrékian, "Bei der Planung des Gartens des Vicomte de Noailles in Hyères," 1929, 331.

[12] Based on Chevreul's 18th century theory of color interaction, simultaneous contrast ("la loi du contraste simultané des couleurs") refers to the varied, mutual visual influences of neighboring colors when viewed at the same time. For instance, colors appear more intense when two complementary colors are seen in juxtaposition; they appear brighter and smaller against a dark background than against a light background; and they tend to take on a hue opposite to that of the surrounding area.

[13] Delaunay considered Cubism's use of color austere intellectualism and, instead, emphasized lyrical, synthetic sensation. See Imdahl, "Delaunay's Position in History," 1967, 79–80.

[14] Ibid., 72, note 17.

[15] Delaunay, "Draft of a Letter to Nicolas Maximovitch Minsky," [1918] 1978.

[16] This work took place in 1912–14. See Imdahl, "Delaunay's Position," 1967, 83; Delaunay, "Simultaneism in Contemporary Modern Art, Painting, Poetry" [1913] 1978.

[17] Imdahl, "Delaunay's Position," 1967, 82.

[18] This patriotic evocation was appropriate to the exhibition's international representation and may also have been an affirmation in the wake of World War I.

[19] The Garden of Water and Light's color specification is based on Forestier, "Les Jardins à l'Exposition," 1925.

[20] Sonia Delaunay commissioned Guevrekian to design a temporary shopfront to exhibit her *simultané* collection, first at the 1924 Salon d'Automne and then the 1925 Exposition of Decorative Arts, where she and the fashion designer Jacques Heim displayed their work.

[21] Sonia Delaunay, "Rugs and Textiles," [1929] 1978.

[22] This and the following two quotations are from Vera, *Le Nouveau Jardin*, 1912, 92–5.

23 Imbert, *The Modernist Garden,* 1993, 61.

24 Vera, *Le Nouveau Jardin*, 1912, 94.

25 Guevrékian, "Une Villa à Neuilly," 1929, 9.

26 Guevrékian, "Propos," 1929.

27 Smith, "Phenomenology," 2018. Phenomenology is a subdiscipline of philosophy, founded by Edmund Husserl, that studies the structure of experience or consciousness and how people experience things in a subjective or first-person point of view.

28 Gestalt theory focuses on people's perception of patterns or configurations rather than individual components. It gained currency in architecture and urbanism in the 1930s.

29 Wigley, *White Walls, Designer Dresses*, 1995, 314.

30 Imbert, *The Modernist Garden*, 1993, 44.

31 Forestier, "Les Jardins," 1925, 526. The exposition featured five international garden idioms, including Persian, Mediterranean, and East Asian.

32 Dodds, "Freedom," 2002, 195, 198.

33 Wilber, *Persian Gardens and Garden Pavilions,* 1962, 33–4.

34 Koliji, "Gazing Geometries," 2016, 120.

35 The five geometries of the traditional *girih* tiles—decagon, hexagon, bowtie, rhombus, and pentagon—vary in complexity, angles, and according to their flat or convex surface application.

36 Wilber, *Persian Gardens*, 1962, 23.

37 Coentro et al., "Hispano-Moresque Architectural Glazes in the Context of Medieval Glass Technology," 2017.

38 Ostadzaman et al., "The Psychological Effects of Stained Glass in Traditional Iranian Architecture," 2016, 36.

39 Ibid., 37.

40 White Pyrethrum replaced two of the begonia beds, at one point.

41 Steele, "New Pioneering," 1930, 164.

42 The most renowned example of mirror effects in a garden was the small trapezium-shaped garden at the Noailles hotel in Paris, designed by Paul and André Vera in 1924. The mirror devised an experience of illusion by increasing depth and creating tension, ambiguity, and distortion. See Imbert, *The Modernist Garden*, 1993, 82–7.

43 The metal and glass artist Louis Barillet designed the sphere and the pylon.

44 Dodds, "Freedom," 2002, 192.

45 Ibid.

46 Steele, "New Pioneering," 1930, 165. Steele initially referred to it as a "night-club trick," but later he deemed it "completely successful in focusing the interest and relieving by its unexpected location what would otherwise be an altogether stiff pattern."

47 Marrast, *Jardins*, 1925, plate 15.

48 Dodds, "Freedom," 2002, 191.

49 Naegele, "Object, Image, Aura," 1998, 3. Purism, embodied in the work of Le Corbusier and Fernand Léger, represented objects as shapes stripped of detail.

50 Imbert, *The Modernist Garden*, 1993, 267.

51 Benjamin, "The Work of Art in the Age of Mechanical Reproduction," [1955] 1968, 238–9.

52 Mattens, "The Aesthetics of Space," 2011, 112.

[53] One of the photographs was published in the official exposition catalogue, 1925, volume XI, plate LXXIV, and in Marrast, *Jardins*, 1925, plate 14. See also *Exposition Internationale des Arts Décoratifs et Industriels Modernes, 1925: The Environment, Street, and Garden,* Vol. XI, reprint of the official catalogue (New York: Garland, 1977).

[54] Baker, "Equivalent of a Loudly-Colored Folk Art Is Needed," 1942.

[55] Dodds, "Freedom," 2002, 197–8. Dodds considered Guevrekian's involvement with CIAM, as a founding member and its secretary, a turning point for his rejection of decorative arts in favor of universal, functional design.

[56] The house was conceived as a work of art. Mallet-Stevens collaborated with artists and architects, including Georges ("Djo") Bourgeois, Theo van Doesburg, Francis Jourdain, and Pierre Chareau, who designed one of the outdoor roof gardens. The Noailles garden was significantly changed in 1934 and, after a period of neglect, reconstructed in the 1990s.

[57] Zahn, "Ein Geometrischer Garten an der Riviera," 1929, 223.

[58] Shand, "An Essay in the Adroit," 1929, 147.

[59] Guevrekian, "Bei der Planung des Gartens," 1929, 310.

[60] For a thorough analysis of the garden, see Imbert, *The Modernist Garden*, 1993, 130–9.

[61] Khosravi, "Discreet Austerity," 207.

[62] Dodds, "Freedom," 2002, note 38.

[63] Jacques Lipchitz noted: "Because of the location and the problem of seeing the sculpture in the round, I suggested installing a machine so that it could rotate. ... It is a culmination of all my findings in Cubism but at the same time an escape from Cubism." See Dodds, "Freedom," 2002, 202.

[64] Imbert, *The Modernist Garden*, 1993, 131.

[65] Dodds, "Freedom," 2002, 178; Vera and Guevrekian, "Sketches for Gardens by Paul Vera and Gabriel Guevrekian," 1926, 27.

[66] Dodds, "Freedom," 2002, 196–97.

[67] The archive at the University of Illinois, Gabriel Guevrekian papers, 1923–34; available at https://digital.library.illinois.edu/collections/6e75f750-9739-0131-1105-0050569601ca-b.

[68] The statue was added after the garden had been completed and the wall at the triangle tip lowered to better display the statue and open the view.

[69] Dodds, "Freedom," 2002, 197.

[70] Imbert, *The Modernist Garden*, 1993, 84.

[71] Guevrekian, "Ein Landhaus," 1929, 298.

[72] For Le Corbusier's modern gardens see Imbert, *The Modernist Garden,* 1993, Chapter 8.

[73] Guevrékian, "Une Villa," 1929, 229.

[74] Dodds, "Freedom," 2002, 209.

[75] Guevrékian, "Une Villa," 1929, 8.

[76] Guévrékian. "Ein Landhaus," 1929, 297–8. Google translation from German.

[77] Imbert, *The Modernist Garden*, 1993, 71.

[78] Tunnard, *Gardens in the Modern Landscape*, 1938, 70–1; Morley, *Contemporary Landscape Architecture and Its Sources*, 1937, 35.

[79] Adams, "Introduction," 1991, 17.

References

Adams, William Howard. "Introduction." In *Roberto Burle Marx: The Unnatural Art of the Garden*, 8–38. New York: Museum of Modern Art, 1991.

Baker, Geoffrey. "Equivalent of a Loudly-Colored Folk Art Is Needed." *Landscape Architecture Quarterly* (January 1942): 65–6.

Benjamin, Walter. "The Work of Art in the Age of Mechanical Reproduction" [1955]. In *Illuminations*, 219–55. New York: Harcourt, Brace, and World, Inc., 1968.

Coentro, S., L. C. Alves, B. Gratuze, R. Trindade, R. C. da Silva, V. S. F. Muralha. "Hispano-Moresque Architectural Glazes in the Context of Medieval Glass Technology." *Proceedings of the 5th GLASSAC* (June 6–9, 2017): 22–4.

Delaunay, Robert. "Draft of a Letter to Nicolas Maximovitch Minsky" [1918]. In *The New Art of Color: The Writings of Robert and Sonia Delaunay*, ed. by Arthur A. Cohen, 62–4. New York: Viking Press, 1978.

Delaunay, Robert. "Simultaneism in Contemporary Modern Art, Painting, Poetry" [1913]. In *The New Art of Color: The Writings of Robert and Sonia Delaunay*, ed. by Arthur A. Cohen, 47–51. New York: Viking Press, 1978.

Delaunay, Sonia. "Rugs and Textiles" [1929]. In *The New Art of Color: The Writings of Robert and Sonia Delaunay*, ed. by Arthur A. Cohen, 199–201. New York: Viking Press, 1978.

Dodds, George. "Freedom from the Garden: Gabriel Guévrékian and a New Territory of Experience." In *Tradition and Innovation in French Garden Art: Chapters of New History*, ed. by John Dixon Hunt, Michel Conan, and Claire Goldstein, 184–97. Philadelphia: University of Pennsylvania Press, 2002.

Forestier, J. C. N. "Les Jardins à l'Exposition." *L'Agriculture Nouvelle* no. 1450 (12 September 1925): 526.

Guévrékian, Gabriel. "Ein Geometrischer Garten an der Riviera." *Gartenschonheit* 10 (June 1929): 223.

Guévrékian, Gabriel. "Une Villa à Neuilly." *Art et Industrie* (July 1929): 7–10.

Guévrékian, Gabriel. "Bei der Planung des Gartens des Vicomte de Noailles in Hyères." *Innendekoration* 40, no. 8 (August 1929): 309–10.

Guévrékian, Gabriel. "Ein Landhaus in Neuilly." *Innendekoration* 40, no. 8 (August 1929): 296–308.

Guévrékian, Gabriel. "Propos de Guévrékian sur l'Art Moderne." *La Liberté* (December 18, 1929).

Guévrékian, Gabriel. *Hotels and Sanatoria*. Paris: Éditions S. de Bonadona, 1930.

Guévrékian, Gabriel. *Bâtiments industriels*. Paris: C. Moreau, 1931.

Imbert, Dorothée. *The Modernist Garden in France*. New Haven, CT: Yale University Press, 1993.

Imdahl, Max. "Delaunay's Position in History." In *Robert Delaunay: Light and Color*, ed. by Gustav Lyriesen and Max Imdahl. New York: Harry N. Abrams, Inc., 1967.

Khosravi, Hamed. "Discreet Austerity: Notes on Gabriel Guevrekian's Gardens." *International Journal of Architectural Theory* 20, no. 34 (2015): 197–212.

Khosravi, Hamed. "The Multiple Lives of Gabriel Guevrekian." *AA Files* 71 (2015): 50–63.

Koliji, Hooman. "Gazing Geometries: Modes of Design Thinking in Pre-Modern Central Asia and Persian Architecture." *Nexus Network Journal* 8 (2016): 105–32. DOI: 10.1007/s00004-016-0288-6

Lurçat, André. *Terrasses et Jardins*. Paris: Éditions d'Art Charles Moreau, 1929.

Marrast, Joseph. *Jardins*. Paris: Éditions d'Art Charles Moreau, 1925.

Mattens, Filip. "The Aesthetics of Space: Modern Architecture and Photography." *Journal of Aesthetics and Art Culture* (2011): 105–14.

Morley, McCann. *Contemporary Landscape Architecture and Its Sources*. Exhibition catalogue. San Francisco: San Francisco Museum of Modern Art, 1937.

Naegele, Daniel J. "Object, Image, Aura: Le Corbusier and the Architecture of Photography." *Harvard Design Magazine* 6 (Fall 1998): 1–6.

Ostadzaman, Mahdi, Fatemeh ZeraatGar Shafiei, and Mohammad Ghomeishi. "The Psychological Effects of Stained Glass in Traditional Iranian Architecture: The Case of Orsi." *Journal of Current Research in Science* 4, no. 2 (2016): 35–42.

Shand, P. Morton. "An Essay in the Adroit: At the Villa of the Vicomte de Noailles." *Architectural Review* 65, no. 2 (April 1929): 174–5.

Smith, David Woodruff. "Phenomenology." In *The Stanford Encyclopedia of Philosophy* (Summer 2018), ed. by Edward N. Zalta. https://plato.stanford.edu/archives/sum2018/entries/phenomenology.

Steele, Fletcher. "New Pioneering in Garden Design." *Landscape Architecture* 20, no. 3 (April 1930): 159–77.

Tunnard, Christopher. *Gardens in the Modern Landscape*. London: Architectural Press, 1938.

Vera, André. *Le Nouveau Jardin*. Paris: Émile-Paul, 1912.

Vera, André. *Les Jardins*. Paris: Émile-Paul Frères, 1919.

Vera, Paul and Gabriel Guevrekian. "Sketches for Gardens by Paul Vera and Gabriel Guevrekian." *Arts de la Maison* 5 (Winter 1926): 26–7.

Wesley, Richard. "Gabriel Guevrekian and the Cubist Garden." *Rassegna* 3, no. 8 (October 1981): 15.

Wigley, Mark. *White Walls, Designer Dresses: The Fashioning of Modern Architecture*. Cambridge, MA: MIT Press, 1995.

Wilber, Donald N. *Persian Gardens and Garden Pavilions*. Rutland, VT: Charles E. Tuttle Company, 1962.

Zahn, Leopold. "Ein Geometrischer Garten an der Riviera." *Gartenschonheit* 10 (June 1929): 223.

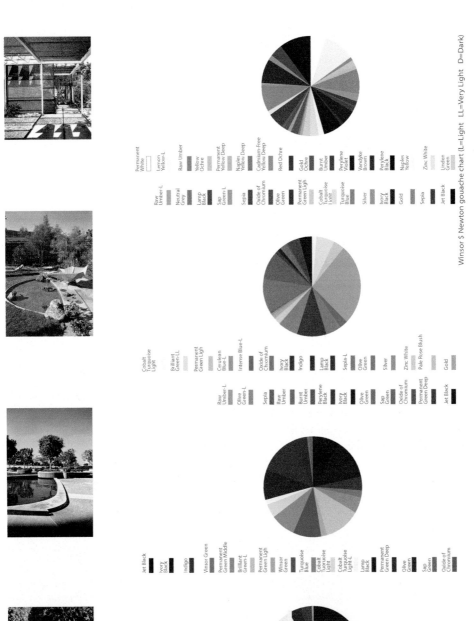

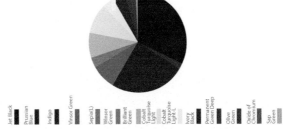

5.0 Diagrams, color analysis, Alcoa Forecast Garden, Los Angeles, photographed by Julius Shulman, ca. 1960 (upper two) and Union Bank Square, Los Angeles, photographed by Garrett Eckbo, 1978 (lower two). Rendered by Asif Khan

(Unless noted otherwise, all drawings and photographs in Chapter 5 are by Garrett Eckbo / The College of Environmental Design archives, University of California, Berkeley.)

5

Spatial Color
A-Chrome,
Garrett Eckbo (1910–2000)

To speak of color first, texture second, and mass third, as does [William] Robinson, is not only to reverse the scale of importance, to stand values on their heads, but also to ignore the primary spatial essence of plants.

Garrett Eckbo, *Landscape for Living*, 1950, 95

Design in the pure color relations of paint or flowers is a kind of highly specialized and sensitized department of the general categories of space and object design. ... As we move toward the clear and rich spatial order out-of-doors ..., we are sure to need such special detail to complete, intensify and subtilize our big conceptions.

Garrett Eckbo, *Landscape for Living*, 1950, 104

In his seminal modern landscape architecture theory, outlined in *Landscape for Living* (1950), the Californian landscape architect Garrett Eckbo made clear his color propositions (he restated them for a lay audience in 1956 in *The Art of Home Landscaping*). In midcentury America, at a time when the new popularity of glass walls in private homes dismantled the boundaries between architecture and landscape and domestic living extended outdoors in suburban homes, Eckbo's theory highlighted the triumph of space and function over all other landscape design considerations (Figure 5.1). He demoted color to the category of "special detail," subservient to space, as expressed in the epigraphs above.[1] Space determined the selection and arrangement of plants and material, underscored physical and psychological well-being, and broadcasted landscape character.[2] Function was fused with line, plane, shape, and volume. Color was a mere interference, its elusive and emotive properties threatened the expression of space. Built structures and architectural materials rivaled plants, a process that had begun in the gardens of the 1920s. Trees and shrubs were mostly valued for their structural and functional capacity, flowers largely avoided.

Born in Cooperstown, New York, Eckbo grew up in Alameda, California, and completed a bachelor's degree in landscape architecture at the University of California, Berkeley in 1935 and a graduate degree at Harvard in 1938. Along with his peers Dan Kiley (1912–2004) and James Rose (1913–91), he rejected the traditionalist Beaux-Arts dogma, which still dominated the department of landscape architecture at Harvard. The three turned for inspiration to the architecture department where modern science and art dominated the course. Back in California, the prominent practice of Thomas Church (1902–78) and the landmark exhibition "Contemporary Landscape Architecture and Its Sources" (1937) at the San Francisco Museum of Art made a strong impression on Eckbo.[3] Five years later, at the museum's second exhibition, "Landscape Design" (1942), Eckbo and his business partner, brother-in-law Edward Williams, took their place among the leading US landscape architects.[4]

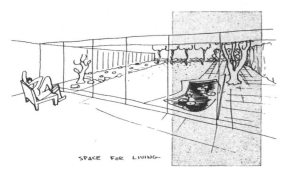

5.1 Sketch, "Space for Living," *Arts & Architecture Magazine*, Oct. 1945, p. 61. © Travers Family Trust

A problem-solving pragmatist with a social bent, Eckbo focused his practice through 1960 on neighborhood and private garden design as generators of both form and human welfare, then turned to larger-scale, urban, commercial, and institutional projects.[5] Of the three colleagues—Eckbo, Kiley, and Rose, all of whom became well-known practitioners with similar attitudes toward color—Eckbo was the most prolific writer. He published five books and numerous articles in professional and popular magazines, influenced a generation of students and practitioners from the 1950s through the 1970s, and brought landscape architecture into mainstream culture.[6] The publications of his most productive decades, the 1940s through the 1960s, established the status of color in his work and, more broadly, in modern American garden and landscape design in the context of suburban expansion and the rising consumer culture and outdoor lifestyle.

For Eckbo, landscape was for living, a purposeful site for the interaction of people and place and people and nature. He rejected the idea of gardens and parks as settings for horticultural display, loci of a stylistic battle between formal and informal, sources of mere visual pleasure. Nature was not mythically or culturally defined but a physical site subject to rational analysis. Science trumped mysticism and romanticism, style was replaced by technique, and form was determined by reason and social good.[7]

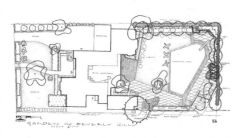

Similarly, color appreciation was not based on the elusiveness of beauty but viewed in practical and rational terms. Regional climate and landscape maintenance served as lenses to assess, accept, or reject color. Paint was shunned in favor of industrially tinted material. The encapsulation of color in material was a way for modernists to make color subservient to space. Predominant landscape colors of browns and greens, tonal and textural contrasts, and an achromatic palette—white, gray, black—were leading choices (Figure 5.0).

But color infiltrated the garden in the 1950s with a barrage of consumer products sponsored by advertisers—outdoor furniture, screens, sunbreaks, and other accessories. Eckbo called on landscape design practitioners to be cautious and turn to experts for help. In contrast to Guevrekian, who collaborated with fashion designers, he called on landscape architects to transcend the appeal of fleeting fashion styles. And while color photography entered publications, aimed at consumerist appeal,

5.2 Eckbo, Williams, Royston, pool garden, Beverly Hills, California, 1946, page spread, *Landscapes for Living*, 1950. Photo: Julius Shulman

Eckbo resisted it, preferring colorless representation in landscape architecture through line drawings and black-and-white photography—they were expedient and had the modern look (Figure 5.2).

Eckbo's "nonuse" of bright, pure, or synthetic color, as he called it, was, of course, its own use of color. The deployment of a largely achromatic palette, together with the enduring earth tones of the natural landscape, is a vital chapter in the history of color in landscape architecture.

Space: Structural Color Revised

Midcentury American modern landscape architecture adhered to the color sensibilities of modern architecture: the zeal for white and self-colored industrial material, as in the architecture of Le Corbusier and Mies van der Rohe. The flat and vibrant color fields of abstract art, De Stijl, and Bauhaus were used sparingly and in highly measured degree.[8] Having eschewed ornamentation, architecture dismissed color as decoration and made function and space supreme. "Chromophobia" was not only a mainstay of modern architecture but imagined as an abstract ideal, a symbol of modern spatial architectural authority.[9]

The modern architectural color code was conveyed by Christopher Tunnard (1910–79) in *Gardens in the Modern Landscape* (1938).[10] Tunnard subscribed to science and technology and made function and space the overriding principles of modern landscape design. He rebuffed traditional gardens that relied on plants for color, calling plant color "a medium for the indulgence of the wildest, irrational caprice."[11] Instead, he proposed an organized, reasoned process that permitted only occasional pure color masses to enliven a garden. He claimed that detaching color from nature and emotive considerations meant "setting color free."[12] Tunnard thus harked back to and refashioned Repton's 18th century "structural color" theory (see Chapter 1). Green, the predominant color, was joined by blue and brown to shape a new coherent spatial landscape composition. Other pure color was to be avoided, lest it interfere with space and composition. Quoting the architectural theorist Adrian Stokes ("isolated from form, sensation of colour does not lead to a pure art of colours, or anything that can be called an art"), Tunnard permitted color to enter only occasionally in clear form and uniform mass.[13]

Both Eckbo and his Brazilian contemporary, Roberto Burle Marx (1909–94), who began their careers in the late 1930s, subscribed to Tunnard's rule, albeit with a notable difference: Burle Marx used color profusely, as a pattern and essential compositional element (see Chapter 6), whereas Eckbo permitted pure color rarely and then only as mere detail.[14] He allowed that "[t]he limited symphony can, of course, have its seasonal crescendos of red and yellow foliage, or pink and white blossoms," but warned against the traditional use of colored plants to create patterns:

> Pattern tends to replace volume, although it too can play a role in space organization: strong contrasts on a plane surface can create considerable sense of form and movement. Thus a bed of scarlet geraniums, a small and ornate pool, or a small and shining smooth terrace placed in the foreground of a large and placid view will tend to disrupt and obscure that view by their stridence. But such a relation is again the result of an over-emphasis on detail and a failure to establish proper overall spatial relations.[15]

Texture and, especially, color were to be judged based on their impact on space. They were relegated to the category of "enrichment," surface finish, "a kind of processing or tooling, polishing or roughing, brightening or making neutral."[16] Eckbo was not alone in this view. Thomas Church simply wrote "color" on planting beds in his plans, leaving it to the client or nursery staff to pick the plants and colors.[17] James Rose labeled flower beds simply "beds." With a few exceptions for flowering trees, Eckbo rarely specified plant names on his published plans. Black line textures—stipples, squiggles, lines, and outlines—distinguished lawn from hedge from shrubs and trees. Flower beds were given a scribbly outline, no color indicated.

Eckbo made a few, general rules concerning color. In *Landscape for Living,* he advanced the color principles and language of Albert Munsell (1858–1915)—hue, tone, and "chroma" (a dimension of color saturation). Hues, he agreed, were safer and less disruptive when in large quantity, lighter or darker in tone, and weaker in chroma. Lighter tones and stronger chromas demanded greater care in terms of quantity and quality as well as an understanding of the observer's psychological reaction.[18] He made a distinction between landscape and pure (i.e., synthetic) colors. Landscape browns, greens, and blues should be dominant. Pure color of intense chroma should be minimized, restricted to finishing, intensification, and refinement, in specially planned locations and in careful relation to other colors.[19]

His most extensive and focused deliberation on color was in the *Landscape for Living* chapter "Plant and Planting" (as in Tunnard's book), where color's minor position in the hierarchy of plant selection and characteristics is made clear. Eckbo described plants as "the last refuge of undisciplined subjectivity and romanticism."[20] They were to be selected and valued first based on their (eventual) size, rate of growth, and form or silhouette, then, in order of importance, by their requirements and maintenance, foliage texture and structural members, and, last, color (followed only by fragrance).[21] Color was also the last item in any discussion about the design of planting and structural elements. In addition to being a spatial disruptor, attention-grabber, and sentimental, color was uncontrollable and subject to seasonal change:

> The "riot of color," that romantic vision of the garden beautiful, is too often, like "informal design", merely *an excuse for sloppy, haphazard, irresponsible planting.* We advocate the use of color, but … in *a disciplined and controlled fashion* which will strengthen, rather than disrupt, the spatial concept of garden or park [italics added].[22]

Echoing Humphry Repton, Eckbo instructed that bright flowers, such as hybrid tea roses and annuals, be planted in functional rows in the workspace or service yard only for indoor vase cut flowers.

Much like his colleague James Rose, Eckbo used plants architectonically, assigning them spatial components: grass as ground cover, shrubs as enclosure, and trees as shade (Figure 5.3). Trees and shrubs were superior to herbaceous plants because of their capacity to create space; herbaceous plants were acceptable only in designated perennial beds. He cautioned that, as long as flowers and fruits were considered the pinnacle of the garden, horticulturists and nurserymen would continue to breed them and thus concentrate less on form, structure, and texture.[23]

In terms of form and structure, plants were considered in the same context as space and building materials, and landscape design became an architectural endeavor of spatial structures and materials. Form-making elements included not only stone and concrete paving, walls, wood, and steel canopies—in Eckbo's words "gravity material"—but also plants or "antigravity material."

> Structure is thought of as THE [sic] art of spatial design, but planting is likewise an art of spatial design—the primary spatial control out-of-doors, equal qualitatively to structural design, though varying in kind; that is, subtler, looser, less positive, less continuous, or with wider variations in degree of continuity.[24]

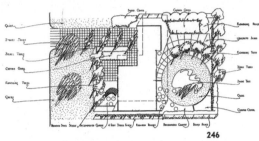

Foliage reclaimed top position: its color was superior to that of bark, flower, and fruit (in that order). Woody plant foliage color, particularly, was reliable for its continuous, usually grayed and toned-down color, unlike pure flower and fruit colors. Eckbo approved of foliage of varied shades, textures, and variegation, insisting:

5.3 Eckbo, Williams, Royston, line drawings, Camp Park Space for migratory agricultural worker families near Harlingen, Texas, 1940 (top). Typical residence garden, axonometry with general references to plants, Co-operative Housing, Los Angeles, 1945–9, *Landscape for Living*, 1950 (bottom)

> All greens are not alike—there is a substantial range from light to dark, from clear to gray, and from dull to glossy textures in the leaves themselves. In addition to special nongreens in spring and fall, there are variations in gray, brown, red, purple, and multicolored forms.[25]

Bark color, too, was acceptable. He favored the white birch and foliated pink river birch barks among others.

He applied the principle of contrast to all design aspects other than color. Textural design was far less complicated than color design, and he sought bold, rather than subtle, tonal and textural plant contrast for a richer, fuller, and more expressive design. A balanced contrast, he wrote, means that man and nature, objectivity and subjectivity, the rational and irrational, meet, merge, and dance together in ever shifting, ever changing, ever variable patterns that are truly the reflection and the fit environment for the dance of life itself.[26]

Eckbo's design for Union Bank Plaza in Los Angeles in 1969 clearly demonstrates the contrast principle in several design elements (described below). His earlier garden plan

5.4 Isometric plan for a model house, *The Californian*, July 1947

for a model house in Crestwood Hills (1948), near Los Angeles, shows the intended interplay in foliage contrasts, and his isometric planting plan for the residence was described thus (Figure 5.4):

> Contrasting patterns of dark and light foliage, ... the gray-green of slender *Melaleuca leucadendra* ..., the orange of persimmons against a graveled site, and a wide expanse of lawn enclosed within the L-shape of the house and contrasted at the border with dark green magnolia bordering ... the shadowed tracery of thin eucalyptus at left and extreme lower right corner contrast with sturdy fig trees, salvia and tamarisk.[27]

Eckbo's praise of Burle Marx's flamboyant Brazilian gardens, in *Landscape for Living*, may seem contradictory, but what he admired was not so much his colleague's botanical and color use as his regional climatic and scientific prudence in selecting, maintaining, and controlling plants.[28] "Climatic regionalism"—the fitness of flora to climate as expressed in terms of grouping, form, texture, and color—was a new concept prominent in the modern theories. It was the scientific replacement of "nature's way" in the premodern empirical and subjective philosophies of Robinson and Jekyll, though on a much larger scale. Eckbo, like Burle Marx, linked the variations in regional climate and light quality with landform and local floral characteristics—including color—and subsequently with the idea of landscape character. But the two men approached regionalism through a different lens: Burle Marx through art, culture, and politics, and Eckbo through natural and social science.

Climatic Regionalism, Rational Color

Eckbo had great faith in science and so subjected color to scientific authority. Science was the overriding aperture to explain the world of not only natural phenomena and social behavior but also aesthetics and creativity. He opened *Landscape for Living* with a clear declaration:

> We live in a world whose advances are based on the continuous expansion of the use of the scientific method, *beyond those fields called exact, to such as esthetics* [sic] *and sociology.* ... [It] is a process of *rational analysis and creative synthesis*, of continuous research, hypothesis, and experiment to prove or disprove such hypotheses [italics added].[29]

Knowledge of local plants and their requirements, always important in landscape design, was now explained by modernists in terms of the science of ecology and climatic regionalism, first developed by Tunnard. To shield planting design from decorative, scenic, and sentimental considerations, as in the work of Jekyll and Robinson, meant to choose ecological rationale; Eckbo explained:

> It is my feeling that the system should eliminate its allusions to botanical or sentimental categories and to design preconceptions. By establishing a simpler and more orderly relation between *ecological and landscape groupings*, it would develop much greater flexibility and usability [italics added].[30]

Plant form and rock formation were subjected to site, regional, and climate analysis. Soft and round forms of bedrock, land, and plant leaf were linked to humidity and old age, while angularity coincided with arid and young formations. The science of ecology also explained chromatic appearance and suitability.

Eckbo deemed the concept of climatic regionalism useful and found support in studies such as those of the naturalist John C. Van Dyke on light effects on foliage color.[31] Different climatic zones—such as the tropics, coasts, desert—differently affect color purity, brightness, and contrast levels. This explains garden and landscape designs in their respective geographies. For instance, Eckbo attributed the pervasive use of colorful herbaceous material in Baroque parterres, Victorian carpet bedding, and Romantic flower borders to the temperate European climate; and, conversely, the use of hardy plants, bulbs, and succulents to the semiarid and arid climates of the American southwest. He similarly rationalized foliage color in terms of "zonal color," distinguishing between colors and textures in humid and dry zones: strong and clear greens and variegations in the humid tropical and temperate forests versus grays, gray-greens, and brown-greens in frigid zones.[32] Because local plant colors govern landscape character and regional expression, Eckbo promoted native plants.[33]

Light quality, too, affected color through the strength and direction of the sun relative to atmospheric matter. Accordingly, Eckbo maintained, in tropical regions light is clearer and stronger and so are color, shadow, and surface contrasts, whereas in temperate regions light weakens and turns softer with increased moisture in the air and clouds, producing paler and muddier colors and weaker contrast.

The main goals of scientific knowledge in landscape design were to establish regional character and to create a balance between regional landscape expression and what Eckbo called a "humanized landscape": "we seek two values in every landscape: one, the expression of the native quality of the landscape, the other, the development of maximum human livability."[34] For the second, he turned to the field of plant sociology for answers.[35] He determined that people instinctively engage in a balancing act to achieve greater physical and psychological comfort in their environment. Plant color and texture play a role in this intricate balancing act that takes climate into consideration: "Line, form, and color are approached and handled with different emphases in different climates."[36] Thus in high-humidity zones, where large-leaf plants of lighter and brighter greens predominate, people prefer their opposites— thinly textured, green-gray and green-brown plants; in cool or overcast zones with plants of mostly fine texture and dull and dark tones, people favor bright greens and silver and gold variegations; and in hot and dry zones, characterized by small and grayed colors, people desire large and rich foliage of darker, brighter, and glossier greens. Clearly, the balancing act concept was intended only to explain rather than promote the habit, since it contradicted regional expression and implied high maintenance and expense, including artificial irrigation in arid zones and the need for constant trimming and weeding in the tropics. In arid zones like southern California, Eckbo endorsed "considerable emphasis on structural elements—paving, seats, screens—to carry the main form or pattern of the garden."[37]

Perceiving that the science of color psychology mostly concerned indoor color, Eckbo expressed the need for a "science of outdoor color and texture, ... such things as the oppressive quality of the dark heavy tree, the cheering quality of the light sparkling tree," and encouraged imagination and independence from natural coloration to enhance human wellbeing:

> If our landscape conception calls for a grove of copper beeches, perhaps contrasted with a block of silver box elders, the former related to a larger background of light clear greens, the latter to dark heavy greens, we will not seek justifying precedent in wild nature, but only in our own imaginative appraisal of the given situation.[38]

Eckbo's outdoor color theory, like Guevrekian's, focused on human physiology and psychology theories, particularly Gestalt psychology.[39] This and other concerns for human perception and wellbeing drew him to the work of the architect Richard Neutra (1892–1970). In his review of Neutra's first published book in the United States, *Richard Neutra on Building* (1951), Eckbo praised the author's handling of site design with skill and sensitivity and emphasis on Gestalt psychology, in terms of the unity of the visual landscape, and in Neutra's words: "what a site produces on our total being is, in fact, a combined total impact ...."[40]

Neutra's study of the surface reflection, outside illumination, privacy, visual perception, and mood of the inhabitants informed landscape architecture. He focused on the psychophysiological effects of the environment, notably, the calming effects of indirect lighting and unrestricted views of the landscape through the glass wall.[41] Eckbo concurred with Neutra's findings on the effects of light and architectural openness to the garden and landscape, and went on to related theories on the sensation of space.[42]

Compared to plants, the more durable and controllable qualities of construction materials were a subject of immense interest to Eckbo. Most appealing were the transparency of glass, the durability and lightness of metal and fiberglass, and outdoor building products that were mass-produced, standardized, and increasingly cost-effective. And the wide range and durability of synthetically colored and tinted products resistant to weathering greatly excited Eckbo. These developments led him to disparage the pervasive bland color choices and lack of responsibility that came with the freedom offered by these innovations, and he attempted to correct them.

Synthetic Material: Stain and Sparkle

Glass was not new in the garden; for example, in 1920s France, Guevrekian and the Vera brothers used glass and mirrors in the garden. But the floor-to-ceiling transparent glass wall was a whole new ball game: it created a seamless extension of indoor-outdoor space, activated outdoor living, and transformed the experience on both sides of the glass. As sunlight reflected, deflected, and penetrated the glass, space turned plastic and expandable. On sunny days, the glass exterior turned into a mirror, doubling the garden space and blocking the view of the inside. At night, the reverse effect occurred as the glass disappeared, revealing the indoor from outside in and alternately blocking the view from inside out (unless outdoor lighting was installed). The glass wall created what has been called "a theatrical experience: in one direction the illusion of the stage ... and in the other direction the perennial world of reality."[43] This optical illusion spectacle in the modern garden elevated landscape to an equal standing with architecture, a development greatly appreciated by landscape architects.

With glass walls came the need for privacy, both indoors and out, and thus the need for built structures. Partitions or screens, sunbreaks, and canopies or pergolas proliferated, creating instant outdoor rooms and making outdoor living possible. New materials for screens included translucent corrugated plastic, frosted Plexiglas, Cel-O-Glass (a plastic-coated wire mesh), and Transite fencing (fiber-reinforced, asbestos-cement board). They also brought color back into the garden.

In the 1930s, Tunnard had already become aware of the superior efficacy and aesthetics of metals over wood, brick, and stone and noted their immaculate and industrial character. In 1950s America, the availability of outdoor materials, both natural and synthetically tinted, grew exponentially, boosted by popular magazines and advertising. Suburban homeowners and landscape architects alike were drawn to inexpensive, mass-produced, low-maintenance products whose lightness, gloss, and modularity made the garden look modern. And these prefabricated materials—colored concrete, cement-bound building units, plastics, metals, and fiberglass,

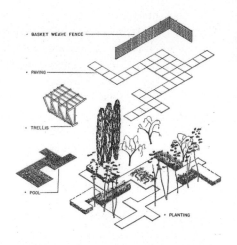

5.5 James Rose, diagram of modular garden (top); small garden mock-up test of scale, modular material, and spring planting color (bottom), *Creative Gardens*, 1958

as well as precast flooring, walls, and other structural units processed with mineral dyes, stains, and acids—greatly enriched the domestic landscape color palette[44] (Figure 5.5).

The new materials were subject to modern architecture's rules: they were to serve a structural function in support of effective and creative spatial organization, while expressing their inherent qualities without seeming decorative or of arbitrarily conceived form. Eckbo felt that letting (nonsynthetic) material express "its true nature" freed it from any imposition of style or cultural association.[45] Synthetic coloring or staining was integral to a material's "truth." The process satisfied the need to enliven as well as preserve the surface quality of the material. It also minimized the need for surface maintenance.[46] Stripping paint and varnish off furniture and structures traditionally made of wood and, instead, staining them to reveal the nature of the material and bring out its grain and shine became the preferred way to feature such items. Except for stucco and industrial sheet materials, such as plywood, hardboard, and corrugated cement-asbestos roofing, extraneous paint coating was discouraged. If it was required, Eckbo advised minimizing it and avoid green:

Much paint color is apt to seem harsh in garden or park: a little trim color, on fence cap or bench will go a long way toward giving that sparkle we are in search of. Green paint is most difficult to combine with vegetation; it seems to kill the natural greens. Blue is also difficult, or any color that is harsh or muddy. *Clear, light, warm earth colors are best with green vegetation* [italics added].[47]

Combining paint with foliage was complicated, requiring sensitivity to color and consideration of regional light quality and sun exposure. Synthetic coloration, too, was an emerging field of design that required well-developed sensibilities for painters, interior designers, and industrial designers, among others. Eckbo referred landscape architects to Munsell's color system and other theories.[48]

The range of metal products both expanded and complicated color choice in the garden.[49] Stainless steel and aluminum used in columns, screens, partitions, and overhead structures were not as flexible as wood during construction but they were more durable, requiring little maintenance. Aluminum in particular appealed to Eckbo: light, durable, easy to maintain, high-performance, and low-cost, it had major advantages over wrought iron and stainless steel.[50] It could produce different qualities for numerous products, such as thin wires, thin foil rolls, rigid perforated meshes, and embossed panels. Importantly, the process of anodizing aluminum with dyes produced a rainbow of colors that went beyond the metallic, bluish silver-white color and prevalent gold, bronze, and silver.[51] The new tints produced sleek and lustrous effects that furthered the bonding perception of color and material. Colored aluminum countered traditional material and added an appearance of newness, of immaculate cleanliness and vigor.

Eckbo grasped the enormous opportunities aluminum presented to designers[52] and turned his backyard into a grand experiment with different forms of aluminum. Known as the Alcoa Forecast Garden (1956–9), it demonstrated the aesthetic and practical applications of aluminum and helped to popularize the material in landscape architecture (see "Alcoa Forecast Garden (Eckbo Garden)," below). The May 1960 issue of *Landscaping*, "The Magazine of the American Landscape Industry," heralded Eckbo's accomplishment as a window into a garden future enriched with a "myriad of forms, colors, and textures, [and] the botanical beauty it will shelter and screen."[53] The Alcoa Garden's lush verdure, cool silvery-olive fountain, and warm bronze, brown, and golden enclosing structures were depicted in many magazines through the color photography of the renowned photographer Julius Shulman (Figure 5.6).

Besides aluminum, new materials like fiberglass, plastics, and heatproof glass became major competitors in the outdoor structure market.[54] Fiberglass was immensely versatile thanks to its lightweight and inherent strength; it could be molded into complex shapes, textures, and diverse outdoor products. As importantly, it introduced brightly saturated rainbow colors to the garden. The Wohlstetter pool garden in Laurel Canyon, Los Angeles (1954), a cheerful and colorful private garden designed by Eckbo, integrated a screen around the bow-shaped pool. With a cellular, grid, wood frame, the screen was fitted with white fiberglass panels with accents of colored panels—deep yellow, red, blue, and darker and lighter echoes of blue and orange-brown speckles (Figure 5.7). It was a hybrid of a Japanese *shoji* screen and a Piet Mondrian painting.[55]

Private swimming pools ushered a new, large, reflective surface of water into the garden. Eckbo welcomed them for their desirable cooling in hot and arid climates, effect of repose,

5.6 Alcoa Forecast Garden, Los Angeles, view toward the office court, 1957. Photo: Julius Shulman

5.7 Wohlstetter pool garden, Laurel Canyon, Los Angeles, 1954

visual interest, reflection of the sky and nearby color and texture, animate water surface, and, not least, the design possibilities of movement, which he compared to choreographing a dance.[56] With growing outdoor recreation, myriad outdoor consumer products flooded the garden: children's playgrounds, mobile furniture, outdoor grills, dining sets, and more. Affordable, mass-produced consumer products promoted by lifestyle magazines and exhibitions in postwar America brought gleeful coloration, subject to changing fashions, akin to indoor furnishing. Landscape architects were thrust into the tastemaker role of fashioning the private outdoor lifestyle.

Consumer Culture, Colorful Lifestyle

In 1961 the landscape architecture theorist John Ormsbee Simonds summed up the American approach to modern color design: "Keep the volume enclosure neutral, in shades of grey, white, or black, and let the objects or person within it 'glow' with their own subtle or vivid colors."[57] The achromatic spatial container was meant to bring into focus the colorful clothing and outdoor furniture and accessories of a new outdoor lifestyle, particularly in the year-round hospitable climates of California and other western states (Figure 5.8).

Color filtered into the suburban middle- and upper-class private garden, becoming an indicator of good taste and class. The markers of class distinction through seasonal and annual flower color, a major preoccupation in garden cultures for centuries, were extended to outdoor structures and furnishing, perpetuated by color photography in monthly magazines and other media.

Eckbo had been highly critical of American commercialism and materialism in the immediate postwar years. He scorned the mass-production system and industrial assembly lines for replacing the social and cultural production of both high art and folk art, and for inflating the ego of the designer.[58] Gradually, though, his work succumbed to the pressure of the consumer ideal of a private outdoor lifestyle and he became a full participant, both reflecting and spreading the outdoor living values of leisure garden culture. Many homeowners, rather than turning to books and professional articles, took advice from popular magazines largely sponsored by advertisers that boosted consumer products along with garden design ideas. The role of landscape architects in suburban landscape design got a lift, too, and Eckbo featured his work in several popular magazines, among other publicity venues. For example, *The Californian* featured an "ideal" modern home and garden design done exclusively for the magazine by the architect Whitney Smith and Eckbo (see Figure 5.4).[59]

Echoing Eckbo's theory, *House Beautiful* instructed its readers to consider the way color and design details impact space, suggesting, for instance, that smaller, narrow boards, finer foliage, and light and clear colors make space feel larger and, in contrary fashion, wide boards, large foliage, and dark, strong colors reduce apparent space.[60] Beginning in 1946, *House and Garden* began publishing an annual color report and forecast each September, coordinating it with manufacturers and retailers.[61]

5.8 James Rose, residential patio, Mineola, Long Island, NY, *Creative Gardens*, 1958

Synthetic fabrics, vinyl, and nylon that were sturdy, water repellent, and therefore ideal for outdoor structures and furniture brought daring pure color to outdoor rooms and were endorsed by professionals like Church.[62] And Rose garnished his work with primary colors. Practicing on the east coast, he used wood frame fences woven with painted wood planks or colored synthetic fabrics to create cheerful gardens where color enhanced rather than disrupted spatial design. Gardens featured in his monograph *Creative Gardens* display contrasting monochromes—light yellow, blue, and pink—in canvases, furniture, and flower beds set against modular white screens and lush green summer foliage (see Figure 5.5).[63] Rose responded to a greater need for color in the northeast coast's more extreme weather, especially during the barren winter season. He suggested using well-defined flower beds in a modular garden system to minimize the impact during the off-season, or pavers that could be lifted temporarily for seasonal flower beds.[64]

Eckbo, on the other hand, guarded against the flood of outdoor consumer products and advised readers that the safe achromes of "[w]hite or black are most reliable, if you have any doubts."[65] He acknowledged that color in exterior furnishing and artwork might, with proper precaution, produce delightful atmospheres, but the task required the combined talents of both a landscape architect and an interior designer.[66] He also complained that "Little has yet been done with the design of fixtures comparable to good modern indoor fixtures": available outdoor furniture was mostly "clumsy, cold, or corny," and in some cases "atrocious."[67] He did, though, approve of artwork that seamlessly integrated into structural elements and of wall mosaics or murals ("spatial color") at proper landscape scale.

Electric outdoor lighting was a further complication. It afforded desirable and prolonged outdoor activity and introduced exciting sculptural and color possibilities for spatial nighttime drama, but it was also expensive and technically complicated, leading homeowners to buy cheap, off-the-shelf products. Fearing kitsch and ostentatious display, Eckbo advised readers that standard commercial lighting fixtures were preferable to decorative or figurative. Frivolous taste and any possible disruptor of the grand design master—space—was anathema.

As his brief polemic on good and bad color taste shows, Eckbo could be quite inconsistent. He was skeptical of acquired taste and the influence of academic color systems, while elsewhere referring to Munsell. Surprisingly, he criticized "the fear of color" he saw in the prevailing "barren, dull, flat, neutral, greyed or pastelled" color in the American home, attributing it to a reaction to the bright chromatic palettes of advertising, billboards, and increasingly bred horticulture varieties, which he too disdained.[68]

Eckbo was similarly inconsistent in his thoughts about color-class stereotypes. He felt that those who preferred clear, bright, or strong colors showed "a kind of dull snobbery."[69] Yet referring to the great, colorful temples of Greece, China, and other ancient civilizations, he wrote: "Those who condemn certain color schemes as 'Mexican,' 'primitive,' or 'vulgar' are merely guilty of self-sterilization." He recognized the "great potential for the controlled use of color to bring harmony and balance to a chaotic landscape,"[70] but, free of meaning and cultural association, achrome was the safest and most consistent with his embrace of modernist, universal truths.

Axonometry Customized, Photography in Color

Modernist landscape architectural design drawings were largely colorless, though occasionally some landscape architects, like Rose, added flat, uniform, transparent, and floating color blocks, in the vein of Henri Matisse or Joan Miró, to their line drawings. Precisely because color had for centuries imitated nature, it was shunned at a time that strived for abstraction. Eckbo used ink pens or "rapidographs" to create line drawings that were precise and had the modern look. Variable lines for tree canopy silhouettes produced a floating quality, also seen in the paintings of Miró and Jean Arp, although the overall impression was more controlled. Color was replaced by an array of patterns—stripes, wiggles, and dots—and by Zip-a-Tone, a new adhesive shading film printed with dots or lines. Its texture and quick cut-and-paste application to the back of a drawing on vellum or tracing paper was popular in cartoons and also proved ideal for landscape architects who desired flat impressions and fast production. Eckbo used the technique extensively from the 1950s onward.

Plan and oblique axonometry were the predominant representation techniques used for a professional audience and publicity.[71] Perspectives, when done, were intended for the client and layperson. Architects used the axon view for its rational and objective representation devoid of sentimentality and chance. In the 1920s landscape architects used 90° or "straight-up" axonometric projection, as did Guevrekian and Paul and André Vera, often rendering it in gouache (see Chapter 4). The straight-up axon emphasized the elevation view with its accurate measurements but exuded spatial ambiguity for the observer. Beginning in the 1930s, however, the expressive straight axon was replaced with a mechanistic 30° and 45° or oblique projection, which explicated constructions and organizations unambiguously.

Eckbo derived his axonometric views from scale models and plans, positioning the 30°/60° projection to show formal and spatial coherence. The oblique axon brought into focus the unity with the house and enclosing spatial planes, so crucial to the modern garden. It also made it possible "to diminish the primacy of scenographic space and eschew any overt references to historical forms."[72] The oblique axon shifted the focus from the subjective eye level to an objective elevated view point, thus confirming the supremacy of the plan.

The three-dimensional analogue of the oblique axon, the physical model, became popular in landscape design as it enabled designers and their clients to "see" space and "walk in" the landscape. But oblique axons and physical models both provided accurate dimensions of a site that was detached from its surroundings and human perception, presenting an unrealistically pristine, self-contained world that couldn't mesh with a continuous landscape and its phenomenal elements.[73] Unlike his architecture colleagues, Eckbo permitted in the axon limited perceptual aspects, such as the sun and shadows (though no people) (Figure 5.9). His obliques were consequently precise and objective and, at the same time, situated. Eckbo and Rose drew very few abstract perspectives, with outlined or "stick" figures more for scale reference than as humans activating a space. People-less drawings were at odds with Eckbo's landscapes for living theory, but aligned with modernist leanings.

The premise of colorless drawings devoid of people coincided with landscape architectural photography. Predominant in midcentury professional publications (unlike the popular magazines), photography did not permit color to enter and disrupt the spatial composition. The mechanical eye of the camera, with

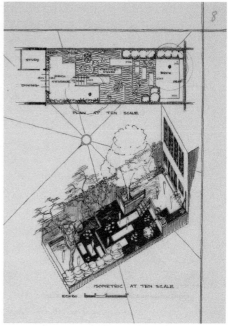

5.9 Axonometric drawing of a garden, from "Small Gardens in the City," *Pencil Point*, 1937

its greater realism and accuracy, dealt the final blow to manual perspective drawings.[74] The *Art of Home Landscaping* is filled with black-and-white photographs, accompanied by a plan marked with numbered shooting locations and arrows corresponding with viewing directions, enabling readers to easily take a sequential "tour" of the garden spaces.[75]

Eckbo's landscapes were all photographed in black and white and absent of people, except in the photography of his neighbor and friend Julius Shulman. Shulman photographed many steel and glass houses for a project conceived by *Arts and Design* magazine, and became the unofficial spokesman of Los Angeles midcentury modern architecture.[76] His pictures of several of Eckbo's early projects and, especially, the Alcoa Garden thrust Eckbo together with the greatest west coast architects whose houses Shulman had also photographed, including Richard Neutra, whom Eckbo admired. Shulman's widely published iconic photographs secured the legacy of Eckbo and his garden.

* * *

The two projects selected to demonstrate Eckbo's modernist color design—the Alcoa Forecast Garden and Union Bank Square, both in Los Angeles—were created at Eckbo's family residence in the late 1950s and downtown in the late 1960s, respectively. The garden, a private landscape of verdure and aluminum (of which only an original fragment remains), and the square, a corporate plaza of concrete, trees, and water (now partly preserved), are among Eckbo's finest and historically significant modernist projects.[77] Although different in scale, material, and context, both projects display the central principles of Eckbo's work: the interplay of forms and layered composition, the use of plants to structure space, experimentation with new materials, attention to climate control and low maintenance, and a contribution to consumerist culture. The two projects demonstrate the way in which color could safely enter modern landscape design, as spatial color as well as Eckbo's use of muted chromatic scheme, contrast, and brightness and preference for synthetic, industrially tinted material. This study is based on archival plans and photographs, secondary sources, and a visit to the project sites.[78]

Alcoa Forecast Garden (Eckbo Garden), Wonderland Park, Los Angeles, California, USA, 1956–9

Eckbo's personal garden, the Alcoa Garden, dubbed "A Landscape of Aluminum," was an experimental ground and show room for new aluminum landscape products.[79] When, in 1956, the Aluminum Company of America (ALCOA) contacted Eckbo to create a garden for the display and publicity of its Forecast collection, Eckbo was enthusiastic about expanding the possibilities for material in the garden. Aluminum, an unconventional garden material, conferred a novel expression that accorded with the age of modernity.

Eckbo lived on a half-acre lot, on the slopes of Laurel Canyon in Los Angeles, from 1952, when the house designed by the architect Josef Van der Kar was completed, through 1965, when he moved to Berkeley.[80] He built the patios adjacent to the house and did the planting in about 1954. The southeast-facing concrete patios extended the living room out through the glass wall and provided an outdoor area for breaks for employees in the on-premises studio, exemplifying the concept of landscape for living. The tree and shrub groupings, which subtly vary in texture and foliage hue, were largely planted at the property boundary to enclose and define the garden and the small open lawn area on the level portion of the lot (Figure 5.10).[81] Two plane trees (*Platanus acerifolia*), a variety with a distinct structure and peeling bark pattern of white, brown, and yellow shades, anchor a southeast corner of the lawn.

Eckbo's use of the garden to explore a variety of pavement shapes, materials, and textures and to demonstrate the enormous plastic possibilities of concrete in multiple

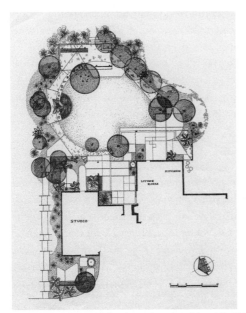
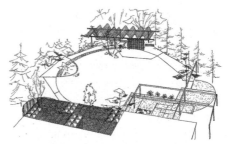

5.10 Alcoa Forecast Garden, plot plan, May 30, 1957 (left) and bird's-eye view (right)

5.11 Alcoa Forecast Garden, paving details, ceramic tiles by Edith Heath (top two) and paving around the pool and fountain (bottom). Photo: Julius Shulman

finishes resulted in a kind of collage landscape. The living room patio was divided by sunken redwood strips into rectangles of varying size, making a geometric pattern that echoes the façade glass frame pattern and reminds one of a Mondrian painting. Also embedded in the pavement were varying stripes of red bricks, bright-white terrazzo pavers, an assortment of colored azulejo tiles, and river pebbles. Eckbo explained that bright and rich material in pavements "can make an elegant foil for certain dark, bold, solid, and rugged rock, plant or wood forms. The final refinement of terrazzo is mosaic paving, the contribution of a specialized artist."[82] Making good on this statement, he integrated colored tile clusters in copper, browns, and light blue by the ceramic artist Edith Heath (Figure 5.11). They harmonized with the colors of the aluminum structure once it was installed. Integration of art with spatial components is evident throughout the garden.

The Alcoa Forecast Garden, completed in 1959, added to the space's already richly textured and nuanced coloration. Eckbo's layout of the backyard as a central open area surrounded by a paved path prefigured the transformation of the garden. As he embarked on the design and integration of the aluminum products, Eckbo subjected the material to performance and maintenance measures, testing it for structural strength, fabrication techniques, privacy, shade, and climate control. The aesthetic treatment of the aluminum was akin to that of the planting and paving, using the material for texture, shadow, light, transparency, and color.[83] The variety of aluminum elements—from rods to trim solid sheets

5.12 Colorful anodized aluminum in Heller Hostessware Colorama tumblers, sherbet dishes, and pitcher, ca. 1950, cat. 4–49 (top). Alcoa Forecast Garden, aluminum details in garden structures (bottom)

153

5.13 Alcoa aluminum products promotional brochure, 1957. Photo: Mira Engler

and meshes of varying perforation shapes and densities and combinations thereof—and of textural and color finishes presented an unprecedented design challenge and opportunity (Figure 5.12). The products both called for and enabled Eckbo to create distinct structures, each with its own character, enclosure, and transparency.

Despite the variety of aluminum finishes and anodized rainbow colors available, Eckbo restricted the products to shades that resonated with landscape colors: anodized and finished in metallic shades, the three aluminum structures in the garden were gold-yellow, bronze-brown, copper, and silver, as specified in Alcoa's aluminum products promotional brochure (Figure 5.13). The first structure, a sunbreak over the two patios set in a wooden framework of posts and beams painted white to match the house, was made of perforated mesh and finished in "architectural brown" (#4020).[84] Four sections of the canopy were crowned with six pyramid modules made of rods and filled with "Egyptian" dimpled sheets anodized in gold on two sides, leaving the other sides open. Under the sunbreak, two vertical screens created three spaces. The first screen, made of mesh like the canopy, was finished in "architectural brown"; its panel modules set in alternating directions were in bronze, cooper, and brown shades. The screen afforded a view of the planting from the living room but blocked the view from the studio patio into the living room and terrace. The second screen, enclosing the studio patio, was made of vertical wooden posts and aluminum channels with varied profiles and transparencies of vertical bronze and brown minimesh planks and gold or yellow smooth sheets. It was the brightest element in the garden.

The second garden structure, a free-standing, ripple-roofed pavilion across the garden lawn, was made of a redwood frame stained dark brown to avoid competition with the splashy silver silhouettes of the mesh panels bent in different curvatures. Both the brown stain and roof form blend with the thickly planted slope behind. Two vertical aluminum screens, one at the rear of the pergola (the only remaining original aluminum element) and a freestanding panel set before the pavilion, were made of woven-like, layered aluminum grids of varied profiles and apertures and finished in architectural brown and bright gold, respectively. The front screen was conspicuously brighter.

The third aluminum structure, an origami-like, folded, flower-shaped fountain, was the focal point of the garden. Fabricated of alloyed plates it was baked in an enamel finish of an unspecified silver tint that registers as teal-silver in several photographs (Figure 5.14). The abstract fountain seems incongruously decorative. Considering Eckbo's disdain of flowers, it may have served as a counterpoint or tribute to the minor role of flowers in his garden. Its color harmonized with the silver waves of the pavilion roof and the dark plants and wood frame but clashed with the bronze and gold of the front screen.

The structures were exposed and visually prominent. The aluminum's heat storage prevented vines from growing over the structures. Although the surface textures reduced reflectivity, except in the smooth planks of the office patio fence screen, the natural light filtering through and bouncing off the sunbreak and screens introduced a new effect to garden design.[85] Eckbo seized the opportunity to bring sparkle and shadow patterns into the garden. The sunbreak pyramids enabled a view of the sky from certain angles and cast sharp geometric shadow patterns on the ground and vertical screens, adding to the layering effect of the already richly textured space. Some contrast was a welcome quality in Eckbo's design, but the new aluminum structures may have been too conspicuous in the landscape and made Eckbo uneasy. An announcement of the completion of the garden by the Alcoa aluminum company described the design as "a composition of standard aluminum shapes, textures, and *colors blended with the beauty of nature's palette* [italics added]"[86] (Figure 5.15).

Alcoa publicized the garden through receptions, publications, and even a weekly television program, "Alcoa Presents," on the ABC network.[87] The publicity sent to newspapers and magazines throughout the country featured the photographs by Julius Shulman,[88] who focused on three aspects to create a powerful sense of space and time: balance of light, camera position, and picture frame. To accommodate the diverse publishing venues and their audiences— product catalogues, lifestyle magazines, professional design magazines, newspapers—Shulman shot the garden in both black and white and color, in close-ups and wide-angles, and with and without people. The aluminum structures, the central focus of the marketing agenda, and their atmosphere were the focus in lifestyle magazines, while space, composition, and detail design served landscape design magazine readers. All the photographs capture the combination

5.14 Alcoa Forecast Garden, fountain and pool, 1957. Photo: Julius Shulman

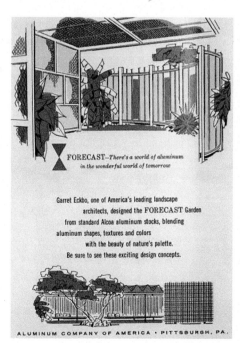

5.15 Announcement for the Forecast Garden on "Alcoa Presents," ca. August 1960

5.16 Alcoa Forecast Garden, view from under the sun break structure looking toward the living room, 1957. Photo: Julius Shulman. © J. Paul Getty Trust. Getty Research Institute, Los Angeles (2004.R.10)

of aluminum and plants and the integration of architecture and landscape. Shulman positioned the camera in one space to frame and look through it into the next space, to make the garden look larger than it really was. Shots, at times from an elevated position, captured the flow, expansion, and contraction of space under the canopies, between the screens, and through the garden rooms, showing multiple frames within the photograph frame.

The widely published photograph shot under the sunbreak, looking from the living room patio toward the studio patio, was taken both with and without people (see Figure 5.6). Seeing spaces populated with people or furniture was desirable for a lay audience, and Shulman used mostly women from Eckbo's family and office in the scenes. One photo showed two women conversing, one seated, the other standing, the scene enlivened by their red and blue clothes, which complemented the golden colors of the fence. In the opposite direction, elevated and from outside the enclosed studio patio, he photographed a young woman sitting on a floor cushion and reading, with several domestic accessories on the side (Figure 5.16). He also featured contemplative scenes, creating a quiet paradisical atmosphere for domestic life in the lush atmosphere of a garden (a classic consumerist device). In contrast, shots of the fountain against the darker background of the shaded patios under the sunbreak let the fountain shine with the bright, light-colored metal and water jets reflecting the sun. Shulman photographed the garden at different times of the day to capture the diverse material and spatial effects under different lighting conditions. His photos higlighted the spectacular range of golden, bronze, and copper colors of the screens and canopies and the textural and light and shadow patterns on the ground.

In its manufactured tinted forms, materials, textures, and light effects, the ALCOA Forecast Garden represented the color palette, production template, and consumerist delivery tactics of American modern residential landscape design. In the 1960s Eckbo applied his early design experiments in residential gardens and suburban planning to urban shopping centers and corporate landscapes. Among these projects was Union Bank Square.

Union Bank Square, Connecticut General Life Insurance Company, Los Angeles, California, USA, 1964–8

Initially called Bunker Hill Square, Union Bank Square sits at the foot of the Union Bank of California Tower on South Figueroa Street. The first component of Los Angeles's modern downtown business district, it was one of many urban renewal projects across the country featuring giant corporate plazas amid once thriving downtown streets. The trend followed suburban expansion, the rise of the automobile and shopping malls, and, subsequently, decaying downtowns.[89]

Five years after the completion of their Union Bank Square project, Eckbo, Dean, Austin and Williams described the three-acre plaza as a space of "dignified quality" that, despite its location over a two-story parking garage flanked by the Harbor Freeway, "presents a remarkable sense of enclosure [with a] water feature of unusual form, … bridge, sculpture, 10' concrete planters, [and] lush peripheral planting"[90] (Figure 5.17). Eckbo's primary design principles of space making and enclosure atop a concrete roof were a challenge solved by "plant material" in raised beds and high planters. No structures were involved in this vast plaza design. It was a meticulously ordered landscape of gray and white concrete paving and mostly green plants, punctuated by a central reflective body of water—a vivid example of Eckbo's rational, practical, and aesthetic sensibilities, especially his pursuit of modern visual and spatial design vocabulary through a mostly achromatic palette.

The square was designed to be experienced by pedestrians at eye level, used for lunch breaks and socializing, and viewed from the windows of the bank tower and surrounding high-rises, notably the Bonaventure Hotel across the street (Figure 5.18). Enclosure and shade were paramount to providing a restful oasis amid the downtown frenzy. The plaza was, therefore, designed as an urban forest. Eckbo described it simply as "[a] grove of boxed trees in a sea of concrete, grass and water." [91] He conceived the plan as an abstract composition that "must be developed in relation to the real existing landscape context and to the willful mobility of the human observer."[92] The main organizing system for the ground plane is a symmetry-defying grid that echoes the urban context and follows the structural grid column under the plaza. The southern part, on three sides of the tower, mirrors the tower's gridded façade, extending the rhythm of its vertical columns so that it looks as if the building is grounded in and rises directly from the ground plane grid. The northern part,

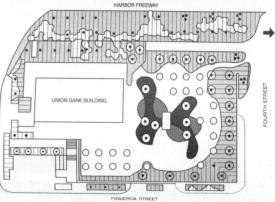

5.17 . View of the square from Hotel Buena Ventura, 2020 (top). Photo: Mira Engler. Eckbo, Dean, Austin, Williams, site plan, Union Bank Square, Los Angeles, 1968 (bottom)

5.18 Photograph looking down on the plaza from Union Bank tower, ca. 1968

157

delineated by a square grid, is dedicated to the square's central open space. An overlay of circles and biomorphic forms on the grid are typical of Eckbo's layered composition, done for visual interest and dynamic movement.

Reliance on trees to build up the formal composition of the flat roof into the third dimension of space was paramount. Thus, three-foot high concrete cylindrical planters, suitable for medium-size trees, are located at intersecting grid lines governed by the structural system of the parking garage. The space is animated by low curvilinear retaining concrete walls that form planting beds and water basins, the gentle topographic undulation of the lawn, and a twisting bridge that flows over a central water and lawn feature. Movement is both grand and sinuous, with views across the freeway and urban vistas. At eye level, the circular planters and the biomorphic island at the center compel a meandering movement counter to the orthogonal gridded paving and planter layout, creating a kind of cinematic parallax experience. The circular and sinuous forms liberate the controlled order of the grid.

Eckbo's affinity for concrete and its functional and versatile material opportunities is on display. The rich textural palette—pebbly concrete floor, deep vertical scores on the cylindrical planters, and smooth curving concrete walls around the shallow pool, grass area, and peripheral beds—offset the utterly uniform concrete material. The grid lines, originally designed as brick stripes, were built with two-foot-wide exposed white aggregates embedded in cement, whitened with acids to contrast the square cells made of exposed gray aggregate mixed in gray concrete. The grid lines make conspicuous the perfect order and repetitive

rhythm across the plaza, creating a sense of calm and linking the design to spatial archetypes in garden design history, as seen in the gridded orchards in medieval courtyards in Moorish Córdoba and the 17th century Safavid royal gardens in Persia.[93]

The trees were organized in classic formation reinforced by seasonal color masses: a vivid, orange-red blaze, double-row allée of coral trees east of the building

5.19 Union Bank Square, model (top). Paving pattern from above in 2020 (bottom). Photo: Mira Engler

and another row west of the building, an evergreen ficus grove in the main square, and a purple-lavender double-row allée of jacaranda to the east and north of the square (Figure 5.19). Tree species were selected based on their capacity for climate control and, not least, color, to offset the roof's achromatic palette and gray urban hardscape.

Eckbo welcomed the coral and jacaranda blossoms as color masses to help define the formal and spatial composition. The ficus (*Ficus retusa*) in the core plaza remained green almost year-round, losing foliage only in a short winter season. The coral tree (*Erythrina caffra*) flanking the tower on both sides formed a dense shaded esplanade inflamed with coral-shaped flowers from late spring to early summer, when its leaves budded. In full blossom, the mature tree was a spectacular sight. Its large numbers of brilliant orange flower clusters in tight, radial patterns graced the naked trunks and twisted limbs. Successive seeds were also brilliant red. By summer the trees were covered with fresh-green leaves. The jacaranda blossoms created purple edge walls from late April, coinciding with the time when the red coral waned and purple took over through the late summer. The deciduous coral and jacaranda trees permitted the sun to enter the plaza during wintertime, when the intertwining branching system of the corals cast shadows on the pavement. The ficus grove kept the main plaza area cool and shaded most of the year.

In addition, the surface effects of the centerpiece fountain were significant. The shallow basins reflected the surrounding trees, built elements, buildings, and sky, creating a mirror effect and a sense of depth[94] (Figure 5.20).

5.20 Union Bank Square, the pool in 1978 (left top and bottom). The same views in 2020 (right top and bottom). Photos: Mira Engler

5.21 Original sketch of the proposed square under tree canopies, 1968 (top). General view, ca. 1970s (bottom)

Despite the intended color effects, photographic documentation of the spectacular flowering events and color effects is hard to come by. Photography was timed in late summer and fall, when the trees were not in bloom. Both color and black-and-white photographs show the square in its pristine green and white, a largely achromatic modern landscape that corresponded with the intended design, as shown in an original sketch of the proposed square that depicts a marvelously quiet and shady retreat from the busy downtown (Figure 5.21). The ficus canopies merged to create a green roof over the plaza, a quality that unfortunately was altered.[95] Photographs at the time of the completion of the project in 1958 (some by Kent Oppenheimer) and color slides from June 1978 and July 1987 (possibly taken by Eckbo) show the changes in the plaza over time.

Whatever the changes from the original drawings and over time, color in the square not only refrained from disrupting the space, it significantly reinforced it. In Union Bank Square Eckbo demonstrated the integration of spatial color in modern landscape design.

* * *

Eckbo eschewed pure color in the modern landscape, where space and function took precedent. An alliance with architecture and attention to emergent ecological and social sciences provided him with the central tenets for color design. He used his writings to shape the profession's resolve to utilize subdued colored material that blended with landscape colors and effects. But in 1969 he wrote: "Color brings the world to life for us, makes it real and positive, lively or quiet, exhilarating or depressing."[96] Again, as mentioned above, his attitude toward color was not monolithic or unchanging.

Eckbo endorsed many architects and only a few landscape architects. To a greater extent than his forerunner, Thomas Church, he was deeply taken by the work of Roberto Burle Marx, the subject of the next chapter. Traveling to Brazil for a speaking engagement in 1975, Eckbo visited a couple of Burle Marx's projects in Rio and was invited to his home, garden, and nursery, which he described as "the great event of my visit to Rio."[97] But in his trip diary, Eckbo overlooked the botanical abundance and poetic craftsmanship in Burle Marx's gardens and grand plant collection. Instead, he singled out the outdoor reception space and shade garden structure by the architects Rubem Breitman and Haroldo Barroso Beltrão. Eckbo's affinity for architectonic spaces trumped all other garden impressions. He and Burle Marx, two great modern landscape architects, could not have been more different.

Notes

1. Eckbo, *Landscape for Living*, 1950, 95, 104.

2. Eckbo, "Pilgrim's Progress," 1993, 210.

3. Eckbo worked at Church's office for two weeks in 1939. He considered Church to be the last great traditional and first great modern designer.

4. Freeman, *Landscape Design*, 1948, 5.

5. During his private practice from 1940–90, Eckbo partnered with Edward Williams 1940–79, Robert Royston (1946–58), Francis Dean 1958–79, and Donald Austin (1964–79). From 1979 through 1990 he formed a series of small practices.

6. Popular magazines where Eckbo was published were *Sunset*, *The Californian*, *House Beautiful*, and *House and Garden*; examples of professional magazines were *Pencil Points*, *Architectural Record*, *Landscape Architecture*, and *Art and Design*.

7. On the events that shaped Eckbo's social consciousness, see Walker and Simo, "Beyond the American (or California) Dream," 1994, 116. See also Treib and Imbert, *Garrett Eckbo: Modern Gardens for Living*, 1997.

8. Posters, billboards, fabrics, and consumer products created by the German Bauhaus all used a minimalist palette of solid color planes, in which primaries and neutral colors dominated. The Bauhaus predilection for flat primaries paired with white and black spread after the immigration of many of its leaders to the United States, including Piet Mondrian, to whom several of Eckbo's outdoor structures can be traced.

9. Manferdini and Griggs, "Color Corrections," 2020.

10. Tunnard, *Gardens in the Modern Landscape*, 1938, 108–17. Eckbo was familiar with Tunnard's 1937 *Architectural Review* essays (compiled in his 1938 book). Tunnard was a lecturer at Harvard in 1949 after Eckbo had graduated, but the two became friends and inspired each other.

11. Ibid., 109.

12. Ibid, 111.

13. Ibid.

14. Eckbo considered the Japanese garden the most developed in the world for its restrictive range of green hues, allowing only sparse and brief seasonal bursts of color.

15. Eckbo, *Landscape for Living*, 1950, 66, 100.

16. Ibid., 77.

17. Imbert, "Of Gardens and Houses as Places to Live," 1995, 114–37.

18. Eckbo, *Landscape for Living*, 1950, 104.

19. Ibid., 126, 256.

20. Eckbo, "The Esthetics of Planting," 1948.

21. Eckbo, *Landscape for Living*, 1950, 96.

22. Ibid., 100.

23. Ibid., 103.

24. Ibid., 95.

25. Eckbo, *The Landscape We See*, 1969, 145.

26. Ibid., 51.

27. Scallon, "Now Is the Time and This Is the House … to Build," 1947, 49.

28. Eckbo mentioned Burle Marx four times in *Landscape for Living*, 1950, 4, 35, 102, 109.

29. Eckbo, *Landscape for Living*, 1950, 1.

30 Eckbo, *Landscape We See*, 1969, 147. Eckbo cited the plant ecologists John Weaver and Frederic Clements when expounding on the appearance of seemingly disorderly plant patterns in nature; Eckbo, *Landscape for Living*, 1950, 36.

31 Eckbo, *Landscape for Living*, 1950, 100–1. Eckbo referenced Van Dyke's book, *Nature for Its Own Sake*, 1898.

32 Ibid., 100. Eckbo made similar observations regarding "zonal texture."

33 Eckbo produced a list of foliage color variations in one California region alone: 190 gray, 36 silver or gray and gray-green, 167 light green, 43 yellow and green, 663 medium green, 31 red and green, 228 dark green, and 68 purple-red. Eckbo, *Landscape We See*, 1969, 145.

34 Eckbo, *Landscape for Living*, 1950, 101.

35 Ibid., 36, 114. Eckbo referenced Josias Braun-Blanquet's *Plant Sociology* (1932).

36 Eckbo, *Landscape We See*, 1969, 201.

37 Eckbo, *Landscape for Living*, 1950, 35.

38 Ibid., 101.

39 Ibid., 63.

40 Eckbo, "Richard Neutra on Building," 1951, 41. Neutra, *Richard Neutra on Building*, 1951.

41 Lavin, "Richard Neutra and the Psychology of the American Spectator," 2000, 61; Lavin, "Open the Box," 1999, 18.

42 Eckbo, *Landscape We See*, 1969, 196–7. Eckbo explored the work of the Hungarian-born British architect Ernő Goldfinger.

43 Lavin, "Richard Neutra," 2000, 62.

44 Eckbo worked tirelessly to prove that concrete was neither dull nor dead but a rich palette for designers' plastic manipulation in both residential and urban projects.

45 Eckbo, *Landscape for Living*, 1950, 76.

46 Ibid., 126.

47 Ibid., 213.

48 Ibid. Munsell's color system was adopted by the US Department of Agriculture as the official color system for soil research in the 1930s; and László Moholy-Nagy and György Kepes also wrote extensively about color in art and design. Moholy-Nagy, *Vision in Motion*, 1947; Kepes, *Language of Vision*, 1944.

49 Harris, "Making Your Private World Modern," 2002, 200.

50 For the development and properties of aluminum, see Nichols, "Aluminum by Design, Jewelry to Jets," 2000, 16–17.

51 Vogel, "Aluminum: A Competitive Material," 2000, 149.

52 For a complete account of the use of aluminum in Eckbo's work, see Treib, *The Donnell and Eckbo Gardens*, 2005, 137–41.

53 Ibid., 175.

54 Ibid., 137.

55 Ibid., 127.

56 Eckbo, "Outdoors and In," 1941, 424.

57 Simonds, *Landscape Architecture*, 1961, 91.

58 Eckbo, *Landscape for Living*, 1950, 253. See Eckbo's early work on migrant worker and social housing in Imbert, "The Art of Social Landscape Design," 1997.

59 Scallon, "Now Is the Time," 1947, 50.

[60] Ibid., 191–2.

[61] Braham, "Color, Power, Velocity," 2010, 50.

[62] Harris, "Private World," 2002, 200.

[63] Rose, *Creative Gardens*, 1958, 36, 65, 97.

[64] Eckbo, *The Art of Home Landscaping*, 1956, 24.

[65] Ibid., 205.

[66] Ibid., 186.

[67] Ibid., 125, 123.

[68] Ibid., 211; and Eckbo, *Landscape for Living*, 1950, 200.

[69] This and the next quotation are from Eckbo, *Landscape for Living*, 1950, 126 and 103.

[70] Eckbo, *Landscape We See*, 1969, 201.

[71] For an extensive discussion of the axon in landscape architecture, see Imbert, "Skewed Realities," 2008.

[72] Ibid., 125. A modified axonometry, called exploded axonometry, was another useful working tool for diagrams showing the modular assembly of structural garden parts. See Rose, *Creative Gardens*, 1958, 25.

[73] Imbert, "Skewed Realities," 2008, 127–9.

[74] Of smaller though not insignificant dissemination, television shows and exhibitions showcased modernist landscape design.

[75] A similar technique called "serial vision" by the illustrator Gordon Cullen was featured extensively in the *Architectural Review* from 1948 onward. See Engler, *Cut and Paste*, 2015, 140–8.

[76] Shulman, "A Vignette," 1996, 181. Shulman invited Eckbo to design his private garden.

[77] Treib, *Donnell and Eckbo*, 2005, 99; Dominick, "Union Bank of California Plaza," 2015; Treib, "Church, Eckbo, Halprin, and the Modern Urban Landscape," 2004, 56.

[78] The author visited the garden in December 2020. Access to Eckbo's archive at the University of California in Berkeley was limited because of Covid-19 closures.

[79] Nichols, "Aluminum by Design, Jewelry to Jets," 2000, 48. Not meant to last forever, the Alcoa Garden died out within 20 years.

[80] The lot was planted as part of a master plan Eckbo prepared for the 67 lots of Wonderland Park community. See Treib, *Donnell and Eckbo*, 2005, 98–179.

[81] For the 1954 planting plan, see Treib, *Donnell and Eckbo*, 2005, 120.

[82] Eckbo, *Landscape for Living*, 1950, 119.

[83] Imbert, "Social Landscape," 1997, 171.

[84] Aluminum material specifications and color codes are from the Alcoa catalogue of products. For a detailed material description and catalogue image, see Treib, *Donnell and Eckbo*, 2005, 171–3.

[85] But in a letter to the owner of the property almost 30 years later, Eckbo refuted this assertion, describing the original effect of the new aluminum as "quite bright." Although he told the owner that "Alcoa could also advise … on how to refresh the finish on all the aluminum," he observed that "[i]t may be that the weathered finish blends more easily to the garden" (letter dated November 26, 1987, from Eckbo to the then former California governor Jerry Brown, the property owner at the time; courtesy of the current owner of the property, Lynne Goodhill).

[86] Alcoa, promotional brochure. Undated.

[87] For the extensive publicity the garden generated, see Treib, *Donnell and Eckbo*, 2005, 169–80.

[88] Ibid.

[89] The Union Bank of California Tower was designed by the firms Harrison & Abramowitz of New York and A. C. Martin and Associates of Los Angeles. For the history of Bunker Hill, see Dominick, "Union Bank of California Plaza," 2015, 8–9. For the urban design background, see Treib, "Church, Eckbo," 2004, 59.

[90] Eckbo, Dean, Austin and Williams, "Banker Hill Urban Renewal Project Master Tree Plan," UC Berkeley archive.

[91] Eckbo, *People in a Landscape*, 1998, 66.

[92] Eckbo, *Landscape We See*, 1969, 202.

[93] Dominick, "Union Bank of California Plaza," 2015, 14.

[94] Ibid., 5. Sometime between 1978 and 1987, the water basins were painted bright blue, typical of swimming pools, dramatically reducing the reflective effect of the water and erasing the quiet atmosphere produced by its darker hues.

[95] Today, the ficus trees are severely trimmed. Of the coral allée only the name remained. They were removed to make space for a new courtyard adjacent to a remodeled conference pavilion called "The Coral Tree Court & Pavilion." The author visited Union Bank Square December 14–18, 2020. For historic photographs, see Dominick, "Union Bank of California Plaza," 2015, 25.

[96] Eckbo, *Landscape We See*, 1969, 196.

[97] Eckbo, *Fifteen Days in Brazil*, 1975.

References

Braham, William W. "Color, Power, Velocity." In *New Geographies 3: Urbanisms of Color*, ed. by Gareth Doherty, 46–53. Boston, MA: Harvard University Press, 2010.

Braun-Blanquet, Josias. *Plant Sociology*. New York: McGraw Hill Book Company, 1932.

Dominick, Hannah. "Union Bank of California Plaza – Historic American Landscapes Survey HALS No. CA-119, July 30, 2015." Washington: National Park Service.

Eckbo, Garrett. "Outdoors and In: Gardens as Living Space." *Magazine of Art* 34, no. 8 (October 1941): 422–7.

Eckbo, Garrett. "The Esthetics of Planting." In *Landscape Design* exhibition catalogue, 17–18. San Francisco Museum of Art, 1948.

Eckbo, Garrett. *Landscape for Living*. New York: F. W. Dodge Co., 1950.

Eckbo, Garrett. "Richard Neutra on Building: Mystery and Realities of the Site." *Landscape Architecture* 42, no. 1 (October 1951): 41–2.

Eckbo, Garrett. *The Art of Home Landscaping*. New York: McGraw-Hill Book, 1956.

Eckbo, Garrett. *The Landscape We See*. New York: McGraw-Hill, 1969.

Eckbo, Garrett. *Fifteen Days in Brazil*. San Francisco: G. Eckbo, Berkeley, 1975.

Eckbo, Garrett. *People in a Landscape*. Upper Saddle River, NJ: Prentice Hall, 1998.

Eckbo, Garrett. "Pilgrim's Progress." In *Modern Landscape Architecture: A Critical Review*, ed. by Marc Treib, 206–19. Cambridge, MA: MIT Press, 1993.

Engler, Mira. *Cut and Paste Urban Landscape: The Work of Gordon Cullen*. London: Routledge, 2015.

Freeman, Richard B., ed. *Landscape Design*, exhibition catalogue. San Francisco Museum of Art, 1948.

Harris, Dianne. "Making Your Private World Modern: Landscape Architecture and House Beautiful, 1945–1965." In *The Architecture of Landscape 1940–1960*, ed. by Marc Treib, 181–205. Philadelphia: University of Pennsylvania Press, 2002.

Imbert, Dorothée. "Of Gardens and Houses as Places to Live: Thomas Church and William Wurster." In *An Everyday Modernism: The Houses of William Wurster*, ed. by Marc Treib, 114–37. Berkeley: University of California Press, 1995.

Imbert, Dorothée. "The Art of Social Landscape Design." In *Garrett Eckbo: Modern Landscapes for Living*, 106–77. Berkeley: University of California Press, 1997.

Imbert, Dorothée. "Skewed Realities: The Garden and the Axonometric Drawings." In *Representing Landscape Architecture*, ed. by Marc Treib, 124–39. New York: Taylor & Francis, 2008.

Kepes, György. *Language of Vision*. Chicago: Paul Theobald, 1944.

Lavin, Sylvia. "Open the Box: Richard Neutra and the Psychology of the Domestic Environment." *Assemblage* 40 (December 1999): 6–25.

Lavin, Sylvia. "Richard Neutra and the Psychology of the American Spectator." *Grey Room* 1 (Autumn 2000): 42–63.

Manferdini, Elena, and Christina Griggs. "Color Corrections." *Log* 49 (Summer 2020): 105–09.

Moholy-Nagy, László. *Vision in Motion*. Chicago: Paul Theobald, 1947.

Neutra, Richard. *Richard Neutra on Building: Mystery and Realities of the Site*. Scarsdale, NY: Morgan & Morgan, 1951.

Nichols, Sarah, ed. *Aluminum by Design*. Pittsburgh, PA: Carnegie Museum of Art, 2000.

Nichols, Sarah. "Aluminum by Design, Jewelry to Jets." In *Aluminum by Design*, 12–57. Pittsburgh, PA: Carnegie Museum of Art, 2000.

Rose, James C. *Creative Gardens*. New York: Reinhold Publishing Corporation, 1958.

Scallon, Virginia. "Now Is the Time and This Is the House … to Build." *The Californian* (July 1947): 48–51.

Shulman, Julius. "A Vignette." In *Garrett Eckbo: Modern Gardens for Living*, ed. by Marc Treib and Dorothée Imbert, 181. Berkeley: University of California Press, 1997.

Simonds, John Ormsbee. *Landscape Architecture: The Shaping of Man's Natural Environment*. New York: F. W. Dodge Corp., 1961.

Treib, Marc. "Church, Eckbo, Halprin, and the Modern Urban Landscape." In *Preserving Modern Landscape Architecture II: Making Postwar Landscapes Visible*, ed. by Charles A. Birnbaum, 56–65. Washington: Spacemaker Press, 2004.

Treib, Marc. *The Donnell and Eckbo Gardens: Modern Californian Masterworks*. San Francisco: William Stout Publishers, 2005.

Treib, Marc, and Dorothée Imbert, eds. *Garrett Eckbo: Modern Landscapes for Living*. Berkeley: University of California Press, 1997.

Tunnard, Christopher. *Gardens in the Modern Landscape*. London: Architectural Press, 1938.

Van Dyke, John C. *Nature for Its Own Sake*. New York: Charles Scribner's Sons, 1898.

Vogel, Craig. "Aluminum: A Competitive Material of Choice in the Design of New Products, 1950 to Present." In *Aluminum by Design*, ed. by Sarah Nichols, 140–65. Pittsburgh, PA: Carnegie Museum of Art, 2000.

Walker, Peter, and Melanie Simo, eds. "Beyond the American (or California) Dream." In *Invisible Gardens: The Search for Modernism in the American Landscape*, 116–42. Cambridge, MA: MIT Press, 1994.

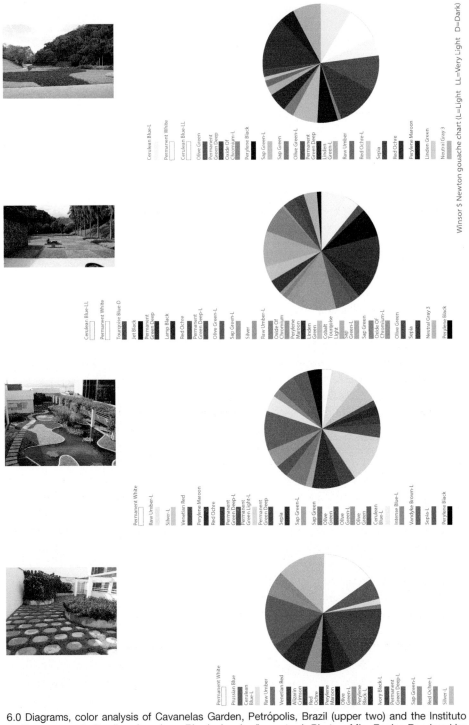

6.0 Diagrams, color analysis of Cavanelas Garden, Petrópolis, Brazil (upper two) and the Instituto de Resseguros do Brasil roof gardens, Rio de Janeiro (lower two). Photos: Mira Engler. Rendered by Asif Khan

(Unless noted otherwise, projects, drawings, and paintings in Chapter 6 are by Robert Burle Marx; photographs are by Mira Engler, May 2019.)

6

Symphony of Color
Tropical Saturation,
Roberto Burle Marx (1909–94)

If I am asked what the most important natural factor in the design of a garden is, I must say: it is light.
Gareth Doherty, *Roberto Burle Marx Lectures, Landscape as Art and Urbanism*, 2018, 108

Climbing the mountains, after traveling over extensive grasslands, I came across a grayish spot of rocks and as I came closer a completely new world opened up to me. An extraordinary society seemed to have been created to form a complete reciprocal harmony. The strong cadmium yellow of the lichen and the Laelia flava *(an orchid) contrasted with the deep violet of the Quaresma trees, harmonizing with the Venetian red of the dorsal side of the leaves of the Mimosa calodendron, … All of this polychrome is seated on a backdrop where form, rhythm, and color are in harmony, emphasizing at each season the character of a certain flowering. Nothing was isolated; it was an orchestra of color … One could speak, even, of a battle of color in which one color would dominate at a particular season, supported by a background whose forms, rhythms, and colors enhanced those of the plants in a very particular way.*
Gareth Doherty, *Roberto Burle Marx Lectures, Landscape as Art and Urbanism*, 2018, 108-9

No landscape architect, not even the quintessential landscape colorist Gertrude Jekyll, felt color as viscerally as the modern Brazilian landscape architect Roberto Burle Marx. His observation of the flora in the interior grasslands of northeastern Brazil, cited above, underscores his instinctual and poetic response to color and infers the centrality of color in his landscape art. "[T]he successful use of color," he once noted, "is one of the most difficult things in the world."[1] His writings are filled with similar enthusiastic observations on form and color, based on numerous plant-hunting expeditions to study Brazil's landscapes, collect seeds, and discover the world's wonders.

Burle Marx's gut impression and imagistic marvel of color and light brought him to a point of ecstasy. His gaze on nature was that of an artist struck by the beauty of the orchestral interplay of forms and colors. The flux he saw in nature fascinated him: "This instability is precisely one of the great secrets of nature, which never tires us and is constantly renewed by the effect of light, rain, wind, and shadows, which shape new forms."[2] He transposed these experiences to his landscapes, creating ever-renewing gardens.

Trained as both a vocalist and a painter, Burle Marx composed his gardens and urban landscapes as chromatic performances. Unlike his contemporaries, he had no preferred color palette, only principles. He drew from an extensive range of bold and muted colors to create tonal contrasts throughout a composition. The opposite of Eckbo, for whom color was a mere detail, color was Burle Marx's primary design element. Like Jekyll, he used plants as paint on canvas, but unlike her, he avoided mixing colors and prescribed harmonies. Like Guevrekian, he joined color and form and used color "en masse" and combined avant-garde and traditional aesthetics, but unlike him, Burle Marx had a prolific knowledge of plants and highlighted their distinct individual qualities.

Burle Marx blurred the line between art and nature and unequivocally sided with art. In his 1962 lecture "The Gardens as a Form of Art" he posited: "A garden should be … a work of art—like painting, sculpture, tapestry, or a symphony."[3] Nature was "a marvelously unruly, incoherent object that needs to be ordered and adjusted before she can lay claim to status in artistic circles."[4] His landscapes therefore walked the fine line of taming and orchestrating nature while fostering its exuberance and mutability. They display two interdependent contrasting tendencies: permanence, a fixed and coherent formal composition, on the one hand, and contingency, ephemeral light, and color effects, on the other.[5] Color, texture, volume, and form were the chief garden elements; plant knowledge was a requisite.

Born in Recife, Pernambuco, Brazil, to parents of German-Jewish and Portuguese origins and well connected to high society and art circles, Burle Marx moved with his family and grew up on a farm in Leme, Rio de Janeiro, where his love of plants, art, and music was nurtured. He received formal education in music in Berlin (1928–30), followed by painting at the National School of Fine Arts in Rio. These vocations were capped with an informal study of botany, which became a lifelong passion in his search of new material for his art. In over six decades of practice, from 1932 to his death in 1994, Burle Marx completed more than 2000 private and public projects on three continents, maintaining an office in Rio with his chief partner, Haruyoshi Ono, and a residence-studio and nursery in his Santo Antônio da Bica estate, known as Sítio Roberto Burle Marx, outside Rio in Barra de Guaratiba.[6] Simultaneously experimenting with an extensive range of media—sculpture, printmaking, tile-mosaic, murals, tapestry, fabric design, set and costume design, jewelry, and landscape architecture, among others—his thoughts on art, music, and ecology intertwined.

Burle Marx did not enjoy writing. However, he gave many interviews, talks, and lectures and wrote 18 environmental manifestos (called "depositions") during his tenure on a federal advisory council on the environment (1967–74).[7] His work should be understood in the context of the emerging modern national identity movement, called variably "Pau-Brazil" and *brasilidade*. It was given expression through his embrace of the richness and contradictions of Brazilian culture, architecture, and botanical diversity, and rejection of the colonial cast of Brazil as an example of exotic primitivism (the country was named by colonists in the 16th century after the glowing ember-red pigment inside the trunk of the *Paubrasilia echinata*). Burle Marx turned colonial exploitation on its head and celebrated the brilliant colors of Brazil's native plants and culture. His sensuous and colorful drawings were a fitting idiom of the intense color of local flora and fauna and the starkness of vernacular art and craft.

Burle Marx's inclusion of opposites—local and universal, traditional and modern, past and present, and native and exotic—produced a hybrid landscape design that has been called "tropical modernism."[8] Hybrid plants, artificial ecologies, bricolage artifacts, and a symphony of color were active agents in his quest for a Brazilian national and regional landscape identity.

Illumination and Regional Identity

The modern concept of regionalism provided Burle Marx with a framework to study regional landscape character—landform, flora, climate, color, and light. The expression of light in a landscape was of utmost importance.[9] Burle Marx described the impact of the dynamic world of light color in the paintings of Van Gogh, which he had seen in a Berlin exhibition: "It was a great shock. It was so brutal. I couldn't forget. ... I got a stroke, an indigestion. It took me a very long time to assimilate."[10]

Light triggered his instincts and thoughts in myriad ways. Physically, light was primal, a life-giving element that fed vegetal growth and made seeing possible. Scientifically, light shaped the characteristics of flora. Aesthetically, light was mysterious, illuminating, a divine phenomenon. Artistically, it was raw material he could shape. To design with light "requires an understanding of the critical difference between pigment color and light color":[11] in painting or sculpture pigment color is static, whereas in the garden, light color is constantly remade by changing lighting.

Burle Marx worked with light to unleash its performative quality and mystique. He marveled at the infinite variations constantly produced and its continual movement that makes landscape come alive. He used light as an agent to produce fortuitous effects and wonder in the garden, while recognizing its challenges:

> Light is a thing that cannot be calculated, cannot be contrived. The use of light, when well thought-out, can bring surprising results. It is the constant change, the capriciousness, of light that makes the landscape architect's work so difficult and satisfying.[12]

Although natural light could not be controlled, the paths of sunlight and moonlight and the ways they registered on and interacted with surfaces, textures, and volumes could be studied and harnessed to illuminate and amplify specific landscape qualities. Lines and forms could be blurred or made sharper, space enlarged, and colors subdued or intensified:

> A tree sunlit from above will look different in the evening, warmed and softened by the setting sun, which lights only the bark and the under surface of the leaves. Lit from the front, trees can seem solid, even sullen; with the sun behind them, they are light and translucent, elegant and witty. A flower, a red peony or a rose, pale at midday, will glow and burn with an inner life in the long, soft light of a northern evening. Light never repeats itself.[13]

Hence, in designing middle- and backgrounds Burle Marx played out front-lit and back-lit drama. Sunlit plant colors that might otherwise go unnoticed became points of interest, while structures and artifacts were accentuated and animated by shadows.

Burle Marx's lavish color displays and light effects were linked to his penchant for the theatrical and gaiety.[14] He often referred to the performative dimension of light in the landscape in theatrical terms, drawing on his experience in set and costume design for theater and ballet performances: "In the theater, the possibilities of lighting have been explored to the utmost: light is controlled, intensified, directed in accordance with the mood suggested by the play."[15] He similarly choreographed the movement of sunlight on plants and artifacts in the garden, like a spotlight following the actors on stage, to elicit a certain mood, controlling its intensity and focus, "showing the nervures and transparencies of the leaves; a tree with an odd form; the texture of a trunk; ... or showing the blossoming of certain plants, ... in rhythmic movements."[16] Thus the lighting spectacle he produced at the Fazenda Vargem Grande, a garden designed for Clemente Gomes in Areias, near São Paulo (1979), featured plants, water, and minerals framed,

6.1 Fazenda Vargem Grande garden, Areias, near São Paulo, 1979

sequenced, and juxtaposed against foregrounds and backgrounds in constantly changing daylight (Figure 6.1).[17]

Burle Marx lamented the failure of landscape architects to see the potential of artificial illumination at night beyond the practical safety consideration of lighting.[18] He drew attention to Japanese garden designers who directed the moonlight on to cherry trees to project shadows on to white sand, and to the use, throughout history and cultures, of candles and fire rituals to engender a feeling of reverence and mystery.

He was also inspired by the new aesthetic possibilities created by neon signs, advertising posters, even traffic lights and parkway lighting. And he was riveted by reflections and light effects on water. In Ibirapuera Park, an unrealized project for the Civic Center square of Curitiba, São Paulo (1953), he illuminated the space with soft light from above and used low, bright spotlights to illuminate high waterjets sequentially and intensely, creating multiple diffractions, reflections, and refractions on the water column (Figure 6.2). Water, itself a versatile material, was sculpted into forms and rhythms and brought life to his gardens with light and movement.

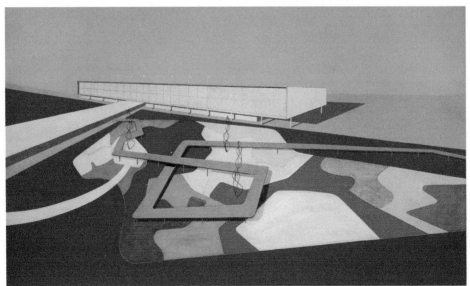

6.2 Ibirapuera Park, Civic Center Square of Curitiba, unrealized project, São Paulo, 1953. Institute Burle Marx

170

Light was not only an aesthetic phenomenon: together with color, it resonated regional identity, and the two became Burle Marx's expressions of the tropics.[19] He wrote that:

> Light is the master touch of nature that suits her colors to her light. In the Brazilian summer, when the light is blue and brilliant, we find flowering together Acacia and the Tibouchina, rich yellow and deep purples, suspended in a sea of saturated greens so intense they are almost black.[20]

Rooting his work in the tropics, therefore, he selected intense plant colors that were not washed out by the strong, blue light.

The region's immense variety of brightly colored birds, insects, and plants found their way into Burle Marx's chromatic schemes. He studied the evolution and function of flora and fauna colors for attraction, communication, and display of vigor, and, convinced that color was linked to plant survival, observed the colors of animals and plants relative to their ambient light environment.[21] In green-dominated forests, environments produced by a combination of yellow and blue light with no ambient red, the brightness and contrast of white, red, orange, yellow, and pink coloration maximize conspicuousness (Figure 6.3).[22] Flowers, such as orchids, found in abundance only in favored spots produce a marked effect of color for a short duration amid the vast masses of green foliage surrounding them. Conversely, dark colors, such as blues and purples, stand out in open landscapes. To be conspicuous in forests, where the light level is diffused by canopies and green dominates, requires brightness and boldly contrasting color, unlike in an open savannah.

6.3 Intense regional colors of the *Ramphastos dicolorus* (Tucano de bico verde) at Fazenda Vargem Grande (top) and *Heliconia* var. at Sítio, Rio de Janeiro (bottom)

The light environment is based on the angle of the light, weather conditions, and time of day. Burle Marx appreciated that radiance and refraction from atmospheric phenomena modify and add intricacy to light quality and affect color contrast:

> Clouds, rain, and wind can change the appearance of a garden. … Atmospheric conditions change surface color into a thousand shades, creating transparencies in the foliage or emphasizing the splendor of blossoming. Light creates variable centers of interest by projecting the shadow of the clouds brought by the wind, and drawing focus to now one and now another detail of the landscape we are contemplating.[23]

Understanding the expression and perception of color and the conditions that render it conspicuous relative to its light environment shaped Burle Marx's choices of color, and visibility through contrast became his chief color principle. He applied this principle to contrasts between plant groups and between the garden and its surrounding landscape, recognizing that for color contrast to be perceptible requires the presence of a fixed and clear formal composition.

Composition: Symphony of Color

While Burle Marx used the theater to describe light in the landscape, he used music to delineate color. The theater gave light presence, music gave color structure. His approach to landscape design was an orchestration or composition of color: "With a garden, one will always know if one is to compose a symphony or a simple motet."[24] As a vocalist and music devotee he was quite familiar with musical concepts. But to conceive gardens in terms of musical composition also required a keen painterly eye. Burle Marx's descriptions of nature and gardens are replete with the lexicon of music—words such as note, key, tone, chord, texture, volume, and, of course, composition.[25] He made analogies between musical notes and plants or colors, and between musical tone and color. The seven notes and 12 octave semitones in music, much like the 12 discernible colors in the light spectrum, were his building blocks for an infinite number of planting design color compositions.[26]

He instructed those embarking on a garden project to consider plants as notes and then decide on the "key signature" and the principal "instruments," taking cues from the surrounding landscape (including the plants' ability to thrive and reproduce in it):

> The surroundings ... will determine if the key is B major or minor; they will help to decide on the pace, the tempo—and whether an andante is to be followed by an adagio or an allegretto .... Once this pattern has emerged, it is better to remain within it. One can change the key, but it must be to a related one; one can change from major to minor, but one must return again [italics added].[27]

The closely related emotional evocation of color and of music reinforced Burle Marx's music-color association. Key and tempo are the most important contributing elements to color-music associations; lighter colors and faster music are associated with gaiety, darker colors and slow music with sadness. Burle Marx promoted consistency of key and mood in the garden. With his preference for joyful impressions, he typically chose reds, yellows, and other warm, light colors.[28]

In addition to color, the orchestral "instruments" in Burle Marx's landscapes were wind, water, birds, animals, and light. Movement of leaves produces sound, falling or still water creates commotion or silence, and birds fill the garden with song. But color was the principal instrument, as is clear in his description of a colorful scene in the Serra do Sincorá, in Bahia:

> there were golden, green, and grayish bromeliads, silver Tillandsias and one with a purplish stripe, ... It was a marvelous symphony in muted tones, the colors a chromatic event, in which the volumes connected and established relationships, textures harmonizing with each other, ... there was an enormous silence, peopled with the tiny, imperceptible sounds that make up the music of nature [italics added].[29]

The acute color discernment and fine-tuned musical analogies in this passage are not merely a lyrical exercise, they informed the way Burle Marx designed landscapes, merging landscape and music concepts to create a chromatic performance or event.

Unlike the fastidiously specified chromatic palettes of Jekyll's gardens, Burle Marx provided no color composition formula. Instead, the principles of repetition and contrast replaced formula. The repetition of colors created "variations on a theme and rhythms that echo one another."[30] Variations or echoes were often produced by mixing a compositional color like ochre with other hues, such as yellow, gold, and red. The resulting yellow-ochre, gold-ochre, and red-ochre hues registered to the eye as chromatic imbrications (imbricated colors were not spectrum-adjacent but overlapped to produce new and distinct colors) (Figure 6.0).

The principle of contrast would be applied to one plant characteristic, say color, that was countered by unifying all the others—yellow and purple plant contrasts were united by similar foliage textures and forms, or grasses of different heights and colors were unified by similar textures, and so on. A plant palette showing, for instance, a group of palms that were similar in kind were differentiated by form, and nearby groups of *Hemerocallis* (daylily) and *Neomarica* (walking iris) that were similar in leaf shape were different in color. Burle Marx did not specify the type of color contrast—complementary or simultaneous; instead, he used multiple contrasting interplays of complementary hues, dark and light tones, bright and dull saturation, and reflective, opaque, and transparent surfaces.

Burle Marx, like Jekyll, was greatly attuned to temporality in the garden, recognizing the dimension of time as part of the art of the garden, including arrangement (composition) in support of the temporal orchestration of blossoms through the seasons and growth. He linked time, climax, and rhythm to concepts in both music and color and to the principles of repetition (or tempo) and contrast. A colorful blossom would dominate for only a short period each year, and the rest of the time serve as a neutral background to other plants.

Climax in the garden produced a "color event," the dramatization of color through volume or mass. For a horticultural composer, he explained,

> [i]t is important to select and dramatize certain passages of a composition by means of plants creating elements of surprise; regulating small, medium, and large volumes; or using more insistently one certain plant, so as to bring out its characteristics to give them value.[31]

Musical rhythm achieved through repeated and accented notes or beats corresponded to dominant colors in time and space. Burle Marx poetically described the rhythm of simultaneous cyclical flowering as "a series of chromatic chords, during each one of which Nature dresses herself as for a festival."[32] The cyclical rhythm of color expressed the "rhythm of life," which he tried to capture. The textures, forms, and volumes of plant groups also had their roles in the production of rhythm.

The coherence of color composition depended on the presence of a consistent, fixed, and conspicuous pattern, a central design concept in Burle Marx's gardens. He created large uniform and contrasting clusters of one plant species which were repeated throughout the garden, reasoning that plants in large groups do not compete or produce visual confusion; they seem ordered, easier to comprehend, and better display and amplify the character of each species, thus producing a coherent overall impact, a mosaic of color patches. Burle Marx went to great lengths to discipline the formal composition precisely because it was subject to the accelerated growth conditions in the tropics, vagaries of weather, and changes in growth and annual cycle. Lest the composition turn incomprehensible, plants were prevented from forming a tangled "jungle" of foliage as they might in their natural habitat. Considering the optimal conditions for growth in the tropics, his chief gardening problem was "not to encourage growth, but rather to discourage the garden's over-exuberance." Chromatic and plant palettes were limited in order "to say the most with a minimum of means."[33]

The formal composition or structure of a garden was an effective way to mark it as an artifact. Burle Marx's forms were orderly, abstract, rational, and enduring, qualities that were captured in the Parque del Este in Caracas, Venezuela: "Everything in the plan, and in the park, is outlined, crisp, and definite. ... The curves are not conciliatory toward context; the park is not a seamless insertion into its environment, but distinct, objectlike, and formal."[34] To form a clear, artificial image and to discipline wandering plants, he often used dividers, usually sunk just below or raised slightly above the ground surface. Invasive groundcovers that, like ivy, strangle trees and compromise boundaries were avoided. Minute disruptions of order were permitted in the form of epiphytic outgrowths that distracted from the linear outline of a tree or column.[35]

Burle Marx showed very diverse chromatic affinities in his work. His color aesthetics derived not only from the local landscape or theatrical and musical insights but also from the palettes of both European and Latin American modern artists as well as the dyes of traditional artisans. This assemblage of sensibilities resulted in novel and distinct color compositions.

European masters—Vincent Van Gogh, Paul Gauguin, Henri Matisse, Georges Braque, Pablo Picasso, Joan Miró, Jean Arp, and Paul Klee—inspired Burle Marx's strong colors, geometric patterns, and large-scale gestures. Latin American modernists—Luis Barragán, Diego Rivera, Cândido Portinari, Alberto da Veiga Guignard, and Emiliano Di Cavalcanti—lured him to the colors of his native culture. Flemish tapestry, Persian carpetry, Chinese porcelain, and Portuguese glazed ceramic tiles inspired his urban and artifice surface color.[36] He combined anew colors from across the spectrum, calling for a "range of tones and brilliance, but *no particular color*. From muddy to pure color" [italics added].[37] Thus in the roof garden of the Ministry of Education and Health in Rio (MES) (1938), he used sienna, yellow, ochre, violet, red, maroon, silver, white, and black; at the Fazenda Vargem Grande (1979), he featured shades of green, cadmium, ochre, umber, violet, maroon, silver, and black; and in the roof garden of the Instituto de Resseguros do Brasil (1939, restored in 2019) he used red, magenta, violet, Vandyke brown, and a range of greens and blues (see Figure 6.0).

Like other modernists, Burle Marx married color and form, and his geometries, like his chromatic palettes, varied enormously. Despite his close association with biomorphic forms, his gardens feature curvilinear, rectilinear, and hybrid forms. Especially late in his career, checkerboard grids appeared together with spirals, helicoids, curves, or countercurves; the gardens he did for Odette Monteiro (Rio, 1948), Clemente Gomes (Areias, 1979), and Edmundo Cavanelas (in Pedro do Rio, near Petrópolis, 1954) displayed biomorphic, rectilinear, and a combination of rectilinear and curvilinear forms, respectively (Figure 6.4).

Many of his plazas and urban hardscapes featured abstract forms of complex geometry. The unifying compositional features, though, were self-contained shapes with closed outlines, where figure and ground were often indistinguishable. They were almost always asymmetric and dynamic: forms evolved and interacted; lines moved, connected, and flowed. In some cases, a small form was contained in a larger one; in others, forms imbricated.

Two exceptions to the asymmetry rule were the checkerboard and wave patterns in lawns and paving, but these rigid patterns constituted only a segment of the site and served as counterpoints to the architecture or the rest of the composition. For instance, the grid in the great lawn of the Cavanelas garden contrasted with the hilly landscape and curved silhouette of the architecture designed by Oscar Niemeyer (discussed below). Similarly, the wave pattern in the paving and lawn at Rio's Museum of Modern Art (1960), no longer decipherable, countered the cubic architecture designed by Affonso Eduardo Reidy.

The inspiration for Burle Marx's abstract biomorphic forms, first seen in the 1938 gardens at the MES building in Rio, has been extensively debated (Figure 6.5). They did not derive from Burle Marx's own paintings at the time but were influenced by the same admixture that inspired his color palette.[38] They may have derived from the sculptural, "arabesque" interwoven forms of plants that he often spoke about, influenced by a bird's-eye view of the Brazilian landscape, with its slow-moving streams and rivers, as well as modern architecture in Rio featuring interconnected curves.[39] Whatever

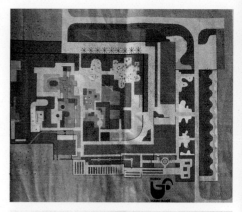

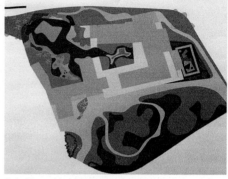

6.4 Fazenda Vargem Grande, garden plan, gouache drawing (top). Walter Moreira Salles residence (now Instituto Moreira Salle), garden plan, 1951, entrance sign (bottom). Photographed by Mira Engler, 2019

the formal origins may have been, the strength of Burle Marx's biomorphic composition lay in its ambiguity—his compositions have been described as blurring the natural with the abstract, the geographic with microbe scales, the figure with the ground, the path with the watercourse.[40]

His landscapes and gardens were composed as symphonies of minimal, yet rich, patterns and colors that borrowed from and mixed different sources. A similar hybridizing approach governed his choice of plant palettes and artificial ecologies.

Hybridity: Artificial Ecologies

At every opportunity Burle Marx flaunted the richness of Brazil's flora: 50,000 species, of which 5000 are trees. Traveling to diverse Brazilian landscapes with botanists (notably Henrique Lahmeyer de Mello Barreto, who studied plants in their natural habitat), his plant-hunting expeditions revealed a world that greatly moved him—a new discovery was an "almost violent attraction, … the revelation of form and color reached paroxysm, a sudden outburst of emotion."[41] At such moments, he was taken less by ecological, scientific truths and more by the beauty of nature, in particular the correspondence of form and color. His discoveries helped him diversify his color palette.

As early as 1934, in his role as director of the Parks and Gardens Department in Recife, Burle Marx planted indigenous aquatic plants and cacti in public parks, among

6.5 Roberto Burle Marx, gouache on board, Ministry of Education and Health (MES), Rio de Janeiro, 1938. Institute Burle Marx

the earliest such plantings in Brazil.[42] His use of indigenous tropical plants at the Fazenda Garcia near Petrópolis was featured in the catalogue of the first modernist architecture exhibition at the New York Museum of Modern Art. From the 1950s on, he made a point of collecting new plants from tropical and temperate zones and devotedly acclimated and cultivated them away from their native habitats. Nurturing new species and showcasing them in his gardens constituted a campaign to expand his artistic palette as well as rescue native plants from obscurity and marginalization. Altogether, he discovered 50 species, of which around 30 bear his name.[43]

Burle Marx's preoccupation should also be understood in the political context of Brazil's search for a modern identity. Burle Marx's position vis-à-vis the European concept of the tropical as "jungle" has been described as a construct of colonial superiority over local primitivism: European colonists considered the tropical flora and culture chaotic, daunting, and exotic, and indigenous plants inferior, symbols of an immoral and unrefined culture.[44] They planted private and public Brazilian gardens with roses, boxwood, and other European species. The term "tropical modernism" characterizes Burle Marx's landscape art as a unique response that at once rebuffed and valorized both the "tropical" and the "modern."

Burle Marx joined other Brazilian artists in the call to decolonialize Brazil's culture, articulated in poet Oswald de Andrade's 1928 "Manifesto Antropófago." Like other Brazilian art and architecture manifestos at the time, it recast Brazilian modernism as both opposition to and cooption of colonial influences to create a truly Brazilian national identity, or *brasilidade*. Burle Marx both celebrated and modernized the perception of Brazil's rich flora and heterogeneous landscape regions—savannahs, deserts, high-altitude grasslands, marshes … and jungles. It has been suggested that Burle Marx's awareness of the consequences of colonization and the contradictions inherent in the country's cultural and economic dependence on Europe led him to embrace the idea of the "self" as a hybrid of nature and culture, a synthesis that combined and reconciled the European artistic vanguard with Brazilian values, traditions, and history.[45] For these reasons his work was seen as political, but Burle Marx was not a political personality.

His early use of Brazilian flora in Recife's public parks, for example, was not indicative of a political or conservationist posture. Rather, he acted as "an artist pursuing innovation in form, color, volume, and textures" at a time when few native plants were used in gardens, and they had the best chances of survival with minimal care.[46] It was only in the 1970s, almost three decades after he began using Brazilian plants, that Burle Marx took up politics, when he advocated against the deforestation of the tropical forest and the ensuing rapid desertification process. His preservationist stance was coupled with a call to create new landscapes "with echoes of the old landscapes, in order to leave and establish an artistic legacy worthy of those who will come after us."[47] His passion for native plants was thus also motivated by a moral obligation to inspire future generations.

Still, he was first and foremost an artist. His incorporation of native plants enriched the landscape material palette with new and distinct forms and colors, like new pigments for his canvas. He likened plants to pigments and, at the same time, opposed the use of living plants merely to provide color:

> In a garden, we should also preserve the beautiful wild plants so often
> neglected. … But a garden is a complex of aesthetic and plastic intentions; and
> the plant is, to a landscape artist, not only a plant, rare, unusual, ordinary or

doomed to disappearance—it is also a color, a shape, a volume, or an arabesque in itself. It is the paint for the two dimensional picture I make of a garden on a drawing board in my atelier.[48]

Burle Marx selected plants for both optimum survival and artistic merit.[49] He was enamored of foliage shapes, textures, and colors and campaigned to create alternatives to the default green, to hybridize and produce variegated, blotched, tainted, dyed, stippled, and painted leaves (Figure 6.6).

He even undertook cross breeding. Claude Vincent, who in the 1940s visited his nursery in Leme, described Burle Marx as:

[A] man whose eyes light up as he shows you a new colour achieved in his keyboard of tones in anthuria plants—he alone has the secret, it seems, of their hybridization—and who almost reverently picks up a tin which once held butter and which now has a tiny, close-furled leaf in it which, he says, he is sure will be purple when it uncurls next week—one of the hundreds of new-veined hybrid Tinhoroes (arums of the Caladium family) he has created in the course of years, in his nursery garden surrounding his old house in Leme.[50]

Early in Burle Marx's career, he was taken with the philodendron sagittate leaf and its reticulated red veins that seemed to him like flowing blood, and was inspired to create different, more unusual patterns and tones of red.[51] His first hybridization experiments were with caladiums and anthuriums. He collected a great number of plants of the *Heliconiaceae*, *Araceae*, and *Bromeliaceae* families, and they became the basis of his extensive specialized collection. He was also fond of ground covers, for their capacity to form low, large color masses, like the carpets of purple Setcreasea and Cortaderia. Structurally distinctive and irregularly shaped plants intrigued him, and he used them to create points of interest in the garden.[52] Fern trees and palms of many varieties were among his favorite trees for their uniquely shaped canopy and columnar character that made them ideal for delimiting space and creating repetition and rhythm.

Burle Marx's study of plants, from the molecular level to the plant community and habitat, taught him how to successfully grow, reproduce, and acclimate them in different regions.[53] He applied to his gardens an important concept of native habitats, which ecologists call "ecological grouping" or "group associations": habitats where certain plants always ally, and therefore appear at their best together. (For instance, banana trees do not belong, and would look horrible, in a forest of sequoias.) Group association also defined the regional expression that Burle Marx pursued, although, as a hybridist, he was not an ecological purist and saw no need for self-restraint. His gardens also featured nonnative and foreign species if "less-favored" geographic conditions arose, native plants were limited, and imported plants offered more and new colors and shapes: "When we find a gap in our plant vocabulary, and this gap can be filled by an imported exotic plant that harmonizes with the landscape, I think that this plant should be used."[54]

Knowing nature's laws and their expressions enabled him to shape his gardens after the essence rather than the image of nature. The knowledge informed his "artificial ecologies," landscapes of new aesthetic compatibilities, with license to alter both group association and natural topography. "To make artificial landscapes," he explained, "means neither to deny nor to imitate nature slavishly. It means, instead, to know how to transport and associate, with personal, selective judgment, the results of a long, loving, and intense observation."[55] Plants and colors not found together in nature thus found new expression in novel and compelling color combinations in Burle Marx's landscapes.[56]

The artificial ecologies were not arbitrary. They followed both practical and aesthetic principles. Burle Marx mixed plants that grew in different regions but had similar needs, whose morphology or other physical characteristics produced a particular artistic effect or formed intriguing patterns or prolonged blossom color. For example, the more than 3000 native, acclimated, and foreign tree species in Flamengo Park (1954) were selected for their resistance to salty sea air and adaptability to Rio's climate as much as for their year-round color interest.[57] Another element of Burle Marx's artificial ecology was *xaxim* columns, vertical sculptures of metal and tree fern bark or cork embedded with bromeliads or philodendrons. These

6.6 Hybrid plants in Sítio greenhouses (left). *Calathea*, *Cordyline*, and *Caladium* (right, top to bottom)

living columns reinterpreted both popular traditions and plant physiology, simultaneously emulating epiphytic plant growth high up in a tree trunk and branches of primary Brazilian forests and alluding to their complete disappearance from certain forests. The columns, recalling indigenous totem poles, can be seen as a protest against modernization and its practices of environmental destruction.[58]

Cross-breeding and constructed ecologies were Burle Marx's expressions of botanical inclusion that synthesized the novel and traditional, foreign and native. His polychrome hybrid landscapes also encompassed a cultural bricolage of modern and traditional, imported and indigenous crafts, materials, and construction technologies.

Tropical Modernism: Cultural Mosaic

Burle Marx's concern for the preservation of indigenous plants extended to indigenous people and the decline of his country's traditional peasant culture: "My work reflects modernity, the date in which it takes place, but never loses sight of the reasons for its own tradition, which are valid and necessary."[59] His work celebrated the ethnic mosaic of the indigenous, European, African, and Asian people of Brazil.[60] It was a passionate agenda to conserve and enrich their lives in their landscapes. Burle Marx's artistic, environmental, and social missions were intertwined as he believed in the capacity of art and landscape architecture to advance society and, more specifically, in the social and pedagogical role of

6.7 Sítio, Rio de Janeiro, bricolage wall of salvaged blocks from a razed building

6.8 Tile murals, azulejos in the Ministry of Education and Health, Rio de Janeiro (top) and Instituto Moreira Salle (bottom)

gardens to teach and connect people with the regional landscape. This pedagogical function is manifested, for instance, in Rio's Salgado Filho Airport Park, where he used native plants from all over Brazil to introduce arriving visitors to the country's flora.[61]

The bricolage character of the artifacts Burle Marx integrated in gardens, an expression of his impulse for "recycling," was totally in keeping with Brazil's diverse and stratified society. His lifelong collection of the country's rich, popular, pre-Columbian/Amerindian art and Portuguese craft inspired the forms, colors, and techniques featured in his gardens' wall and paving compositions as much as avant-garde art.[62] The large-scale, eclectic, and colorful free-standing wall ensembles he created in his gardens often integrated discarded architectural elements and found objects that recall Incan, Aztec, and Portuguese cultures. These acts of recycling were sometimes done on site without prior design. The sculptures in the garden of the Fazenda Vargem Grande include stacks of old stone mill wheels that the owner had and harks back to the ancient totems of native people. For the wall in his own estate, Burle Marx salvaged old pieces of curved blocks from a razed building in Rio (Figure 6.7).

Wall crevices and extrusions were planted with epiphytes or creeping plants and other rock-loving species, appearing to have been colonized over time by wind or the dispersion of seeds by birds. Like modern-era collages, Burle Marx's bricolage walls consist of disparate fragments of materials, combined into a composition that has a new meaning, not inherent in any of the individual fragments. Their metaphorical value and visual ambiguity both reflect and produce multiple and contradictory associations, suggesting new, nonlinear narratives, dialogues, and temporal durations.[63] The juxtaposed fragments are suspended between their original essences and the new roles evoked in the poetic ensemble.

Burle Marx also tapped the rich Moorish-Portuguese decorative traditions, especially glazed ceramics called *azulejos* and mosaic pavement known as *calçada portuguesa* or *pedra portuguesa*. Both became popular among modern expressionist artists and muralists in Brazil. Burle Marx used them extensively in private and public projects as monumental vertical and horizontal canvases, on a scale previously unseen—another example of a Burle Marxian collage.[64] Portinari, a professor at the art institute, taught Burle Marx the *azulejo* technique when he assisted in the production of the MES murals (Figure 6.8). Burle Marx's *azulejos*—both traditional intricate blue color patterns and modern abstract forms—were not used in the traditional fashion for ceramic-tiled indoor surfaces but in the garden as freestanding walls.[65] With distinct color schemes and forms— geometric, organic, figurative, and abstract—they add drama to the garden, often giving off reflections in pools and both complementing and contrasting with the foreground or background.

The *pedra portuguesa* offered a wonderful opportunity to lay out a huge horizontal painting on the city floor

6.9 Calçada portuguesa, Copacabana Beach promenade, Rio de Janeiro

(Figure 6.9). Basalt or limestone were hand-cut following an ancient craft in which minute mosaic stones were inlaid, compressed with a wooden pole into sand or cement to create black-and-white patterns, sometimes with an additional red. Burle Marx combined an old craft with modern design in many projects, including Largo da Carioca (1981) and the famous Copacabana Beach sidewalks (1969–70). Constructed when Avenida Atlântica was redesigned in the 1970s, Burle Marx's Copacabana beachfront promenade at once preserved and magnified in scale the turn-of-the-century black-and-white wave pattern pavement of a segment of the beachfront walk, inspired by the Rossio Square in Lisbon. In contrast, in the median and the opposite sidewalk of the avenue, Burle Marx created distinct abstract patterns and added a reddish-brown stone to the white and black palette (Figure 6.10). The multicultural expression of the project featured the indigenous flora

6.10 Copacabana Beach promenade (left); median (middle) and opposite sidewalk of Avenida Atlântica, Rio de Janeiro (right)

181

of coconut trees, pre-Columbian figures, and Portuguese craft—an Indo-African-Iberian synthesis; even the *calçada*'s red, black, and white colors might be seen as representing the three races that constitute the Brazilian people: Amerindians, Africans, and Europeans.[66]

Burle Marx's landscapes constructed a Brazilian cultural identity through the deliberate inclusion of diversity. His "tropical modernism" both safeguarded and reinvented Brazil's heterogeneous landscapes, cultures, and polyvalent voices and colors. The artifacts, plants, water, and mineral ensembles in his gardens resonate polytonal and polychromic impressions, while remaining ambiguous. His photogenic landscapes are open to interpretation and adaptation, as are his drawings.

Medium: Art and Landscape

Burle Marx's abstract and colorful gouache plan drawings bear only scant resemblance to the final built landscapes. To those who expected his gardens to be a direct translation of his paintings, he responded: "That's why I fight hard: I will not do a painting that is a garden."[67] Juggling many artistic media, each on its own terms, he endowed his landscape drawings with a unique role in the design process, with a purposefully tenuous relationship to his landscapes.

His plan drawings are indicative of his thought process and use of color in the landscape. He usually communicated the design using color only—no lines, just pigments (although occasionally his plans show minor labels and symbols, such as paving texture and tree canopy in the plan for the Fazenda Vargem Grande). He trusted in the efficacy of pigment to convey multiple ideas and information about the designed landscape.

Landscape was a large, complex, and costly production, which he could not simply experiment with, toss "drafts," and "make" himself. But as an artist, he was a "maker," and directly engaged in and mastered the primary medium of each of his multitude of artistic productions; if the primary medium for a painter was pigment, for the landscape designer it was the landscape itself—light, minerals, plants. Also as an artist, he considered conventional landscape design drawings that included information such as orientation, topography, texture, plant location, type, and height irrelevant to his creative thinking process. His sketches merely supported the actual creation; they were not intended to be used by the client or contractor. As with his oil paintings, drawings were both an end in themselves and a laboratory for garden color and form.[68]

The first large gardens he designed—for Odette Monteiro in Correias (1948) and Ralph Camargo in Teresópolis (1955)—were created on site, almost without preliminary drawings, although he later acknowledged that he started a project with a rough plan in pen or pencil, then a sketch in color, followed by conceptual iterations.[69] The conceptual plan enabled him to see the totality of the landscape and work out the underlying garden structure, its form and color composition, as in a painting.

The urge to directly engage the medium—the landscape—kept Burle Marx thoroughly involved in the construction and planting phases, making and remaking a project. His interest in landscape architecture as a creative act, a process rather than a static artifact, meant the original plan (if produced) was no more than an intention, a point of departure, not a document to be followed exactly. Even when he had presented clients with a drawing of what he intended to create, he did not always use it during the construction of the garden. Changes ensued as he supervised and made different decisions at critical points to accommodate modifications or address a limiting circumstance or new opportunity in situ, and as the concept and character of each garden evolved and matured in his mind.[70]

The color drawing of the unbuilt garden that he designed for Mr. and Mrs. Burton Tremaine (1948) in Santa Barbara, California (Figure 6.11), was in fact intended only to serve as a color chart and for museum exhibit, he explained:

> The flora was suitable to Santa Barbara but the colored chart for this garden ... is a permanent exhibit in the Museum of Modern Art in New York; and it has brought me many letters that suggested that people all over the world are seeking solutions to a problem identical with my own—that of finding a garden style to meet contemporary needs—artistic, social, and economic, for the man in the city as well as the country dweller.[71]

Thus the value of a Burle Marx landscape representation was in its abstraction, which made the design adaptable to other situations as well as suitable for an art exhibit, a marketing strategy to "sell" his design and boost his reputation. Often done in the office during the project or even after it was completed, these representations were largely intended for publication and exhibition, and, with the appeal of artwork, were admitted to national and international galleries, traveling exhibitions, and

6.11 Gouache on board, garden design for beach house for Mr. and Mrs. Burton Tremaine, Santa Barbara, California, 1948. © Museum of Modern Art/Licensed by SCALA/Art Resource, New York

premier art institutions. His work was extensively exhibited from the 1940s onward, and Burle Marx was the first landscape architect to mount a solo exhibition at New York's Museum of Modern Art in 1991.[72]

With his growing reputation and expanded office and workload in the 1960s, Burle Marx's design assistants turned his visual descriptions and rough sketches into final drawings and perspectives for clients, publications, and exhibition displays, and created working drawings for builders. They also helped him produce painterly renditions and models of his gardens as artworks alongside his paintings, sculptures, tapestries, or fabrics.[73]

Burle Marx's abstract gouache drawings present a snapshot of his creative thinking and making. The use of pigment color helped detach the primary medium, the landscape

183

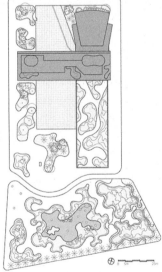

6.12 MES, terrace garden and street-level garden, view from the tower roof (top); plan of the gardens and the unbuilt park to the south, 1938, © Catherine Seavitt Nordenson, drawing from contemporaneous documentation (bottom)

itself, from the drawing, leaving it ambivalent, open to adaptation and interpretation.

* * *

The two projects selected for detailed study, the gardens at the MES building, in downtown Rio de Janeiro (1938), and the Cavanelas residence (1954), are from Burle Marx's early career. The garden built at the prestigious MES building, a modernist architectural landmark in the center of Rio, was his first prominent public commission. It is here that his distinctive design of bold colors and amoebic forms filled with tropical plants clearly emerged.[74] The Cavanelas garden, one of the few well-preserved private gardens, is a clear and graceful example of Burle Marx's form and color principles. Composed of two geometric gardens of contrasting curvilinear and rectilinear compositions on opposite sides of Niemeyer's building, they harmonize beautifully with the architecture and surrounding landscape. Both projects were extensively photographed over time and featured in numerous publications, making it possible to follow their development and change. The author of this book visited both gardens in July 2019.

Ministry of Education and Health Gardens, Rio de Janeiro, Brazil, designed 1938, implemented 1943

Burle Marx's landscape project for the MES is best known on account of its exuberantly polychromatic plan-view gouache drawing of the terrace garden, one of three gardens he created at the site (see Figure 6.5). The plan-drawing was done after the garden was built, for exhibition purposes. Its vividly colored abstract blobs depict no flower grouping, color, or season; foliage tints and textures are unnoted; and most of the year this garden only displays shades of green. The intent of the drawing was purely to reveal the essence and spirit of the garden.[75]

The forms in the drawings are similar in character to the garden bed layouts, but the color blobs only roughly represented the plant groups in the built garden—there were more blobs than planting areas and a greater variety of colors than species. And yet the drawing provided ample information: the pigments generally resonate with the range of flower colors when in bloom; color contrast coincides with contrasting plant qualities—texture, structure, or shade;

and the imbricating sinuous forms in the drawing largely echo the built structure (Figure 6.12).

Both the drawing and the garden feature a range of warm tints and induce a cheerful mood. The color palette in the drawing incudes lemon yellow, yellow ochre, red ochre, burnt sienna, perylene maroon, Venetian red, brilliant violet, and a greenish oxide of chromium. In in contrast, the garden's flowering plant palette consists of white, yellows, oranges, reds, magenta, and purples, with the proviso that not all flowers bloom at once. Each of the low-lying ground covers and slightly higher flower masses boast bright colors in cyclical but asynchronous chromatic events. The flowers then disappear for a long period of time, leaving the garden covered in shades of green.

A colorless planting plan for the MES gardens lists 34 species of plants, chosen for their Brazilian tropical origin, distinct forms, and diverse foliage shades and textures as well as their warm flower color.[76] On the south-facing terrace garden structurally distinct green specimens in groups of two to five emerge from beds filled with one or two low flower patches and two medium-height shrubs. The sculptural *Dracaena marginata* and *Nolina recurvata*, among other specimens, bring accents and rhythms to the garden. The large sculptural foliage of the *Philodendron undulatum* and *P. bipinnatifidum*, among others, introduce textural interest. During the summer, bright groundcover and low flowers, notably two varieties of *Hemerocallis flava*, boast yellow and orange hues in concert with the magenta *Schizocentron elegans*. Other times, the white and red-purple flowers of the *Tibouchina radula* and *T. vermelha* shrubs join the concert. In fall and winter, shades of green foliage include the distinct gray-rose and yellow-linden greens of Burle Marx's favorite bromeliads, *Vriesea imperialis* and *V. regina*.

6.13 MES, terrace garden, June 2019. Photos: Mira Engler

The terrace garden has been regularly photographed from the 16-story tower rooftop above, giving the impression of a flat abstract painting in a frame. But what looks like a colorful garden is green most of the year (and it is far from flat) (Figure 6.13). The conspicuous absence of green in the plan was considered surprising, although it largely showed Burle Marx's original intention.[77]

Designed on three levels—the street-level plaza, the terrace garden just outside the minister's dining room and above the exhibition wing, and the dining room roof terrace atop the main building—the garden complex was conceived as staggered, synchronized planes. The frame of the terrace garden just about succeeds in isolating it from its setting—but it becomes apparent from the plan or aerial view that the planting bed pattern starts at the rooftop, continues in the terrace-garden, and spills down to the lower garden at street level.

On the street-level public plaza, pedestrians daily experience the curving island beds, tropical varieties, contrasts, and color events, subject to sun or shade. Several flowering plants, like *Hemerocallis*, are repeated and new ones are added, such as the red, orange, and yellow *Heliconia psittacorum*, yellow-orange *Canna indica*, light purple *Neomarica coerulea*, and *Yucca elephantipes* with its cluster of white flowers. As the terrace and roof gardens could not support trees, in the plaza Burle Marx planted clumps of short, multitrunk, and tall columnar palms (*Chrysalidocarpus lutescens*, *Roystonea oleracea*, *Arecastrum romanzoffianum*, and *Rhapis flabelliformis*)—and the national tree of Brazil, *Paubrasilia echinata* (commonly known as Pernambuco wood or brazilwood). The choice of tropical plants and the symbolism of the *Paubrasilia* tree made a political statement that aligned with Burle Marx's tropical modernism and support of Brazil's national identity.

Burle Marx became involved in the building in 1937, as an assistant to Portinari (who executed a series of frescoes and *azulejos* on site), when he was asked by Lúcio Costa to design the gardens. Costa, who led an architecture team that included Niemeyer, Affonso Reidy, Jorge Moreira, and Le Corbusier (as consultant), mentored Burle Marx in his formative career phase and this European and Brazilian modern architecture circle had a decisive influence on Burle Marx's work. Burle Marx's novel tropical plant and color palettes and biomorphic composition emerged during lengthy discussions with Costa. He also aligned himself with the teachings of Le Corbusier as well as the nascent "Pau-Brazil" modern movement and set out to create landscape art that was part of the growing collection of traditional craft and avant-garde art by both Brazilian and European artists.[78]

Scholars have debated Burle Marx's design vis-à-vis Le Corbusier's modern architecture and his early landscape drawings for the site, and speculated on whether Burle Marx's design intended to challenge the rectilinear architecture or was simply his way of creating harmony through contrast. Analysis of Burle Marx's three early proposals reveals a progression from the first draft of a rectilinear garden and rectangular beds, to the second draft with rounded surfaces, and then to the third, a draft of the built version.[79] With his hybrid working mode or "bricolage" method, Burle Marx's MES gardens likely reacted to the rigid architecture, created an independent statement, and were inspired by the meandering outline in Portinari's *azulejo* in the ground-level wall.[80] The cultural hybrid of native and European influences expressed through Burle Marx's form, plants, and, particularly, color befitted the hybrid spirit of the MES building itself.

Edmundo Cavanelas Residence Garden (now Strunk House), Pedro do Rio, Petrópolis, Brazil, 1954

The Edmundo Cavanelas garden was one of several project collaborations between Burle Marx and the architect Oscar Niemeyer.[81] Located in a valley, the modest but dynamic building is the center and focus of the garden. Burle Marx sounded somewhat self-deprecating when he said in 1947, "Basically, and following the modern architects, the garden is nothing but the extension, the continuation of the dwelling. It is in truth the outdoor dwelling."[82]

The Cavanelas garden is of course more than simply a continuation; it is an arresting dialogue between the architecture and the landscape (Figure 6.14). The building looks minuscule relative to the vast garden and landscape beyond, and at the same time it anchors the whole. The garden is surrounded on one side by north-facing slopes of dense forest (a barren pasture at the time of construction) and, on the other side, by south-facing open grassland with isolated tree clumps. The descending approach to the garden is lined with a columnar row of palms that raises the observer's eye to a sweeping view of the estate and surrounding hills. Burle Marx surely marveled at this bird's-eye view of the ensemble of architecture, garden, and landscape beyond the colonnade of palms. From this viewpoint, the garden seems to flow under the building's saddle-shaped roof and through the glass structure, stretching on both sides toward the foothills. Suspended between two vertical, triangular, free-standing walls made of local stone, the concave roof echoes the architecture in the basin-like landscape. The building seems to be levitating.

The gardens on opposite sides of the house strike a dialogue between its contrasting east and west parts. It is a masterful dialogue of opposition and balance, one that Burle Marx consistently played out in landscape projects (Figure 6.15). From the living room and outdoor seating areas just beneath the wide roof canopy, one can see the two contrasting gardens at once. They are essentially parterres where large color patterns made of low plants and occasional tall specimens are embossed like a tattoo on the earth's surface. Burle Marx's desire to simultaneously bring the facing hill slopes into the garden

6.14 Cavanelas Residence (now Strunk Residence), Petrópolis, Brazil, 1954, view from the upper entrance in 2019

187

6.15 Cavanelas Garden, planting plan (top). Institute Burle Marx. Views from the house of west garden (left) and east garden (right)

and oppose them resulted in a unique solution of two distinct gardens: one rectilinear, with a rectangular swimming pool and planting beds set in a checkerboard-patterned lawn to the west, and to the east a gracefully curving garden of sinuous planting islands and stripes and a pond. The grassland, one of the garden's unifying elements, descends from the foothills into the two gardens, and the architecture of the house serves as a bridge between the gardens.

The contrasting formal layouts of the two gardens, in keeping with Burle Marx's principle, are united by colors and other qualities. On both sides there are solid green and variegated varieties of *Stenotaphrum*, a linear stripe of red *Iresine herbstii*, and lime green *Duranta repens*. The silver groundcover foliage of *Helichrysum petiolare* adds further variety to the east garden's chromatic palette. Because of their shapes, the two gardens are thought to represent masculinity and femininity, respectively.

Burle Marx took advantage of the sun-exposed terraces on the sloping north bank of the garden and planted large groups of grasses, including *Cortaderia selloana*, yellow and orange *Hemerocallis* carpets, and cacti (*Yucca aloifolia*, *Agave americana*, *Dracaena largestroenia*, and *Dracaena indivis*). To the palm row he added the red-flower tree *Erythrina verna*, among others. Along the bank, large groups of philodendrons form a wavy stripe that echoes the gently curving roof and rolling hills (it reappears in later gardens, such as the one at the Fazenda Vargem Grande). There are only 15 tree species in this extensive garden. In the summer, purple *Agapanthus africanus* and orange *Hemerocallis* flowers mark the edge of the lawn.

The east lawn is traversed by two-color parallel stripes of lime green *Duranta repens* and purple-magenta *Setcreasea* and punctuated by a circular bed of red canna. The sinuous stripes flow like a river from the house terrace down to the pond, where a grass island is furnished with a stone picnic table and a group of *Vriesea imperialis*. The east garden also features wet and shade plants like the yellow orchid *Cyrtopodium andersonii*, purple *Vellozia plicata*, white African lily, *Moraea iridioides*, the iris *Morea grandiflora*, and pink-purple *Verbena hybrida* (Figure 6.16). Each side is anchored by a sculpture, a softly curved reclining woman in the rectilinear garden and a perforated metal sphere in the opposite garden, creating an internal contrast in each garden.

Photographs taken over many years show the gradual growth of and minor changes to planting throughout the Cavanelas garden. But its core—the two formal garden compositions—remains fixed, etched in the ground with their distinct plant colors.

* * *

Burle Marx used the agency of light and color in the construction of an idiosyncratic modern Brazilian landscape identity. Casting aside color composition formulae and advancing principles learned from nature, art, and culture alike, he attempted with the colors and gestures of his hybrid landscapes to critically synthesize traditional with contemporary culture, indigenous with modernist, past with present, and universal with local. Celebrated by design professions and high-art institutions worldwide and appreciated by the ordinary citizens of Rio and São Paulo, Burle Marx's landscape architecture oeuvre has been far-reaching and lasting. His passion for color is a legacy that continues to guide the prominent postmodern successors discussed in the following chapters.

6.16 View from the west garden pond toward the house in the early 1960s (top), *Tropical Gardens of Burle Marx*, 1964 by P. M. Bardi. Photo: M. Gautherot. The same view in 2019 (bottom)

Notes

1 Doherty, ed., *Roberto Burle Marx Lectures*, 2018, 138, 113–4.

2 Ibid.

3 Ibid., 105.

4 Bardi, *The Tropical Gardens of Burle Marx*, 1964, 10.

5 Berrizbeitia, *Roberto Burle Marx in Caracas*, 2005, 60.

6 Roberto bought Sítio Santo Antônio da Bica, a small farm of about 200 acres south of Rio, in 1949. Studio Burle Marx continues his work to this day, trying to preserve and maintain his built landscapes, although a large number have disappeared or are poorly maintained.

7 A dozen lectures in English (nine originals and three translated) that he delivered at various schools and institutions between the 1950s and 1970s are collected in a 2018 volume edited by Gareth Doherty. Burle Marx's environmental manifestos are reprinted and discussed in Nordenson, *Depositions*, 2018.

8   Stepan, "Tropical Modernism," 2000; Vaccarino, *Roberto Burle Marx: Landscapes Reflected,* 2000, 229.

9   Doherty, ed., *Lectures,* 2018, 108.

10 Doherty, "On Burle Marx and His Lectures," 2018, 58.

11 Doherty, ed., *Lectures,* 2018, 109.

12 Ibid., 108.

13 Ibid.

14 Bardi, *Tropical Gardens,* 1964, 44.

15 Doherty, ed., *Lectures,* 2018, 200.

16 Ibid., 201.

17 See Vaccarino, "Interpreting and Preserving the Work of Roberto Burle Marx," 2002, 22.

18 Doherty, ed., *Lectures,* 2018, 198.

19 Stepan, "Tropical Modernism," 2000, 82.

20 Doherty, ed., *Lectures,* 2018, 108.

21 For the implications of the color of light on habitat coloration in the tropics, see Endler, "The Color of Light in Forests," 1993, 1, 7.

22 In both RGB and CMYK color printing systems the color hex #00755e, which has 0 percent red tint, is called Tropical Rain Forest.

23 Doherty, ed., *Lectures,* 2018, 198.

24 Ibid., 116.

25 One shared term in color and music is "tone," which in color means the darkness or lightness of the hue, and in music means the quality or "coloring of the sound," such as rich, dark, or mellow. OnMusic Dictionary. https://dictionary.onmusic.org/terms/3614-tone.

26 The distinguishable light colors are red, (red-orange), orange, (orange-yellow), yellow, (yellow-green), green, (green-blue), blue, (blue-indigo), indigo, (indigo-violet), and violet. Sir Isaac Newton was the first to demonstrate the equation of color intervals and music notes. The analogy was carried on by Albert Henry Munsell, known for the Munsell color system, who maintained that the music scale, like the color scale, comprises successive notes of ascending or descending key and color. Munsell's 12-note chromatic scale is based on the 12 semitones of a musical octave, while volume is indicated through shades of color.

27 Doherty, ed., *Lectures,* 2018, 116.

28 Of lesser importance for Burle Marx was the symbolism of colors.

29 Doherty, ed., *Lectures,* 2018, 114.

30 Ibid., 116.

31 Ibid., 158.

32 Ibid., 168.

33 Doherty, ed., *Lectures,* 2018, 172. The neglect and disappearance of many of Burle Marx's gardens clearly show the results of poor maintenance and lack of resouces.

34 Berrizbeitia, *Burle Marx in Caracas,* 2005, 61.

35 Eliovson, *The Gardens of Roberto Burle Marx,* 1991, 189.

36 On Burle Marx's paintings and sources and influences, see Frota, "A Planetary Modernist," 2011.

37 Doherty, ed., *Lectures,* 2018, 168.

38 Adams, *The Unnatural Art of the Garden,* 1991, 21; Doherty, "On Burle Marx," 2018, 62.

39 Burle Marx only traveled and saw that part of the country in 1950.

40 Fraser, "Cannibalizing Le Corbusier," 2000, 185.

41 Doherty, ed., *Lectures*, 2018, 166.

42 Burle Marx was first inspired by a cactus garden he saw at Berlin's Dahlem Botanical Garden in 1937. It is possible that he was familiar with the work of Victor Brecheret and Mina Klabin, who created the first abstract cactus garden and founded the Brazilian tropical garden movement in São Paulo in 1927.

43 For a discussion of his work at the Museum of Modern Art exhibition, see Goodwin, "Brazil Builds," 1943, 38. For a complete list of plant species linked to Roberto Burle Marx, see "Appendix: Plant Alphabet" in Cavalcanti et al., *The Modernity of Landscape*, 2011, 321.

44 This discussion draws on the work of Stepan, "Tropical Modernism," 2000, 76. She borrowed the term "tropical modernism" from William J. R. Curtis, who used it to describe Le Corbusier's vision of architecture for Brazil.

45 Vaccarino, "The Inclusion of Modernism," 2002, 210.

46 Tabacow, "Science of Perception," 2011, 65. Tabacow notes that despite Burle Marx's apolitical approach to his work, his planting of red canna in a park in Recife was perceived as indicating communist sympathies by some political factions, and the associated tensions led to his ouster from the directorship of the Parks and Gardens Department.

47 Doherty, ed., *Lectures*, 2018, 118.

48 Ibid., 188.

49 For an extensive list of plants that Burle Marx frequently used, see Eliovson, *The Gardens,* 1991, 60–5.

50 Vincent, "The Modern Garden in Brazil," 1947, 166.

51 Bardi, *Tropical Gardens,* 1964, 13.

52 Eliovson, *The Gardens*, 1991, 270.

53 Doherty, ed., *Lectures*, 2018, 127.

54 Ibid., 115.

55 Ibid., 138.

56 His mix-and-match approach to plants and to garden design might be viewed as a tribute to the long history of international plant exchange and adaptation. Stepan, "Tropical Modernism," 2000, 85–6.

57 Doherty, ed., *Lectures*, 2018, 125.

58 Vaccarino, *"Inclusion of Modernism,"* 2002, 220.

59 Doherty, ed., *Lectures*, 2018, 89.

60 Doherty, "On Burle Marx," 2018, 143. This interest also manifested in his early paintings.

61 Social concerns also triggered Burle Marx's entrepreneurial skills. At Sítio he employed many locals from the village of Guaratiba, teaching them to cultivate and hybridize plants and maintain his built gardens as they matured. The previously poor fishing village is now a thriving suburb with many nurseries tended by those who worked with Burle Marx and their descendants. Ibid., 163.

62 Leenhardt, "From Modernism to Ecology," 2011, 61.

63 Shields, *Collage and Architecture,* 2014, ix.

64 Vaccarino, "Inclusion of Modernism," 2002, 217.

65 For Burle Marx's wall mosaics and murals, see Hoffmann and Nahson, *Roberto Burle Marx: Brazilian Modernist*, 2016, 28–43.

66 The critic Edgardo Mario Ruiz made these observations, cited in Leenhardt, "Roberto Burle Marx: *The City as Landscape,*" 2005, 193.

67 Frota, "A Planetary Modernist," 2011, 141.

68 Hamerman, "Roberto Burle Marx: *The* Last Interview," 1995, 178.

69 Eliovson, *The Gardens,* 1991, 67; Hamerman, "Last Interview," 1995, 168.

70 Vaccarino, "Interpreting and Preserving," 2002, 11–12. Vaccarino, who studied Burle Marx's original drawings for the purpose of preserving his gardens, found that very few of the finished gardens, including plant species, matched the original working plans.

71 Doherty, ed., *Lectures,* 2018, 178.

72 Adams, *The Unnatural Art of the Garden,* 1991, 31. Earlier, Burle Marx contributed to the architecture exhibition "Brazil Builds" (1943) at the Museum of Modern Art in New York. His first solo exhibition in the United States, in the gallery of the Pan-American Union Building (headquarters of the Organization of American States), in Washington, DC, was in 1954.

73 Vaccarino, "Inclusion of Modernism," 2002, 230.

74 Although he had used curvilinear forms before, it was in the Ministry project that Burle Marx's formal signature first emerged most clearly. Fraser, "Cannibalizing," 2000, 189, note 53.

75 Leenhardt, "From Modernism to Ecology," 2011, 59.

76 Although plant species were changed over time, the form and design principles of the gardens have been preserved.

77 Leenhardt, "*City as Landscape,*" 2005, 186.

78 Burle Marx was working in Recife during the planning period of the MES building, but he returned frequently to Rio and met Le Corbusier in team consultations and at public lectures.

79 Cavalcanti, "Roberto Burle Marx: The Permanence of the Unstable," 2011, 33.

80 For an explanation of the Law of the Meander, see Fraser, "Cannibalizing," 2000, 187. Le Corbusier's sketches show a single row of imperial palms and several raised rectangular beds set in the lower paved square. He repeated the beds on the roof of the exhibition wing, adding a giant statue of a reclining woman on a high pedestal. The distinct background of the surrounding mountainous landscape and Guanabara Bay were the focus of the drawing. Ibid., 188.

81 The residence is now owned by the artist and designer Gilberto Strunk.

82 Rambert, "An Aesthete Between Species and Spaces," 2011, 279.

References

Adams, William Howard, ed. *Roberto Burle Marx: The Unnatural Art of the Garden.* New York: Museum of Modern Art, 1991.

Bardi, P. M. *The Tropical Gardens of Burle Marx.* New York: Reinhold, 1964.

Berrizbeitia, Anita. *Roberto Burle Marx in Caracas: Parque del Este, 1956–1961.* Philadelphia: University of Pennsylvania Press, 2005.

Cavalcanti, Lauro. "Roberto Burle Marx: The Permanence of the Unstable." In *Roberto Burle Marx: The Modernity of Landscape,* 31–36. Paris and Barcelona: Institut français d'architecture and Actar, 2011.

Cavalcanti, Lauro, Fares El-Dahadah, and Francis Rambert, eds. *Roberto Burle Marx: The Modernity of Landscape.* Paris and Barcelona: Institut français d'architecture and Actar, 2011.

Doherty, Gareth. "On Burle Marx and His Lectures." In *Roberto Burle Marx Lectures: Landscape as Art and Urbanism,* 56–83. Zürich: Lars Müller Publishers, 2018.

Doherty, Gareth, ed. *Roberto Burle Marx Lectures: Landscape as Art and Urbanism.* Zürich: Lars Müller Publishers, 2018.

Eliovson, Sima. *The Gardens of Roberto Burle Marx.* New York: H. N. Abrams/Sagapress, 1991.

Endler, John. "The Color of Light in Forests and Its Implications." *Ecological Monographs* 63, no. 1 (1993): 1–27.

Fraser, Valerie. "Cannibalizing Le Corbusier: The MES Gardens of Roberto Burle Marx." *Journal of the Society of Architectural Historians* 59, no. 2 (2000): 180–93.

Frota, Lélia Coelho. "A Planetary Modernist." In *Roberto Burle Marx: The Modernity of Landscape,* ed. by Lauro Cavalcanti, Fares El-Dahadah, and Francis Rambert, 141–8. Paris and Barcelona: Institut français d'architecture and Actar, 2011.

Goodwin, Philip L. "Brazil Builds: Architecture New and Old, 1652–1942." New York: Museum of Modern Art, 1943.

Hamerman, Conrad. "Roberto Burle Marx: The Last Interview." *Journal of Decorative and Propaganda Arts* 21, no. 21 (1995): 156–79.

Hoffmann, Jens, and Claudia J. Nahson. *Roberto Burle Marx: Brazilian Modernist.* New York: The Jewish Museum, 2016.

Leenhardt, Jacques. "Roberto Burle Marx: The City as Landscape." In *Cruelty and Utopia: Cities and Landscapes of Latin America,* ed. by Jean-François Lejeune, 183–95. New York: Princeton Architectural Press, 2005.

Leenhardt, Jacques. "From Modernism to Ecology." In *Roberto Burle Marx: The Modernity of Landscape,* ed. by Lauro Cavalcanti, Fares El-Dahadah, and Francis Rambert, 57–62. Paris and Barcelona: Institut français d'architecture and Actar, 2011.

Nordenson, Catherine Seavitt. *Depositions: Roberto Burle Marx and Public Landscapes under Dictatorship.* Austin: University of Texas Press, 2018.

Rambert, Francis. "An Aesthete Between Species and Spaces." In *Roberto Burle Marx: The Modernity of Landscape,* ed. by Lauro Cavalcanti, Fares El-Dahadah, and Francis Rambert, 277–80. Paris and Barcelona: Institut français d'architecture and Actar, 2011.

Shepheard, Peter. *Modern Gardens: Masterworks of International Garden Architecture.* London: The Architectural Press, 1953.

Shields, Jennifer. *Collage and Architecture.* London: Routledge, 2014.

Stepan, Nancy Leys. "Tropical Modernism: Designing the Tropical Landscape." *Singapore Journal of Tropical Geography* 21, no. 1 (2000): 76–91.

Tabacow, José. "The Science of Perception." In *Roberto Burle Marx: The Modernity of Landscape,* ed. by Lauro Cavalcanti, Fares El-Dahadah, and Francis Rambert, 63–68. Barcelona: Institut français d'architecture and Actar, 2011.

Vaccarino, Rossana. Roberto Burle Marx: *Landscapes Reflected.* New York: Princeton Architectural Press, 2000.

Vaccarino, Rossana. "Inclusion of Modernism: Brasilidade and the Garden." In *The Architecture of Landscape, 1940–1960,* ed. by Marc Treib, 206–32. Philadelphia: University of Pennsylvania Press, 2002.

Vaccarino, Rossana. "Interpreting and Preserving the Work of Roberto Burle Marx: In Search for New Approaches" (conference paper). *Paisagem Ambiente: Ensaios,* no. 16, São Paulo (2002): 9–41.

Vincent, Claude. "The Modern Garden in Brazil." *Architectural Review* 51, no. 605 (May 1947): 165–72.

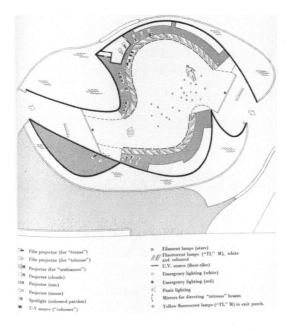

⊏ Film projector (for "écrans")
⊏ Film projector (for "tritrous")
Projector (for "ambiances")
Projector (clouds)
Projector (sun)
Projector (moon)
Spotlight (coloured patches)
U-V source ("volumes")

○ Filament lamps (stars)
Fluorescent lamps ("TL" M), white and coloured
— U.V. source (floor-tiles)
○ Emergency lighting (white)
● Emergency lighting (red)
∝ Panic lighting
{ Mirrors for directing "tritrous" beams
○ Yellow fluorescent lamps ("TL" M) in exit porch.

III.1 Le Corbusier, Philips Pavilion, World Expo, plan with schematic of lighting sources, Brussels, 1958, from *Philips Technical Review*, 1958/1959 (top). Le Corbusier and Iannis Xenakis, "Poème Électronique," performance at the Phillips Pavilion, 1958 (bottom). © F.L.C./ADAGP, Paris/Artists Rights Society (ARS), New York

Part III
Postmodernism Onward
From Pigment to Affect

The New Sublime, Minimal and Land Art

Color became ever more radiant in the latter part of the 20th century. Three significant developments transformed color in art and, subsequently, in landscape design: (1) amid the social unrest and economic and environmental crises of the 1960s and 1970s, artists abandoned the ivory tower of art galleries and studios in favor of mundane and spoiled landscapes, such as polluted rivers and landfill, exploring new scales, matter, and phenomena; (2) the intensification of consumer culture inspired artists to use cheap, off-the-shelf material and paint that resembled the goods people were increasingly buying; and (3) electronic mass media—film, television, and then the internet—propelled artists to give color more autonomy, freeing it from form, surface, and emotion to become an all-consuming ethereal space, light, and atmosphere.

The first artist to anticipate some of color changes was Hungarian-born László Moholy-Nagy (1895–1946) in the 1940s. He said that color would transition from pigment to colored light and most visual work in the future would be handled by the "light painter," who "will have the scientific knowledge of the physicist and the technological skill of the engineer coupled with his own imagination, creative intuition and emotional intensity." He wrote:

> Many painters already use re-evaluated psychophysical effects such as optical illusions, changes in size, automatic complementaries, halo effects around negative shapes, new relations of hue, chroma, and value. But *to enhance the radiance of color*, besides these, more experiments are needed—with polished surfaces, with translucencies which allow a combination of pigment and direct light effects [italics added].[1]

He said that the search for radiant color would involve material and immaterial light effects including natural and electric light. Although Moholy-Nagy died in 1946, he had already espoused specific ideas about the way color in the form of picture-sound would invade every aspect of design once it had become available in motion pictures and television.

Two of Moholy-Nagy's contemporaries, Le Corbusier and Iannis Xenakis, fulfilled part of his prophecy by designing a temporary, experimental visual-spatial-auditory show at the 1958 World Expo in Brussels. They designed a pavilion for Philips, the electronics manufacturer, where "colour was not only allowed free reign without adherence to form, but also appeared in piercing and luminous *electronic* form."[2] Titled *Poème électronique*, the installation is regarded as the first immersive multimedia environment that relied on sophisticated electronic circuits (Figure III.1). Accompanied by electroacoustical sounds, Le Corbusier and Xenakis choreographed an illusion of movement, a continuously shifting play of projected pictures, colors, and atmospheres.[3]

The extravagant color-light experiment of the Philips Pavilion presaged the use of color in architecture, urbanism, and landscape design that would occur more than 30 years later, in the 1990s.[4]

In the intervening decades of the 1960s, 1970s, and 1980s, artists combined pigment and light effects, fusing color and space and making color look like air—just as Moholy-Nagy foretold. Donald Judd (1928–94), a multimedia minimalist, was the first to merge color with space: "More than the so-called form, or the shapes, colour is the most powerful force. … [T]he century's development of colour could continue no further on a flat surface. … Colour to continue had to occur in space."[5] In Judd's work, color became a material in and of itself, an immediate sensation and phenomenon devoid of predetermined meaning. Newly invented for commercial and industrial use, vivid and artificial color emanated from transparent Plexiglas, anodized metals, and iridescent industrial paint (including motorcycle lacquer) in his art.[6] Judd and his contemporaries, Dan Flavin (1933–96), Andy Warhol (1928–87), and other minimalist, conceptual, and pop artists stripped color from materials and surfaces and made it an object of spatial exploration.

Looking to the mundane and popular for beauty, Warhol began working with luminous material for mass media and advertising, like Day-Glo paint and fluorescent light. Color was playful, radiant, and increasingly branded for consumption. The painter Yves Klein (1928–62) registered his deep blue hue paint formula under the name International Klein Blue at the French Institut National de la Propriété Industrielle in May 1960, and Pantone, which began as a commercial printing company in the 1950s, established its standardized Matching Color System in 1963.[7] Improved color reproduction systems—CMYK, a standardized method of printing color using cyan, magenta, yellow, and black inks in printing, and RGB, which uses red, green, and blue colored light in photographic color film and cathode-ray tubes—dominated commercial markets, and they continue to shape art and design production today.

The eruption in the use of stridently pure, nonneutral, even vulgar shades of cheap paint in the mid-20th century was part of the move to the vernacular and the popular. The period also gave rise to a search for glossy material and natural light effects. Earthworks and Land Art artists abandoned traditional art materials, including paint and electric light, and left the studio to work outdoors. Robert Irwin (b. 1928), Walter de Maria (1935–2013), Nancy Holt (1938–2014), Robert Smithson (1938–73), and James Turrell (b. 1943), among others, composed works of unprecedented scale using dirt, plants, and natural spectral light in remote landscapes.

The awe-inducing light became a central element in the work of de Maria, Holt, and Turrell.[8] De Maria's *Lightning Field* (1977) near Quemado, New Mexico, creates the spectacle of a lightning event using a giant grid of stainless steel poles. In the northwestern Utah desert, Holt's massive and elegant *Sun Tunnels* (1976) frames the landscape and casts shadows that mark solar and lunar configurations of light. Turrell's art, almost exclusively defined and shaped by natural and fluorescent light, creates ethereal environments that induce and evoke new levels of awareness and transcendence in viewers using constructed apertures that dematerialize space, turning it into air. In *Roden Crater* (created in 1977), a long-extinct volcano near Flagstaff, Arizona, Turrell has fashioned a series of connected underground viewing chambers open to the sky to mark and frame external experiences of changing skies and celestial elements. Crossing the boundaries between matter and ether and interior and exterior, his work set the stage for architecture and landscape architecture to enter the era of affect in the last two decades of the 20th century. The Earthworks and Land Artists engaged Edmund Burke's centuries-old idea of the sublime. But whereas Burke's sublime inspired a sense of terror that engendered instinctive self-preservation, 20th century artists awakened a technological sublime of pure spectacle.

Architecture, too, underwent changes in the course of entering the postmodern phase. A mix of new and old ideologies in the field gave color a new lease of life. Rejecting the modern dogma, postmodern architecture charted a world of "complexity and contradiction."[9] Interest in both high- and low-brow architectural aesthetics coexisted and, in the 1960s and 1970s, architecture embraced two opposing color expressions. On the one hand, the pervasive whiteness and metallics that dominated modern architecture were replaced with the "classy" colors of natural, time-proven materials—the subdued yellows, beiges, and browns of granite, travertine, marble, and brick.[10] On the other hand, architecture in commercial strips, suburban malls, and urban public spaces was embellished with gaudy colors and neon lighting. Caught up in the alluring advertising and commercial product design so vividly manifest in pop art, architecture put all the colors on display, none more prominent than the others.[11] But the turn to showy color intensified the white image of modern architecture and validated the return of color as a superfluous ornament.[12] Representative of the era is the Piazza d'Italia (1978) in New Orleans, Louisiana, by August Perez and Associates and Charles Moore. Built below a casino tower as a gift from the Italian community to the city, it comprises an eclectic collage of classical Italian symbols and archetypes and showy fountains. Old and new materials, from marble to stucco to neon, are carefully situated to create a dramatic sequential experience. The project celebrates the new freedom and permissiveness of architectural postmodernism.

Landscape architecture, meanwhile, came under the influence of city and regional planning as well as environmental and social science. Cognizant of the consequences of expanding urbanization, many designers followed Ian McHarg's *Design with Nature* (1969), which championed large-scale land use, in which more ecological factors could be considered. Sociology and environmental psychology stirred landscape architects to focus on the pedestrian scale and community participation and to counter traffic engineers and top-down modernist planning.[13] These approaches largely produced formulaic design, naturalistic landscapes, and design by the community. The pressure on landscape architects to change course increased as artists and architects breached disciplinary confines and entered park and urban landscape design territory. Critics sounded the alarm—landscape architecture was neither advancing an operational theory nor shaping new landscapes.[14]

Artistic considerations of color continued to be absent in landscape design in the 1970s. The competition for attention with other cultural practices ultimately forced landscape architects to reverse course and renew its ties with art and architecture. The year 1980 signified the fulcrum of change, when the bold moves of the young American landscape architect Martha Schwartz and the editor of *Landscape Architecture Magazine* (*LAM*), Grady Clay, joined forces.

Radiant Architecture, Luminous Landscapes

Slow to awaken to the sea changes in art and architecture, *Landscape Architecture Magazine*, the chief discursive platform of the American landscape architecture profession, didn't acknowledge them until January 1980. The featured essay and cover image of Martha Schwartz's Bagel Garden—created as a joke in the front yard of her Boston home and office—shocked practitioners and sparked productive debate about the direction of the profession in the postmodern age (see Figure 7.2). Two rows of bagels she bought at the corner bakery, waterproofed with glazing from a hardware store, lined her mundane and vividly colored garden. She arranged the bagels on a rectangular strip of purple aquarium gravel between clipped boxwood hedges, bringing surprise, humor, fun, and freshness to the garden.

Although the content within the magazine, which set the tone for the profession, changed little—it took two years for *Landscape Architecture Magazine* to devote an issue to postmodernism[15]—a small group of young landscape design professionals, recent graduates from Harvard University, including George Hargreaves, Jory Johnson, and Schwartz, among others, began calling their work postmodern and made a notable shift toward bold colors. They studied under Peter Walker (b. 1932) and practiced in his Sasaki Walker Associates (SWA) Group offices,[16] breaking with established functional and scientific conventions, renewing the classic debate over landscape as nature versus landscape as artifact, and arguing that landscape form and color shouldn't look natural. Walker, who had lost interest in functionalist and mechanistic landscape design in the mid-1970s, encouraged his students to seek inspiration in art, especially sculpture.[17] Walker opened ways to rethink landscape as art, taking cues from the field compositions of sculptors and the marking of postindustrial and desert landscapes by land artists, and he revisited the grand formal gestures of 17th century Versailles and 19th century Central Park.[18] For him, art became a way of lifting landscapes from being merely functional and pleasant to exciting artifice.

If the modernists—Guevrekian, Eckbo, and Burle Marx—took inspiration from the form, material, and color of Cubists, Constructivists, and Surrealists, the young postmodern landscape designers followed conceptual, minimalist, pop, and land art. They searched for ways to apply contemporary art to the expanding practice of urban, corporate, and institutional landscapes. Walker and his energetic apprentices went on to produce significant projects that featured innovative water and steam fountains, illumination, artificial materials (like "silica" rocks glowing in bright colors), and, most significantly, vast ground plane color patterns with repetitive arrangements of objects.[19] Among these projects, the IBM Solana corporate park at Westlake-Southlake (1988), Texas, was the most daring in color.[20] Although color was clearly present in Walker's work, it was not his focus; he rarely spoke of it until the 1990s. Walker's geometric, continuous, and layered floor "carpet" integrated the 17th century French garden parterre and the early 20th century modernist garden with new stimuli that came from architecture.

The influence of the first and second prize projects of the Parc de la Villette design competition in Paris (1981–2) by the architects Bernard Tschumi and Rem Koolhaas, respectively, proved contagious to landscape architects. Breaking with romantic and modernist park models, both Tschumi and Koolhaas created a three-layered design. Tschumi's overlays of lines consisting of promenades, walkways, and bridges emphasized movement through the park; fields comprised large lawns and thematic gardens for play; and a grid of points or follies made of 35 bright red, enameled steel structures established activity hubs and branded the park in a new era of consumer entertainment. Independent programmatic layers of highly geometric patterns came to dominate large landscape architectural floor plans in the 1980s.

As importantly, drawing on cultural allusions, historical references, and the spatial lessons and expanded design vocabulary, landscape projects showcased visual ambiguity, cultural criticism, fun—and a lot more color. Fanciful parking lots, rooftops, and gardens featured a fresh approach to color that was artificial, loud, lavish, and uncompromising. For their color explorations landscape architects turned away from architecture, toward the plastic arts and natural light.

Postmodern art gave landscape designers the freedom to explore color without the confines of structure. Natural light became a new design material. Devoid of preconditioned associations, color leaped from objects to surface, space, and atmosphere, becoming more emphatic. Light reflection and optical illusion enhanced the experience and created strangeness and playfulness. The Harlequin Plaza (1980–2) in Englewood, Colorado, designed by SWA Sausalito (with Hargreaves as team lead designer), was a suburban office court suffused with color and optical tricks. A black-and-white, harlequin-patterned terrazzo pavement is ricocheted by two mirror-

III.2 Harlequin Plaza, Englewood, Colorado, George Hargreaves lead designer, Sasaki, Walker Associates (SWA) Sausalito office, 1980–2. © SWA Group / Gerry Cambell

surfaced office buildings on either side and juxtaposes a high red wall that tapers down through the plaza, running into a purple wall (Figure III.2).[21] Tiffany Plaza (1983), designed by Lee Weintraub in South Bronx, New York, featured a playful constellation of eclectic historical architectural fragments and ethnic motifs, showy fountains and materials, soft and elegant colors, and a play of light and shadow.[22] The postmodern harbingers garnered praise: "Landscape architecture desperately needed the jolt of [Schwartz's] Bagel and Necco gardens, and the Tiffany and Harlequin plazas. One cannot but admire the open-mindedness that was a prerequisite for the creation of these places," said Steven Krog, a key critic. But he also expressed skepticism about the depth and viability of these projects in the long run.[23]

While postmodern landscape color may have appeared superficial, it had a revolutionary effect on the profession. Bold colors proliferated in landscape projects and garden festivals after the first annual Chaumont-sur-Loire Garden Festival in 1992 and its many offshoots throughout the world. The common denominator of these works was a conceptual grounding, the "harnessing of an idea, or a set of related ideas, as the starting point for work that was characterized by the use of colour, artificial materials and witty commentary on a site's history and culture," Schwartz said in a retrospective essay.[24] Unsurprisingly, these landscape characteristics increasingly appealed to corporate customers and city councils, who saw in them an opportunity to "brand" their outdoor space. It was the projects' agency of narrative, interrelated allusions, and iconic form and color that gave them conceptual lift and visibility, although several of them were criticized for putting form and color ahead of function.

In the late 1980s, landscape design's representational techniques reflected the postmodern shift. Designers began using the surrealist Xeroxed collages and composite drawings of Archigram, Superstudio, and Rem Koolhaas, deconstructed and layered axons of Bernard Tschumi, and naive, eclectic, and colorful models of the Dutch architectural firm the Office for Metropolitan Architecture (OMA), which had been heavily used in architecture since the 1960s. The 1986 Harvard Graduate School of Design exhibition, "Transforming the American Garden: 12 New Landscape Designs," was considered to be a breakthrough.[25] The exhibition and its accompanying museum-style catalog intended to let the designers think of themselves as artists free from practical considerations. The range of visual explorations—notably collage or composite drawings, dioramas, and other objects—clearly built on and expanded those used by architects. Advances in photocopiers and color ink-jet printers supported the new experiments. Within a decade, the massive shift to personal computing and digital drawings, using standardized computer-aided design (CAD) software and the luminous red, green, blue (RGB) light-color system, opened new creative avenues for some, while slowing down creativity for others. The promotional and marketing materials of landscape architectural firms adopted the form of glossy, color-saturated, self-published monographs with images bleeding off the page, and little text.

In the final decade of the century, luminous architectural glass façades began reflecting the same digital screens that were used to design them. The 1995 Museum of Modern Art exhibition "Light Constructions" heralded the change. For contemporary designers, working with light and glass wasn't a passing fashion; it became integral to their search for new materials and techniques: "Today, every project begins and ends behind a layer of glass—from computer screen to glass façades"; signaling a more pluralist, media-saturated world, the focus has turned "away from objects themselves toward their impact upon us."[26] As design increasingly relied on special light and color effects, the importance of form diminished.

In 1999 Rem Koolhaas forecasted that:

> It is only logical that, with the incredible sensorial onslaught that bombards us every day and the artificial intensities that we encounter in the virtual world, the nature of colour should change, no longer just a thin layer of change, but something that genuinely alters perception. In this sense, the future of colour is looking bright.[27]

In the 21st century, where little if anything is experienced, produced, known, or felt that is not in some way affected by or connected to digital technology, where life exists in part in an illusionary world of images, color as affect (immersive color, devoid of signification) has gained primacy. Koolhaas's forecast of a bright future for color as a tool to alter perception remains true 20 years later.

Notes

1. These two quotations are from Moholy-Nagy, *Vision in Motion,* 1947, 166, 168.
2. Kane, "Broken Colour in a Modern World," 2015, 9 [italics in original].
3. Kalff, "The Light Effects," 1958/1959, 38.
4. The architectural theorist Mark Wigley posits that atmosphere has always eluded architecture because of its reliance on physical matter and fixity. See Wigley, "The Architecture of Atmosphere," 1998, 25.
5. Judd, "Some Aspects of Colour," [1994] 2008, 205. Judd began working with one or two pigments and moved to polychrome in the last decade of his career.
6. Temkin, *Color Chart*, 2008, 177.
7. Klein's Blue realized the artist's concepts of immaterialized and spatialized image and color. Pantone's Matching Color System has been widely adopted by graphic designers and reproduction and printing houses.
8. Beardsley, *Earthworks and Beyond*, 1984, 39.
9. Venturi, *Complexity and Contradiction in Architecture*, 1966.
10. Koolhaas, "The Future of Colours Is Looking Bright," 1999, 13.
11. Ibid.
12. Wigley, *White Walls, Designer Dresses*, 1995, 330.
13. A leader among community participation advocates was the landscape architect Randy Hester. One of the leading practitioners, Lawrence Halprin, directed focus to the human dimension. He was inspired by a range of fields—including modern dance, behavioral psychology, and natural history—as evident in many of his civic squares and pedestrian malls in the 1960s and 1970s.
14. Krog, "Whither the Garden?," 1991, 96.

15   The *LAM* editors of the January 1982 issue on postmodernism acknowledged the profession was behind the curve. Still, they presented confusing and contradictory arguments about postmodernism. On the one hand, they claimed that it is the kind of practice that landscape architects already engaged in and ridiculed architects who considered postmodernism brand new and suddenly "rediscovered" the history, context, and genius loci of their building site. On the other hand, the editors criticized landscape design for its lack of inventiveness and considered it a genuine search to fight and overturn puritanical functionalist rules: "Post Modern means design freedom" through ambiguity, inversion, and strangeness—and landscape designers should look more closely at the evolving postmodern architecture." See, Johnson, "Post Modernism," 1982, 53. See also, Eastman, "Coining a Phrase," 1982, 55.

16   SWA was the office Walker founded with Hideo Sasaki after he graduated from Harvard in 1957. He worked at SWA until 1983.

17   Walker admired the minimalist work of Judd, Carl Andre, and Robert Morris, the Earthworks of Smithson and Holt, the vast temporary installations of Christo, and the phenomenological engagement of Turrell.

18   Walker, "A Gallery Exhibition," 1982.

19   Walker, "Peter Walker: A Personal Approach to Design," 1989, 10; Walker, *Experiments in Gesture, Seriality and Flatness*, 1991.

20   Solana was a collaboration with the architect Ricardo Legorreta, who is known for his bright monochromatic stucco walls, after Luis Barragán.

21   Kassler, "Since 1964," 1984, 107. The plaza has since been completely redesigned.

22   The jury that selected the project for an urban design merit award in 1983 remarked: "The fountains answer the spectacle and ceremony suggested by the church, while the lions evoke its sovereign themes, whimsy and delight. … Tiffany hints that something new is about to break" in design. *LAM* editors, "Tiffany Plaza," 1983.

23   Krog, "Whither the Garden?," 1991, 99–100.

24   Schwartz, "Forward," 2009, 9.

25   Van Valkenburgh, "Transforming the American Garden," 1986, 6.

26   Gannon, "Light Constructions," 2007.

27   Koolhaas, "The Future of Colours," 1999, 16.

References

Beardsley, John. *Earthworks and Beyond: Contemporary Art in the Landscape*. New York: Abbeville Press, 1984.

Eastman, Susan Rausch. "Coining a Phrase." *Landscape Architecture* 72, no. 1 (January 1982): 54–61.

Gannon, Todd. "Light Constructions." 2007. Paper draft.

Johnson, Norman K. "Post Modernism: Questions Not to Ask." *Landscape Architecture* 72, no. 1 (January 1982): 52–3.

Judd, Donald. "Some Aspects of Colour in General and Red and Black in Particular," [1994]. In *Colour*, ed. by David Batchelor, 201–7. London: Whitechapel Gallery, 2008.

Kalff, L. C. "The Light Effects." *Philips Technical Review* 20, nos. 2/3 (1958/9): 37–42.

Kane, Carolyn L. "Broken Colour in a Modern World: Chromatic Failures in Purist Art and Architecture." *Journal of the International Colour Association* 14 (2015): 1–13.

Kassler, Elizabeth B. "Since 1964." In *Modern Gardens and the Landscape*, rev. ed., 94–110. New York: Museum of Modern Art, 1984.

Koolhaas, Rem. "The Future of Colours Is Looking Bright." In *OMA 30 Colour: New Colours for a New Century*, 13–16. Blaricum, the Netherlands: V+K Publishing, 1999.

Krog, Steven. "Whither the Garden?" In *Denatured Visions: Landscape and Culture in the Twentieth Century*, ed. by Stuart Wreke and William Howard Adams, 94–105. New York: Museum of Modern Art, 1991.

LAM editors. "Tiffany Plaza." *Landscape Architecture* 73, no. 5 (September/October 1983): 82.

McHarg, Ian L. *Design with Nature*. Garden City, NY: Published for the American Museum of Natural History [by] the Natural History Press, 1969.

Moholy-Nagy, László. *Vision in Motion*. Chicago: P. Theobald, 1947.

Schwartz, Martha. "Foreword," In *Avant Gardeners: 50 Visionaries of Contemporary Landscape*, ed. by Tim Richardson, 8–9. London: Thames & Hudson, 2009.

Temkin, Ann, ed. *Color Chart: Reinventing Color, 1950 to Today*. New York: Museum of Modern Art, 2008.

Van Valkenburgh, Michael R. "Transforming the American Garden: 12 New Landscape Designs," exhibition catalogue. Boston: Harvard University Graduate School of Design, 1986.

Venturi, Robert. *Complexity and Contradiction in Architecture*. New York: Museum of Modern Art, 1966.

Walker, Peter. "A Gallery Exhibition: Peter Walker Explores Art into Landscape." *Landscape Architecture* 72, no. 1 (January 1982): 62–3.

Walker, Peter. "Peter Walker: A Personal Approach to Design." *Process* 85 (October 1989): 10.

Walker, Peter. *Peter Walker: Experiments in Gesture, Seriality and Flatness*, ed. by Linda L. Jewell. New York: Rizzoli, 1991.

Wigley, Mark. *White Walls, Designer Dresses: The Fashioning of Modern Architecture*. Cambridge, MA: MIT Press, 1995.

Wigley, Mark. "The Architecture of Atmosphere." *Daidalos* 68 (1998): 13–26.

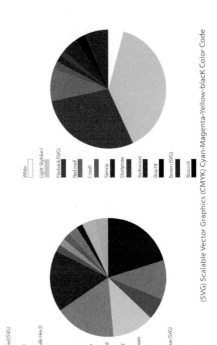

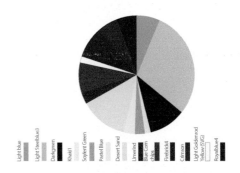

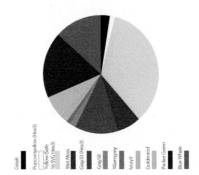

(SVG) Scalable Vector Graphics (CMYK) Cyan-Magenta-Yellow-blacK Color Code

White | Light Skyblue1 | Firebrick (SVG) | Red roof | Coral1 | Sienna | Dustyrose | Burlswood2 | Bisq18 | Brown (SVG) | Broccoli

Passion Fruit | Palevioletred (SVG) | Sqtsalmon | Firebrick (Safe Hex3) | Pink3 | Grape | Nikko Blue | Golden rod | Indianred2 | Soylent Green | Od Green | Lightskyblue (SVG) | Battleship

Light blue | Light Steelblue3 | Darkegreen | Khaki1 | Soylent Green | Pastkel Blue | Desert Sand | Limestine | Blue Corn chips | Firebrick4 | Citrimon | Light Goldenrod Yellow (SVG) | Royalblue4

Grey6 | Popcornyellow (Hex3) | Yellow (Safe 16 SVG Hex3) | Wet Moss | Gray33 (Hex3) | Gray58 | Warmgrey | Ivory3 | Goldenrod | Packer Green | Blue Whale

7.0 Diagrams, color analysis of Davis Garden, El Paso, Texas (upper two) and the Mesa Arts Center (MAC) public space, Mesa, Arozona (lower two), 2021. Photos: Mira Engler. Rendered by Maryam Maddahzad

(Unless noted otherwise, drawings and projects in Chapter 7 are by Martha Schwartz Partners.)

7

Conceptual Color
Purely Synthetic,
Martha Schwartz (b. 1950)

Color rocks. Color in my career is the most difficult design move. It is highly emotive, and it has cultural meanings. There's so much complexity about how we feel about color, probably just because we feel it. We are very sensitized to color.

Martha Schwartz, interview, 2020

Living on Crosby Street, New York, in the late 1970s, Martha Schwartz, recent Harvard landscape architecture graduate, began testing the efficacy of color using the simple act of spray painting. Her account of Untitled, an artwork done in her backyard parking lot, discloses the transformative sway of color she discovered:

> It was a parking lot filled with cars, gravel, and then ailanthus trees, the weeds. So I went out and painted them in purple. Then I just watched people walking along react to them. It made them see the whole space very differently, asking 'what is going on here in this parking lot?' That was a way of putting something upfront but in a very minimal way.[1]

Her spray painting of weeds soon joined other small design moves that similarly demonstrated the power of color to transform the experience of everyday space and objects. Expanding the color repertoire from self-colored material to paint, Untitled entered the belated phase of postmodernism in landscape architecture.

Then in January 1980, the *Landscape Architecture Magazine* cover image and story of Schwartz's "Back Bay Bagel Garden" transformed the landscape architecture profession overnight. Schwartz had created a temporary installation in the front yard of her brick townhouse-office in Boston, featuring 48 pairs of glazed bagels arrayed on purple aquarium gravel between two concentric rectangular boxwood hedges and an inner rectangle planted with a grid of 30 pink geraniums, all surrounded by a typical iron fence. It was a garden like no other (Figure 7.1).[2]

The photographs in *Landscape Architecture Magazine* were seductive. The essay explored witty yet practical arguments about the aptness of bagels in gardens, and (to rebuff anticipated counterarguments) Schwartz's measured plan and elevation drawings showed how one incorporates bagels in a garden.

The project ignited deeper than expected emotions and heated debate about the nature and culture of landscape architecture in the magazine's "Cut & Fill" pages. Among the casualties were the pragmatic reticence of the profession and (eventually) the post of the magazine editor, Grady Clay.[3] One observer wrote that "The debate gave the Bagel Garden a polemical heft that overshot its original aspirations. ... [the Bagel Garden] was

The Bagel Garden

7.1 The Bagel Garden, issue cover, *Landscape Architecture Magazine*, Jan. 1980. © Martha Schwartz Partners

unapologetic, bold, provocateur and, at the same time, a lighthearted and pithy little garden installation."[4] It launched Schwartz's career at an unusually steep pitch. Reminiscing on its impact on the profession and her career, she mused, "It is difficult to live with, like being a child star, [yet] really important."

The Bagel Garden carved for landscape design practice a new space between art and landscape. It cracked open the canons of beauty and assumptions about material and message in a profession gripped by modern functionalism, science, and elitism. Still new to landscape architecture, Schwartz freed landscape designers to imagine that a garden can be about and made of anything.

The Bagel Garden's agent provocateur was clearly the bagels (from a corner bakery) *and* their display on the purple aquarium gravel. Schwartz explained: "If it had not been for the purple gravel, the level of perception would have turned the heat down." The purple—the color of royalty—not only created contrast, making the bagels visually prominent, but also both vivified the transgression and made the mundane bagels elegant. Endowed with cultural and poetic meanings, all colors are highly emotive—people *feel* color, says Schwartz, and feelings may forge both hindrances and openings. Schwartz hones these openings and exploits color to draw attention, affect emotions, and probe cultural meanings and disciplinary assumptions.

Born in Philadelphia to parents of Russian Jewish descent, an architect father and a real estate saleswoman mother whose brothers were architects and graphic designers, Schwartz fused her parents' vocations with a dose of art. Her upbringing in the sophisticated and aesthetic environment of her father's architectural office (Milton Schwartz and Associates Architects), and childhood art classes at the Philadelphia Museum of Art, shaped her early interest in art and eventual resolve to opt for the less structured arena of an artist rather than an architect.[5] She enrolled in printmaking in the School of Art and Architecture at the University of Michigan in the late 1960s and early 1970s, but was drawn to the large-scale Earthworks of the likes of Robert Smithson, Walter De Maria, Michael Heizer, Mary Miss, and Richard Long. Intent on acquiring technical tools to build Earthwork art, she transferred to the landscape architecture department. Her sentiments were bolstered after meeting Peter Walker as an intern in the SWA summer student program in 1973. She earned a master's in landscape architecture at Harvard's Graduate School of Design in 1977, at the time that Walker came to Cambridge to kick-start the landscape design curriculum. Walker hired Schwartz at SWA East in San Francisco, an office he founded and directed, and supported her artistic approach to landscape design. They married in 1980.

Like Walker, Schwartz rejected pseudoscientific environmental planning and modernist problem-solving models and was drawn to minimalist artists like Robert Irwin, Carl Andre, and Donald Judd, who manipulated space through seriality and gesture. Her work with Walker, a prominent landscape architect with an established career by the time they met, was indispensable.

In 1983 Schwartz opened her own New York office, Martha Schwartz Inc., and four years later founded a joint office with Walker, Peter Walker/Martha Schwartz, where each worked on different projects and with separete teams. In 1990 Schwartz and Walker parted ways, and Schwartz opened an office with Ken Smith and David Meyer. Two years later she began teaching at Harvard and founded Martha Schwartz Partners (MSP), which now has offices in Boston, London, and Shanghai. With four major monographs and numerous lectures, essays, and interviews, she has been a formidable force in the profession.[6]

When Schwartz began her career in the late 1970s, landscape architecture was dominated by men, the established position on landscape was functional, and architects had little regard for landscape architects. She set out to raise the status of landscape architecture. As a political figure and a feminist, she fought to be accepted as a woman artist in a sexist profession, secured tenure at Harvard, and has sustained a high-profile career as a woman who is continuously vocal about her culture, profession, and gender.

Of her novel applications of color, Schwartz says, "I have used color much more politically than as a painter. It is there for a reason." Her color design does not simply decorate but transforms, critiques, puzzles, provokes, delights, and brands. It alters the appearance and experience of a landscape, unleashes a child-like sense of fun, and makes a place imageable and often marketable. Pure, bright colors are a Schwartzian trademark (Figure 7.0). Like Loudon and Guevrekian before her, she uses bold colors to announce human handiwork and proclaim the garden artifice. And much like those of Burle Marx, Schwartz's landscapes teem with color. But her color scheme is minimal—one to four monochromes that do not rely on plants—her colors are neither classical nor harmonious, and they derive mostly from painted and colored material other than plants.

Digital computation and its corresponding RBG color system entered Schwartz's work in the early 1990s, enhancing her chromatic opulence and audacity. Grown out of the postmodern turn in landscape architecture and bolstered by digital sophistication, Schwartz's landscapes radiate hypnotic color power and offer visual tricks. She explores the cultural depth of color as a concept that is devoid of fixed signification. In moving away from or countering signification, she allows color not only to contest disciplinary and cultural ideas about nature and art, but also to register new, more complex conditions and forces of materiality, gender, consumerism, technology, and taste.

Schwartz's work has been described as a "transfiguration of the commonplace," jolting viewers out of a state of distraction, compelling awareness of their values and assumptions, and calling them into question.[7] Color is a central player in Schwartz's transfigurations.

Transfiguration, Pop Color, and Day-Glo

With the eye of an artist, Schwartz sees potential beauty everywhere and value in things that others may discard. Through the 1980s, she often worked with nonstandard materials from junkyards, hardware stores, and popular catalogues, from colored gravel to plastic plants and Astroturf, from garden ornaments to tires, fishing nets, and fairy balls. "Color transforms things that are very everyday and not considered to be good materials" she explains. Coat or spray painting, as in her early Untitled piece, is a basic defamiliarization tactic of making the familiar unfamiliar. It yields dramatic change in an object's form and appearance, covering without concealing. It may beautify, but it does not decorate (wrapping may yield a similar outcome, without permanent disfiguration). Art has proven concealment through paint and wraps to be effective devices to focus attention on and elevate the status of everyday objects, surfaces, and spaces.

Christo (1935–2020) began wrapping objects like chairs and oil barrels as early as the 1960s. With his wife, the artist Jeanne-Claude (1935–2009), he created large-scale, site-specific temporary installations—wrapping a coast with white cloth in Sydney, Australia; surrounding islands with pink nylon sheeting in Florida; and covering bridges in white or gold fabrics in Rome and Paris, among many others. The color choice is always pure, brilliant, and visually prominent relative to the context, and the fabric interacts with the local light. By wrapping, the artists unraveled, compelling people to see places with new eyes. Furthermore, the act of wrapping was itself a kind of performance art. The sites were major attractions for the duration of the installations and, even after the cover was removed, continue to carry the memory of the event.

Schwartz too creates temporary installations, an artform that she introduced to landscape architecture. Her installations unravel and focus attention on common, mostly ignored, and undervalued landscapes, such as roofs, parking lots, strip malls, and road medians. Like those of Christo and Jeanne-Claude, they are performances during construction and spectacles through their duration.

An early Schwartz project, reclamation of a roof—wasted common space—involved several color techniques: wrapping and covering, painting and whitewashing, and reflecting and shining. In 1979, on the small, empty roof of their four-story, brick townhouse at 190 Marlborough Street in Back Bay, Boston, Walker and Schwartz, with John Wong, created a place for sunning, eating, and enjoying the views of Boston's skyline. With a limited budget, they used Astroturf and gravel to cover parts of the roof, whitewashed the shed and lightwell windows, painted the inside of empty clay pots on a grid blue, reflected the sky on a grid of mirrors, and, at night, shone colored light through the lightwell windows. The sky and cloud reflections in the mirrors animated the space, and the small gridded mirrors and pots produced a greater sense of depth. The designers appropriated the 18th century English landscape concept of "borrowed landscape" and incorporated the grand view of city roofs, walls, chimneys, and skyscrapers.

An inexpensive coat of paint was especially important in many of Schwartz's early projects of low or no budget. It became a veneer for cheap material. "Color was a way of giving a design a power. ... I would use colors because of really not having the budget to do much. I made things out of nothing." For her, design and art do not depend on material quality but rather on how things are put together and how materials interact. "Cheap and colorful equals beautiful," declared Schwartz.[8] Her "economy of means" approach is especially relevant at the landscape scale, where creation of a conspicuous effect typically requires a grand intervention involving quantities of material.[9] Schwartz uses cheap, off-the-shelf paint and factory-colored products, along with scrapings and recycled material. Spray paint and fluorescent Day-Glo paint, such as that used in safety applications and signage, came in handy. It was inspired by the color of everyday consumer products and landscapes—neon lights and commercial strip signs, bright traffic signs, and pavement marking—Schwartz's bright industrial colors have become her design signature.

Schwartz's work resonates with Andy Warhol's (1928–87), who used synthetic Day-Glo in the mid-1960s, initially in his commercial art and advertising and later in his artwork. It echoes the rawness and humor of Dan Flavin (1933–96), who used fluorescent color tubes he bought from the hardware store. And, it is guided by Frank Stella's (b. 1936) application of fluorescent and industrial canned paint directly on to monumental canvases or metal wall constructions that are then spattered with glitter on top. As inspiration, Schwartz points to Stella's interlacing, circular cities he created with a protractor, where color alterantes for contrast, instead of following some sort of color theory, forces the viewer to absorb it as a non representational part of the piece (Figure 7.2). She demonstrated this on vast surfaces in Snoopy's Garden (1991) and the Moscone Center Competition (1990). The Stella Garden (1980), a project created in the backyard of her mother, Stella, outside Philadelphia, in turn, echoes Frank Stella's colorful relief constructions.

The Stella Garden flaunted the transformative power of color (Figure 7.3). Using color and light, in 1980 she transformed the small, dreary backyard, an old garage wall flanking it, and even the garbage cans into "a fantasy environment for viewing, much as one can gaze into a Fabergé egg."[10] With junk from her mother's garage—chicken wire and rickety wooden ladders as well as a fishing net canopy, colored aquarium gravel, and colored Plexiglas scraps—color and light entered the garden in multiple guises: through paint, factory-colored material, transparency, reflection, shadow, and artificial light. Schwartz replaced the old garbage cans that stood along the driveway and entrance to the garden with five new ones that she painted with pink glitter and epoxy to sparkle in the sunshine: "I figured that if my mother had to walk past garbage cans to get to the garden, at least they were going to be beautiful garbage cans."[11]

Through innovative color techniques and effects, the Stella Garden thwarted the modernist pressure to use durable and expensive material. The colored aquarium gravel laid on the ground in an amorphous pattern, disregarding the layer of strict grid cells made of lumber, lends the color freedom and the space dynamism. The two tall tree trunks at the

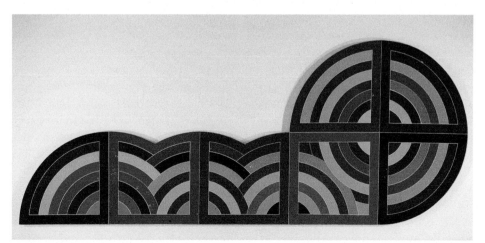

7.2 Frank Philip Stella, "Raqqa II," 1970, synthetic polymer and graphite on canvas. © North Carolina Museum of Art, Raleigh, Gift of Mr. and Mrs. Gordon Hanes, 82.16 / 2022 Frank Stella / Artists Rights Society (ARS), New York

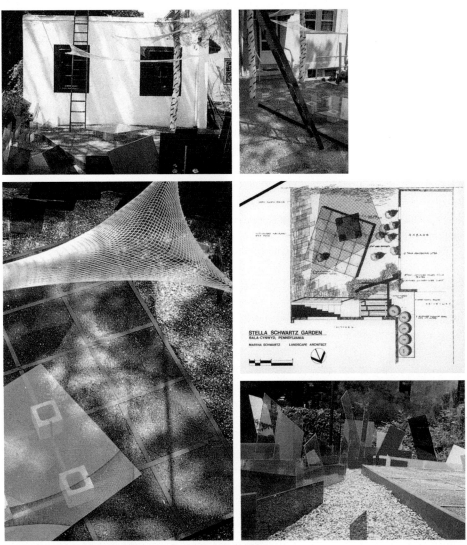

7.3 The Stella Garden, Philadelphia, Pennsylvania, 1980

entrance to the yard were painted white with red and green dashes to blend in with the colorful chaos of the rest of the garden, such that a cloud of white spray-painted chicken wire supported by the trunks appears to float alone, blending in with the colorful chaos of the rest of the garden.[12] A ladder salvaged from the garage was painted dark green and propped against the whitewashed garage wall, introducing a surrealist, trompe l'oeil effect—the garage wall looked eerie and longer, and the left black-framed window appeared smaller than its corresponding right window when viewed from the house. To better join the house with the garden, Schwartz repainted the stone foundation of the house and concrete stairwell down to the basement with light lavender and covered the stairs to the back door with turquoise and green Astroturf strips.[13] She placed a small wire glass table at the center under the canopy to reflect light and the blue sky, substituting it for a high-maintenance water feature. Finally, she arranged colored Plexiglas slabs in the border and graded them from clear to warm to cool colors to look like a colorful flower bed.[14] The early morning sun, shining through the panels, casts colored shadows across the gravel. At night, light through the colored panels produces a magical garden atmosphere.[15]

Sidelining expensive materials and valorizing lowly materials and discarded objects was Schwartz's way of critiquing mainstream landscape architecture, much as pop artists critiqued mainstream art. Moreover, by rethinking design materials, she believed landscape architecture could move forward and expand its language and design concepts:

> We could increase our conceptual language; granite curbs could be reconstituted plastic, glass, marbles, or Astroturf. In language, one's lack of vocabulary limits what one can think. Make something remarkable out of humble materials. Trying to find virtue in lowly inexpensive materials is inevitable if one wishes to proceed into the future with optimism. In the same way, the lack of material possibilities limited conceptual thinking in landscape architecture.[16]

Schwartz's exploration of new and unconventional materials was also coupled with the desire to be part of a consumer culture that feeds on mass-produced, cheaply available, and disposable products. As importantly, she sought to continue the modernists' push to steer the profession away from plants—and thus away from "green architects" who plant trees after the architect has left the scene.

Schwartz is driven by challenge: "I wanted to challenge conventional thought and beliefs long before I ever knew landscape architecture existed."[17] Critique is her stimulant and device to improve the world.

Critique: Green and Other Landscape Jokes

Critique begets critique. Critics deemed Schwartz's landscapes "unecological" or "antinature," disparaging their synthetic material and artificial gaudy color. They saw the work as a ridicule of and a threat to what was considered appropriate for the profession. The censure served as both irritant and energizer for Schwartz, who mocked the critics' ill-conceived assumptions and questioned their judgments as she affirmed that ecology and artistic expression in landscape are not mutually exclusive:

> [C]ritics wrongly attribute to my designs a lack of ecological responsibility. I am often stunned by these criticisms, particularly because they come most often from within the profession, where styles such as naturalism or "eco-rev" are fashionable, easily understood and highly marketable. It is falsely believed that if a landscape looks "natural," it is in fact natural, ecological or even sustainable.[18]

In a lecture she delivered in 2004 Schwartz deemed the criticism to have risen from several misguided cultural and professional forces. Among them are the American idea of "wilderness" fed by the environmental movement's powerful preference for naturalistic imagery—a fantasy that grips the profession; the widespread belief that landscapes are somehow an inappropriate medium for art; the pragmatism of the American corporate and institutional markets that regards art as superfluous and unruly; and the shortsightedness of architects, who accept landscapes only as benign backdrops that do not compete with their buildings. These ideas, said Schwartz, created "landscape tokenism," the symbolic and minimal effort to "green" acres of urban concrete, like highways, parking lots, and garage roofs.[19] Schwartz doubled down: "Ideas must be challenged in order to prove their viability in a culture. Much of the art … may be important only in that it creates discussion and in the end critical self-reflection."[20] Her work, especially in the 1980s, has been described as "a form of built criticism and construction, simultaneously challenging existing norms and imagining new landscape worlds to replace the old."[21]

Schwartz's acts of artistic transgression subject forms, materials, and objects to an array of tactics: juxtaposition, inversion, mutation, aggrandization, excessive repetition, and ironic commentary, often simultaneously. Color is used both as a perceptual tool and in support of a design concept; "there is so much power in color, because there is so much meaning in it." As an artist, she puts color to work on the senses; as a cultural critic, she uses its transcultural relativity to challenge social and cultural ideology, code, and symbolism. Internationally, rules about color change because of what it means to a particular culture:

> In Northern Europe, everything is very subdued. Big bold pieces of color are okay if there's enough grey, black, or white around, but when there are too many colors it is really upsetting. That shows that you are from a different culture or have bad taste. … In China and the Middle East, people tend to be very colorful, the culture wants and loves it."

The idea of color as a social phenomenon has been the subject of the historian Michel Pastoureau's work:

> It is society that 'makes' color, defines it, gives it its meaning, constructs its codes and values, establishes its uses, and determines whether it is acceptable or not. The artist, the intellectual, human biology, and even nature, are ultimately irrelevant to this process of ascribing meaning to color."[22]

Schwartz works carefully within the confines of each culture. Her musing on color echoes the difficulty and uncovers the arbitrariness of ascribing meanings.

Green, especially, presents Schwartz with an ideological conundrum. It has been imbued with the meanings of nature, health, and rebirth, at least since the renewed attraction to nature as part of late 19th century Romanticism. Goethe considered green a soothing color and recommended its use for decorating places of rest and conviviality, an idea that has persisted.[23] Plants, the prime medium of landscape architecture, have thus relegated the profession to the business of "green therapy," often in opposition to the city.

For Schwartz landscape is always designed; it is inherently unnatural. Yet for most people in the Western world nature or landscape equal green, even when many arid landscapes are not green at all. Furthermore, corporations have used green in the guise of politics and profit, attributing to it a distorted ethical dimension.

Schwartz cannot stomach any pretense of false nature. She contests the use of terms like "natural," "artificial," "native," and "exotic."[24] The small rooftop Splice Garden (1986) at the Whitehead Institute for Biomedical Research in Cambridge, Massachusetts, is an early example (Figure 7.4). Taking the idea and image of green nature to an extreme, Schwartz constructed an all-green garden—no other color was permitted. The roof space was filled with green aquarium glass chips and furnished with Astroturf-covered benches and planters with plastic plants, including one mounted perpendicularly on a

7.4 The Splice Garden, Whitehead Institute, Cambridge, Massachusetts, 1986

wall. Schwartz's acerbic rationale for barring living plants centered on the tokenism of a garden in a tiny space that had no weight capacity to carry a living garden, no water access, and no plan for maintenance. She linked the formal concept to landscape gardening traditions, drawing typologies from French Baroque and Japanese Zen gardens that she mixed and grafted. It was a commentary on the deceit inherent in the concept of nature, the artificiality of gardens, and the danger inherent in the genetic splicing work carried out by the institute, including the possibility of creating a monster. The Splice Garden itself was described as a "monster" that spoke to two different entitled manipulators: landscape architects and gene scientists.[25]

The Splice Garden entered the landscape debate of natural versus artificial through image, material, and, notably, color. Schwartz explained:

> Once [artificial] color is there, it signals that this is not natural nature. The idea that we even consider color as artificial is weird. Many things natural are full of color, and most of nature is color coded. So the issue is not so much nature and natural color as how humans view color in terms of what's right and wrong in society, and what rules are made up about what is appropriate and not appropriate. *Color is anathema for landscape architecture* [italics added].

Turning color anathema on its head, green's indissoluble association with nature was particularly apt for Schwartzian manipulation: she included green in her work *only* as unnatural and as a joke. Astroturf was handy for both "greening" and commenting on landscape architecture and architecture.

Schwartz's Turf Parterre Garden (1988) in the grounds of the newly built World Financial Center complex in lower Manhattan is made entirely of Astroturf. The minuscule portion

213

of land allocated by the architect for a garden prompted her to utilize instead the vertical surface of the building as the ground plane—she referred to her piece as "landscape wallpaper" for building façades. In presenting an honorable award to the installation, the 1989 *Landscape Architecture Magazine* jury recognized Schwartz's clever and critical take on landscape design.[26] The commentary and the new award category, Landscape Art and Earthwork, in which the project was judged were indicative of the growing cracks in the establishment's resistance to new ideas about landscape, even when it was the subject of a joke.

Low budget, demand for low maintenance, and desire for "instant" gardens further buttressed Schwartz's rationale for constructing synthetic landscapes. Her favorite loud, synthetic colors contrast with their context, in part to counter the general chromophobia of Western (especially American) society, and to make an unambiguous statement about the artificiality of gardens and landscapes.

Although mostly intuitive, her emphasis on project concept led to extensive experimentation with the ways in which colors communicate messages. In the King County

7.5 King County Jailhouse Garden, Seattle, Washington, 1987

Jailhouse Garden (1987) in Seattle, Washington, pastel colors of blue, pink, mauve, purple, and yellow, with gray and black accents, projected a restrained sense of gaiety and hope (Figure 7.5). Pastels are associated with candies, girlish stuff, and Easter or the Christian idea of resurrection. Schwartz's use of pastel colors in the severe environment of a jailhouse garden was a way to "sweeten" the bitter pill of incarceration, project a hopeful mood, and inject a feminine softness in a place dominated by men. The small garden space functions as an entry and "lobby" for jailhouse visitors and lawyers, but the prisoners can only see it as a picture from above. Again cognizant of the lack of maintenance budget, Schwartz designed a garden with no real plants. It consists of traditional topiary shapes made of concrete and covered with broken black ceramic tiles. The ground, a pastel mosaic carpet, reinforces a phantom garden atmosphere. The ground, topiary, and faux fountain mosaics merge with a wall tile mural that frames a trompe l'oeil gateway, an exit in a place with no real one. The pastel colors corroborate the hopeful concept and bring a light-hearted mood in a place shrouded with despair. With the pastel prison garden Schwartz aligned message and color within the complex web of professional and cultural meanings.

For the 1986 Harvard Graduate School of Design exhibition, "Transforming the American Garden: 12 New Landscape Designs," participants were asked to rethink the American garden and its loyalty to classical European models. Schwartz's submission did so with a commentary on contemporary urban lifestyle as her New York City Bulb Garden spelled out words in flower colors.[27] The high-rise rooftop garden consisted entirely of potted bulbs arranged in a rectangular bed. During each of New York's four growing seasons one of the four bulbs in each pot flowered—yellow daffodils in early spring, purple anemones in summer, orange Peruvian lilies in early fall, and red amaryllis in late fall—and they were arranged to spell out a word each season: "greed," "evil," "ignorance," and "bliss," sequentially. The color choices hinged both on the meaning of the word and the season's mood; for example, the yellow spring daffodils brightened the spirit after the cold and barren winter even as they alluded to the gold of greed. Schwartz's American garden proposal was subversive, witty, and practical, with its low maintenance requirements and the plants' ability to withstand seasonal variability. It also conveyed a democratic stance: anyone can create an instant garden with pots bought at a nearby nursery.

Some of MSP's recent projects in China, where red is a beloved and considered a blissful color, use grades of red-orange for central, oversized elements, as in the Fengming Mountain Park in Chongqing (2013) and Zigong Dongxingsi Waterfront in Sichuan (2019). In the West, though, she has used red for its more forceful meanings of anger, war, blood, lust, and power. An example is the temporary installation Power Lines (1999) for the International Building Exhibition in Germany's industrial Ruhr region, where she wrapped giant hay bales in bright red and black plastics, the red alluding to the electric power lines that crisscross the region as well as the site's history of war and the black alluding to the major local industry, coal.[28] The bucolic green agricultural landscape created a complete contrast and cut out background "noise." The installation's color scheme intentionally touched on cultural and historical meanings.

In comparison, the red and green swaths that crisscross Grand Canal Square in the reclaimed docklands of Dublin (2017) bring both liveliness and formality to this postindustrial site. The colors allude to the literal red carpet leading to the city's newly built theater and to the river estuary that once lay beneath the reclaimed land. The square's red concrete path is punctuated by 23-foot-high, "drunkenly" slanted, red light poles, and green swaths of native plants and bright green perforated metal benches are in sharp contrast to the gray city, its industrial past, and its often cloudy skies. The unusual angles of the poles and the programmed lighting that dances up and down them bring energy to civic plaza events. They have become the most identifiable feature of Grand Canal Square.[29]

Schwartz's capacity to expunge outmoded cultural referents from color and construct a more open-ended interpretive value system is often achieved with wit and fun. Even, and especially, when color is used to test common clichés, her disarmingly light-hearted presentation defuses conflict.

Humor, Wonder, and Bliss

In Schwartz's work mockery, irony, and humor often overlap. These traits come from her family's Jewish tradition, where, she says, "humor is a powerful tool that allows people to face issues too painful to confront."[30] Physiologically proven to be a socially acceptable method of giving vent to anger and frustration, humor opens people up and relieves stress through laughter. Schwartz uses it effectively to confront, agitate, and make serious points while at the same time educating and entertaining people. "People are more afraid to use color than to look at it. In fact, people are happy to see color. Bright color signals a permission to be free to act," she explains. Her landscapes resonate with the spirited and innocent world of a child. Reminiscing about her child-like delight in color, Schwartz says that she has not allowed herself to outgrow that delight. In her view, grownups are culturally conditioned and act

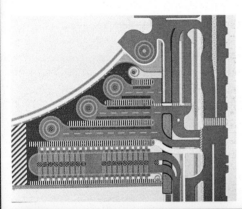

on preconceptions of what is tasteful and approved of in order to be accepted. "As a child, one just gut reacts to color and experiments and invents with it. Leaving yourself open, perhaps vulnerable, is a gift."[31] She wants to trigger in people a child's fresh and open-minded response to color, to feel joyful and even silly.

Humor brings out a surprise element by reframing and exaggerating ideas and stories. Schwartz elicits surprise through exaggeration of scale and unexpected, bright saturated color. For the east entry esplanade at Disneyland Theme Park (1998) in Anaheim, California, she drew on basic, highly visible, brightly colored objects for pedestrian and vehicular road markings and traffic paraphernalia to address the problem of traffic safety at that entrance (Figure 7.6).[32] The plan resembles her favorite French Baroque parterres with yellow road pavement tape, a black-and-white zebra-pattern pedestrian crossing, and traffic cones, all of which are oversized. Recalling French garden topiary, she painted the oversized

7.6 Disneyland, Anaheim, California, computer drawings, East Entrance Plaza, Plan (Top) and perspective (Bottom), 1998

reinforced-concrete traffic cones green (instead of the usual orange). She then flanked each traffic island with formal rows of standard highway lighting in different colored lights to complement the palette, aid wayfinding, and create a fantastic and playful atmosphere.

Pink is Schwartz's ideal muse. It introduces a range of codes and feelings that can prompt a smile and at the same time challenge gender-related biases. The color has been described as bringing an intensity that activates the senses and emotions: "Pink radiates warmth and vitality that elicits the sense of touch, the sense of closeness, the sense of taste (sweetness and fruitiness), and the sense of smell (the fragrance of blossoms)."[33] The biological aspects of pink—the color of sensitive parts of the body—suggest "nakedness," linked to self-awareness and vulnerability.

Schwartz used pink in the playful community gardens at the Kitagata Apartments in Gifu, Japan (2000), and the candied May Day installation (1980) in Cambridge, Massachusetts. Her attraction to the color's gender referent explains why phallic-shaped pink rocks ended up in the prominent circular stone garden and children's play pool in the Kitagata gardens (Figure 7.7). The story behind the pink rocks is as telling as it is entertaining. The original idea for pink granite rocks in a big bowl-shaped fountain was too expensive and so pink granite was changed to pink fiberglass. When the Japanese firm that was commissioned to produce the rocks sent photographs of the product, the pink rocks surprised, even shocked, everyone.

> I think they took our terminology of "pink granite" too literally. We were shocked at the images of these pink … things. The men in our office were most shocked. It was a really embarrassing moment. So I took a vote on whether to keep them. All the men said repaint them …. All the women said they looked nice pink. There were more women than men, so I kept them pink. It was a cross-cultural misunderstanding that worked out brilliantly.[34]

The story may be as straightforward as it sounds. However, when Schwartz is involved, it seems more likely it was a soft coverup for a planned happy ending.

In addition to the circular pink stone fountain, Schwartz created a series of sunken, age-specific garden "rooms" or mini landscapes where everyone could be in his or her own space while being together. The spaces' season-specific materials, texture, and color form a polychrome tapestry to the visual delight of residents looking at them from apartments in the surrounding high-rises. The Four Seasons Garden comprises four miniature spaces that capture the spirit of each season and are enclosed by colored Plexiglas walls in yellow (spring), green (summer), red

7.7 Kitagata Apartments, the circular stone garden and children play pool (top) and bird's-eye view of garden series (bottom), Gifu, Japan, 2000

(fall), and blue (winter). Each room was also fitted with season-related features: the yellow Spring Garden has a yellow S-shaped love seat; the green Summer Garden has a tree, grass, and wall-mounted lugs for a couple of hammocks; the red Autumn Garden is filled with a burning bush (*Euonymus alatus*) and wooden birdhouses; and the blue Winter Garden is a field of gravel and bamboo marked by a central stone cylinder with a small depression for a water freeze.[35] The transparent Plexiglas rooms work as colorful lanterns at night, joining the dramatic illumination of other objects in the complex, including the pink rock fountain.

In the May Day Necco Garden (1980), a daylong art installation in Killian Court at the Massachusetts Institute of Technology in Cambridge, pastel shades were used to arouse sensorial indulgence and capture the traditional spring-focused spirit of May Day.[36] Schwartz overlaid two pastel-colored giant grids: a line grid made of Necco candy wafers aligned with the neoclassical courtyard building columnar façade and a point grid of color-matching tires pointing to a newly installed Michael Heizer sculpture that was inaugurated at the same time. The tiny Necco candy, which was produced by the nearby New England Confectionery Company and donated to the installation, came in many pastel colors and sweet flavors that filled the site in the sweet whiff of spring and Easter bunnies. Schwartz reminisced: "The candy evoked strong associations with childhood pleasures and afternoons at the movies."[37] The pastel shades of the painted tires offset their usual distinct black rubber smell. Together the Necco Garden's festive mood, material, fragrance, and color fully invoked the day's festivities.

In Schwartz's hands color is a device to produce not only fun but also mystery, drama, and fantasy in the landscape. At the Paul-Lincke-Höfe Apartment complex (2000) in Berlin, Schwartz filled the five residential courtyards with enticing colors and fashioned each into a vignette inspired by a Grimm Brothers' fairy tale.[38] To encourage people to engage with the work, Schwartz introduced "a certain kind of mystery, a puzzle that may explain the unconventional design, and one that is hard to figure out, … that is not quite handed on a plate." Wonder and imagination might generate a feeling of connection with the place in visitors. Night illumination adds to the drama, as Schwartz explained: "Lighting the landscape at nighttime creates another life and changes the experience. Like the dual nature of Dr. Jekyll and Mr. Hyde, it is a way of making negative positive and positive negative."[39]

Schwartz prefers lighting that emanates from and through things instead of shining spotlights on objects. Perforated sheet materials work especially well in capturing and diffusing colored light. An example is the series of mountain-shaped "follies" in Fengming Mountain Park, where giant red-orange pavilions, raised on "dancing" legs, line the entrance to draw people into the arrival plaza. They create shade during the day and, lit from within, a spectacular glowing lantern effect at night. Schwartz's approach to lighting is discussed again in the section below on the Davis Garden.

Color Wars, Branding, and Image Making

The graphic nature and brightness that Schwartz endows her landscapes with reflect her training as a printmaker. Her cunning allusions together with bold formal and chromatic palettes elicit intense positive or negative reactions; some people are even offended by them. However, the brashness, peculiarity, visibility, and publicity appeal to corporations and city councils that see an opportunity to brand their outdoor space in landscape. The growing use in the 1970s and 1980s of "green ethics" to project a positive corporate image added a new dimension to landscape commodification.

In Fengming Mountain Park, the residential landscape was overtly used, at least initially, to attract customers and draw attention to the development sales center through the use of strong images and a distinctive identity. In the Kitagata low-cost housing project, the client and government agency were pleased with the national and international attention the project garnered, perhaps the reason behind the commission of Schwartz's work in the first place. The project's heightened visibility also made landscape architects and architects aware of the importance of landscape architecture both in the realm of housing and in general.[40]

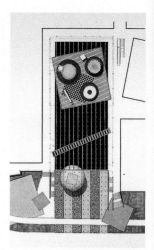

The Rio Shopping Center (1988–9) in Atlanta, Georgia, designed with Arquitectonica, was perhaps Schwartz's most daring, but alas short-lived, branding experiment (Figure 7.8), intended by the developer to generate new life and development in the area and to push against the conventional image of a shopping center. In Schwartz's highly unusual, one-of-a-kind commercial project, the courtyard was marked by alternating grass and white riprap stone stripes, and an adjacent colorful square plaza set askew in a large black rectangular shallow water

7.8 Rio Shopping Center, courtyard plan (top) and courtyard view (bottom), Atlanta, Georgia, 1988–9

basin with a bright red elevated crosswalk projected a striking image. But it was the field of 350 gilded frogs in the basin and on the slope, all facing a geodesic dome that doubled as a mist fountain, that made the lasting impression and branded the place. As if worshipping the globe, the golden frogs brought both humor and mystique. Fiber optic lines across the pool and between the frogs added glow and motion. Despite being described as kitschy and quirky, the Rio Mall received several prestigious awards.[41] Unfortunately, after initial economic success, the mall failed to catch on with the buying public for complex reasons independent of the design; it closed and was demolished in 2000.

Unfortunately, most projects are encumbered by color wars with clients and Schwartz had to change or scrap color altogether during the design or construction phase numerous times. Negotiations over color always threaten to sap the energy out of a project, though Schwartz always persevered and often prevailed.

In the revitalized Forecourt Plaza of the Department of Housing and Urban Development (HUD) (1988) in Washington, DC, the blazing color light scheme was initially accepted but then became a sticking point (Figure 7.9). The original 1960s barren plaza located above an underground garage was designed to showcase the modernist building by Marcel

Breuer. A new design was sought to express the agency's mission of creating habitable spaces for people and to make the unused space usable by HUD employees. Because the space had no capacity to support soil for trees, Schwartz introduced a cluster of 14-foot-tall "mechanical trees," lifesaver-looking and with colored canopies made of vinyl-coated plastic, to bring shelter, shade, and a riot of color. But the effect of the built outcome is captured in an essay titled "White out: HUD pulls the color—and life—from a Martha Schwartz design at its Washington, D.C. headquarters": "When completed, they were glowing in soft white, a bleached version of the original proposal— seven glowing, circular canopies radiant with bright, juicy colors— red, orange, yellow, and violet."[42] In Washington, where politics dictate what gets built, the essay continued, "architecture stands as a lasting metaphor for how power moves." Schwartz's early design for the plaza was shockingly funny within the severe context of 1960s federal architecture in Washington. Henry Cisneros, the HUD secretary at the time of the commission, "understood Schwartz's Pop Art humor and embraced the project." But his replacement, Andrew Cuomo, "thought Schwartz's design might detract from the department's mission and make HUD look frivolous on his watch." Assisted by a powerful ally, Commission on Fine Arts chair J. Carter Brown, Schwartz saved the project but had to compromise and agreed to the white canopies. More than simply neutral, white was a statement, an act of defiance. The color erasure was as political as the antiforces at play. While the

7.9 US Department of Housing and Urban Development (HUD), Forecourt Plaza, three night scenes, computer modeling drawing (left) and built project (right), Washington, DC, 1988–97

final design is elegant, as the white disks seem to float over the plaza offset by deep green grass circular planters, it is also a monument to chromophobia.

In 1997, while the HUD project was on hold, Schwartz sounded pessimistic about the ability of government projects to rise above bland, merely pleasing, noncontroversial color to avoid political problems. Her adventurous stance attracted enlightened patrons who supported the artistic intent behind the design, but in the public realm she struggled to find people willing to take a risk and stand by her through the process. "Unfortunately," she observed, "most people who work in the public realm are risk averse."[43]

For Schwartz color is a necessary ingredient for the creation of place identity, which in turn promotes attachment, care, and, ultimately, the viability of a project in the long run. She has always believed that a strong image—desired by for-profit corporations, institutions, and sales developers for branding and marketability—also applies to public places and neighborhoods: "If the landscape does not inspire or disturb people, they don't really see it: it does not matter, and they do not care."[44] She maintains that a space that performs as the face of a neighborhood or city is as important as all other pragmatic and programmatic requirements. The designer's task is to decipher how an image that is unique to a particular place can reflect or create an identity embraced by the public.[45]

But image alone, often linked to strong form and bold color contrast, is not enough to sustain a project and build attachment. Despite their imageability, several of Schwartz's projects have failed.

The design of the high-profile Jacob Javits Plaza (1997) at the heart of Manhattan, New York, was replaced with a conventional design 20 years later. The plaza was previously host to Richard Serra's infamous "Tilted Arc," a sculpture loathed for being forbidding in scale and obstructing pedestrian movement. As the plaza had nowhere that people could sit, Schwartz considered the revitalization project in practical terms, as a problem of seating first and foremost. She used the ubiquitous New York park bench for the conceptual, formal, and whimsical aspects of the project and as the icon of the plaza. The cheap bench selected from stock items of the city's Parks Department approved list was configured in exaggeratedly long, double-sided twisting strands. Sinuous lines curved around miniature turfed hills and resembled parterre de broderie, a favorite model of Schwartz's. The swirling lines of benches painted bright green and lit from below by bright green nightlight and six-foot-tall grassy hemispheres lit in green at night and emitting mist on hot days energized and added mystery to the plaza. A bright magenta paving band under the benches, seen in the original computer drawings, was to highlight and vivify the flowing green bench lines as they faded over time. Exaggeratedly long poles for light fixtures sporadically spread in the plaza were slated for pink, but ultimately painted black.

Schwartz's Javits Plaza design may have been of its time, but it was a limited time.[46] The design was rigid and inflexible and didn't meet the requirements of increasingly diversified and desirable public programs.

Considering that the only consistent urban condition is change itself—in demographics and needs—Schwartz wondered whether it was desirable or even possible for a design to last more than a couple of decades. Questions of time and change are also questions of color, which is a matter of fashion. If color announces the present, then it cannot be timeless.[47] But the fact that color, or a design, falls out of favor does not worry Schwartz:

> If I worry about it, I would pretty much have to stop doing it. Things do not need to last forever. And maybe it is a good thing. Things come and go. Most of

the places where I worked, people do not want to invest, and materials will fail. … [A]t least it will have one shining moment. And that is okay, because I do not believe that only things that last forever are better. Sometimes when something is fleeting, it is more beautiful. Nature is like this, it too changes.

At the same time, she is not oblivious to the costs of and responsibility for material and color wear and tear. Color, in particular, "is a flash point":

> Putting color into the landscape is the hardest thing to pull off, because the materials that we use in our culture are not made to be colorful; usually landscape materials are pretty dull natural colors, … not intended to be colorful. … [C]eramic is the best way to get color on the ground or elsewhere. But it is expensive. [italics added]

Durability of bright color in the landscape is still difficult to accomplish. Not so in landscape representation. Schwartz's colorful drawings, both analog and digital, have their own color stories.

Pantone, RBG, and SuperPaint

During Schwartz's four-decade career, representation technology has shifted dramatically. Computer software—computer-aided design (CAD), formZ, and Photoshop—replaced the pencil and drafting table, and computer color systems— RBG and SuperPaint—replaced Prismacolor and markers.[48] The bright colors of virtual computer space, a medium that employs light, supports her color affinity, however she has not fully embraced the computer and its color system, preferring to work intuitively and empirically. Analog drawing at the conceptual phase gives her more control over the colors before others develop them into computer models; "Computer algorithms do not allow you to turn things around, turn things inside out, to come up with ideas and concepts." Algorithmic processes are rarely singular; they are mathematical, prescribed, and nonspontaneous, so users cannot determine how colors work or how different people see them differently in different contexts.[49]

In the 1980s Schwartz kept her drawings abstract, refraining from realistic or metaphorical expression. Pencil or ink drawings—mostly plans, sections, and elevations, rarely perspectives—were rendered lightly in Prismacolor and projected a dream-like and mellow flair, in contrast to the exuberantly bright built projects. In her publications, though, color-saturated photography is dominant. When in the early 1990s she and her partners embraced computation and digital modeling to work out spatial concepts, drawings were directly generated from AutoCAD. Plans featured straight lines with occasional black shadows for depth, but without labels, so as to not interfere with the pattern. Other drawings, including axons, bird's-eye views, and perspectives, were converted from CAD and rendered with greater realism in Modelshop, formZ, and other software to project a vision of reality. All this software came with standardized digital colors.[50]

One of the earliest CAD drawing Schwartz did with her partner Ken Smith was for the Los Angeles Center (1990). It displays earthy and realistic-colored material that hardly matches Schwartz's bold and abstract sensibility. Advanced CAD graphics with added fly-through animation were first done for a presentation to the client of Snoopy Garden (1991), an amusement park north of Tokyo. The client rejected the original proposal, so Schwartz and Smith collaborated for the first time with a computer graphic consultant, Franz Israel, on the second proposal. It met with the client's approval. The drawings resonated luminous colors and were true to the desired exuberant atmosphere. Instead of working directly with the limited computer color system, Schwarz and colleagues first selected colors from a Pantone book and then applied them to CAD-generated images.[51] The typical RGB rendering system, which only approximates the variation in spectral distribution and surface-scattering properties present in the real world, has proven insufficient for Schwartz. She uses the licensed Pantone Matching Color System as her reference chart for landscape color, so that she is not limited by a built-in computer color program. And the use of noncomputer color charts resolves the discrepancies between screen, printed, and built colors.

Schwartz may have been slow to embrace CAD and other computer tools, but her saleswomanship was galvanized by the power of the image and the mass media that accompanied her Bagel

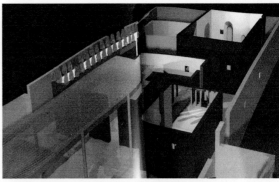

7.10 Davis Garden, El Paso, TX (1996), computer modeling

7.11 Visitors taking pictures against the yellow screen at the Mesa Arts Center (MAC), Mesa, Arizona.
(Photographs in Figures 7.11–7.21 were taken by the author in March 2021.)

Garden, and led to a series of bold portfolios for outreach and marketing. Since the published drawings of the Davis Garden in 1997 and then the HUD and Javits Plaza projects in her first monograph, seductive color photography and computer-rendered drawings have displayed equal energy (Figure 7.10). Taken from multiple angles and as close-ups, powerful images bleed off the glossy pages. The pressure to produce sleek images was an outcome of a new overabundance of visual content, brought on partly by the democratization of architectural publishing.

Using little text, Schwartz's monographs, like Repton's Red Books, serve as the company's portfolio and coffee table books for visual consumption. The principles of editorial salvage and recycled images, consistent with the marketing operational mode common in architectural publishing, were underscored by the conceptual shift that has occurred with computer publishing. A review of MSP's latest monograph, *Recycling Spaces* (2018), noted the two approaches used in the book design—the reuse of images and the cooption of images from internet sites like Flickr and Google Image. Whereas the first reuse approach overlooks the time-based change of color in built projects, the second shows the attraction to color of the people who use these spaces (Figure 7.11).[52] Today,

7.12 Davis Garden, hallways between the rooms (top three) and view from the top of the garage (bottom), El Paso, Texas, 1996

yearbooks rich in imagery and spare in text are published online by MSP and other firms to showcase their latest productions.

* * *

The two projects discussed below—Davis Residence Garden in El Paso, Texas (1996), and Mesa Arts Center in Arizona (2005)—distill Schwartz's color and light design sensibilities in a residential garden and an urban public space, respectively. The Davis Garden is arguably Schwartz's most concerted experiment with color and light. Its minimalism is austere, its light contemplative, and its color intensely stimulating. The result is a powerful spatial-visual chromatic experience at once supported by and independent of color signification. The public complex of Mesa Arts Center is an experiment with movement and flow activated by people, water, and, notably, light and shadow. It is an urban marker and a gathering space that is both dynamic and calming, with a sensory kinesthetic and thermal experience. The descriptions below are informed by the author's visits to the project sites, original drawings, project statements, and secondary source publications.

Davis Residence Garden, Sam and Anne Davis, El Paso, Texas, USA, 1996

> Architecture that envelops us like a physical presence, simple and dense, defying description, imitation and photography; universal and present. ... Talking seems superfluous; ... The light is relaxing, or ecstatic. And the colour? It matches variable states of the soul, it is never definite.[53]

7.13 Davis Garden, Spike Room or Drying Room

This account of Luis Barragán's architecture applies to Schwartz's Davis Garden, itself a homage to the brilliantly colored courtyard gardens of Barragán.

Color and light are the essence of the Davis Garden. Color is thick, intoxicating, and fleeting. Illumination is both meditative and arousing. The garden is a theatre of effects. The protagonists—cacti, metal spikes, broken shards, gravel heaps, and other "constructions"—are staged in a six-act drama, each act set in an open-air room surrounded by high, color-saturated stucco walls. While the sets are static, the passage of sunlight, shade, and shadows across the day animates and dramatizes the garden. Drama unfolds through myriad itineraries across passages, openings, and rooms.

Sam and Anne Davis hired Schwartz in 1994 to design an addition to their 25-year-old, two-acre English landscape garden in suburban El Paso. Anne, a trained horticulturalist, saw an image of Schwartz's Dickinson Garden (1992) in Santa Fe, New Mexico, on the cover of a gardening magazine and grew to like it; her first impression of oddity turned into an appreciation of cleverness and innovation.[54] Schwartz was asked to design a low-maintenance, visually separate garden with Mexican echoes to house Anne's cactus collection; she could do whatever she liked provided she stayed inside an allocated "box" of 37 by 60 feet, a space bound by a gray perimeter wall between the garage and an amoeba-shaped pool.

Schwartz inserted six boxes in the space, creating an ensemble of small, high-walled outdoor garden rooms of varied shapes and sizes (Figure 7.12). The Davis Garden design conjures multiple tropes, among which several relate to garden history archetypes or "quotations," typical of Schwartz's work: the "folly" in an 18th century English garden; Jekyll's one-color garden rooms, which inspired the garden design of Sissinghurst Castle in Kent, England, a favorite of Anne Davis; and a playful maze.

The basic concept of containment that structured her design resonates three spatial typologies, of which two have color associations. The first spatial typology borrows from the serial, open-air box installation of the minimalist artist Donald Judd in Marfa, Texas, three hours away. Like Judd's maze of roofless rooms, the constellation of boxes at the Davis Garden distorts preconceptions of interior-exterior and public-private boundaries; inner walls become the outside walls of other rooms.[55] The second typology emulates in miniature a Mexican village with narrow, colorful walled streets leading to space with a typical livestock drinking trough. The walls contrast with the surrounding green garden as they display Mexican hacienda-style colors—bright pink, golden yellow, ochre, indigo, cobalt blue, and purple—that transform, express, and individualize their environment.[56] The third spatial typology, a house floorplan of six rooms and adjoining narrow hallways, is Schwartz's brainchild.[57] She assigned each room a domestic trope associated with the nearby pool: a towel and swimsuit drying room with a wall of metal spike hangers (Figure 7.13); a changing room with a mirrored wall and a grid of upright *Trichocereus* cacti; a contemplative room with a small gravel cone in the middle; a stall-like bathroom with shower and toilet;[58] and two garden rooms, one with a barrel cacti (Figure 7.14), the other with a saguaro (Figure 7.15). A "patio" space with two wooden planks for seating was created at the intersection of four rooms in the middle.

The Davis Garden wall paint specification was selected from Pantone's catalogue. The outer walls for the narrow hallways, including their tops and opening frames, are of darker hues: deep blue, dark purple, reddish brown, dark tan, dark green, and dark brown. Suffused in deep shadows, the hallway floors are lined with grayish-pink gravel and areas of Utah red sandstone pavers. In contrast, interior room wall colors are lighter, brighter, and warmer—pink, orange, gold-mustard, and white—and meant to look like glowing lanterns with intense sunlight. The spiky drying room walls are painted Coral Pink (Pantone #184-U), with light gray concrete pavers on the floor.[59] In the changing room across the way, one wall is completely covered with a mirror, while the other three are again painted Coral Pink; the floor is laid with concrete pavers, with a rose quartz bed for the *Trichocereus* cacti. The contemplative room walls and gravel cone are spray painted in gold with glitter.[60] The bathroom, initially slated for blue walls (Pantone #2718) and a black obsidian rock floor, has whitewashed walls and a white gravel floor; the walls are capped with large azure-colored glass shards, made of recycled glass bottle residue from the Coca-Cola Company (Figure 7.16). Their color refracts onto the walls on a sunny day, and

7.14 Davis Garden, White Room (upper two), Barrel Cactus Room (lower two), Meditation Room (upper two, following page), and Mirror Room in different times of day (lower, following page). Photo of Mirror Room is by Sam Davis

7.15 Davis Garden, Saguaro Room in different times of day

on certain days and in particular lighting conditions the azure shards are washed in brilliant orange-pink, as if on fire.[61] The walls of the golden barrel cactus room are light green-cyan (Pantone #572) and the floor features white quartz. The saguaro room walls are painted orange (no Pantone specification), with matching orange aquarium gravel (later replaced with lava rocks painted orange). The outer perimeter wall was painted gray to match the existing house paint.

The Davis Garden is a spectacle of changing shades, textures, shadows, and tonal sequences. Coated in thick plaster, the walls have a solid, textured, and absorbent surface. Color is illusive, changing from one moment to the next. With

7.16 Davis Garden, glass shards crowning the White Room

intense light in the heat of the day, surface color thickens into the air and atmosphere. As light falls across the walls tonal gradations materialize and shadows come to life. The interplay of silhouettes of the walls, sculptural plants, objects, and shadows of the surrounding trees creates a theater of moving shadows. The saguaro room seems to vibrate in red-orange as the erect cacti turn into ghostly black shadow figures (see Figure 7.15). In the white bathroom, at certain times the shadows cast by the upper shards align on a stainless-steel shelf that Anne installed as a homage to Donald Judd (see Figure 7.14). Strategically placed 12-foot by 12-foot cut-out openings add to the drama by framing "pictures" of colors inside colors. Where two or three openings align, they invite a pause and peer through—and evoke a Rothko painting (Figure 7.17).[62] Passages and hallway walls create forced perspectives that drive movement. Looking up from inside each room, even the sky is framed (recalling James Turrell's Skyspace installations). Reflections, too, play a dramatic role: mirrors in the changing room double the space, and a constellation of walls is reflected in the pool. Night illumination is low-key, with one soft spotlight in each room (and three safety lights mounted in the hallways).

The immersive effects are interspersed with humor, as in the grid of phallic-looking cactus towers in the changing room. Objects and colors carry double and triple meanings that support the assigned function and statement of each room. But political, regional, environmental, or cultural meanings do not overtly intrude on the experience, which is left to personal interpretations. The 12-inch, gridded spike wall in the towel drying room can be seen as a play on cactus spines. The pink walls that often turn red may conjure up a picture of the barbed wire and rage at the nearby Mexican border. The golden cone of granite gravel from the region's bedrock may allude to the volcanoes of Central America, the nearby heaps of industrial waste, or the cone of salt, a Shinto symbol of purity found in Japanese dry gardens. The white bathroom radiates cleanliness, while its shard-topped walls recall those used in Mexico to deter vandals. The sky-blue walls in the golden barrel cactus room confer

7.17 Davis Garden, three wall openings resembling Rothko paintings

7.18 Mesa Arts Center (MAC), computer modeling, with Boora architects, Mesa, AZ, 2005

7.19 MAC, entry plaza, views in daytime (top two) and nighttime (bottom)

a spiritual ambience. The cactus plants play a role as sculptures, with fleeting flowers—a day- or week-long spectacle when in bloom. In the Davis Garden, Schwartz questions the concepts of nature, garden, and culture in a desert, suburban, and Mexican border-town context.

The Davis Garden is more exotic than it appears in pictures. Photography cannot capture the fleeting chromatic effects; a video might do better. Designed during Schwartz's office transition from analog to digital drawings in 1994–5, the blueline prints of the early design proposals, drawn in ink and rendered in Prismacolor, were redrawn digitally for publication (see Figure 7.10). An early computer-generated drawing (by Rick Casteel), a 3-D model from which axons are taken, shows the rooms in bright RBG colors. To further dramatize the color effect the background of the renderings is black, the inverse of the garden's apotheosis in daylight.

Mesa Arts Center Public Space, Mesa, Arizona, USA, 2005

The public space at the Mesa Arts Center (MAC) complex is neither exotic nor whimsical. It does not challenge or question nature, landscape, or culture. Instead, it participates in the art and the performing arts functions of the center. It also creates a strong urban identity for sleepy, suburban Mesa, to invigorate development and density in the core of downtown.[63] The spatial concept plays out the idea of staging: materials, water, light, shadow, and color are orchestrated as stage sets for people and activities at the center. The master plan for the eight-acre site, designed by Bora Architects and Martha Schwartz Partners, focuses attention on the active streetside and the arc-shaped linear space of the grand promenade that links MAC's three theaters, eight galleries, contemporary arts center, and art education studios (Figure 7.18).[64] The public space weaves through and at different levels of the building complex, providing a rich spatial program for large and small group gatherings as well as places for quiet relaxation.

Color is produced by the imposing architecture, paving, and screen glass walls. Given the region's blazing sun and bleaching light, the façades of the three theaters are covered with colored glass tiles in lavender, olive-green, or light terracotta orange. A tall, curved lavender stucco wall provides enclosure and background to the plaza's corner entry. It is juxtaposed with dazzling, long-lasting flowering magenta bougainvillea and interspersed with curved strips of planting beds lined with colored glass pebbles, elevated water troughs, and large cubic glass lanterns of changing lights (Figure 7.19). All ground surfaces conform to the strong arc gesture of the buildings with parallel curving bands of alternating pavers and gravels in various porous and smooth textures and colored materials—gray volcano and light ochre granite pavers of different sizes, and strips of planting beds and grass. The colors of the plant foliage and blossoms are strategically complemented by brightly colored gravel, Schwartz's favorite aquarium glass chips.

Given the arid landscape of Arizona, the unifying ideas of the site and architectural design were to provide thermal delight and energize the space. Wind, water, and people register movement and imbue the space with dynamism. Every surface, tree, building, and visitor is part of the flow. Two large, sail-like tensile shade structures connect the arts and theater complexes and cast their shadows over the central "Shadow Walk," as Schwartz calls it.

Schwartz's contribution focuses not on color but on light and shadow design. To create a refuge from the sun, the Shadow Walk is

> a place where the rich interplay of overlapping shadows, trees and architectural canopies create a cool and inviting environment. Long, curving lines of trees, shift back and forth as one walks along the promenade, throwing different shadow forms on the ground and creating different qualities and quantities of shadow.[65]

Also following the curve are linear bands of diverse water features—a trough, arroyo, classical Roman and Renaissance water table, and Chadur (a Mughal garden water chute). They add a cooling effect and

7.20 MAC, shadows cast by pergola canopy at the north end of the Shadow Walk (upper and lower) and paving reflected on canopy (middle)

7.21 MAC, totem pole cacti against turquoise glass screen (top) and same cacti's shadows seen on the back of the screen (bottom)

a calm and peaceful atmosphere, reinforce the sense of motion, and bring music to the space.[66]

Whereas in the Davis Garden Schwartz explored the power of color and light to dramatize the space, at the Mesa Arts Center she tested the dramatizing capacity of light and shadow. She staged the protagonists (plants, screen walls, and pergolas), scripted the sun, and choreographed shadow movement. Other sources of natural and artificial lighting are used to produce diverse effects, from dazzling luminosity to reflections to black shadows. Shadows are cast on the ground and on translucent colored walls to register movement palatable to the senses. At either end of the Shadow Walk shiny polished canopies made of metal bands woven like a basket cast wavy shadows on the ground and, like a mirror, reflect up onto the canopy. Bits of colored glass embedded in the canopy pepper the shadows with color (Figure 7.20). Running along the Shadow Walk is a long banquet water table (recalling the cardinal's table at Villa Lante in Bagnaia, Italy); its blue glass pebbles refract blue light onto the ground. Also along the path are three raised glass walls in yellow, turquoise, and red. They are frontlit by the morning sun, backlit in the afternoon, and spotlit at night, and serve as a luminous background to a row of local cacti planted on one side. Totem pole cacti in front of a sloping grass amphitheater are set against the turquoise glass (Figure 7.21); vertical *Cereus* cacti are set against the red screen and prickly pear cacti against the yellow screen. The latter flank the green and yellow polka dot garden plaza, the most playful, Schwartzian spot in the complex (Figure 7.22). Light projectors are paired with individual cacti, extending the daily shadow performance to nighttime. The vertical shadows on the yellow, red, and blue panels have become a popular stage backdrop for visitors, who perform shadow plays for their friends and families.[67]

MSP's treatment of light and shadow as basic design materials at MAC is a noteworthy experiment, and the center is a popular place to take pictures and celebrate events and rites of passage, such as graduation ceremonies. Unfortunately, largely because of insufficient maintenance and the fragility of fixtures and plants, built details have deteriorated and shadows faded. A designer's ability to control and impact light and shadow, in public as opposed to private space and in large as opposed to small space, requires material durability, additional testing of spatial scenarios, and budget.

7.22 MAC, prickly pear cacti against the yellow screen at the polka dot garden plaza in daytime (left two) and nighttime (right)

* * *

Beginning in 1979 Schwartz used color to assail a profession that refused to acknowledge its entanglement in the cultural as much as the natural. Her efforts yielded fruits. By 1989 other practitioners had caught up with her groundwork and, for the first time in 15 years, *Progressive Architecture Magazine* devoted an entire issue to landscape architecture, documenting and explaining new developments.[68] A decade later, as landscape design as art practice was accepted by the public, the sting of Schwartz's work gradually abated. She emerged from the periphery into a new mainstream that she helped shape.

Over the past decade, MSP commissions have grown in scale, scope, and budget, adding a new focus on climate change. Schwartz described the move as "a pivot, a move away from the field into science and bioengineering, a fall into an Alice in Wonderland hole, down and down into climate change, a real new adventure." In the most ambitious project of her career, she has founded Mayday.Earth, an organization to tackle social and climate change challenges. At least for now, she says, color gets lost.

"Color comes in the art of making. It links abstract concepts with the sensorial dimension." Schwartz is an "alchemist," who mixes color to stir curiosity, provocation, humor, and emotion and to build a landscape image.

Notes

1   Zoom interview with the author, December 10, 2020. Unless otherwise attributed, Schwartz quotations in this chapter are from this conversation.

2   Martha Schwartz, "Back Bay Bagel Garden," 1980. The photographer Alan Ward, who recorded the garden and convinced Schwartz to publicize it, was integral to the garden's success.

3   This and other "controversial" decisions cost Clay his position in 1984.

4   Osler, "Beyond the Bagel," 2012, 133.

5   Schwartz, "My Mission," 2004, 81.

6   Schwartz's four monographs are *Martha Schwartz: Transfiguration of the Common Landscape*, Landecker, 1997; *Martha Schwartz Partners: Landscape Art and Urbanism*, MSP, 2004; *The Vanguard Landscapes and Gardens of Martha Schwartz*, Richardson, 2011; and *Recycling Spaces: Curating Urban Evolution: The Work of Martha Schwartz Partners*, Waugh, 2018.

7   Meyer, "The Transfiguration of the Commonplace," 1997, 5.

8   Schwartz, "Landscape and Common Culture Since Modernism," 1993, 264. Schwartz was also drawn to the work of pop artists Jasper Johns, Roy Lichtenstein, and Claes Oldenburg.

9   Schwartz, "My Mission," 2004, 85.

10   MSP, *Landscape Art and Urbanism*, 2018, 28.

11   Deitz, "Planting Plastic," 1985.

12   Ibid.

13   S.R.F., "Garden Against the Grain," 1984, 73.

14   Ibid.

15   Deitz, "Planting Plastic," 1985.

16   Meyer, "Interview with Martha Schwartz," 1997, 106.

17   Schwartz, "My Mission," 2004, 125.

18   Ibid., 123.

19   Duffy, "Better than Nature," 2004.

20   Schwartz, "Landscape and Common Culture," 264.

21   Meyer, "Transfiguration," 1997, 5.

22   Pastoureau, *Blue: The History of a Color*, 2001, 10.

23   Pastoureau, *Green: The History of a Color*, 2014, 171.

24   Waugh, *Recycling Spaces*, 2011, 136.

25   Gillette, "On the Subject of Human Nature," 1997.

26   *LAM* editors, "Turf Parterre," 1989, 92.

27   Schwartz, "New York City Bulb Garden," 1986.

28   See Waugh, *Recycling Space*, 2011, 134–49.

29   Ibid., 19–43.

30   Meyer, "Interview," 1997, 109.

31   Ibid.

32   Richardson, *Vanguard*, 2004, 182.

33   Nemitz, *Pink*, 2006, 27.

34   Richardson, *Vanguard*, 2004, 129.

35   Treib, "A Constellation of Pieces."

36   See Schwartz, "MayDay! MayDay!," 1982, 60.

37   Ibid., 62.

38 MSP website, https://msp.world/paul-lincke-hoefe-berlin-germany/#.

39 Ibid.

40 Treib, "A Constellation," 2002, 92.

41 Among the awards was an ASLA award. See *LAM* editors, "Landscape Architecture Awards: Rio Shopping Center," 1989.

42 McKee, "White Out," 1998.

43 Meyer, "Interview," 1997, 109.

44 Zoom interview, 2020. Also see Meyer, "The Performance of Aesthetics," 2011, 173.

45 Schwartz, "The Role of the Public Realm Landscape," 2011, 126.

46 Meyer, "Transfiguration," 1997, 9.

47 Lavin, "What Color Is It Now?" 2004, 100.

48 The RGB color model is an additive color model in which the red, green, and blue primary colors of light are combined to reproduce a wide range of colors. SuperPaint was a pioneering color paint system in which users could control and choose which tool, color, or brush to use with only a mouse click, akin to Photoshop commands.

49 Kane, *Chromatic Algorithms*, 2014, 1.

50 Digital color was democratized first through hardware, then through commercial "off-the-shelf" software with color tables, and finally through standards established by the World Wide Web. Ibid., 159.

51 *LAM* editors, "Portfolios," 1993, 63.

52 For a thorough review of the monographs, see Osler, "Beyond the Bagel," 2012, 140.

53 Siza, "Barragán," 2003, 11. Barragán's spatial and color influence derive from the Spanish-Moorish-Andalusian world.

54 Author interview with Anne and Sam Davis in El Paso, March 9, 2021.

55 Richardson, *Vanguard*, 2004, 33.

56 Pauly, *Barragán*, 2002, 188.

57 Richardson, *Vanguard*, 2004, 33.

58 Several features and functions of the original design, such as the toilet, were not implemented or changed overtime, in part for city codes and budget.

59 All specifications for colors and material are taken from construction documents dating to 1996 in the possession of Anne and Sam Davis.

60 Originally the walls and rocks were to be coated in gold metalflake paint, and the floor stones were to match a series of standing rocks, but according to Sam Davis this was a bit expensive and "outlandish."

61 Author interview with Anne and Sam Davis, 2021.

62 The Davis Garden photographs in Figures 7.10 and 7.12–7.16 were taken by the author in March 2021.

63 Waugh, *Recycling*, 2011, 263–5.

64 All photographs of the Mesa Arts Center in figures 7.19–7.21 were taken by the author in March 2021.

65 MSP website, https://msp.world/mesa-arts-center-mesa-az-usa

66 For a description of the water features see Waugh, *Recycling*, 2011, 269.

67 Ibid., 273.

68 Boles, "New American Landscape," 1989.

References

Boles, Daralice D. "New American Landscape." *Progressive Architecture* 89, no. 7 (1989): 51–5. https://link.gale.com/apps/doc/A7714681/AONE?u=iastu_main&sid=AONE&xid=c0b9c94b

Deitz, Paula. "Planting Plastic: A Landscape Architect Looks to Art for Inspiration." *New York Times*, September 22, 1985. Accessed December 1, 2020. https://www.nytimes.com/1985/09/22/magazine/planting-plastic.html

Duffy, Ellie. "Better than Nature." *Building Design* 30 (April 2004): 24. Accessed November 26, 2020. http://bi.gale.com/essentials/article/GALE|A116667808?u=iastu_main

Eckstut, Joann, and Arielle Eckstut. *The Secret Language of Color*. New York: Black Dog and Leventhal Publishers, 2013.

Gillette, Jane Brown. "On the Subject of Human Nature." *Landscape Architecture* 87, no. 8 (1997): 72–89. Accessed December 1, 2020. www.jstor.org/stable/44677497

Kane, Carolyn L. *Chromatic Algorithms: Synthetic Color, Computer Art, and Aesthetics after Code*. Chicago: University of Chicago Press, 2014.

LAM editors. "Landscape Architecture Awards: Rio Shopping Center." *Landscape Architecture* 79, no. 9 (1989): 91. Accessed February 12, 2020. https://www.jstor.org/stable/44666252

LAM editors. "Landscape Architecture Awards: Turf Parterre." *Landscape Architecture* 79, no. 9 (1989): 92. Accessed February 12, 2020. https://www.jstor.org/stable/44666253

LAM editors. Portfolios: Drawings of Landscape Architects. *Landscape Architecture* 83, no. 5 (1993): 57–63.

Landecker, Heidi, ed. *Martha Schwartz: Transfiguration of the Common Landscape*, Washington: Spacemaker Press, 1997.

Lavin, Sylvia. 2004. What Color Is It Now? *Perspecta* 35 (2004): 98–112.

McKee, Bradford. "White Out: HUD Pulls the Color and Life from a Martha Schwartz Design at Its Washington, DC Headquarters." *Architecture* 87, no. 8 (1998): 45. Accessed November 26, 2020. https://link.gale.com/apps/doc/A21073210/PROF?u=iastu_main&sid=PROF&xid=7ceaada5

Meyer, Elizabeth K. "Interview with Martha Schwartz." In *Martha Schwartz: Transfiguration of the Common Landscape*, ed. by Heidi Landecker, 106–10. Washington, DC: Spacemaker Press, 1997.

Meyer, Elizabeth K. "The Transfiguration of the Commonplace." In *Martha Schwartz: Transfiguration of the Common Landscape*, ed. by Heidi Landecker, 5–10. Washington, DC: Spacemaker Press, 1997.

Meyer, Elizabeth K. "The Performance of Aesthetics, Interview with Martha Schwartz." In *Recycling Spaces: Curating Urban Evolution*, ed. by Emily Waugh, 170–7. Novato, CA: ORO Editions, 2011.

Martha Schwartz Partners (MSP). *Martha Schwartz Partners: Landscape Art and Urbanism*. London: Edition Axel Menges, 2018.

Nemitz, Barbara, ed. *Pink: The Exposed Color in Contemporary Art and Culture*. Berlin: Hatje Cantz Verlag, 2006.

Osler, Peter L. "'Beyond the Bagel,' book review. *Recycling Spaces, Curating Urban Evolution: The Work of Martha Schwartz Partners*." *Landscape Architecture* 102, no. 11 (2012): 132–40. Accessed November 26, 2020. www.jstor.org/stable/44795126

Pastoureau, Michel. *Blue: The History of a Color*. Princeton, NJ: Princeton University Press, 2001.

Pastoureau, Michel. *Green: The History of a Color*. Princeton, NJ: Princeton University Press, 2014.

Pauly, Danièle. *Barragán: Space and Shadow, Walls and Colour*. Basel: Birkhäuser-Publishers, 2002.

Richardson, Tim, ed. *The Vanguard Landscapes and Gardens of Martha Schwartz*. London: Thames & Hudson, 2004.

S.R.F. "Garden Against the Grain." *Landscape Architecture* 74, no. 3 (1984): 70–3. Accessed December 2, 2020. www.jstor.org/stable/44670009

Schwartz, Martha. "Back Bay Bagel Garden: Le Petit Parterre Embroiderie." *Landscape Architecture* 70, no. 1 (1980): 43–6.

Schwartz, Martha. "MayDay! MayDay! Neccos in the Garden!" *Landscape Architecture* 72, no. 3 (1982): 60–3.

Schwartz, Martha. "New York City Bulb Garden." In *Transforming the American Garden: Twelve New Landscape Designs*. Exhibition catalogue, ed. by Michael Van Valkenburgh, 16–19. Cambridge, MA: Harvard University Graduate School of Design, 1986.

Schwartz, Martha. "Landscape and Common Culture Since Modernism." In *Modern Landscape Architecture: A Critical Review*, ed. by Marc Treib, 260–5. Cambridge, MA: MIT Press, 1993.

Schwartz, Martha. "My Mission." In *The Vanguard Landscape and Gardens of Martha Schwartz*, ed. by Tim Richardson, 80–7. London: Thames & Hudson, 2004.

Schwartz, Martha. "The Role of the Public Realm Landscape: The Softer Side of Sustainability and the Hard Working Urban Landscape." *Citygreen Magazine* 3 (July 2011): 122–7. Accessed November 26, 2020. https://www.nparks.gov.sg//media/cuge/ebook/citygreen/cg3/cg3_19.pdf?la=en&hash=4BFD47698A68A3DC90F496E7E70F4BC3EB10BA8C

Siza, Álvaro. "Barragán." In *Barragán: The Complete Works*, ed. by Raul Rispa, 11. Hudson, NY: Princeton Architectural Press, 2003.

Treib, Marc. "A Constellation of Pieces." *Landscape Architecture* 92, no. 3 (2002): 58–67, 92.

Waugh, Emily, ed. *Recycling Spaces: Curating Urban Evolution: The Work of Martha Schwartz Partners*. Novato, CA: ORO Editions, 2011.

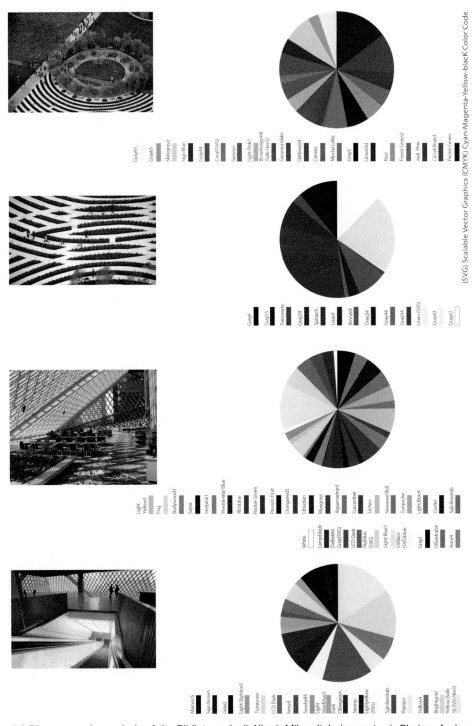

(SVG) Scalable Vector Graphics (CMYK) Cyan-Magenta-Yellow-black Color Code

8.0 Diagrams, color analysis of the Biblioteca degli Alberi, Milan, Italy (upper two). Photos: Andrea Cherchi. Color analysis of the Seattle Public Library interiors, Seattle, WA (upper two). Rendered by Maryam Maddahzad

(Unless noted otherwise, drawings, photos, and projects in Chapter 8 are by © Inside Outside.)

8

Affective Light Color
Translucence,
Petra Blaisse (b. 1955)

We felt that an engaging and energetic environment would help trigger a mood of ownership and activity from the future public. Colour seemed an attractive tool with which to achieve this. At the same time, colour can help break down the boundaries between past and future, learning and enjoying between one culture and another. ... Green was the colour we envisioned for the library gardens; fruitful, protective, mysterious, poisonous green; arsenic, malachite, methyl, iodine green; jade, frog back, mi se, celadon, emerald, sea, olive, apple, grass, ...

Petra Blaisse, *Avoiding Architecture*, 2007, 203

Everything is defined by light. Our state of being is connected to light. Mostly all that is living depends on light. Colour is light. ... All our work has to do with time. So with the change of natural light through the day and the seasons, our work is about catching, reflecting, filtering, dimming or excluding daylight.

Mondo Arc editors, "Lighting Talk," 2014, 38–9

Light, time, and color, among other factors, are central ingredients in Petra Blaisse's work.[1] They enable her to move freely between inside and outside, interior and landscape design, and multiple mediums—curtains, carpets, and plants. She alternates between scales and disciplines—exhibition, lighting, textile, interior, and landscape—working on each project in many different capacities. For Blaisse two and three dimensions and horizontal and vertical planes are interchangeable: floor is landscape, landscape is carpet, wall is curtain, curtain is tree, and vice versa. In her monograph *Inside Outside* (2007), she similarly aims to leave her readers "favorably impressed without always being sure exactly what is being shown."[2]

Blaisse refuses to use the label "designer," considering herself a "producer," "choreographer," and "curator" of sensory environments.[3] Born in London to a multitalented family—her Dutch parents were musical and artistic—she moved to the Netherlands at the age of 10. She studied at the Hammersmith College of Art in London and the Minerva Art Academy in Groningen. Lacking the temperament of an artist, she started her career at the Stedelijk Museum in Amsterdam in the Department of Applied Arts, in 1978. There, she developed an intimate understanding of color and lighting effects, acoustics, spatial composition, and how people use and move in space. She began freelancing in exhibition design in 1986 and applied her ideas to traveling exhibitions of industrial design and architecture, notably the works of Rem Koolhaas and the Office for Metropolitan Architecture (OMA). She remains interested in new ways to display objects and plants and create rewarding experiences.

The first garden Blaisse designed, in the early 1980s, illustrated her affinity for color. Designed for a chef from southern France at a remodeled restaurant on a small, dark canal

8.1 Lina Bo Bardi, "L'interno di un giardino d'inverno con piante esotiche ed in grande acquario a parete," page spread from *Lo Stilo,* October 10, 1941. © Instituto Lina Bo e P.M. Bardi / Casa de Vidro

in Amsterdam, the garden was intensely bright and colorful to evoke the warm climate and colors of the chef's homeland. Asked to brighten the restaurant's backyard with "lots of color," Blaisse recalled, "I painted the existing fence pink, orange, yellow, and light blue, and I made the concrete floor pink with holes, where I planted bamboo with apricot-colored stems. I made the chef happy." She forgot to take pictures of the work.

The first curtain Blaisse made, in 1987 for a dance theater in the Hague, showed her material and light sensibilities. Called "Liquid Gold," the textile, with lines of dots made of gold foil and attached to a heavy, gray wool velvet, shimmered. The ever-changing reflective curtain actively conditioned, filtered, and registered time, light, and shadows. Beyond its essential functions, it was a producer of affect:

> The effect of [the] "floating" metallic dots on that soft, undulating surface of velvet is that of a waterfall, rain, fire, sunrise, a silver moon or a plane full of holes. Because we control the lighting in theatres very carefully, it is exciting to introduce chance, to let the outside enter the interior. Natural things such as the changing light from morning to night, spring through winter and the shadows of passing clouds; … all play an important role in the changing character, structure and overall effect through time.[4]

Blaisse quietly nurtured her skills over the next few years and in 1991 opened her own firm, Inside Outside, in Amsterdam, which now has a multidisciplinary and multinational team.[5] Its global reach, including many project collaborations with OMA, requires her to speak a language that transcends cultural boundaries.

Blaisse's idealistic, romantic nature is encapsulated in her approach to gardening: she uses her work to search for an equilibrium among all living creatures and optimize their physical and mental well-beings.[6] Her gardens are sensual, cheerful, contemporary, and, at the same time, practical and scientific. In addition, her biological and social sensibilities enhance her awareness of and appreciation for the psychic resonance, material condition, and social energy of places. An avid gardener (like her mother and aunt), she is fascinated by the New Perennial Movement in garden design, a movement that originated in Holland and Germany.[7]

Inside Outside's ambition to dematerialize architecture and blur interior and landscape goes beyond the visual reciprocity and psychological lift afforded by the modern glass wall. She aims for something more intriguing that neither architecture nor landscape alone can do.[8] She emancipates architecture from structure and landscape from pictorialism by intervening in surfaces to generate a field of effects and flow through space and time.[9] In an age of sophisticated and flashy architectural façades, she does not compete with architecture for attention, but rather creates what Koolhaas calls "a kind of universe of quietness and disappearance."[10] Blaisse's diverse working mediums and postdisciplinary outlook reveal new landscape design potentialities for making color and light both affective and tactile (Figure 8.0).

Curating Textiles and Landscapes

Developed during her early exhibition design career, Blaisse's ambitions involve mediating the realm of display within space and context to create new ways for experience and social function to unfold:

> The interesting thing about making an exhibition, especially in applied arts, is that you can completely influence the meaning of an object with the environment you create around it. Even with the height you position it, the light you shine on it, or the background you provide, you can make it much more than it actually is [italics added].

8.2 Curtains, private house, Oslo, Norway, 2011–13 (top). Jubilee in Gold, installation, GTA Zürich, Switzerland, 2017 (bottom)

She is particularly interested in fashioning ways to shed new light on objects and landscapes and to engage the viewer. She adapted this concept from the early exhibitions of the Italian-born, Brazilian modernist Lina Bo Bardi (1914–92), who participated in the art and design fields of architecture, exhibition design, and gardening (Figure 8.1), and the American art collector and philanthropist Peggy Guggenheim (1898–1979). Blaisse was especially inspired by the daring move of one of Bo Bardi's exhibitions, in which paintings stood loose in space and people could walk around them and see the back of them. She also admired Guggenheim's experimental exhibitions in the 1930s: "Guggenheim operated between the artist and the viewer, saying to the artist 'it is really good for your work that people will see it a completely different way than you're used to.'" In one of these exhibitions (designed by the architect Frederick Kiesler), paintings were hung on universal joints, enabling viewers to turn them and view them in different angles and light. It created a more intimate relationship between the viewer and the work. Blaisse similarly challenges expectations about materiality and gravity by displaying things that are not grounded but rather float in the air ("I have a weak spot for floating buildings"). For example, in 2014, for a chamber music performance of *Narcissus*, she created a large fleece-like silver curtain that was suspended in space from a row of dancing helium balloons and adjusted for the different sets.[11]

She also seeks to engage people by curating and dramatizing the theater of everyday gardens, streets, and parks, and by bringing the botanical luxury of plants indoors. To elicit new experiences she treats her objects—curtains, floors, and landscapes—to new possibilities through two distinct moves: physical emancipation and physical, almost chemical interaction with the surroundings (Figure 8.2).[12] In her manifesto "Avoiding Architecture," she wrote: "To talk about curtains is to defend their emancipation from servicing, obedient, passive objects to self-regulating, active, and independent actors that improve the performance (spatial, theatrical) and physical (audible, visual, climatic) quality of a space or building."[13] She locates her curtains, much like her landscapes, both indoors and outdoors. For Inside Outside's first solo exhibition, organized in 2000 by Storefront for Art and Architecture in Soho, New York, Blaisse hung on the Storefront façade a three-story-tall, blazing red curtain of knitted plastic, typically used for scaffolding. The soft, pliable, and translucent material was subject to the wind and changing light effects.[14] She has written of her curtains:

> They filter or reflect light. A temporary presence, sensitive to UV light, drought, moisture, dirt and mismanagement. Dependent on maintenance and human interaction. Their Achilles heel: fragility. … When curtains catch air, they become walloping volumes, changing from one rounded, sensual shape to the next. Never repetitive, always a surprise.[15]

Through careful consideration of medium, structure, and display relative to their environment, Blaisse exteriorizes interiors and interiorizes landscapes. Extensive links and analogies between curtains and plants and, more broadly, between textiles and landscapes are evident in Blaisse's work and language, incorporating yarn, fiber, and the natural dyes of plants and minerals.

The interplay of the myriad shared properties of textiles and landscapes is displayed in her proposal for Textile City Park in Prato, Italy (2016), which called for the creation of a productive landscape and invited people to learn about both making textiles and the plants (and animals) that provide the ingredients needed to produce textile fibers and natural dye (Figure 8.3). All the park plants were to be directly linked to textile making. The park's tree planting plans echo diverse fabric weaving and stitching patterns. The myriad shared properties of textile and landscape are evident in Blaisse's designs. Curtain and plant mediums are subject to climate and time; they are unpredictable and thus counteract a monotonous, fixed environment; they create privacy and control light and acoustics, although they cannot be completely controlled; they can be backgrounds or dividers, or

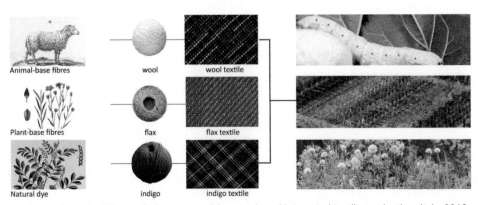

8.3 Parco Centrale di Prato, design proposal for a park and integrated textile production, Italy, 2016

create their own flexible space and envelop the body; they produce sound, move, perform, and can be an event themselves; they are inviting to touch; they create atmosphere; they are sculptural and have a personality; they communicate an image, message, and tradition—and, as is often the case in public landscape installations, they are subject to the program, the economy, and politics.[16]

Textile carpets (and other interior flooring) and landscape ground cover—paving and planting—are subjected to similar physical and sensorial treatment, which involves tactile, sound, and climatic qualities, spatial definition, optical illusion, dynamism and movement, communication, and durability. Design strategies involving curtains, carpets, and landscapes often intermingle in Blaisse's work.

In Inside Outside's design for the Glass Pavilion at the Toledo, Ohio, Museum of Art (2005), the beauty and technical performance of both textiles and trees were harnessed to aesthetic and practical aims. Curtains in the interiors and trees around the building (in the park and the two patios) were strategically selected and positioned to wrap the building in a translucent "mesh" of fabric and foliage. The purpose of the mesh was to insulate—to mitigate glare and heat—the highly exposed glass pavilion, create flexible spaces and changing views, and produce special light and shadow effects.[17]

Inside Outside's more recent project in Tilburg, the Netherlands (2019), of a retrofitted, defunct, train repair building, joined a built "landscape" of stairs and curtains to structure the vast space into flexible rooms for a public library, flexible work spaces, and cultural performances and exhibitions. In addition to the glass façade, confluence between outdoor and indoor space is achieved by the use of three elements: a modulated topography of stairs that stream down and into several floors, three pairs of curtains that hang from roof to floor, and several "garden wagons" that slide into different positions from outside to inside.

Textile and landscape designs in Blaisse's work also reciprocate through imprint and path. She has continued the tradition of using textile weaving and print in landscape and garden patterns—i.e., parterres. The choreography of movement through space manifests in her use of similar mechanisms in curtains and landscapes:

> With curtains we use the track, the path, and the motor. The motor controls the speed of opening and closing the curtain itself. The track and its path delimit and shape space and choreograph the movement of people and social interaction in space. The track of a curtain is comparable to the path in the landscape, which also choreographs movement and scenarios through the landscape.

The path and imprint, two important devices that tie together disparate elements in the structure, produce the bold graphic composition of Inside Outside. The imprint introduces repetition and rhythm, the path creates gesture, and both move people through space using bright, conspicuous colors. "I'm quite a control freak, so we're mostly very graphic in our gardens," Blaisse says.

Lines and Imprints: Color Itineraries

The line of movement in Inside Outside's designs participates in the search for reciprocities between different spaces. It is also an exploration of color. The path concept and choreography in Blaisse's landscape projects can be traced to a trajectory that began in picturesque landscape garden strolls, passed through early modern film and the works of filmmaker Sergei Eisenstein, continued in the 1920s with Le Corbusier's "architectural promenade," and led to the midcentury Townscape serial vision.[18] Blaisse's paths are different from picturesque garden strolls, Le Corbusier's mostly architectural interior itineraries (with occasional framed views to the landscape), and Townscape's urban serial vision. They are closer to the experience of the parallax motion technique in film. They move between exterior and interior spaces, mixing inside and outside and, in the process, create multiple itineraries and narratives. Color sequencing plays a key role in triggering sensations and building changing ambiences and narratives, as seen in the prison in Nieuwegein and the public park in Milan.

At the new Nieuwegein State Detention Centre (1999), the concept of a path in the garden offset the restricted movement and forfeited freedom of the incarcerated (Figure 8.4).[19] Borne of Blaisse's concern with the political, social, psychological, physical, and visual aspects of the prison environment, the path is meant to be seen as an antidote to the condition of the place and of the people in it. Conspicuously orange, it meanders through six differently colored spaces around the building, connecting or running through or under outdoor shade structures, benches, and planting beds, and crosses the fence, leading to the parking lot outside. The path branches, loops, knots, and weaves through the garden, and even crosses

 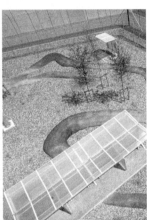

the boundary fence leading to the corporate environment outside. It choreographs physical movement, shifts direction, stages changing views and "accidents" along the way, and provides visual interest from the cell windows. Its intended effect is to loosen the rigidity of the place and the tension within and among inmates. Blaisse set out to create an undulating, eccentric path, "a strong and very visible continuous form, [that] could orchestrate the gardens, attract the view and invite unexpected movements," and liberate the space.[20]

To determine the layout of the path, Inside Outside created a site model of colored paper cut into long and twisted organic forms. The proposed orange concrete path was ultimately replaced with black asphalt because of budgetary and technical issues, partly related to maintenance. But Blaisse acknowledges that "The black asphalt is material color itself … it still stands out and contrasts with the ground material." The six "garden rooms" connected by the path suggest different kinds of activities and ambiences. Each is covered with mineral and herbal carpets of a different material and color: white, blue, orange, ochre, green, or mixed colors.

8.4 State Prison Nieuwegein, ground cover of blue mussel shells around men's ball field (top left) and Sport Court path seen from above (top right), the Netherlands, 1999. Photo: Hans Werlemann. Inside Outside, collage-plan (bottom)

The ground and planting color help orient strollers and personalize the spaces.

The women prisoners' space is a white garden with a mound covered in white shells, spring bulbs—snowdrops, anemones—and lady's mantle (*Alchemila mollis*); Blaisse described the latter as "a beautiful lime green plant whose leaves have furry hairs that catch every raindrop. The droplets glitter like tears or pearls, depending on how you look at them."[21] The garden around the men's ball field is blue made of mussel shells—dark blue with black-and-white mother-of-pearl— and bluish Dutch dune grass. Other spaces include a warm orange room covered with terracotta granulate, an ochre space laid with sand, and a green room with both Astroturf for soccer and real grass mixed with bulbs and wildflowers. The last two rooms are mixed-color wildflower gardens with subtle topographies that catch the light in different ways. Complying with the many government prison regulations concerning durability, visibility, and security presented a major challenge, but did not hinder the dynamic and playful outcome. Blaisse appreciated that the path

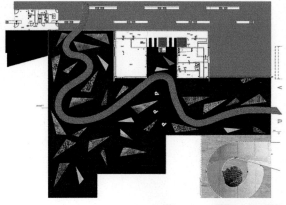

8.5 De Plussenburgh, residential plaza garden, planting plan (top) and elevated walk over pool (bottom), Rotterdam 2008

configuration seemed to match several "prisoners' tattoos pretty well!"[22]

Compared to the prison, the path running through a residential garden at the De Plussenburgh in Rotterdam (2008) is restrained, gentle, and elegant (Figure 8.5). The garden is situated over an underground garage in the space between an eldercare building and two new housing projects. The bright orange gestural line is inscribed on the entire plaza: it starts at the street, crosses a shallow water basin near the entrance to the building, cuts through a stand of reeds and allows a view over the water, meanders across a vast smooth black asphalt platform and between wooden benches and triangular planting beds in the concrete, and ends at the foot of a wavy wall by the water's edge. The contrasting orange line on the black asphalt animates the space day and night while giving presence to the persistent wind at the site. With calligraphic precision, the gently undulating path is meant to accommodate easy wheelchair movement, given the proximity of the eldercare facility. Slanted rail tubing over the path-bridge portion mimics grasses swaying in the wind. Inside the glass recreation center, the plaza's textural grassy beds continue in the carpet imprint, another notable organizational system of Inside Outside's design.

Inside Outside's imprints, repeated marks or patterns applied to and reproduced indefinitely on a surface, are linked less to movement and more to a narrative, a local history, or a concept behind the design. In her landscape projects, Blaisse thinks of the ground as an

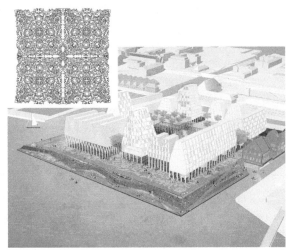

8.6 Christiansholm, paper island, floor papercut pattern (top) and bird's-eye view (bottom), Copenhagen, Denmark, 2015–ongoing

imprinted carpet that occasionally escapes strict boundaries. Her garden imprints hark back to 1920s European modern garden experiments, notably those of the graphic and landscape designer Pierre-Émile Legrain and Gabriel Guevrekian's Garden of Water and Light (1925) in Paris (in collaboration with the textile designer Sonia Delaunay), as well as Jean-Charles Moreux's Grosvenor Gardens (1952).

Weaving the pattern in- and outdoors, however, Blaisse lends spatial ambiguity to her ground surface material. The graphic language of imprints in particular is an important starting point on roofs, where the ground plane is carte blanche and trees cannot do well. The visual interest created by bold and colorful graphics on a roof offsets the lack of three-dimensionality that would be created by trees, and the roof perimeter neatly delimits the imprint as picture frame. A good example is the roof gardens of the Shenzhen Stock Exchange (2013), where Blaisse combined an overscaled flowery motif with the symmetry and rhythm of French carpet-like parterre patterns (Figure 8.6). The idea for the "Sino-European" gardens, as she calls them, draws on four centuries of cultural exchange of ideas, plants, and aesthetics between the Eastern and Western worlds—in a place of international money exchange. The embossed roof garden imprint, visible from the windows of the central tower, extends to a long, lush indoor "living wall" embedded with plants and to the lobby. Varied in texture and height—short lawns and 2–3-foot grasses and trimmed hedges of varied height and thickness—the planting beds create a range of green hues and tonal variation. Like tactile fabrics woven with different threads, the roof garden imprint projects a strong tactile quality, even though it is mostly experienced visually.

The ground imprint for the peninsula of Papirøen ("Paper Island") in Christiansholm, Copenhagen (2015, ongoing), again took its cues from the location. Its design is based on that of a papercut by the city's famous fairy-tale author, Hans Christian Andersen, whose lesser-known hobby was papercutting, and it also sustains the island's historical role as the city's paper store. The intricate pattern will be etched across the entire island and under the buildings, like a tattoo, using off-white and dark gray concrete pavers (see Figure 8.6). The achromatic imprint will have many contrasting colors: the blue seascape panorama from the perimeter promenade; flowering trees, shrubs, perennials, and vines in the neighboring streets and roof gardens; and lush green circular flower carpets in the central plaza.

In all of Inside Outside's projects color choice is a sensitive matter and varies greatly, based on the "couleurs trouvées." Color choices are drawn from biological and cultural sources, the project site, local flora and fauna, clients and users, and impromptu moments during the design process. Color is often selected to contrast with the pervasive surrounding color, as in the endlessly monochromatic desert of Qatar, where the isolated green pockets, bluish-silver shrubs, and bright yellow blooms of the desert's parasitic plants become a visual sensation, or in lush Shenzhen and Hong Kong, where bright synthetic color can rescue green monotony. Personal color preference and the temperament of individuals can influence choice, as can material and technique, area size and shape, local light and temperature, and viewing distance.[23] Cultural penchants and aversions are a vital part of the decision process. In the Netherlands, strong red, yellow, and orange colors are acceptable, but in other cultures they trigger resentment, shock, even fear because of political associations, fashion trends, or a chemical pigment base perceived as environmentally harmful. For example, the proposed black-and-white stripes for the stage curtain at London's Hackney Empire Theatre were fiercely rejected, while a red counterpart was accepted because red is an innate biological sign of health and potency that guarantee reproduction and survival.[24] Blaisse therefore hardly ever ends up with the color she started with. (Her personal preference is warm and energetic colors; her favorite is lime green "because of its absolute positive energy, its sunny glow, its imagined smell.")[25]

The color selection of Inside Outside projects creates an identity and enhances attachment to a place; it is designed to prevail even through periods of low maintenance and neglect. But graphic color strength cannot be the sole criterion. "In some [projects]," Blaisse has noted, "the focus is on colour and imagery; in others all is about colourless structures and invisible veils."[26]

Luminosity: Color-Sphere

A second Inside Outside body of work involves manipulation of light and production of atmospheres. For example, the "ever-unraveling patterns of the paper-cut and the different layers of the lighting systems" in Copenhagen's paper island design are meant to "house a heterotopia of atmospheres."[27] Blaisse likes to work with colors that are soft, translucent, luminous, and "broken" or "virtual." Through the interaction of surfaces with light and air waves, color solidity is broken and weakened.

The theory of color solidity developed by the artist Amédée Ozenfant (1886–1966) during his post-Purist period is useful for elucidating the color light quality in Blaisse's work. Ozenfant's theory aimed to enhance architectural form and space, and thus to increase the solidity of color. His dual focus on the objective and subjective effects of color, largely based on the 19th century chemist Michel Eugène Chevreul's theory of the interaction of color, led him to articulate a theory of virtual color.[28] "Virtual color" refers to the optical, or virtual, phenomenon created by simultaneous contrast, whereby neighboring bright and dull colors seen together produce complex and vivacious color. Ozenfant's theory of color solidity is based on three principles: (1) very bright hues are chemically, and appear visually, less solid than more neutral hues, (2) the purest pigmented color is the most solid, and (3) translucent hues are less solid than opaque ones.[29] To preserve the integrity of architectural space, Ozenfant favored pure, dark, and neutral hues; he rejected luminous and translucent broken color. Blaisse's preference for luminous and translucent color is to achieve the exact opposite, to destabilize spatial perception, to blur architectural confines, and to produce dynamic and evanescent effects. Her color is vivacious and virtual not by way of simultaneous contrast and solid reflection of color but through illumination techniques—and it is formless.

Blaisse has said, "Everything is defined by light. ... Colour is light."[30] Her work is about catching, reflecting, filtering, dimming, or excluding daylight, as it changes through the day and season. The luminosity of her colors propagates atmosphere or affect, the sensuous, intangible, and ephemeral emission of light, sound, heat, smell, and moisture that envelops people. Although, like color, atmosphere challenges language or description, Blaisse discusses it in both aesthetic and functional terms, and explicitly considers it for each project. Her affect-producing surfaces interact with and manipulate light as it is filtered and configured through the built structure and surface openings, like traceries or stained-glass windows in a church. Of the churches she visited as a child, she recalled: "[T]he sun comes through, and patches of color go all over the place. They shifted with time during the long mass." Daylight enters her space through slits, cuts, holes, tiny perforations, or wide-open planes, and at night light flows out from within. "The play of light and shadow and the shift in direction and intensity of light throughout the day mark the time, causing a variety of effects, moods and experiences."[31]

Technically activating surfaces to affect light waves necessitates attention to every surface design detail: pattern, texture, material, structure, openings, and color. For example, as Blaisse explained, while also chosen for aesthetic reasons, textures and structures

> are more often programmed to catch light and sound waves, to allow them through or to absorb or scatter them. Patterns can do the same, as in direction and distance of yarn or the effect of 3-D forms and openings.[32]

Modulation and the internal structure that holds a surface together govern the performance of light in space, which in curtains is done through the fabrication techniques of folding, pleating, overlapping, knotting, weaving, cutting, tearing, and more.[33] Different screening and degrees of tissue porosities produce different translucencies; different forms and sizes of openings (e.g., dense perforations or a few large windows) and textures (e.g., smooth, rough, shiny, matte) regulate the way light projects, absorbs, reflects, and alters the shadow play, giving it different depths and tone.

The landscape equivalent of a curtain surface is a "plant curtain" and mass, involving the selection of plant characteristics and construction of "planting curtains or walls," seen in the work of Blaisse and a few other landscape architects.[34] The result is luminescent, phosphorescent, and iridescent volume, where physical space dissipates into air and the distinction between architecture and landscape disappears (see Figure 8.2).

With light effects Blaisse dramatically retools traditional ideas of space and form. Her focus on atmosphere displaces the architecture itself. Inside Outside has joined the radical shift of the 1990s, experimenting with the production of affect to formulate principles and techniques for the 21st century. Instead of structure, fixity, and control, architecture "is now treated as a system of hydrodynamic flow, projects have become complex weather systems."[35] In Blaisse's work, the weather metaphor has been extended to chemistry, which is concerned with processes, probabilities, interactions, reactions, transformation, and ambiguities.[36] The flow, chance, interactions, and ambiguities brought about by light yield the special ambience and optical intrigue that Blaisse seeks:

> The balance, or lack of balance, between darkness and light introduces change, mystery and illusion where heavy becomes weightless; massive becomes transparent; colourful becomes colourless. A wall opens up; a thin fleece changes into a wall; an elegant figurine turns into a frightening Dracula; a poppy field into a deep dark forest; a dark corner in the garden into a sunny playground. This is what light and darkness can do, time and again.[37]

The visual-spatial ambiguity she created with light reflection in the temporary installation at the Sonneveld House in Rotterdam (2015) is a case in point. By covering the floor with mirrors and taking down the gauzy curtains at the windows, she exposed the hidden qualities of the house. Daylight enters unfiltered, the mirrored floors fly from one space to the next, boundaries disappear, space turns upside down and inside out, and the visitor's views inside and outward are unobstructed.[38] Blaisse's quality of light resonates with Rem Koolhaas's projection in 1999: "at the end of the 20th century, we are committed to the authenticity of materials or even more, to materials that announce their own dematerialisation."[39] At a time when glass façades "dematerialize" architecture, color is ethereal, transparent, and radiant. Nighttime architecture, too, has been radically reshaped by new lighting and digital technologies, a world fused in hybrid digital and physical effects.

More easily calibrated and controlled, artificial light sources can be manipulated for nighttime atmospheres. For a 2012 temporary installation, "Blues Before Sunlight," in the historic Vondelpark in Amsterdam, artist and film director Steve McQueen replaced all the park streetlamps with blue bulbs; Blaisse said: "All of a sudden this whole park turned spooky, becoming a very interesting space." Similarly, Blaisse produced a mysterious effect in Almere's Swamp Garden (2007), where low lights in the underground parking lot interact with occasional mist in the area, light up tree crowns, and accentuate shifting shadows.

Blaisse focuses on the color and intensity of artificial lighting and on the position of the light source, "as low and as soft as possible."[40] Direct, indirect, reflected, broken, dispersed, or colored, artificial light and shadow affect the experience of space. In Blaisse's recent collaboration with Hou Hanru on an exhibition design celebrating the tenth anniversary of MAXXI in Rome, four spaces were bathed in colored light: blue, yellow, pink, and white. Located behind two, black-and-white, curved walls that defined a narrow, central space, the bright colors leaked through narrow slits and invited people in. Each room offered visitors a different experience that combined video projections and objects. For instance, blue created endless space, yellow projected energy, and white created a clinical, laboratory-like space.[41]

The affect generated by the designs of Inside Outside differs from the intended universal psychophysical responses sought by modern landscape architects like Gabriel Guevrekian. Today's affect—created by a new surface design of confounding mediums, such as projection and architecture, but deeply immersive—has been framed as neophenomenology, internalization of perception, rather than feelings prescribed by cultural codes, sentimentality, and emotional reaction to a phenomenon.[42] The blue cathode ray, light that emanates day and night from high-definition plasma computer and cellphone screens, is not simply another color but the affect of contemporary architecture.[43] Inside Outside exploits the affective potential of color and light not only to transform space but to denote the present, or contemporaneity, and produce an immersive environment.

Tactile Color and Contemporaneity

Blaisse invests her curtains, carpets, and gardens with intimacy. The visual-tactile appearance of material texture and depth in her work invites touching. In fact, touching her textiles and plants is irresistible. Few could resist pressing the floor-to-ceiling bubble wrap curtain, "Don't Pinch!" (2018), that she hung for an exhibition at the Swiss Institute in Manhattan, or rubbing the concave wall made of brush at the Mercedes Benz Museum in Stuttgart, Germany (2006), or touching for verity the "Touch" Wallpaper Series (2003) in a gallery on Long Island, New York. "Touch" comprised close-up photographs of soft materials produced for previous

 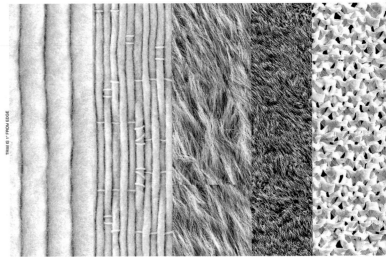

8.7 "Touch" Wolf Gordon Gallery, wallpaper, New York, 2003 (left and middle). Mercedes Benz Museum, curtain, Stuttgart, Germany (right)

projects printed in super-high resolution on vinyl, producing a trompe-l'oeil effect—tactile seduction resulted from deceptively real-looking images (Figure 8.7).

The sensorial environment engendered by Inside Outside's work derives from the perception of material weight, movement, texture, color, and scent. Sensation is invigorated by unusual and coarse surfaces, shimmering skins, varied transparencies, and contrasting combinations of diverse materials—heaviness with light, hard with soft, cold with hot. Inside Outside's textiles convey softness, sensuality, coziness, and ambiguity, while curtains induce movement through their own motion, rhythm, and sound. Blaisse uses both curtains and plants as veils to hide, reveal, mute, wrap, or unwrap space.

Like their curtain and wallpaper counterparts, Blaisse's carpets and landscapes produce tactile sensation. Indoor fiber carpets and outdoor mineral carpets not only soften sound, darken or lighten, warm a space, or communicate intentions, they can also invite the pleasure of movement, a pause, or rest. Crisp and vivid color imprints create an optical illusion of depth and urge touch. Landscape, too, can be like a curtain: "A curtain billowing in the breeze and grasses or willows swinging in the wind create dynamism and music. Tree leaf and bark texture invite touch, and flower scent compels smell."[44]

Partly because of her affinity for textiles, Blaisse's work has been discussed in feminine terms—its attributes cited as softness, healing, practicality, libidinal, and flow, even seduction, where truth of space is revealed only through a veil.[45] The veil and its performance, however, are familiar to the landscape architect, recall the Chinese garden tradition of wall tracery (or leak window), which separated yet enabled women to gaze from their designated courtyards into the garden of a male counterpart. Blaisse's veils also evoke the Muslim world's *mashrabiya*, a perforated decorative wooden screen that divides private and public space. Blaisse's veils, linking different domains, treat males and females alike to a world of wonder and truth.

Unlike Schwartz's fierce and witty feminism of protest, Blaisse's feminism is gentle and celebratory as much as it is assertive. Like Schwartz, she uses material and color to challenge conventional definitions of disciplines and gender identity. Her reproach of masculine-

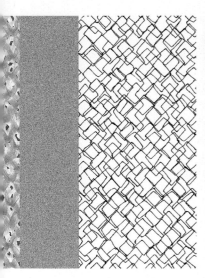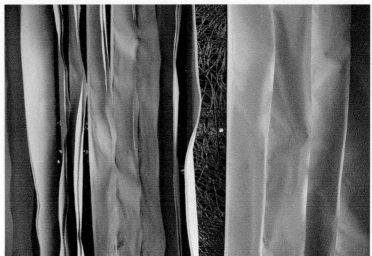

dominated architecture and pictorially based landscape design is also demonstrated through her working mode and sensuality.

Blaisse's tactile working methods apply to both textile and landscape design. Textile requires direct engagement with the material: "Feeling what you are doing, realizing by drawing, cutting, folding, ... sewing, ... to understand scale, what the material wants to do." She works with plant material with similar intimacy, unlike many landscape designers who rely on plant experts:

> I've always been interested to stick my hands in the soil and really understand how plants or animals or insects ... work, even as a child. I wanted to know how the roots of a plant behave in a certain soil, or how much you can influence its growth by improving it. In a roof garden project, we tell the architect, "Okay, you want to grow a garden on top of your parking, you want trees to block the wind, all right then, please, you have to create this in these conditions because a tree is not a plastic element." That's why Martha Schwartz uses plastic plants and it's fantastic. But if you want things to live you need to have the right soil and moisture conditions.

For Blaisse, living plants are not just design materials and instruments but a source of well-being and a way of knowing the world. She is deeply interested in plant sciences and philosophy, in the "intelligence of plants."[46] The death of bamboos a year after she planted them in one of her first garden projects, Villa Kralingen in Rotterdam (1988), prompted her to learn the practicalities of gardening. She befriended Lily ter Kuile, who taught at various landscape gardening schools in the Netherlands, and helped the ter Kuile family transform their three-hectare plot into a garden and nursey. Kuile also introduced her to anthroposophy, a gentle way of treating and collaborating with nature. Blaisse appreciates that

> Nature is about the collaboration between all living organisms. It is about air, change of season and time, light and darkness, sound and smell and ever-

changing views and perspectives. The connection between all forms of life, other than human beings, is critical.

Time and change, light and darkness, the visible and invisible are the basic ingredients of nature that she labors to make visible in her designs.

Although both gardens and textiles will degrade in time with use and lack of upkeep, their timeline, she says, is opposite. A fabric is at its best when newly installed and slowly degrades thereafter, whereas a garden may take 50–100 years from creation to look its best. Color, too, is a matter of time and lifespan. Blaisse recognizes that people may tire of a color because it falls out of fashion, or fades or scrapes off, eventualities she has tried to address through continuous involvement with projects. In fashion, maybe more than in other fields, color changes fast to stay fresh and increase sales.

> If you look around, the colors that one saw everywhere in the fifties and sixties—the colors of Technicolor—simply don't exist any longer; they literally disappeared from our general color scope—even in the color charts of large paint firms they are no longer included.[47]

At the same time, some colors—those that are warm and soft—never fail. People are also less likely to tire of colors in gardens, even those that are bright and pure, because they constantly change appearance by way of the natural cycle and are perceived as "natural." To emphasize that gardens are not natural, and green is not merely a filler, a decoration, or a softener of harsh architecture, Blaisse conceives of garden greenery as fields, carpets, or planes that are folded, slanted, woven, or pleated with plants.

Blaisse considers fear of color and chance a problem of our time. She cites color-saturated walls, decoration, and layers of visual narratives that were an integral part of architecture from ancient Rome through the first half of the 20th century. Murals and mosaics on walls, ceilings, and columns added color, dimensionality, light, illusion, and spatial effects to both interior and exterior spaces. But in the 21st century, she observes, people feel the need to predict and control.[48] She is not, however, worried about the dictates of color fashion. She welcomes and uses color strategically to signify its time. Her design drawings project a similar sentiment. With simple lines and luminous tones they explain the vision of the world to which Blaisse wants to give color, one that goes beyond gray tones while accommodating clients' sensibilities.

Multimedium: Bricolage, e-Collage, and Montage

The drawing repertoire of Inside Outside is as multivalent as the firm's project types and scales. Drawings use varied techniques—manual and computer, collage and e-collage, montage and video—and range in type—from abstract, diagrammatic, and cartoonish to impressionist, realist, and superrealist—to match the project medium, spirit, culture, and client. So does their color.

Blaisse's hand drawings, particularly her urban and landscape drawings, are rendered in her signature loose, cartoonish, colorful style. The simple sketches, displaying a fairy-tale, childlike flair characterized by the presence of human figures, show a strong affiliation with Bo Bardi's highly eclectic, atmospheric, and color-filled drawings.[49] Like Bo Bardi, Blaisse's spontaneous, instinctive, and free-style illustrations synthesize her thoughts and project conceptual, practical, and scientific ideas using pencils, crayons, or markers. For example, her simple diagrams explained the water pressure through the concrete that shaped the Swamp Garden Almere design. The more refined children's-book-like computer drawings for the Chocolate Factory project in Kyiv's Roshen Park capture a child's delight in the rich brown chocolate color for the paving (Figure 8.8). The unsophisticated drawings with exaggerated color display Blaisse's optimistic world. "Exaggerated," she says, "because it's fun. I don't see why we would do a kind of photographic representation of landscape."

Compared to curtain or interior design drawings, Blaisse finds landscape representation difficult. In textile design she uses simple sketches to show details and measurements of fabric structure or pattern, spatial constellation, and mechanism of motion (Figure 8.9). In contrast, atmosphere and color are impossible to communicate through drawings. "[In landscape design] I don't communicate color. I choose the plant or a flower. The plant has a specific family and each species in the family has a specific color." For example, drawings explain her choices in tree selection:

> I draw the trees, the characteristics of the bark and the color of the leaves or the special character of the roots. … I draw each tree as a kind of children's book with its special characteristics, and color it. So everyone can see that they are there for a reason, and that they have certain qualities.

The children's book approach is, in part, an antidote to digital renderings where attempts to draw a specific tree, like a

8.8 Chocolate Factory, computer drawing, Roshen Park, Kyiv, Ukraine, 2016

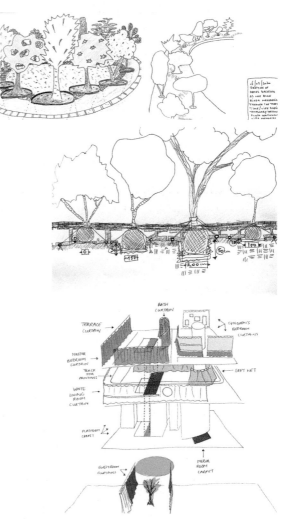

8.9 Sketches by Petra Blaisse. Radura della Memoria, Genoa, Italy, 2020 (top three). Maison à Bordeaux, Villa Floirac, Bordeaux, France, 2011–12 (bottom)

birch, always fail. In her proposal for the temporary memorial, Radura della Memoria (2020) in Genoa, a commemoration of a collapsed bridge tragedy, she drew the character of individual trees, showing them in a circular embrace around the memorial clearing. To illustrate their formal, textural, and color qualities, as with material palettes in interior design, she created a pictorial planting palette of the 43 local trees. Another analog drawing shows a measured section of the size of the planting hole needed for each tree (see Figure 8.9).

Representations that "give a kind of atmosphere and energy and ideal" communicate a vision for a landscape project, says Blaisse. Here, the drawings and model style of the French landscape architect Yves Brunier (1962–91) serve as guide (Figure 8.10). His conceptual, boldly colored collages of mixed drawing techniques, combining plans, perspectives, and bird's-eye views, made a powerful impression on Blaisse. Their highly tactile mixed media—color photographs, hand drawings, and photocopies overlaid with vigorous strokes of crayons, markers, or watercolor—were greatly appealing. They were not precise; rather, they communicated the concept and atmosphere of the landscape. Blaisse worked with Brunier in the late 1980s to make eclectic and colorful models for the Museumpark in Rotterdam, using screws, pieces of wood, paper, and fabric, among other found material. She considered his bricolage and tactile operations expressions of freedom and surprisingly effective.

Blaisse's tactile affinity is also evident in her monograph *Inside Outside*. Printed in high resolution, the 500-page volume and its numerous color-saturated

8.10 Yves Brunier, garden plan (top) and perspectives of back garden (middle) and front garden (bottom), house no. 2 designed by BEEL Architecten, Antwerp, Belgium, 1990. © Yves Brunier

images immerse readers in a meandering, visual-tactile experience. Its intent to "lead everyone to the touch, the smell, the movement, the real thing" is spelled out in the introduction.[50] The images often bleed from the page and are layered and woven with text. Blaisse's essays display a stream of consciousness style, with poetic section headings and project names such as Silk Rock, Milky Way, and Liquid Gold. The last 90 pages of the volume provide factual and visual information about each project, through a mosaic of vignettes that read like a material sample palette. The dominant color of each project (e.g., the lime green of the Seattle Public Library project) appears at the corresponding outer page margin and is visible on the front edge of the closed book, serving as project identifier and locator.

Inside Outside continues to use playful analog landscape sketches and models, even as more models are done in AutoCAD and collages are now computer-generated, or e-collages. Representation varies in each project depending on the expectations of the client and the culture. Blaisse has found that clients in the Middle East and China want highly realistic representation; in Japan, conceptual drawings suffice; in the Netherlands abstract drawings are accepted, although this is changing due to commercialism. The change from analog predigital collage to hypermeld realistic e-collage, done in Photoshop, involves the erasure of the tactility and identity of the distinctive medium and genres that constitute it. It further erases real world materiality and the metaphoric experience it brought to the picture. But as the e-collage tests today's fusion of reality and virtuality, it may lead to new a kind of intimacy and interactivity.[51]

Since 2000, video has emerged as a new mode of representation in Inside Outside work.[52] Camcorders and the ubiquitous iPhone can easily catch the transient and performative characteristics of Blaisse's curtains and landscapes and those who experience them. Unlike photography, video can convey the sensual qualities of fabrics—movement, changes in color and shadows, and the radiant and translucent effects that charge a space.[53] For Swamp Garden Almere on the company's website, the camera records the sway of grasses in the wind and a child indulging in a kinesthetic experience on the slanted pavement, and then pans across the site from an elevated position. These cinematic montage techniques, using color, lighting, framing, composition, and camera position and angles, expose the disciplinary overlap between landscape architecture, film, and theater, and are enhanced by software montage and modeling techniques.

Landscape computer models now add the fourth dimension of time through animations and dynamic light and time 4D models. And computer color rendering systems can perform illumination calculations for image synthesis, although the RGB model introduces inaccuracies during color rendering and printing, resulting in an image that is substantially inferior to an analogous image rendered with full spectral information. Furthermore, the fluorescence of an object is difficult if not impossible to convey using the RGB system. Because the RGB model can only give an approximation of the wide variation in spectral, surface-scattering properties present in the real world, Blaisse is reluctant to use it to communicate her colors.

The studio of Inside Outside is full of color and material samples. In interior design, Blaisse attaches the material sample or color "chips" on a white page. "If you want somebody to make a color for you in whatever material," she says, "you need to send a physical example." In landscape design, though, this is more complicated, as demonstrated in the pictorial plant palette of the flowering calendar in the Library of Trees in Milan.

* * *

Blaisse's two milestone projects—the Central Public Library in Seattle and the Biblioteca degli Alberi (Library of Trees) in Milan, both located at the heart of their respective cities— illuminate her color design sensibilities and processes. The first is an interior and landscape design for an innovative public building; the second, a complex infrastructure public park.

The "library of books" and the "library of trees" projects share and differ in their color concepts and strategies. In both projects, Blaisse uses strong and bold colorful graphics as organizational systems. In the Seattle central library, the sequencing of color surfaces and gardens from exterior to interior is a fluid and voluptuous sensorial feat unequalled in any other public institution. In Milan's public park, the plant patchwork of color fields and circles follows a choreography of year-round color display, making visible the dimension of time and seasons at the heart of the city. Apparent in both projects is Blaisse's fascination with plant collection and taxonomy. Her strategic grouping of plant families and species isolates and amplifies color and textural effects.

Her color selection and design processes for the two projects were quite different, reflecting cultural sentiments and different attitudes to artifactual versus natural plant color: in Seattle, the decision making was lengthy and often accompanied by heated deliberations; in Milan, the plant color selection was based on aesthetics and science and devoid of controversy.

8.11 Seattle Public Library, main floor (Living Room) (top) and planting beds crossing glass wall and turning to plant carpets (bottom), Seattle, Washington, 2005

Seattle Central Public Library, Washington, USA (2000–5)

Color was a major design ingredient in the ten-story Seattle library. The rich palette of green, red, and mauve shades Blaisse selected for the project's interior "carpet gardens" (described in this chapter's first opening quotation) is an instrument to energize space, produce atmosphere, engage the spectrum of senses, and break down boundaries between people, cultures, and mediums (Figure 8.11).[54]

The project scope developed early on for each outdoor and indoor space. "The people's library," as it was called, was to be welcoming and inclusive. OMA, with Loschky, Marquardt and Nesholm (LMN) Architects, developed a radical architecture, an open, flexible, and visually connected spatial scheme that could adapt to new future uses.[55] The diamond, steel-faceted glass façade, likened to a fishing net, encrusts the building and floods the interiors in intense light, casting constantly moving shadows that animate the interconnected floors. The steel structure color, light blue with a hint of gray, was chosen to contrast with the cloudy, gray city and mostly gray and brown surrounding buildings. The interior colors were selected for multiple functions and effects: as area delineators, codes for activity zones, spatial scalers in the enormous space, way finding guides, and, importantly, a highly tactile and immersive sensation. The stunning connected floors, vertiginous internal views, illumination, and brightly colored floor planes have made the building popular for film shoots and photo snaps. It has been described as "the 'most Instagrammable' library in the world."[56]

Inside Outside worked as carpet and curtain designer and advisor on landscape design and interior materials and finishes.[57] Attention focused on "the unification of the building's volumes through the manipulation of the horizontal planes—floors and ceilings—and through the one vertical structure that choreographs both sound and space in a single movement, which was the auditorium curtain."[58] The carpets, which were used to scale down the space, delineate activity areas, participating in a narrative about a fluid landscape-interior, for which Blaisse used the metaphor of "flying carpets" (Figure 8.12). The narrative followed the dynamic architectural maneuver of the transparent shifting floors of the building, which followed the sloping streets flanking the building and the views toward the ocean and mountains. As at the Kunsthal in Rotterdam, another building designed by OMA with Blaisse as an advisor, where the park flows into the building to reappear on the roof, the Seattle library both invites the landscape in and makes its interiors visible to the exterior.[59] The landscape infiltrates and folds into the interior through the glass façade and flows from one level to another. Blaisse noted:

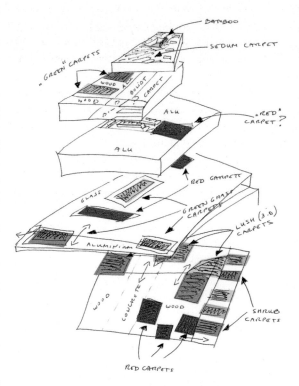

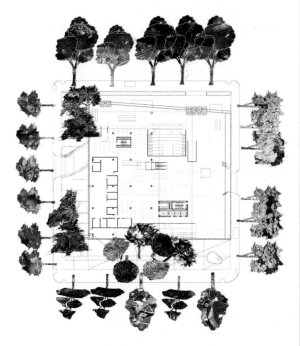

8.12 Seattle Public Library, concept drawings, "flowing carpets" (top) and street tree planted in small "bosquets" of family tree groups (bottom)

The most important discussions we had with the architects here were about the continuation of landscape in the interior and the coherent sequence of ambiences and functions throughout the building: the choice of colours and materials; and how to coordinate this on every level.[60]

In terms of color choice, "Green was the colour we envisioned for the library gardens." Around the building was a strip of patches of gardens, with shifting, tectonic color fields or planes that were sometimes covered by the building's folded façade. The strip widens at the 5th and 4th Avenue entrances, where the living green carpets appear to cross the transparent façade and enter the building to the Living Room, where they transform into fiber carpets printed with large-scale plant patterns. Daylight accentuates the color and textures of the plant carpets and nurtures several living plant beds indoors—a visual play between real and imagined nature. "The carpets become gardens and gardens become carpets that catch the visitor's eye from all angles and levels," Blaisse explains.

The municipal trees lining the surrounding streets were planted in family groups of oak, maple, magnolia, and beech, among others, creating small "bosquets" over planes of wild grasses, ferns, and perennials (see Figure 8.12). Blaisse's interest in taxonomy and in creating bold effects led to "clans of trees," where one genus is represented by several species. Planted in groups, the specific plant characteristics produce a stronger impression of form, texture, and color, much like in Burle Marx's gardens. Time and change, important principles in Blaisse's work, manifest in the plants' seasonal displays of color outside and through animation by the fleeting shadows on the plant-imprinted carpets inside.

8.13 Seattle Public Library, view down to the main floor from the computer floor balcony. Photo: Mira Engler, 2011

To invigorate the sensation of color Inside Outside choreographed an interior design sequence of movement through the contrasting colors of red, blue, and mauve plant carpets. "Our aim here was comparable to the landscape-like exhibitions we designed: to keep the public alert and interested by leading them not only from one space to another but also from one experience to another."

Upon entering from either 5th or 4th Avenue, one encounters the auditorium space, a void at the center of the space that connects the first and third floor entry levels via a slope of rows of green chairs and brown polyurethane stairs. The auditorium is defined by a two-sided curtain that is closed or opened to suit the activity. Inside, the curtain features a fin-like texture in apple green with cream, while outside it is lined with a bearskin imprint. Blaisse referred to the auditorium curtain and chair color choice as an afterimage of the outside green, which "creates another garden-like space in the heart of the building."[61] As in the striped effect of bulb fields, the color and depth of the curtain change as one walks by.

The Living Room's green plant-imprinted carpets, complemented by undulating chains of red lounge chairs and a central circular black "water pool" of reflective

8.14 Seattle Public Library, sequence of color atmospheres. Green and earthy colors in auditorium. Photo: © Parikh (top left). Glossy red stairway leading to the workspaces (top right) and chartreuse escalator space leading to digital library (bottom). Photos: Mira Engler, 2011

polyurethane, create a very light, fresh, and relaxed atmosphere. As they mitigate noise and bring softness underfoot, they put people at ease, inviting them to sit and read. Low bookshelves crisscross the green carpet, introducing an intimate living room atmosphere (Figure 8.13). To define the Teens Library on that level, the floor changes from white-stained wood to red polyurethane.

To take the hard-to-miss elevators, beaming in chartreuse or green-yellow fluorescent light like a highlighter, one enters a womb-like space, whose curvy hallway walls and floors are soaked in intoxicating glossy red (Figure 8.14). It is a soft and warm organic space with red, dark red, pink, orange, and orange-brown surfaces and a narrow winding corridor. "From this boiling hot and pumping space, doors open into brightly lit, clinic-like workspaces (white, light grey and blue; with here and there a brown or black plane)."[62] Taking the stairs, one climbs up to the steel-cold fifth floor, the digital library or Mixing Chamber, with a sharp transition from "hot" to "cold." As Blaisse explained in our interview, "It was all about the trajectory. It's very red, but when you open the door, it's all of a sudden blue or white … it's a different world. And so it's all about color sensation." Looking down from the Mixing Room onto the Living Room, the plant carpet makes a fantastic impression of depth and realness. It also affords a seamless visual connection between the exterior garden and the garden representation woven into the carpets. The top floor reading rooms are furnished with one of three carpets, printed in greens, pinks and reds, and mauves and blues, while on the first floor the Children's Library displays a cheery pink, red, and yellow color scheme, and a ceiling field of "starry sky" hanging bulbs.

Blaisse attributes the daring color scheme of the library to the participatory design process, in which clients, library staff and volunteers, and future users ultimately inspired and trusted each other. But convincing the library board and the public that furniture could help bridge the gap between outmoded and contemporary architecture, and that color could help break down boundaries between past and present and inside and outside, took time. It was a process whereby everyone involved came to terms with their biases. Initial surveys and conversations with future users about their color preferences, and photographs of Seattle architects' interiors, pointed to a dislike of orange and preferences for brown, beige, dark green, and burgundy (Figure 8.15).[63] These colors reminded Blaisse of "hunting cabins: wood, leather, rugs, open fire, hunting and sports trophies on the walls; being one with the forest, the soil and the field; pointing to Seattle's Scandinavian inheritance more than to the Indian predecessors," penchants that did not resonate with the designers' intentions.[64] Puzzled by the color preferences and the discovery that in public buildings all over America, colors seem muted, mixed with white or black, Blaisse wondered about Americans' fear of bright, pure color. She concluded with several hypotheses, of which the most convincing was that Americans' relationship with nature complicates their ability to imitate it.[65] She decided to use digital imaging to create a trompe l'oeil effect of nature on the garden carpets.

8.15 Seattle Public Library, photograph taken by local project architects of their parents' interiors (left). Collage of the interiors' color analysis (right)

8.16 Seattle public library, carpet imprint for production in red, green, and blue-mauve palettes

8.17 Biblioteca degli Alberi (Library of Trees), bird's-eye view (top) and aerial view (bottom), Milan, Italy, 2018. Photos: Andrea Cherchi

The American fear of color translated to unsatisfactory samples from US carpet manufacturers of plant carpet imprints based on Blaisse's photographs: "Not only were the colours reduced to grey, beige, and olive green, but the photographic images kept turning into corporate-looking patterns, totally dead."[66] So the job of printing the crisp digital photographic images on a rug in a way that vividly displays the plants in plan-view was given to a Danish firm.[67] The photos were enlarged to the maximum possible size without losing image resolution. The difficulty of transferring a picture onto a carpet, Blaisse explained, is that a carpet, whether knotted, tufted, woven, or printed, can only be built up of 8–12 colors, compared to a photograph of just greens, which is composed of almost 400 colors (Figure 8.16).

Drawings and models of the Seattle Library multidisciplinary and multimedium design exhibit eclectic techniques: loose diagrams showing the fluid movement of the plant carpet from outside to inside and across the different floors; mixed drawings, reminiscent of Brunier's drawings, depicting the main floor plan with surrounding trees in elevation view; photographic collages of the color palettes for each carpet, projecting the ambiences of the different library spaces; technical, measured drawings specifying the auditorium curtain's make-up and hanging mechanism as well as the street tree planting holes; and eclectic multimedia models.[68] Color and light effects resonate in the robust photographic documentation of the finished project.

Biblioteca degli Alberi (Library of Trees), Central Park, Milan, Italy (2003–4, 2010–18)

Six years after the firm's first prize-winning proposal entered in the competition for Milan's Giardini di Porta Nuova ("the gardens of the new city gate"), the project was revived.[69] Located between two main transportation centers, Stazione di Porta Garibaldi and Stazione Centrale, and other municipal, commercial, office, and high-rise residential buildings (including a lush green pair named "Bosco Verticale," or vertical forest, by Stefano Boeri), the ten-hectare park is the beating heart of the city. A designated center of cultural venues, particularly the Città della Moda, it includes a fashion academy, fashion museum, and textile pavilion. The link between plants and fashion was strengthened through the design by Blaisse and her team, which matched the fashion center with a botanical garden.

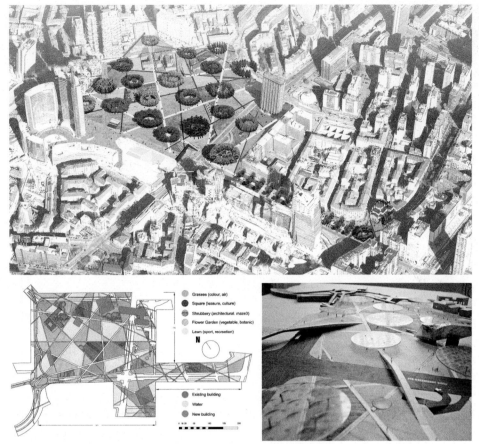

8.18 Biblioteca degli Alberi, proposal drawings (top and bottom left) and model (bottom right)

The Library of Trees proposal resembled a patchwork of "textile gardens" made of different textural planting patches, adorned with circular bosques, and stitched together by paths and a meandering wrought iron fence (Figure 8.17).

Because Milan's historic botanical garden, the Brera, had fallen into decay, the main idea of the firm's competition entry was to create not only a new public park in the urban landscape but a new version of a botanical garden—a Library of Trees. The proposal drawings display Inside Outside's eclectic representation: collages showing the diversity of planting, lettered paths, and vegetal screens; diagrams of color planting calendars featuring the months in which key plants are in color; tree material palettes; and abstract models, including one made of a patchwork of wood parts of diverse textures and tints and plexiglass-printed circles of tree canopies (Figure 8.18).

The graphic layering of the path network and colorful circles yields a powerful impression typical of Blaisse's work (Figure 8.19).[70] The path network also yields multiple connections, movements, and views for small and large impromptu happenings. The space ties together park and infrastructural programs and accommodates cultural, recreational, and educational buildings at the site without interfering with the integrity of the design. As in the prison project, the paths are designed to string together narratives in

265

8.19 Biblioteca degli Alberi, aerial view of two tree circles and maze (top). Photo: Andrea Cherchi

8.20 Biblioteca degli Alberi, tree palettes of individual color rings. Designed with Piet Oudolf

scenarios that unfold through movement. At times, the paths continue through buildings, blurring the boundaries between inside and outside. They climb and fall, following the space's topographic manipulation and, together with the slopes and variety of plants and trees, create both enclosed spaces and open views over the park and toward the city.[71] "By folding some of the plots downward," Blaisse explained, "we created sloping gardens which at their lowest point open the visitor's view to the subterranean canal that runs right through our site, or to the trains passing by underground."[72] The public can experience the park from multiple viewpoints: sidewalks, cars, buses, trains, airplanes, and high-rise offices and residences.

267

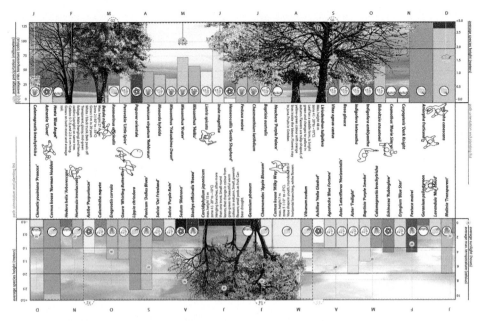

8.21 Biblioteca degli Alberi, planting plan calendar. Designed with Piet Oudolf

For park strollers Inside Outside created a theatrical experience. Screens of vegetation are used as curtains:

> When you walk through the park, you experience layers of screens, from translucent to opaque, from thin to thick, giving a feel of dense complexity, although the garden's organization is actually really simple. And speaking of curtains, we also planned a real curtain made of stainless steel that closes off an area in the heart of the park at night.[73]

The theatrical experience is further bolstered by narratives, poetry, botanical names, and wayfinding information inscribed in the concrete paths. The texts, inspired by similar garden traditions and designed by Irma Boom, create a montage or filmic experience when read in sequence while moving through the park.[74] Originally, the paths—the 16-foot-wide concrete paths are light gray and the 8-foot-wide paths dark gray—were to be black and white. The proposed extreme contrast was exaggerated to ensure some degree of tonal difference in the end.[75]

The park transcends heavy perimeter traffic and underground infrastructure, as color and texture enter through fields of plant cover and tree canopies. The fields between the paths comprise gardens, orchards, squares, and water. The canopies of the bosquets create open-air pavilions and display distinct foliage, flowers, and fruit colors in different seasons (Figure 8.20). As their crown color changes through the seasons they contrast with the park's dominant green (Figure 8.21).

Blaisse's affinity for the simple, systematic organization of botanical collections is clearly displayed. The park is a place for people to walk with their dog, meet, relax, play—and learn about local plants. The tree selection consists of common street trees and fruit trees that represent Milan's agricultural tradition and are chosen for color, sound, scent, profile, and scale as well as their capacity for screening, wind breaking, sound absorption, and air filtering.[76] The planting design of each of the 13 gardens and 23 tree circles, done in collaboration with Dutch garden designer Piet Oudolf, offers a different type of visual experience:

> Each circle is one kind of tree and color coordinated. The paths between the plots and trees circles are organized as seasonal routes or planting type routes through grasses, lawns, meadows, herb gardens, a maze, trimmed shrubbery, and a number of colorful perennial gardens. There is a reddish route and a whitish route. We worked with planting screens and their heights. ... So there are different seasons and forms of transparencies.[77]

The "color itineraries"—red, white, green, yellow, and orange—connect trees of similar colors. The reddish route, for instance, connects circles of Magnolia Heaven Scent, crab apple, red maple, and two other red fruit-producing trees. The whitish route connects circles of Callery pear, the European hornbeam, and three other white bark and flower-producing trees.

Bold synthetic paving delineates two circular bosquets of intense activity: a bright red-pink playground and a light blue sports exercise track. A black-and-white maze, which began as a technical solution to an emergency and exhaust ventilation exit point of the underground train tracks and Metro, has become the park's major attention grabber. The alternating curvy dark green shrub strips and white paths are spaced to accommodate maintenance vehicles. The height of the labyrinth "walls," which determined the plant types, was limited to 50 centimeters by security and transparency codes (but raised a little)—too low for an effective maze, but people nonetheless enjoy wandering through.[78]

* * *

Petra Blaisse's postdisciplinary work has opened new ways for color to enter landscape design, as affective color light. It transgresses physical boundaries and evaporates materiality and spatial confines. It is sensual and tactile. The luminous, translucent, and phosphorous effects perfectly fit the aura of today's digital environment. The following passage from "Avoiding Architecture" best captures these ideas:

> When one's life's work is avoiding architecture by creating spatial effects with other means; when these effects tend to be more flexible, less costly and easier to realize; when they introduce narrative, tactility and unpredictable, un-stable, ever-changing volumes and shapes to a place; when the work connects inside to outside or forms a flexible membrane between the two; when it enhances perspectives and view-lines or creates openings; when it organizes movement, use, climate and acoustics; when it adds softness, colour, structure and scale; when it filters, spreads or obstructs light or sound; when it introduces the aspect of time and change, of life and decay; ... then we can speak of a radical design intent.[79]

Notes

1. Multiple other factors inspire and direct the work of Blaisse's firm Inside Outside, including movement, change, sequence of experience; soil, climate, and sustainability; and technical aspects and maintenance.

2. Ota, ed., *Inside Outside*, 2007, preface, no page number. The monograph (edited by Kayoko Ota) was designed by Irma Boom.

3. WebEx interview with the author on April 2, 2021. Unless otherwise attributed, Blaisse quotations in this chapter are from this conversation.

4. Beattie, "Interview with Petra Blaisse," 2010, 40.

5. Peter Niessen, a fashion designer, has worked with Blaisse on curtain design all along. In 2016 the firm was joined by two partners: Aura Melis, architect, and Jana Crepon, landscape architect.

6. She was taught the art of gardening and botany according to the logic of the moon calendar, invented by the Austrian esotericist Rudolf Steiner (1861–1925).

7. The New Perennial Movement, associated with the Dutch garden designer Piet Oudolf, is an extension of Gertrude Jekyll's perennial drifts but with bolder compositions and color. For Blaisse's planting design, see Taylor, *Women Garden Designers*, 2014, 238.

8. Richardson, "Petra Blaisse," 2008, 42.

9. Lavin, "Petra Envy," 2008–9, 88.

10. Koolhaas, "The Future of Colours Is Looking Bright," 1999, 13.

11. Blaisse, "Avoiding Architecture, a Manifesto," 2016, 118.

12. Unless otherwise noted, drawings and projects in this chapter are by Inside Outside.

13. Ibid.

14. Barreneche, "Curtain Call," 2000, 57.

15. Blaisse, "Avoiding Architecture," 2016, 118.

16. Several analogies are discussed in van den Heuvel, "A Choreography of Reciprocities," 2007.

17. Blaisse, "Invisible Presence," 2007. The proposal was rejected, lest it interfere with the architecture and the museum display.

18. For the links between gardens, film, and urban sequencing techniques, see Colomina, *Privacy and Publicity*, 1994, 77; Bruno, *Atlas of Emotion*, 2002, 28.

19. Van den Heuvel, "A Choreography," 2007, 281. Blaisse's first proposal, which was rejected, was to flank the prison's exterior wall that faces the corporate office park with mirrors to reflect the outside world and make the prison invisible. The subversive proposal of an optical illusion was intended to protest the controlled, corporate world that often denies or ignores the existence of social problems and prisons. This kind of social protest is atypical in Blaisse's work, which is overwhelmingly vested with positivity.

20. Blaisse, "The Path as Spatial Tool," 2007, 254.

21. Ibid.

22. Ibid.

23. Beattie, "Interview," 2010, 40.

24. Ibid., 44.

25. Ibid., 38.

26. Blaisse, "Undoing Boundaries," 2007, 208.

27 Inside Outside webpage, https://www.insideoutside.nl/Landscapes/Paper-Island-Copenhagen

28 Kane, "Broken Colour in a Modern World," 2015, 10.

29 Ozenfant, "Colour Solidity," 1937, 243.

30 *Mondo Arc* editors, "Lighting Talk," 2014, 38.

31 Ibid. For more on Blaisse's curtain effects see Kwinter, "The Garden and the Veil," 2007, 500.

32 Weinthal, "Bridging the Threshold of Interior and Landscape," 2008, 69.

33 Balmond, "Dialectics of the Tangible and the Intangible," 2007, 406.

34 Most notable is the work of the Dutch landscape architect Adriaan Geuze of West 8. In his 1997 Cypress Garden, a swamp garden around the city of Charleston, South Carolina, he created a perforated screen wall made of moss hung on wires. And in a monastery garden in Padua, Italy, where pine trees shed their cones constantly, he built a wall of pinecone-filled gabions. In both gardens the filtered, changing, ethereal light produced awe-inspiring illumination.

35 Wigley, "The Architecture of Atmosphere," 1998, 19. The Icelandic-Danish artist Olafur Eliasson produces similar effects in his light installations using machines.

36 Kwinter, "The Garden and the Veil," 2007, 500.

37 *Mondo Arc* editors, "Lighting Talk," 2014, 38.

38 Inside Outside website, https://www.insideoutside.nl/Interiors/Huis-Sonneveld2-Rotterdam

39 Koolhaas, "The Future of Colours," 1999, 13.

40 *Mondo Arc* editors, "Lighting Talk," 2014, 38.

41 WebEx interview, 2021.

42 Lavin, *Kissing Architecture*, 2011, 21.

43 Ibid.

44 Barreneche, "Curtain Call," 2000, 125.

45 Kwinter, "The Garden," 2007, 500.

46 On Blaisse's gardening passion, training, and influences, see Taylor, *Women Garden Designers*, 2014, 240.

47 Beattie, "Interview," 2010, 39.

48 Ibid., 44.

49 Ippolito, Paulini, and Attenni, "The Social Poetry Drawing of Lina Bo Bardi," 2020.

50 Ota, *Inside Outside*, 2007, Introduction.

51 See Stafford, "To Collage or e-Collage?," 1998.

52 All videos of curtains and gardens are by Frans Parthesius.

53 Ronald, "The Effect of Curtains," 2007, 102.

54 Blaisse, "Undoing Boundaries," 2007, 203.

55 Ibid., 194.

56 Davis, "Seattle Has the 'Most Instagrammable' Library in the World," 2018.

57 Landscape architect collaborators were Kate Orff's Scape, New York, and the local Jones & Jones Architects.

58 Blaisse, "Undoing Boundaries," 2007, 209.

59 At the Kunsthal in Rotterdam the surrounding public park flows into the building, turns into tree trunk columns, a group of colorful chairs, and a trunk-like curtain, and reappears as a garden on the sloping roof.

60 Blaisse, "Undoing Boundaries," 2007. This and the following quotations in these paragraphs, until otherwise noted, are from pages 200–5.

61 Ota, *Inside Outside*, 2007, 432.

62 Blaisse, "Undoing Boundaries," 2007, 207.

63 Beattie, "Interview," 2010, 37.

64 Blaisse, "Undoing Boundaries," 2007, 200.

65 Ibid., 207.

66 Ibid.

67 Danish pigment regulations allow for brighter colors than in the Netherlands or United States.

68 Ota, *Inside Outside*, 2007, 432–39.

69 Among several collaborators on the 2003–4 competition entry were the architects Mirko Zardini and Michael Maltzan, Piet Oudolf, the graphic designer Irma Boom, and local landscape architect Studio Giorgetta. The much anticipated Library of Trees finally opened in December 2018 following several years of administrative and planning delays.

70 The complex layered park approach had precedents in OMA competition entries for Parc de la Villette in Paris (1982) and Downsview Park in Toronto (2000); Blaisse was involved in the latter.

71 van den Heuvel, "A Choreography," 2007, 281.

72 Blaisse, "Complex Urban Park," 2007, 133.

73 Ibid.

74 Ibid., 150–1.

75 WebEx interview, 2021.

76 Blaisse, "Complex Urban Park," 2007, 141.

77 Ibid.

78 WebEx interview, 2021. The local landscape architects took the liberty of raising it to 80 centimeters, assuming no one would be able to tell the difference.

79 Blaisse, "Avoiding Architecture," 2016, 120.

References

Balmond, Cecil. "Dialectics of the Tangible and the Intangible." In *Inside Outside: Petra Blaisse*, ed. by Kayoko Ota, 406–7. Rotterdam: NAi Publishers, 2007.

Barreneche, Raul A. "Curtain Call." *Architecture* 89, no. 12 (2000): 57.

Beattie, Nicole. "Interview with Petra Blaisse." In *New Geographies 3, Urbanisms of Color*, ed. by Gareth Doherty, 38–45. Cambridge, MA: Harvard University Press, 2010.

Blaisse, Petra. "Complex Urban Park: Giardini de Porta Nuova, Milan, Italy." In *Inside Outside: Petra Blaisse*, ed. by Kayoko Ota, 128–51. Rotterdam: NAi Publishers, 2007.

Blaisse, Petra. "Invisible Presence: The Glass Pavilion, Toledo, USA." In *Inside Outside: Petra Blaisse*, ed. by Kayoko Ota, 18–38. Rotterdam: NAi Publishers, 2007.

Blaisse, Petra. "The Path as Spatial Tool: State Detention Centre, Nieuwegein, the Netherlands." In *Inside Outside: Petra Blaisse*, ed. by Kayoko Ota, 250–79. Rotterdam: NAi Publishers, 2007.

Blaisse, Petra. "Undoing Boundaries: Seattle Central Library, Seattle, USA." In *Inside Outside: Petra Blaisse*, ed. by Kayoko Ota, 194–209. Rotterdam: NAi Publishers, 2007.

Blaisse, Petra. "Avoiding Architecture, a Manifesto." *Materia Arquitectura* 14 (2016): 116–20. www.materiaarquitectura.com/index.php/MA/article/view/27

Bruno, Giuliana. *Atlas of Emotion: Journeys in Art, Architecture, and Film*. New York: Verso, 2002.

Colomina, Beatriz. *Privacy and Publicity: Modern Architecture as Mass Media*. Cambridge, MA: MIT Press, 1994.

Davis, Brangien. "Seattle Has the 'Most Instagrammable' Library in the World." Crosscut, December 3, 2018. https://crosscut.com/2018/12/seattle-has-most-instagrammable-library-world

Ippolito, Alfonso, Marcelo Mott Paulini, and Martina Attenni. "The Social Poetry Drawing of Lina Bo Bardi." In *EGA 2020: Graphical Heritage*, ed. by L. Agustín-Hernández, A. Vallespín Muniesa, A. Fernández-Morales, 51–62. Springer Series in Design and Innovation, vol. 6 (2020). Cham: Springer. https://doi.org/10.1007/978-3-030-47983-1_5

Kane, Carolyn. "Broken Colour in a Modern World: Chromatic Failures in Purist Art and Architecture." *Journal of the International Colour Association* (April 2015): 1–13. www.aic-colour-journal.org

Koolhaas, Rem. "The Future of Colours Is Looking Bright." In *OMA 30 Colour: New Colours for a New Century*, 13–16. Blaricum, The Netherlands: V+K Publishing, 1999.

Kwinter, Sanford. "The Garden and the Veil." In *Inside Outside: Petra Blaisse*, ed. by Kayoko Ota, 500–3. Rotterdam: NAi Publishers, 2007.

Lavin, Sylvia. "Petra Envy: The Designs of Petra Blaisse." *Harvard Design Magazine* 29 (Fall/Winter 2008–9): 87–94.

Lavin, Sylvia. *Kissing Architecture*. Princeton, NJ: Princeton University Press, 2011.

Mondo Arc editors. "Lighting Talk." *Mondo Arc* 177 (2014): 38–9. Accessed February 16, 2021. https://www.arc-magazine.com/mondoarc-febmar-2014-issue-77

Ota, Kayoko, ed. *Inside Outside: Petra Blaisse*. Rotterdam: NAi Publishers, 2007.

Ozenfant, Amédée. "Colour Solidity." *Architectural Review* 81, no. 237 (1937): 243–6.

Richardson, Tim, ed. "Petra Blaisse." In *Avant Gardeners: 50 Visionaries of the Contemporary Landscape*, 42–7. London: Thames & Hudson, 2008.

Ronald, Tim. "The Effect of Curtains." In *Inside Outside: Petra Blaisse*, ed. by Kayoko Ota, 102–3. Rotterdam: NAi Publishers, 2007.

Stafford, Barbara Maria. "To Collage or e-Collage?" *Harvard Design Magazine* 6 (Fall 1998): 32–4.

Taylor, Kristina. *Women Garden Designers: 1900 to the Present*. Woodbridge, Suffolk: Garden Art Press, 2014.

Van den Heuvel, Dirk. "A Choreography of Reciprocities." In *Inside Outside: Petra Blaisse*, ed. by Kayoko Ota, 280–3. Rotterdam: NAi Publishers, 2007.

Weinthal, Lois. "Bridging the Threshold of Interior and Landscape: An Interview with Petra Blaisse." *Architectural Design* 78, no. 3 (2008): 64–71. https://onlinelibrary.wiley.com/doi/abs/10.1002/ad.676

Wigley, Mark. "The Architecture of Atmosphere." *Dailalos* 68 (1998): 19–26.

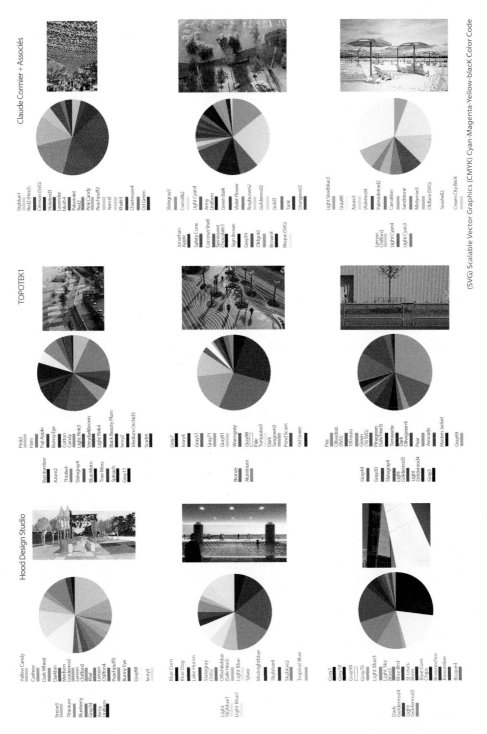

9.0 Diagrams, color analyses of Pink Balls and Sugar Beach in Toronto, Canada, by Claude Cormier + Associés (upper row); Superliken, Copenhagen, and Evergreen Heerenschürli, Zurich, Switzerland, by TOPOTEK 1 (middle row); and Urban Diaries book drawings, the International African American Museum, Charleston, South Carolina, and Double Sights, Princeton, New Jersey, USA, by Hood Design Studio (lower row). Rendered by Maryam Maddahzad

9

Color Now
Gender, Skin, and Screen

The three landscape architects covered in this chapter—the Canadian Claude Cormier of Claude Cormier + Associés, the German Martin Rein-Cano of TOPOTEK 1, and the American Walter Hood of Hood Design—began their practice in the mid-1990s and acquired renown in the new millennium. Educated between the late 1970s and early 1990s, they came on the heels of the dissenting generation of conceptualist designers of the 1980s, who rejected empirical, social, and ecological dogma in favor of art and cultural praxis. The younger generation continue to vocally repudiate the 18th century English landscape garden tradition that has persisted as a point of reference. They counter the natural pretense of designed landscapes with bold design that celebrates landscape's artificiality, and shift the focus to the politics of identity and social equity. The Romantic version of nature and its green insignia are replaced with extravagant and assertive gestures of color. Color has intensified its role as central design ingredient and active instrument in social negotiations, place-making, and digital culture.

Martha Schwartz looms large over the three practitioners, two of whom—Cormier and Rein-Cano—practiced or interned with her. While escaping the Schwartzian force of gravity and building their distinct professional signatures, all three share her contention that color frees them to explore a broader range of possibilities in landscape design and defy conventions, like artists.

Working at the intersection of public art, landscape architecture, and urban design, Cormier, Rein-Cano, and Hood have used color as a communicative and subversive tool to energize, create mood, and expose and challenge color biases (Figure 9.0). Cormier and Rein-Cano also use color to invest their work with humor and irony and loosen people up. What distinguishes the three from Schwartz and her generation is their active engagement in social justice and the virtual world. Color is activated in Cormier's politics of gender identity, Rein-Cano's politics of ethnic identity, and Hood's racial politics and its contemporary voice, Black Lives Matter.

Color is prominently present in entertainment landscapes, an integral part of contemporary consumer and digital culture. Urban events and installations compete for attention, not the least, through color. Instantly mirrored on Instagram, color permeates our real and virtual worlds. Cormier + Associés and TOPOTEK 1, at times, forcefully and surreptitiously work to surprise and alter reality. They employ visual games, optical illusion, and camouflage to alter the perception of the observer. Their color whimsy and color stories engender, expose, and diffuse tension, channeling it to creative ends and transporting people to a fantasy, blended real-surreal world. Hood is unconcerned with fantasy and the surreal. Instead, he stays close to reality by exhuming the past and shedding light on social wrongs and illuminating future possibilities.

Naughty Color: Monochrome, Claude Cormier (b. 1960)
Claude Cormier + Associés, Montreal, Quebec, Canada

We realized early on that color is actually extremely loaded, and we challenge that aspect within each project. ... It's amazing when you open up that possibility and try to bring a kind of magical element within it. When you start playing with this, you realize how much potential it has.

Interview, *Harvard Design Magazine*, 2013, 46

In 1994, during his study at Harvard Graduate School of Design (GSD), the Canadian landscape architect Claude Cormier read an article in the *New York Times* about painting burnt grass green during the summer. He had an idea for a lawn project at the Canadian Center for Architecture (CCA) in Montreal, where a decade earlier as a junior landscape architecture student at the University of Toronto he had done a landscape management project. The CCA lawn, burnt from winter frost, was yellow in the spring and looked dreary for the museum's opening in early May. Armed with new ideas, Cormier thought of a new solution: painting the CCA lawn blue. He described his rationale:

> Green is made of yellow and blue. If you remove the yellow from green, you get blue. Additionally, blue is the color [brand] of this institution. It represents and gives it identity. So I thought it would be great to paint the lawn blue in the early spring, and when the grass grows back, the blue will disappear, and the green will come back. It was the idea of composing a tableau, a landscape experience for the visitors. By taking the yellow out of the green pigment, the whole perception of landscape is completely challenged. And for a short time, you create something completely new.[1]

Following his graduation from Harvard, Cormier proposed the idea to the CCA director (Figure 9.1). The spray-painted blue grass sample they tested was well received, but there was little time and no budget to protect and wrap everything around the lawn—paths, walls, poles—during the spraying. The project was never realized.

The blue lawn design was Cormier's first major encounter with color, which would remain one of his most productive landscape design elements. It was the context at Harvard, however, that more broadly invigorated him to think through color. Much like Martha Schwartz, his mentor at the GSD and with whom he worked in 1993 and 1994, who had discovered the power of color by spray painting the ailanthus trees in her parking lot purple, Cormier discovered the magic effects of painted objects on human perception, as he recounted in the epigraph.[2] Although Schwartz's work set Cormier on the road to developing his style, history and theory classes he took at Harvard with professors Elizabeth Meyer, Mirka Benes, and Linda Pollak freed him to explore landscapes as artifacts. Cormier realized that, although they worked a century apart, both Schwartz and the 19th century landscape architect Frederick Law Olmsted built artificial landscapes—Schwartz with reference to culture and the visual arts and Olmsted to nature. Gaining an understanding that Olmsted's Central Park and Schwartz's Bagel Garden are equally artificial was a breakthrough in his career development and he decided to marry the two. "It is a kind of postmodern attitude. I take a bit of this and a bit of that and bring them together. This is where the notion of genetics comes into play."

Cormier grew up on a dairy and maple syrup farm outside Quebec City. His early interest in plant breeding—his dream was to invent a new flower—led him to enroll in agronomy at the University of Guelph in 1982.[3] "In genetics you cross two equal things together and create an improved hybrid that will respond and adapt to a new reality, such as sugar or salt spray. Like in genetics, I cross ideas together to create something new." When he opened his own studio in Montreal in 1995, Cormier felt that crossing contemporary and historical ideas yields a strong signature, one that did not feel historical but was loaded with history. After 25 years of practice, his first monograph, *Serious Fun: The Landscapes of Claude Cormier* was published in 2021.[4]

Cormier's work aims to wake audiences up and forces them to take a fresh look at their surroundings. Projects are idea-driven, with a clear and simple concept that "meticulously guides all aspects of the project, from global organization to the finest construction detail. This results in complex, consistent environments that communicate loudly and clearly."[5] Communicating the concept and personality of each site is important, and "As a conceptual tool, color can be essential to reinforcing and referencing that idea, creating mood, forming an image, and defining the persona of the project. If rightly done, it can be impactful." Together, idea, materiality, and color create an experience that people can describe. Color is not simply decoration; it has meaning.

9.1 Blue Lawn, design proposal, plan (top) and sample test of spray-painted blue grass (bottom), Canadian Center for Architecture, Montreal, Canada, 1996–7.

(Unless noted otherwise, drawings and projects in Figures 9.1–9.10 are by Claude Cormier + Associés.)

Gender, Identity Politics

Operating between urban design, public art, and landscape architecture, Cormier's landscapes evade convention and celebrate the artificial—artificial but not fake: not being fake means being original and authentic. A good example is the temporary Blue Stick Garden (1999–2009) at the Métis International Garden Festival in Quebec. Cormier elaborated on his ideas:

> People will not drive six hours from Montreal to see the same flowers they can see at the local botanical garden. They expect to see something new about gardens, something exciting. So, instead of planting flowers, like Gertrude Jekyll, we thought we would plant sticks, but with the same principle. We used the two colors, blue and red, to reference the poppy that grows in Métis.

The Blue Stick Garden, a rectangular space "planted" with 3500 garden stakes of varying heights on a grid, is a pointillist version of Jekyll's flower borders. Each stick was painted blue on three sides in reference to the Métis signature flower, the Himalayan blue poppy, with the fourth side painted red-orange, like the poppy's stamen[6] (Figure 9.2). The painted wooden stakes gave festivalgoers the experience of a garden in blossom from day one and throughout the year. As people walked around the garden, they experienced a slowly shifting gradient from blue to orange, unevenly across the field—some parts completely red or blue, others part blue and part red. Moreover, because of their varied positions relative to the sun and one another, the hue on each stick changed at any point in time and across days and seasons, much like a flower. As photography over the years attests, the Blue Stick Garden never looked the same.

Cormier is intuitive yet highly calculated about color choice and material. His color-saturated projects—Pink Balls, Lipstick Forest, Blue Tree, Blue Lawn, Blue Stick Garden, and others—derived their color from a simple concept and identifiable reference. Since color is always referential, it can be used as a subversive tool. He explained: "We realized early on that color is actually extremely loaded, and we challenge that aspect in each project."[7] Challenging preconceived ideas about color, as in the CCA lawn proposal, is one of Cormier's color strategies. He admits, though, that in his early career, color was also a way to be loud. It was about self-affirmation; with age and renown, it became less important. As he acknowledged:

> I look at the earlier work, it was very gutsy. I love that. But it's youth that did that. … I think at some point you stop having to scream to show that you exist, and … aging does that to me.

The use of pink, a signature color of Cormier's, is unmistakably related to contrast and meaning; it's visual-physical seduction. Pink contrasts well with gray, beige, blue sky, and green foliage, which are present by default. In the iconic Pink Balls in Montreal (2011–16), pink conveys both softness and powerfulness. As a strong feminine color, which does not represent nature, it can be used to challenge accepted professional concepts of natural and unnatural. In public space, the soft, intimate, sexy, and feminine pink participates in the political and cultural discussion of gender. Gender plays a key role in the color overtones of Cormier's work. He has confronted color gender associations head-on and has made great strides.

A defining precedent to the Pink Balls was Lipstick Forest in Montreal's Palais des Congrès (1999–2002). A winter garden had been commissioned for the building's north lobby; partly because there was no interest or budget to maintain a real indoor garden, Cormier introduced the idea of artificial nature instead. A comment by the Minister of Culture that the building was very masculine triggered Cormier's somewhat seditious proposal defying the status quo of gender reception and discrimination: 52 majestic, concrete tree trunks painted hot pink, a color that will be highly visible from the outside. To sell his idea—Cormier says he is a salesman—he took the logo of Montreal, the hot pink, lipstick-painted kissing lips, that attracts international tourism to the city, and recycled it for the project, pointing to its popularity, sex appeal, and European flavor. He recalled the logic:

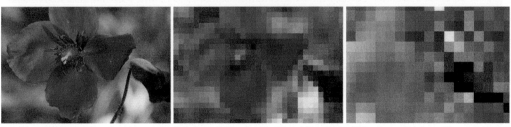

9.2 Blue Stick Garden, temporary installation, Métis International Festival of Gardens, Quebec, Canada, 1999 (top and middle) and concept drawing (bottom row) drawn by Claude Cormier + Associés and Louise Tanguay

It was different from the rest of American culture and Canadian English culture. I thought, let's borrow that pink and make this artificial forest with big trunks, floor to ceiling. Let's use tree trunks that would reference a forest that we have in our mountains and boulevards to create a force within the room. Instead of making it brown, we would do lipstick color, a hot pink that would somehow make reference to this Montreal logo.

Cormier uses simple naiveté to "naturalize" his rationale. Borrowing and fusing the prevalent silver maple street trees (i.e., nature) and the city lipstick color logo does not seem radical to him (Figure 9.3). The unspoken gender allusion of the lipstick and color did not escape anyone—and early project reviews did not go well.[8] Nonetheless, the leading architect of the building trusted Cormier's vision and rescued the project. Cormier's crew built and brought one trunk into the hall for a test; the scene created commotion, and construction workers called his crew "faggots." The incident deeply angered Cormier, who continued fighting for the project. It was approved and built, only to be greeted by a media ruckus of both contempt and acclaim. Now, 20 years on, still standing, the forest is a loved icon of Montreal. Seeing people on television news lining up to get their COVID-19 vaccine in the Palais des Congrès with the forest in the background brought Cormier great joy. "If the color is right for the project, it is not going to fall out of fashion," Cormier observes philosophically.

Eight years after the Lipstick Forest and other successful projects, the Pink Balls installation (2011–16) at Sainte-Catherine Street East in Montreal's Gay Village met with no resistance. The village's Business Association launched the project to revitalize the declining neighborhood, calling for projects to create a "signature threshold" that would be experienced day and night.[9] Cormier's proposal, Pink Balls—170,000 recyclable resin balls in a ribbon-like canopy hovering 20–30 feet over ¾ mile of the street—cleared all the fire codes and functional hurdles and engendered great enthusiasm (Figure 9.4). Neither the public nor the city asked why the installation was pink. "But they all knew why. It could not have been green or yellow. It was a gender identity question that I just wanted to put forward, … and they did not object to it." The bold oeuvre drew throngs to the neighborhood. The five subtle shades of effervescent pink balls created a striking visual and atmospheric experience. It became a source of pride and a social and economic catalyst for the community.[10] The installation remained for six years, until its color faded—and was replaced by Cormier's 18 Shades of Gay (2017–20).

At first, Cormier resisted the rainbow scheme of the LGBTQ community flag for the follow-up installation; he wanted to find a different way to talk about gender identity. Ultimately, he catered to the colors of the flag, extending its 6 spectral stripes into 18 gradations, keeping the same linear progression of hues. It was flamboyant and strikingly photogenic. The color spectrum represented identities as plural, diverse, inclusive, and nuanced. Crowds came to the many music and art events under the multihued canopy and took innumerable selfies of the spectacle. The different colors of the canopy created different atmospheres of modulated light and shadow. The piece touched a political chord and gained international attention, branding the neighborhood. The Italian magazine *Domus* featured the rainbow street project in an issue titled "Room for Diversity."[11]

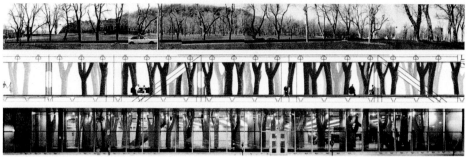

9.3 Lipstick Kiss, concept drawing, drawn by Claude Cormier + Associés and Paprika (top). Lipstick Forest, permanent installation, Palais des Congrès, Montreal, Canada, 2010, 2002. Street trees, collages drawn by Claude Cormier + Associés and Jean-François Vézina

9.4 Pink Balls, views from below and above (top) and installation plan (bottom), Montreal, Canada, 2010, 2011–16. Photos: Marc Cramer

In these and other projects Cormier's landscapes make visible things kept under the carpet, thus awakening latent preconceptions. At a fundamental level, though, he operates on human perception through optical games or tricks, whimsy, and simple joy.

Visual Games, Camouflage, Pun, and Flavor

Cormier likes to play games with the viewer. His work has been characterized as "explorations into the mechanics of vision and the manipulation of the viewing subject's expectations in confronting a landscape."[12] Techniques for manipulating observation through camouflage have been integral to landscape design since its establishment in the 18th century. Among them, plantings to hide undesirables, trenches to replace boundary fences, and topography to disguise the artificiality of landscapes, favored by Repton, are the principal techniques.

To make landscapes look artificial, Cormier uses camouflage to subvert, trigger thought, and produce spectacle or pun. Color is central to the optical disguise and to the reference it carries. The green paint of the fountain in Dorchester Square in Toronto was chosen to mimic the color of the tree foliage in the background and blend the fountain with the landscape. In the summer the fountain almost disappears, visually melding into its background; in the winter it is vibrantly present against the naked brown trees and white snow, coming to life when everything around it (including its water jets) is asleep. The color also dazzles people, defies visual expectations, and introduces a subtle irony, a commentary

9.5 Blue Tree, concept drawings (left) and temporary Installation (right), Cornerstone Festival of Gardens, Sonoma, California, USA, 2004. Photo: Geneviève L'Heureux

on the city's initial desire to get rid of the fountain to ease traffic. The camouflaging color compliments the fountain's self-concealing shape: viewed from the park, the fountain looks like a classic Victorian-era fountain; from the road, it looks like someone sliced a fountain-shaped cake and attached a sculpture of a pileated woodpecker on its flat backside.[13]

Cormier's optical game of making objects disappear is most compelling in the Blue Tree (2004), an installation at the Cornerstone Garden festival in Sonoma, California, where he completely covered an old tree in Sonoma sky-blue resin balls. Blue, a color he had used extensively for referencing and blending with the hue of the sky, also referred to the status of the tree: it was slated to be taken down, and (from afar) the blue balls effectively made the tree disappear; a closer look suggested that the tree had contracted a parasite that disfigured and transfigured it (Figure 9.5). The Blue Tree against the blue sky was an awe-triggering attraction.

In another project, the unrealized Commissioners Park in Toronto (also named after its concept, Camouflage Park), Cormier used a military camouflage pattern to organize the park's complex spatial composition. In a twist, the camouflage design was intended to make visible the site's invisible history as a munition storage site.

The play on visual expectations in the rose garden project next to Toronto's Four Seasons Hotel Plaza (2012) employed semantics to create a mischievous pun for spectators. The garden is in the form of a rose and displays chairs painted in rose, but no roses. It is green year-round. In the adjacent plaza, with an elaborate "carpet" whose pattern references a Victorian jewelry box, colored granite cobblestones surround a super-scaled crimson cast aluminum Victorian fountain.[14]

Another visual game plays out in Berczy Park (2017), located between Toronto's Old Town and Financial Districts. Here, Cormier's typical limited artificial color palette diverges, with a clash of real and superreal color (Figure 9.6). The park redesign needed to accommodate a rapidly diversifying community with seemingly incompatible demands—dog walks, children's play, strolling, and seating. Cormier addressed the conflicting demands through a single focal point, a fountain that creates a unifying experience for all. Combining traditional and contemporary, Olmsted and Schwartz, the classic dark blue-gray cast-iron fountain is surrounded by 27 sculptures of life-size, superrealist dogs and one cat, all painted glossily in superrealist colors. Waterjets in each dog's mouth aim toward a cast golden bone atop the fountain, while the cat appears riveted by two cast birds on a lamppost on the opposite side of the plaza. As owners show up with their dogs, the mix of real and superreal

9.6 Berczy Park, real and "super-real" dogs at the fountain (top) and drawing of centerpiece fountain and accessories (bottom), Toronto, Canada, 2017. Photo: Industryous Photography

283

produces a hyperreal *mise en scène* for a hyperrealist society.[15] In addition, the surrounding three-tone, granite, checkered paving pattern is skewed, stretched to amplify the triangular shape of the block and to extend the view, a typical optical trick to make a small park feel big.

Cormier's design for Sugar Beach in Toronto plays on the color of flavor and conjures sweet taste, like Schwartz's pastel-colored Necco garden, with its sugary whiff from the nearby Necco factory in Boston. A mile west of the HTO Urban Beach, where Cormier teamed up[16] to create the iconic yellow umbrella beach, Sugar Beach features its own iconic sugar candy color of light pink. At a beach where no swimming is permitted, the sugar-boat moorings at the Redpath sugar refinery across the slip were targeted as a viewing spectacle for those relaxing, walking, or gathering for events (Figure 9.7).[17] "In Sugar Beach, the sugar-coated color came first, and then the fiberglass of the umbrellas, and all the rest," said Cormier. The 2012 Canadian landscape architecture Honor Award described the novelty of the project:

> With the fragrance of sugar in the air, the park's conceptual reference is experienced in both sight and smell. Sugar as concept was used to establish a language for many

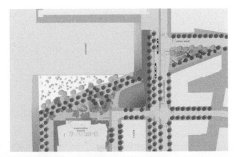

9.7 Sugar Beach, plan (top) and aerial view (bottom), Toronto, Canada, 2010. Photo: Jesse Colin Jackson

of the elements throughout the park, from the red and white bedrock candy stripes on the park's two outcroppings, the soft confection-like pink of the umbrellas, and even the candy cane pattern on the stainless steel ventilation pipes for the fountain mechanical room buried under the promenade.[18]

At Sugar Beach, the protagonists are 36 permanent umbrella-shaped shade structures the color of pink bubble gum (Figure 9.8). Designed by the industrial designer Andrew Jones for all-season exposure, they dot the "white sugar" sand, which was brought by barge from Chardon, Ohio (local sand did not look good, and turned almost gray when it rained). The imported sand is luminescent, even in the rain; it feels soft underfoot and compacts well. It is dotted with 150 recycled white plastic Adirondack beach chairs. The "color flavor" is a tour de force:

> The pink animates the space year-round and in all sorts of weather, against the pure blue sky and grey sky, alike. And when the sugar factory is in shadow and the umbrellas in sunlight, you have these hot pink disks against a dark background … pops against the white snow in winter.[19]

All other material colors, including the promenade's paving pattern, are muted to avoid competition with the soft pink and white scheme except at night, when a dynamic water feature is illuminated in bright pink light.

Adding to the sweet flavor are two large granite rock outcrops in the event space. These ancient rock formations were carefully cut, relocated, transported, and pieced together at the site. They recall the outcrops that Olmsted appropriated for Central Park in 1857 and the more recent neighbor in Yorkville Park (1994), Toronto, created by Martha Schwartz, Ken Smith, and David Meyer. At Sugar Beach, though, the rocks (and ventilation pipe of the nearby fountain) assume a new "persona," that of a "Candy Cane Rock," through the application of thermoplastic red and white stripes across the rock's cuts (Figure 9.9). Cormier's drawing of a barefoot woman in a soft pink dress seated on the candy-rock on the beach, with a palm tree and ocean backdrop, captures the surreal quality of the site, of being transported from the city to a balmy ocean beach. The drawing appeared on the poster of the exhibition

9.8 Sugar Beach, pink umbrellas in winter (top) and summer (bottom) scenes

285

9.9 Sugar Beach, aerial photograph of candy outcrop and grass hills

"Erratics" (2010), which also featured the firm's work, and has become an icon of the project (Figure 9.10).[20] Spare in details, its flat and abstract cartoonish style has become Cormier's favorite representation—"It forces you to enter the drawing in a different way."

Photographic Mediation, Cartoon, Collage, and Superrealism

The website of Claude Cormier + Associés has no project descriptions, only photographs of built projects and drawings: the images explain the project. The drawings Cormier uses for design development, representation, and selling of a project vary from abstract cartoon to collage to superrealism (the latter is used primarily for developers, never for a design competition). "A drawing does not need to represent and sell reality. I like drawing as art form. It could suggest something other than reality. A good drawing, like an artifact, should be open to interpretation." Collage and abstract drawing strategically reveal important details, whereas realist drawings do not produce that level of attention, he explained.

Many of Cormier's representations are "visual citations," photographic precedents from nature and art that explain his ideas.[21] To sell the Sugar Beach proposal he used Georges Seurat's painting *Bathers at Asnières* (1887), which shows people lounging along the Seine with billowing smokestacks in the background. It encapsulated the "soul of the park," the democratic idea of summertime urban recreation, and being in the city and able to look out at water and the horizon. To appease those who opposed the naive fountain scene at Berczy Park, considering it kitsch, Cormier presented several paintings populated with dogs, and created a miniature mock-up of the fountain with charming ceramic figurines of all 27 dogs.

Cormier also plays with makeovers of famous paintings or scenes to familiarize or defy objectors to his eccentric ideas. To convince review panels and developers, he often uses lengthy slide lectures of artworks replete with subjects or color that are deemed inappropriate, such as the presence of dogs in art for the Berczy Park project. His paper and

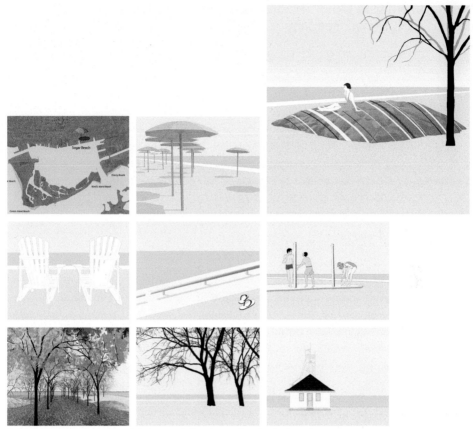

9.10 Sugar Beach, cartoonish concept drawings of main design elements

cardboard collage over David Hockney's reproduction of *Paper Pool 25* (2013) was done for the 52 Garrison Point project in Toronto to show the spectacular view of the city's towering skyline over the grand public pool. He created and sent a postcard of the nativity scene, showing figurines of the Holy Family and wise men under a pink umbrella canopy, to thumb his nose at an objector to the size and color of the pink umbrellas.

In today's hypervisual culture, the experience of both project site and website are mediated through the (photographic) frame of both computers and camera lenses, so Cormier relies heavily on photographic representation.[22] To demonstrate the translation of Jekyll's flower gardens into a field of sticks in the Blue Stick Garden, Cormier enlarged an image of a poppy flower into its pixelated version; the tacit reference to the Impressionist brushstrokes that inspired Jekyll is readily recognized (see Figure 9.2). For the Blue Tree, he used Photoshop to progressively erase portions of the existing tree and, instead, simulate the gradual covering of the tree with blue balls using a format akin to film montage. In both cases the tree seems to evaporate (see Figure 9.5).

For Place Ville Marie in Montreal, where the city's Museum of Contemporary Art resides during its transformation, Cormier's proposal for a permanent installation, L'anneau/The Ring, to be constructed in spring/summer 2022 "throws a wrench at the entire color discussion." "It's colorless, and yet it has a huge presence and ability to speak about timelessness."

Instagrammable Color: Radiance, Martin Rein-Cano (b. 1967)
TOPOTEK 1, Berlin, Germany

Color is visibility. Color is immediacy. Color is assertiveness. . . . Color is fantasy. . . . Color can cultivate the strange, like in Alice in Wonderland.

Color makes people feel present and human in the age of blended real-surreal. The romantic English landscape referenced pictures. Today, our point of reference is the internet, the contemporary medium of seeing and drawing. Color creates a crossover between the real public space and the new public space — the internet. . . . As landscape architects, we need to provide both the poetic and the instagrammable. The [internet] manipulates our places. In turn, we can misuse it. Color can be a driver, a connector, or a catalyst of this process. It works because it moves people, it's instagrammable.

WebEx interview with the author, 2021

Martin Rein-Cano, the founder of TOPOTEK 1, began his love affair with color in his first large commission, the Postindustrial Park State Horticultural Show in Eberswalde, Germany (1998–2002), where full-blown experiments with an idiosyncratic program, scale, surface marking, details, and color began in earnest.

Among the show's small, fantastical exhibition gardens—inspired by a 19th century "cabinet of curiosities," retrofitted industrial vestiges, and other entertaining venues—were two bold color design moves: a very long orange bench, modeled after the ubiquitous *Berliner Parkbank*, and a plaza for special events with an asphalt surface painted in a pink and purple camouflage pattern (Figure 9.11). The elongated bench seamlessly weaves through the park, projecting ambiguity about its meanings and giving its users a sense of ease and unease alike.

All the design elements were installed during the day, except the pink and purple plaza, which was done under cover. TOPOTEK 1's first daring color move entered the project mischievously, and just a little deceitfully. To secure its approval and lest the client reject the pink surface, TOPOTEK 1 submitted a black-and-white version of the plans, with the color scheme written in very small print. "It was easily overlooked, and the plan was authorized without any problems," recounted partner Lorenz Dexler.[23] When the client came to document the installation process with a television crew, the painting team put a paint roller in the client's hand and encouraged him to join in. The story goes the expression on his face was one of absolute horror. Bold color choice became the firm's design signature—there was no need to hide it in future projects.

Color plays a central role in the design narrative and visibility of TOPOTEK 1. "One of the big problems of landscape architecture is its nonreadability and nonvisibility," explained Rein-Cano, echoing Martha Schwartz, one of his models.[24] He aims to put the craft of the designer on display and erase the seeming "naturalness" of the lingering practice of 18th century Romantic English landscapes. "Architects are allowed to be loud; we are expected to be quiet, invisible, a little bit pretty, and always cute. And that's not a role that works for every project, definitely not for me," he said, adding "Color has been truly a question of visibility."

Rein-Cano traces the origin of the landscape architecture tradition of color to its landscape painting origin and to André Le Nôtre's elaborate parterres de broderie,

9.11 Postindustrial Park and State Horticultural Show, alternative floor color concept drawings for special events area (top left), photographs during and after construction (top right), and views of extra-long "Berliner Parkbank" (bottom), Eberswalde, Germany, completed 2002

(Unless noted otherwise, drawings and projects in Figures 9.11–9.19 are by TOPOTEK 1.)

which used plants as pigment and etched graphics on the ground. TOPOTEK 1's shift from plant color to asphalt color is part of the evolving romantic and baroque garden traditions. As Rein-Cano put it, "The idea that we create pictures is related to our work with colors. Colors are part of the design palette and the way we work; they are at the core of that tradition." More broadly, art and color provide greater freedom to expand the possibilities and definitions of gardens. The pigmented asphalt coating at Eberswalde Park proved a breakthrough for the firm's color design; the color charts of the pink and purple surface are proudly displayed near the studio's central events hall. Negotiations over landscape color design are common and inevitable. What is less common is the centrality of color stories that frame and live on in many projects and fill many pages in the publications of TOPOTEK 1.

The name TOPOTEK 1 is derived from the merger of *topos*, the Greek word for "place," and "tek," from "architecture" or "tectonic." Rein-Cano coined "topo-tecture," shortened to "topotek," to position his practice in the realm of making places as opposed to buildings. Since Frederick Law Olmsted and Calvert Vaux coined the term "landscape architecture" in 1863, generations have tried and failed to replace the profession's indistinct and partly plagiarized name. Rein-Cano insisted on a new name: "Landscape architecture is something that has left us under the radar, because we are not real architects. We are like the wife of someone," assuming the spouse's last name. Brimming with confidence, he capitalized and numbered his firm's name, TOPOTEK 1, in anticipation of more Topotek firms to come.

Like its contemporaries, the studios of Schwartz, Blaisse, and Cormier, TOPOTEK 1 operates at the margins of the profession, overlapping with art, urban design, and architecture, the latter division recently added to the firm. This insider-outsider professional position reflects Rein-Cano's personal history.

Born in 1967 in Buenos Aires, Argentina, to a Jewish Polish-Lithuanian father and a Spanish mother, he moved with his family to Germany in 1980 at the age of 13. He founded TOPOTEK 1 in Berlin in 1996, after studying art history at Frankfurt University and landscape architecture at Karlsruhe Institute of Technology and Leibniz University Hannover. The medium of landscape as an artform that is subject to change and time appealed to him, providing an alternative path to the prevailing functionalist, quantitative research and ecological landscape design approaches. His internships with the Swiss landscape architect Dieter Kienast for a year and at the office of Peter Walker and Martha Schwartz in San Francisco in 1993 led Rein Cano to emphasize strong graphic design. He grew fond of op art, which uses optical illusions, and of land art (Earthworks); both have been influential in his surface design.[25]

Literature is another source of inspiration. The postmodernist philosophical thoughts on the fantastical and the act of interpretation of the Argentinian Jorge Luis Borges, one of Rein Caro's favorite writers, have had an enormous impact on his work. The firm's design signatures—a mixture of fantastical and associative and the use of ambiguous, strange, and at times extreme elements, touched by humor, irony, and the surreal—find their origins in Borges. Like him, Rein-Cano and TOPOTEK 1 question the primacy of the "original text" of a site and engage in purposeful fragmentary and mistranslations. This approach produces narratives that enrich the original text and the identity of the place.[26] Not unlike the mediation of English gardens through the paintings of Nicolas Poussin and the imaginary landscapes of Claude Lorrain, TOPOTEK 1's response to the reality of a site is mediated through literary and cinematic concepts and images from the internet.[27]

"Chemotherapy," Visibility, and Ambiguity

Color is central to the immediacy and staged artificiality of TOPOTEK 1's landscapes. Rein-Cano wants landscapes to show quick results. He appreciates that rhythm and time may be poetic, but in the competition for visibility in today's world immediate results are just as desirable:

> I like the idea of color as an immediate momentum, an attraction that unlike plants does not take years to become beautiful. Some places just need some plants and a little bit of aspirin. But a poor neighborhood can't wait years to get results. *Certain projects are so sick, they need chemotherapy*. [Synthetic] color has exactly this immediacy of presence that plants sometimes cannot produce [italics added].

Designing a quiet refuge from the world is not TOPOTEK 1's response to the world getting louder. Rather, it competes and creates even louder places. Instead of hiding the artificiality of the landscape, it uses color and other means to draw attention to it through visual contrast and brightness simultaneously distracting and mystifying it through ambiguity. The computer screen and its built-in color system inspire the choice of bright colors TOPOTEK 1 makes.

Castle Park in Wolfsburg (2004) is an example of the ways color makes statements about artificiality through ambiguity (Figure 9.12). Working with Wolfsburg's existing English landscape park, TOPOTEK 1 borrowed, emphasized, and inverted several inherent concepts, including its natural deceit and historical falsehood, by using color and other optical tools. The English park's cinematic stroll and concept of follies were accentuated, and adapted to modern time. New follies were made of polished stainless steel to reflect and thus "dissolve" them in the surrounding landscape.[28] The historically inaccurate existing park bench was exposed with pink paint, to puzzle visitors, and draw attention to the fact that the seemingly historical bench is in fact fake, dating to a later industrial period than the original castle. Trash cans near the park benches added to the ambiguity, drawing both attention and smiles. Wrapped with artificial turf, they alluded to habitually camouflaged utility elements. TOPOTEK 1 thus turned on its head Repton's deception strategy, making visual folly anchors invisible, traditionally unsightly elements prominent, and hidden falsehood visible. The color concept for the entire park, Rein-Cano explained, participated in the subversive scheme, showing "that these items are actually singular intrusions in the park and not historic."[29] By deploying color to blur artifice and nature, historic and fake, and past and present, TOPOTEK 1 bewildered and thus engaged visitors in a mental dialogue with the site.

The overriding color scheme for Castle Park hinged on an image model—the color seen in the multilayers of a halved red cabbage—a strategy the firm occasionally uses. TOPOTEK 1 transferred the reddish gradient of the vegetable to multiple elements in relation to their position in the park: dark red asphalt at the fringes becoming a lighter, earthy aubergine at the center. Two shades of pink were featured in rose beds, fences, and benches. The park's color design, Martha Schwarz noted, is nuanced and "brilliant as a visual disturbance."[30] Ole Hartmann, a TOPOTEK 1 team member, described the team's discipline for the color scheme: "not a single tulip was allowed to step out of line. The park reflected this stringency, and that is what made it unique."[31] The

9.12 Castle Park, concept drawings showing reddish color gradient of the red cabbage (top left) corresponding plan showing color gradient of paths (top right), and three views of multiple park elements: benches, horse paddock fence, and "inflatables" (top to bottom), Wolfsburg, Germany, 2004

design of Castle Park "translated" the existing site "text" by questioning, elaborating on, and conveying the readings in built form and color. Straightforward and simple, they dazzle, amuse, confuse, even irritate, but they do not impose. They are open to multiple interpretations and, sometimes, contradictory allusions that are devoid of preconceived, preclusive symbolism.[32]

TOPOTEK 1 is distinguished by its idiosyncratic attitude to signification. It uses markings and color to flout and evade the "meaning trap." The architect Pietro Valle has identified three rules that TOPOTEK 1 uses to assign color codes at a site: (1) arbitrary fixing of a specific meaning or value to a color; (2) transfiguration of the inherent color that gives meaning to an object; and (3) manipulation of color to affect perception of distance, space, and time.[33] Color thus gives presence to and estranges us from conventional codes and meanings as well as altering perception. Rein-Cano stressed "Significance derives from cultural ideas and social class, but it is not inherent in a color. It can change," adding:

> You can't escape meaning, but you can play with it. You can create new understandings. There are certain underlying meanings to colors, I think of red as blood, of heaven as blue, of green as vegetation. They are like the color's DNA. But still, even those meanings can be manipulated and read in very different ways. For example, green can also be the color of Islam.

At Castle Park, the usually brown or green bench was assigned new meanings by painting it pink, which produced mixed readings alluding to flesh, girlishness, sweetness, and more.

Perceptual discrepancies arising from visual ambiguity through contradictory readings, unexpected scenes, and surprise can also produce humor and irony. Humor, intended to disarm and loosen people up, is an integral part of TOPOTEK 1's kit of design tools. "Humor is in short supply in our daily life. Conflict comes in ample supply. What better place to invoke a laugh, a smile, than in public space," commented Rein-Cano. Among his tools are exaggerated scale, distortion, illusion, and misdirected and misused functions and rules.

Color jokes often produce a mixture of humor and irony (or perhaps anger, depending on the viewer's age and background). The Pink Inflatables, a temporary installation first used at Castle Park, is a prime example. In stark contrast to the green surroundings, 24 oversized, eye-catching, and moving inflatable sculptures in pink and baby pink evoked fascination, play, fun, and irony, simultaneously. Some kids saw in the air-filled rings, cubes, wands, balls, and bouncy mats a Barbie Dreamhouse or fantastic land of giants. For them, the pink inflatables were fun. Conversely, adults thought they were kinky, evoking adult sex dolls. Rein-Cano believes that whereas children can play with everything because their mind is free to imagine, adults find it difficult to play.

TOPOTEK 1's landscapes aim to kindle playfulness in everyone. Its public places are designed as playgrounds for mixed ages, instead of separate designated areas for adults and children. The outsized yellow picnic tables that TOPOTEK 1 designed for the National Horticultural Show in Schwerin in 2009 were placed in the water at the lakeside. The somewhat unusual bright yellow wading tables gave people permission to take off their shoes and have fun (Figure 9.13). Placing a common picnic table in the water might have been thought to be an oversight or bad planning, but the exaggerated size and unusual

9.13 National Horticultural Show, submerged yellow picnic tables, Schwerin, Germany, 2009

color helped to get the mischievous message across. Together, design and color instilled a sense of freedom, fun, and looseness.

The strategy of mixing commonly separate uses, such as playground and sculpture or picnic and water wading, invigorates activity and charges places with energy. In the case of the neighborhood revitalization project of Köpenick Old Town in Berlin (2007), TOPOTEK 1 proposed to convert two parking lots into public squares with dual functions: parking and playground at one, parking and market at the other. The needs of the neighborhood were incorporated. The layered everyday uses received a makeover through "chemotherapy treatment." The asphalt of the KAiAK (Kunst und Architektur in Alt-Köpenick) Market/Parking was painted blazing red, with standard parking lines in lilac and giant numbers (Figure 9.14). The flamboyant red of the vast ground surface was also used for the caravan ticket booth and a giant parasol. Rather than serving as a source of shade, the parasol acts as a messenger: when open, it means it's market day and the area is closed to cars; when closed, it means the square is available for parking.

TOPOTEK 1 imbues the surfaces and structures of spaces with messages responsive to thought and behavior, messages of function, history, and identity, or simply of beauty.[34] Built form and color, then, activate and tell stories. Stories, both inherent in a place and invented, are revived and created through the design process and thereafter. Color supports and engenders a place's stories and identities.

9.14 KAiAK Market/Parking, red painted asphalt and parasol open for events and closed for parking (vignette), AltKopenick, Berlin, 2007

Color Stories, Identity, and Marking

The narratives behind the project site and design are vitally important. "Places are both made of and make stories," says Rein-Cano:

> As designers, we need to create the story as much as the place. The story is part of the design, not something that will be created later. I think the identity of gardens or places becomes much stronger if they have a strong story that is told over and over. Obviously, we create part of the story. The story is then continued by someone else.

Open-ended stories make for successful projects that live on. Rein-Cano cites Lucius Burkhardt, a Swiss sociologist and economist, drawing on his theory of how people construct an image of a landscape, based on how they interact with their surroundings and interpret what they see. Burkhardt's idea of "tactile knowledge"—interactive reciprocity constructed by means of literary or cinematic narrative—convinced Rein-Cano that the perception of a landscape is highly dependent on the stories told about it.[35] He seeks to engage people in mental-tactile-kinesthetic experiences through stories, touch, and movement.

Among other design elements, TOPOTEK 1 exploits the implicit and pliable semantics inherent in color: its capacity to tell stories about people's reactions to it, the color decision-making process, and the origin or derivation of color. Color is the first thing people see, to which they react and on which they love to remark. Color decision making can therefore be fraught with conflict. Color choices are influenced by the site and by personal and cultural preferences.

> Color ... alters the atmosphere, it touches people .... Color charges people the same way that iPhones do. Color sets up the mood, like the overture in opera, or an appetizer to a meal. It triggers your eyes and appetite in preparation for what's to come.

In Superkilen in Copenhagen (2007–12), designed by TOPOTEK 1 in collaboration with Bjarke Ingels Group (BIG) and Superflex, the triad color scheme of red, black, and green plays a crucial role in the concept of the overall project (Figure 9.15).[36] In a linear sequence of public spaces, color defines the identity of each of three activity zones and, as importantly, of the users: the Red Square, a plaza for large parties and events; the Black Market, a formal urban living room and trendy meeting place; and the Green Park, a grassy area for picnics and sports, with paths for biking and walking. Superkilen's vast color floor surfaces intermittently infiltrate the adjacent vertical building façades.

Superkilen is located in an ethnically diverse, mostly immigrant, working-class neighborhood. The Red Square, Rein-Cano explains, is meant

> clearly to create contrast to the grey city of Copenhagen, to make a clear statement about being different. 'I came here. I am an immigrant. I am foreign, but I am joyful. And it's fun to be here. I can contribute even if I am different. I do not have to become the same.'

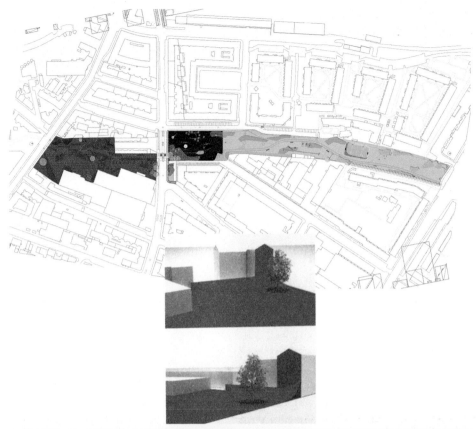

9.15 Superkilen, designed with Bjarke Ingels Group and Superflex, plan of linear color-coded public space sequence (top), CAD-Design concept rendering (middle), and aerial photo of the Red Square (bottom), Copenhagen, Denmark, 2012

Contrast has become part of Superkilen's story over time.

Rein-Cano's fondness for reds is seen in other projects. He likes it because, in contrast to other colors, like blue and green, red is ambiguous, unfriendly, and agitating. Red "is life and death, at once. It feels aggressive. But it is also the color of love, Christmas, lipstick … and so, it is a very ambiguous color." An anecdote about Superkilen's signature red demonstrates his point:

> When we tried to push the red for Superkilen, most of the people were against it, saying that red is aggressive. In that area, aggression was a problem. … But then, in one of the meetings with people from the neighborhood, around November, an old lady with a loud grandma voice said, "red is the color of Christmas." Then the whole discussion was over, and everyone was convinced that red was the right color.

Bjarke Ingels elaborates on the story about the debate over the red:

> The discussions about colour were amazing, and the amount of suspicion was enormous. … When they complained about the red—"Red is the colour of death and blood"—I answered, "It is also the colour of Christmas and love." One of the representatives in the jury got truly offended, because he thought that the colours were referring to the Palestinian flag: red, black, and green. And they also thought that the plan looked like a Kalashnikov. … Luckily, there was a veiled woman from some Middle Eastern or African background who supported us. She was quite silent, and then she said … that the colour in the project is very refreshing, and she recommended that we fight for it.[37]

The color debate continued. After the color coating company produced the color samples—four shades of red: two more orange in tone, two more magenta—people in the community thought the colors were too loud.[38] They were invited to propose alternatives in the spectrum of red, but when their color choices were printed, their brown shades were unacceptable to the designers. For Rein-Cano brown is a color of status quo, an incoherent mixture of a world that has become less coherent. It tries to gloss over the cultural differences of people living next to each other. Ultimately, the client broke the logjam and convinced the community to trust the specialists. There are likely several variations of Superkilen's color narrative; what is important is the inevitable stories that built colors trigger. "Convincing people," added Rein-Cano, "is part of the story."

The black of the Black Market has its own story. Its color and name reflect its early function as the main place for selling drugs in Copenhagen. This was not a selling point for the community. Fortunately, Ingels recalled, the community meeting in which the color was discussed took place in a new building the black floor of which was very attractive.[39] The Black Market's color reinforced and materialized the story about the place and, at the same time, erased its bad reputation. Like a blackboard, the black asphalt surface invited markings. White stripes, like those on common roads, animate the space, choreographing movement among dispersed objects and trees (Figure 9.16).[40] Akin to topographic contour lines on a map, the spatial illusion

9.16 Superkilen, Black Market, view of small hill with road markings on blacktop asphalt (top left).
Photo: Torben Eskerod. Skateboarding on the asphalt hill (top right). Aerial view (bottom)

9.17 Superkilen, Red Square, wall and paving color (top left), color samples (top right), street view (middle), and aerial view (bottom)

effectively turns two into three dimensions, changing flatness to volume through optics and kinesthesia. The ground appears to be pressed by force and to swell, an effect reinforced by a small asphalt hill, called "the bump," which is enjoyed by skateboarders. The bump turns into a green hill and leads into the Green Park. TOPOTEK 1's use of the vast, dark ground surface as a drawing medium with added topographics creates spatial ambiguity and encourages visitors to explore directions and scale.[41] The lines (and sometimes numbers) also suggest codes of behavior, which become catalysts for activity and negotiation.

The pavement at Superkilen is entirely asphalt, TOPOTEK 1's favorite paving material. With color applied to the unpretentious, ubiquitous asphalt, the surface appears to belong in the domestic realm of the living room, as a soft and welcoming carpet (Figure 9.17). The effects are due to painstaking experiments with pigment durability. The Red Square's color coating is made of polyurethane with sand and red pigment, the Black Square's asphalt is mixed with aggregate black stones, and the bicycle and pedestrian paths in the green zone are asphalt with liquid polyurethane coating in two different green colors.

The colors, objects, and planting in each zone are carefully coordinated with the dominant red, black, or green. For instance, in The Red Square, Royal Red Maple and cherry plum accord with the red surface, and in the Black Market, Atlas and Lebanon cedars and windmill palms tend toward the gray (Figure 9.18). The color backdrops unify the many different objects dispersed in each zone, many of which were selected by community members and brought from different countries.

Superkilen's built form and color thus offer both visual coherence and disruption. The expression of color is entirely appropriate to the heterogeneous and fragmented community. Its notable presence on the internet both perpetuates and reconstructs the narrative and shapes its experience.

Real/Surreal, Alice in Wonderland

TOPOTEK 1's landscapes straddle the real and the surreal. Rein-Cano maintains that the idea of constructed atmospheres through imported objects, of creating alternative or "surreality," has always been part of the garden tradition. The Romantic garden, too, felt like an otherworld. Scenes, edifices, statues, plants, and cultural traditions from around the world have found their way into the garden. The design and experience of gardens have always been mediated, shaped through drawings, paintings, photography, magazines, story books, film, and now the internet. They have been a place of illusion, imagination, divergence from reality. TOPOTEK 1 continues this tradition, creating otherworldly atmospheres with contemporary means, where color looms large.

"Someone said about Superkilen that it looks like Photoshop," Rein-Cano observed. "Superkilen is an updated English Romantic garden, following a similar principle of copy and paste, a modern way to bring surreality into reality. Color has much to do with that." Color produces moods and stimulates the imaginative power of the beholder.

> It can cultivate the strange and surreal, like in Alice in Wonderland. There, things change in scale and color, reality is distorted, rabbits are speaking …. Superkilen has been photographed so much. … it is present on the net more than in reality. It has a double life …, it is both a dream and a real place.

Rein-Cano provides an alternative to both the prevalent position—"I am landscape, I am real, and I don't need Instagram"—and its poetic counterpart—"I want nature, I am calm, a counterpoint to the hectic world." He considers reality and the internet to be closely linked, even interchangeable, and exploits this duality, using and manipulating the internet.

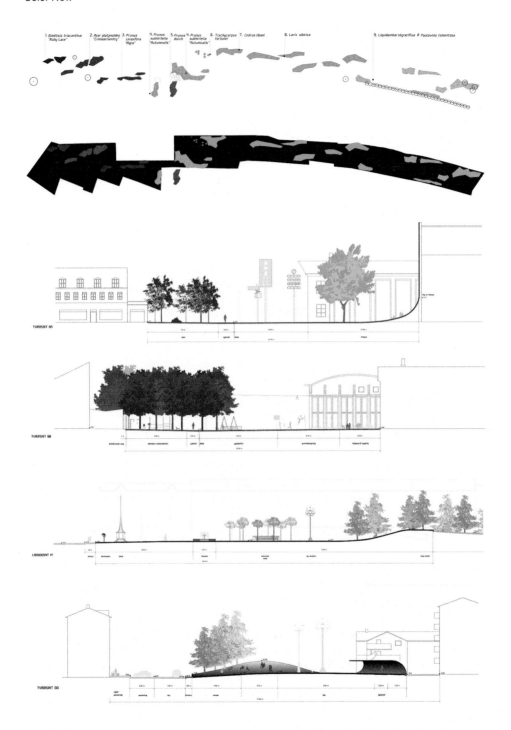

9.18 Superkilen, planting plans (top two) and sections through the Red Square and Black Market (lower four), 2009

Rein-Cano loves the fantastic staging of the banal, following Borges's literary genre. Whether highlighting the romantic and bizarre in Eberswalde Park or the functional and odd scale in KAiAK Market/Parking, TOPOTEK 1's landscapes are created with eloquent expression in response to the basic requirements of communication, visual and social activation, and humanity's place in time. The firm inhabits and amplifies the present. Rein-Cano explains: "If you are in the moment, you are more eternal than if you try to be eternal. That's my strategy of eternity. The present will change for sure. Change, not fixity, is eternal." Then he ponders, "if the red in the Red Square survives several years, will it become classic?"

By countering green with conspicuous radiant color TOPOTEK 1's landscapes leap out visually and announce their artificiality. Considering the loaded meaning of nature carried by green and the stigma of landscape architects as green planners, green is not an expected color in its projects. But it is not rejected outright either.

9.19 Evergreen Heerenschürli, detail of wall and rails (top), bird's-eye view (middle), and detail of double-layered fence (bottom), Zurich, Switzerland, 2010

In Evergreen Heerenschürli, in Zurich (2005–10), green has taken over the entire sports complex and neighborhood park, except for the gray roads and paths. Entirely artificial, the place stays green and active year-round with artificial turf in several fields and it is light both day and night (Figure 9.19). Arranged like city blocks and streets, the design consists of planes in shades of green. What is commonly a functional, gray sports facility was turned into a lively place by framing each field with double fences made of highly durable polyethylene terephthalate (PET) colored coating on metal wire: an inner yellow green layer and an outer dark green layer, producing a dynamic moiré effect.

TOPOTEK 1 color design exploration interrogates the dualities of nature and artifice, past and present, authentic and fake, communal and fragmented society, real and surreal, and analog and digital.

Rhythms of Color and Light: Black, White, and Blues, Walter J. Hood (b. 1958)
Hood Design Studio, Oakland, California

Painting was a way to get away from green. It was a way to stop doing these plans where everything was green. At the time, it also meant moving away from the ethnographic work that I was doing [in academia]. It was a way to differentiate myself, from Martha [Schwartz], George [Hargreaves], or others. That's where I got really interested in jazz and blues and ways of incorporating multiple rhythms in the work. One of those ways came about with color. Color kind of freed me up to create multiple rhythms.

WebEx interview with the author, 2021)

When "Urban Diaries" (1995–7), a traveling exhibition by Walter Hood, showed at Iowa State University's College of Design, it made a powerful impression on my colleagues, students, and me. I knew Walter from our master's study at the University of California, Berkeley in the late 1980s. By the mid-1990s he was doing work no one else did and established himself as a rising landscape architect of a different kind: dynamic, unrestrained, and deeply committed to racial equality.

The "Urban Diaries" exhibit of hybrid watercolor-photo-drawing collages and mixed-media models and constructions displayed small neighborhood interventions in Oakland, California—miniparks, playgrounds, and community centers—based on daily encounters and observations of locals and their stories. Hood's landscape redesign projects were humble, joyful, and idiosyncratic, providing the backdrop for the colorful drama of everyday life. The exhibit showed a riot of color rare in landscape architecture and urban design representation and was published in a book-catalogue of the same title (1997).[42]

In an earlier publication, *Blues & Jazz: Landscape Improvisations* (1993), Hood—searching for a personal response to the environmental inequities of the Black community, his community—tapped African American daily rhythms through the arts, notably music, as expressed in the epigraph.[43] Blues and jazz foddered his imagination and creativity. "As a design process in the African American arts and craft tradition, improvisation reveals as much about accepted culture parameters as it does about an individual's creative process."[44] *Blues & Jazz* featured composite drawings of black-and-white photography and line drawing as well as photographs of design models and people, the latter by the photographer Lewis Watts. In *Blues & Jazz* Hood was still somewhat restrained, ensuring the drawings' recognizable architectural rigor. But by the time he got to *Urban Diaries*, he says, "I was just painting." A decade later, in the mid-2000s, his iconic polychrome design expression shifted focus to material and light. An idiosyncratic artist, a member of the Black community, and a member of academia and scholarly discourse, his career has been a balancing act, a three-prong maneuver between defiance and subversion, caution and innovation, art and intellect.[45]

Hood grew up in Charlotte, North Carolina, in a segregated neighborhood. When he attended an integrated school in junior high, for the first time he started being around people who didn't look like him. He was drawn to the arts but, as the first in his family to go to college, an art degree was not an option. Instead, he enrolled in architecture at a historically Black college in Greensboro, but then switched to

9.20 Courtland Creek, perspective concept drawings, oil pastel on board, Oakland, California, USA,1996–7.

(Unless noted otherwise, drawings and projects in Figures 9.20–9.28 are by Hood Design Studio.)

landscape architecture. Working for a few years in private and public offices, Hood felt at odds in conventional practice and decided to return to the rigorous, intellectual world of academia to develop his own distinctive art practice. After earning double master's degrees in landscape architecture and architecture from Berkeley, in 1991 he founded Hood Design Studio in Oakland.

Hood's self-expression was influenced by Watts, whom he met in 1992, and the architects Herzog & de Meuron and the artists Andy Goldsworthy and James Turrell, with whom he worked on the de Young Museum in San Francisco in 2005. Watts' black-and-white photographic characters changed how Hood looked at Black landscapes and people. Watts' portraits and landscapes showed familiar people, circumstances, and places that Hood saw in his own neighborhood and had recorded in his diaries for some time.[46] He was intrigued by Herzog & de Meuron's design, which was done with actual material and mock-ups and few drawings, by Goldsworthy's close attention to the medium of landscape, and by Turrell's use of light as an art medium. These practices inspired Hood to pursue a Master of Fine Art at the Chicago Arts Institute to further center his landscape design practice in the cultural arts. His early color-saturated drawings and recent focus on material color and light are vested with the power of improvisation and invention.

For Hood, light is linked to the idea of double consciousness, positive and negative, life and death, hope and despair, joy and sorrow. If color intrigues, light reflects. If color frees, light grabs. Hood's shift from bright colors to light and shadow and to black and white resonates with a deeply held conviction about shedding light on Black history and racist institutions. In addition, it reflects a deliberate refrain from color stereotypes and evanescence. He prefers to focus on things that last.

Painting versus Drawing, Field versus Figure

One of Hood's early projects, Courtland Creek Park in Oakland, California (1996–7), was the first one in which he was intent on bringing color to a place. In the former streetcar corridor in an underresourced neighborhood, he planted a circle of redwood trees and created a promenade with 150 purple-leaf plums in a double row over a sidewalk of cracked reddish-brown granite. Densely planted—15 feet apart rather than the standard 30–50 feet—the trees are a dark red-purple most of the year. But in the spring, the formal allée bursts into life with clouds of pale pink blossom against the creek's wild green background and eclectic neighboring yards. The park's monoculture planting plan was disapproved of by environmentalists who prefer diversity of plants. But Hood insisted on a more powerful effect, on difference rather than diversity. "I wanted color to manifest in a bold way in a place that didn't have color," he wrote.[47] This approach "started to resonate in [my] work," he recalled, "and every [low-income housing] project that I was working on, ... I mean, the most mundane projects I was working on, came alive through color. Even the renderings that I would do for them were more [like] paintings." Color entered these sites through planting and painting, steeped in a kind of speculative dream that both lifted communities from obscurity and distinguished his practice.

The initial drawings he presented to the residents of the Courtland Creek neighborhood were typical landscape architecture office drawings that bored everyone. Hood remembered: "There was nothing exciting. I remember going home and saying, 'I need to make people excited,' and I took crayons ... and [colored] the purple trees purple on whited-out areas of black-and-white photos." The final "drawings" were then done with oil pastels on top of black-and-white photos of the neighborhood (Figure 9.20). In perspectives or axons, the oil pastels "brought both the drawings and the people who looked at them to life." Hood was looking for ways to inspire people in disinvested environments, where he worked at the time. He wanted to make beautiful things to look at, and the drawings he did were transformative.

> Through collage, I constructed nine perspective drawings, highlighting houses and other familiar elements. The drawings were crude—for instance, I showed red trees vividly rendered in oil pastel. They conveyed not a pretty[,] homogeneous park, but something different. They included people's lives, and their context. The collages, with black-and-white photos I had shot juxtaposed with the mix of colors, proved arresting. Unknowingly, I was embracing the cultural turn in design and planning. I was seeking ways to bring in new narratives and representations.[48]

The beauty of the drawings and the landscapes represented their environment through the collage technique, yielding new narratives rooted in place. When he presented several of his early images to colleagues at Berkeley, he remembers one of them saying, "'How dare you experiment on these people?!' They looked at the work and they thought I was doing this crazy art." Using bold colors and expressing artistic freedom seemed a travesty to genteel academics, who typically expect paternal solutions in marginal places like community gardens. Not Hood. "Color," he explained, "was the thing that I used to improvise. It allowed me to reshape things and to create things anew. With color I can create double negatives. I can create things that intrigue people."

The drawing techniques that Hood used in the 1990s were inspired by a couple of architects: the Italian Aldo Rossi (1931–97) and his mentor at Berkeley, Lars Lerup (Figure 9.21). Their hybrid drawings—composites of mostly oblique perspectives, plans, and elevations saturated with color—were both painterly and architectural. The two architects occupied the margins between architecture, design, and art and displayed an enigmatic position that recalled the metaphysical resonance of the painterly smudge of the futurist artist Giorgio de Chirico (1888–1978), among others.[49] Some of their drawings feature paint or thick watercolor with heavy black lines, dark shadows, and color contrast. The colors are intense, luminous, and dramatic. Other drawings display fine lines that speak to conceptual rigor while flouting graphic conventions. Their drawings had "a kind of power that was neither standardized nor Pop," says Hood.

Hood stopped doing line drawings and started painting around the time he was in Rome and completed the Courtland Creek project in 1997.

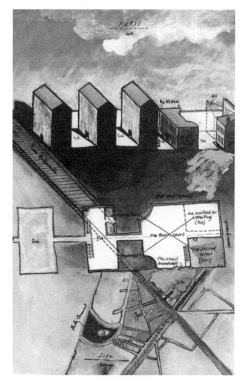

9.21 Lars Lerup, "Planned Assaults," 1987

307

Drawing requires looking at line and profile rather than seeing the space and atmosphere which is what interested Hood. In his essay "Color Fields," he described the act of painting color fields as a kind of reverse sketch, from figure to field:

> Danger: landscape architects can become trapped and confined to the lines of the sketch they first put upon the page. At this point the drawing ceases to be the vessel for experience and observation in the environment, and becomes itself a subject of uncritical appreciation. To better understand the ideas possessed in the sketch, it can be useful to reinterpret what we have first drawn. One method is to reverse the relation of figure to field, by painting the negative space, by treating it as a positive.[50]

The color field distills the essence of the landscape by translating forms into fields that project a personal experience and ambience. Drawing, according to Hood, is independent of the self, to a certain degree, because one can practice and get good at drawing forms. But in painting fields, "one, literally, has to see the space, not just fill it; one has to be able to feel the space." He recommended oil pastels over pen and ink, often in combination with black-and-white Xeroxed photography with parts of them whited out. The rich colors of oil pastels felt the closest to painting; their flexibility enabled improvisation.[51] Painting, then, was a way of seeing landscapes anew. Hood embraced color as a painter and enjoyed sharing his paintings with others, free of the constrictions of landscape architecture.

This is when *Urban Diaries* emerged, its tenets perhaps the articulation of Courtland Creek Park's design. Community everyday patterns are enhanced and bolstered; activities range from social and communal to illegal to inappropriate—from drug dealing to car repair.[52] Among the programmed and unprogrammed areas are youth meeting spaces with hard-paved surfaces for ball games and a peewee basketball court, a lawn along the creek edge for field games, dog play, and neighborhood parties, and walls allowing for garden terraces and seating (Figure 9.22).

Urban Diaries tailored design interventions to a portfolio of local characters and circumstances around West Oakland, with color and everyday narratives central to the design. Hood's journal entries of the daily life of neighborhood residents describe

9.22 Courtland Creek, perspective drawing of double row purple-leaf plums (left) and photograph of same view a few years later (right)

experiences at the corner liquor store, in the front yard and on playground, clandestine meetings on the street or in the backseats of cars, liminal transactions on sidewalks, and more (Figures 9.23). By examining ordinary people and mundane spaces and objects around him, Hood found new meaning in the everyday.

The *Urban Diaries* became an outlet for his expression and shaped very different landscape design proposals that reinforce Black history and culture. "Colonialism is about sameness. It takes difference and makes it into sameness. It does that to promote and maintain its construction," Hood explains.[53] People who have been overlooked for generations, reduced to a group demographic, and subjected to planned landscapes that never worked were suddenly given individualized attention. Hood turned each diary entry into a programmatic layer in local park or street projects, producing vibrant and nonnormative spaces: "Many of these proposals transgress the boundaries of normative societal norms and planning in neighborhoods and open spaces. They validate 'familiar'

9.23 Durant Minipark, Day Three: The Perch, page spread, *Urban Diaries*, 1997

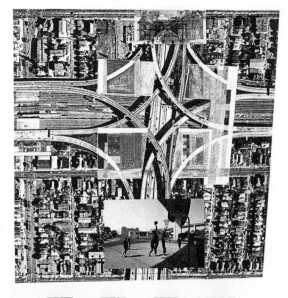

9.24 Grove Shafter Park/Freeway Park, Day Three: Community Center, site analysis of the freeway interchange (top), composite plan (middle), and community center over the freeway (bottom), *Urban Diaries*, 1997

activities, events, and patterns of life without applying moral judgments."[54] The drive-through brothel neatly fits in the neighborhood street, the prostitute's home is next to the church, and the church and a recycling center nestle under the freeway interchange viaduct. All is brightly colored to set the right tone and mood.

The drawings and models in *Urban Diaries* are filled with everyday joy. Hood's enjoyment of reds, blues, yellows, and purples is evident. "Once I stopped using green, I started using primaries. You can't get it wrong with primary colors." Durant Park glows in blue with purple and blue walls on day three ("The Perch") and is equipped with yellow recycling bins on day five ("Recycling Bins") (Figure 9.23). At the 25th Street Park tripartite programmatic areas are delineated with color: the children's play yard has polychrome asphalt blocks and concrete paving, two treehouses in red and yellow anchor a steel tension bridge, and wood plank tables grace the park's corner, anchored by a red concrete block hearth with two surface grills for barbecues. And in Grove Shafter Park, the main space of the community center that spans one of the nine quadrants of the freeway interchange, is painted golden. Its façade, a steel frame structure with thin cut marble inlays, catches the light and shadow as it spans the scar of the freeway (Figure 9.24).

Hood's work has continued to raise difficult questions about the ways landscape design can play a more significant role in people's lives. He does not attempt to solve problems, he tries to make them visible. Making things visible has become central to Hood's work, and not necessarily through color.

In-Visibility, People of Color

Coming to California's open, brown landscape from North Carolina's green, enclosed woodland gave rise to a major change in Hood's appreciation of color and light:

> When I was back East, I never had this kind of predilection toward color, because the light was just different, and also you're *in* the landscape. On the West Coast you are always looking out at the landscape, and so color and changing light became just amazing. My biggest question was, 'Why don't landscape architects use color in the same way?'

He began studying color and light in paintings by California painters, and looking at light through color. This practice coincided with the early, low-income projects, where color helped people to see light. But as his commissions grew larger in scale and budget and included projects in well-to-do areas, color was no longer needed. "With more investment and funding, color doesn't figure as predominantly as some other things that bring light to places." Gradually, Hood began looking at light, rather than color, in space. He still paints in the studio, but light is what engages him most in landscape projects.

Light is both a concept and a design tool in Hood's goal to expose and undo manifestations of years of racist planning doctrines:

> It's important to allow these issues and histories *to come to a greater light and clarity*, because now more people are interested in trying to understand this predicament than I've ever seen. ... I'm trying to put something out in the world that has been covered up, erased, which might allow people to see the world and themselves in a different way [italics added].[55]

Hood's latest book, *Black Landscapes Matter* (2020), and his recent projects focus on unearthing hidden layers.[56] For example, his master plan for the Rosa Parks neighborhood in Detroit explores the history of the movement for racial equality.

The idea of light was also inspired by Robert Farris Thompson's 1983 book *Flash of the Spirit*, which elucidates the death rituals and grave decorations that came out of Africa, particularly West Africa. Several rituals relate to the idea of light and the spirit of the dead or evil spirit—lamps used to lead the spirit to heaven, glittering glass bottle trees to block or ward off evil spirits, and flowerpots adorned with tinfoil turned inside out to evoke the flash of the departing spirit.[57]

Shadow comes with light, and Hood is interested in the relationship between the two. In his Shadow Catcher Commemoration (2004), with landscape architect Cheryl Barton, he created a layered, skeletal steel pergola that marks the site of an African American homestead on the South Lawn of the University of Virginia campus in Charlottesville; the shadow of a solid overlaid cutout on the grid outlines on the ground the house of the seamstress Kitty Foster. Other interventions include the depressed gravesites of Black laborers who served the university and the removal of strips of turf to reveal buried stone pathways and porch areas.[58]

The racial events of 2020–1 gave renewed prominence to Black history and entrenched inequities in the United States. But for Hood Black people have remained invisible. The association of dark skin with uncivilized and subordinate status and the preference for fair skin persist. Hood does not avoid these realities:

> Within the American context a black body is feared in space. I've walked down sidewalks where people just literally cross the street in front of me. You see five black people on a corner and people are freaked out. The idea of the pigmented body in space is something that's been marginalized on one hand, and characterized on the other. That creates its own kind of spatial fear. It is a kind of spatial neglect, that you're almost invisible to a certain degree.

The Black body in space has become a subject for Hood's investigation. He appreciates that Watts' photographs document Black landscapes and people unapologetically and show them as omnipresent, "not as spectacle." He adds that "[i]n this way, we become familiar with the image of the Black male as a person, the Black youth as children who run and play, the Black woman as beautiful, and the elderly as possessing beauty and dignity, people who exist in the same space as everyone else."[59]

His design for the International African American Museum (IAAM) in Charleston, South Carolina (under construction), explores the presence of the Black body at the site of the notorious Gadsden's Wharf, where it is believed that at least 40 percent of Africans landed, were sold, or died. It is a somber and yet hopeful landscape in black and white, set against the blue of the Atlantic Ocean and skies (Figure 9.25).[60] The paved floor of hallowed ground of the museum site is embedded with seashells, used in African tradition to enclose the soul's immortal presence. Visitors strolling between two black marble walls will encounter two rows of sculpted Black kneeling slaves against their own silhouettes on the reflective walls (Figure 9.26). They will then arrive at a shallow pool that extends into the ocean. At the bottom of the pool they will see the outline of unimaginably crowded bodies in the hold of the transport ship. White, curved lattice walls will evoke the memory of "hush harbors," secret spaces where slaves would gather to share stories and keep traditions, away from the watchful eye of slave owners. Unlike Hood's other landscape projects, bright colors, often associated with traditional African American arts and crafts, did not enter the IAAM color scheme.

Color Stereotypes, Material to Last

The equation of bright colors with "primitivism" lingered through modernist architects. Frank Lloyd Wright, for instance, characterized Black people as being childlike and simply enjoying music, dance—and bright colors; about a school building he was designing in 1945, he wrote, "The Darkies would have something … exterior of their own lively interior color and charm."[61] Cognizant of this history, Hood refuses to succumb to such stereotypes:

> For [places with] people who look like me and other minorities, many designers' immediate go-to is color. At times, this attitude infuriates me because they don't spend any time trying to understand the place and people. The first response is, 'Oh, let's do a mural, let's paint the columns.' And I go, 'Well, you wouldn't do that in North Berkeley. They wouldn't let you do it in North Park.' I mean, you wouldn't do it in these other places where people invest in real material.

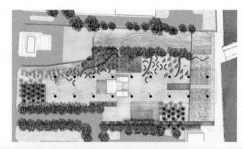

9.25 International African American Museum (IAAM), plan (top) and perspective drawing (bottom), Charleston, South Carolina, USA, 2021, under construction

9.26 IAAM, perspective drawing

9.27 Seventh Street Transit Village, Dancing Lights, Oakland, California, USA, 2012

He avoids unrestrained polychrome schemes, using instead monochrome and primary colors. Blue, with its sky, water, and music connotations, is the most prominent color in Hood's projects. The sky-blue rain catchers in Baisley Park, Queens, New York (2008) allude to water, while at the Seventh Street Transit Village in Oakland (2012) the royal blue dancing light poles with their bright blue and red nightlights remind one of the once prominent local blues and jazz, reflecting the music's melancholy (Figure 9.27). The massive gateway that spans Seventh Street displays pixelated+, black-and-white portraits of prominent Black leaders, with gray-blue areas changing to bright purple at night.

As a designer, Hood does not look to imitate the vernacular. Bright colors in African American or Latino neighborhoods, he explains, can turn into pastiche. Luis Barragán created amazing walls and atmospheres based on what he had seen around him, not through imitation. The tried and tested vernacular is an authentic process of generations. Hood wants to understand how a process has transpired and changed and extend that tradition.

Shared and celebrated vernacular landscapes have produced distinct physical environments, such as the iron and bricks of Savannah and Charleston or the "shotgun houses" of Black families in the South. As in music, fashion, and the culinary arts, landscape improvisations, not copying, can reshape something new out of the old and familiar.[62] In the Awakening installation (2001), part of Project Row House: Shotguns 2001, Hood took inspiration from African American quilts to evoke the spirit of the shotgun house. The quilts, made of circles, squares, strips, and diamonds from discarded clothing and fabric scraps pieced together by women in multicolored compositions, inspired in Hood an understanding of the improvisational design process. He improvised using poplar wood strips fashioned into five objects with different rhythms, patterns, and compositions. Instead of the traditional polychrome quilts, he painted the wood orange, a color he selected so that it would stand out against the context.[63] The shotgun house was white outside, the interiors were pale yellow, and the orange wood strips glowed through the windows. Hood's color choices originated from the specific context, culture, place, and time—and avoided stereotype.

The primary colors Hood used in early projects to escape the spatial and propositional green tropes of landscape freed him to find "nonobjective fields" of place, culture, and atmosphere. In places with no investment or maintenance, color came with plants and was cheap and had an impact. He avoided using pigmented material, like concrete, which fades and looks cheap over time, exposing neglect. "I want to make things that last. I want real material." Materials like stones have their own coloration. In larger projects with bigger budgets Hood uses durable and more expensive material. For example, the green sandstone paving at the de Young Museum came from Scotland; its blue and brown veins reflected as many different colors, from green to ochre to yellow.

Recently, Hood completed Double Sights (2019), a public art installation on the campus of Princeton University. Two shiny stainless steel columns, a white column leaning on a vertical black column, are each etched with images and positive and negative quotations by former US president Woodrow Wilson, who was also the university president. The black and white columns reflect the light and the buildings—and the people around (Figure 9.28). Color enters through reflection and refraction. The Courtland Creek and Double Sights projects, a generation apart, seemingly make opposite color statements but, in fact, are quite similar: the early project brings color and beauty to a gray place, and the more recent project sheds light on covert history. Both create contrast through a design that reflects the dualities of Hood's practice—real and metaphysical.

9.28 Double Sights, Princeton University, Princeton, New Jersey, USA, 2018

As more vibrant colors permeate the public realm and digital formats are tethered to a given mode of computer color representation, Hood retreats further from color into the rhythm of light and the quietude of material color. He prefers real material mockups and fewer drawings. The cultural pulse and color rhythms seen in the drawings in *Landscape Diaries* have given way to the standardized computer drawings of Hood Design Studio. "With the loss of the original it just seemed like filling in or rendering drawings," Hood reflected. But while his color seems to have lost its beat, material's juncture with light forms a new beat. Light matters.

Notes

1   WebEx interview with the author, May 7, 2021. Unless otherwise attributed, Cormier quotations are from this conversation.

2   *HDM* editors, "Claude Cormier + Associés," 2013.

3   In 1986 he received a bachelor's degree in landscape architecture from the University of Toronto.

4   Treib and Herrington, *Serious Fun*, 2021.

5   Claude Cormier + Associés website, https://www.claudecormier.com/en

6   See Herrington, *On Landscapes*, 2008, 14–16; O'Connell, "Layers Revealed," 2001.

7   *HDM* editors, "Claude Cormier + Associés," 2013, 46.

8   Ibid.

9   LILA, "18 Shades of Gay, Montreal," 2021.

10 See Palavecino, "The Best Architecture and Design," 2011, 42.

11 See Bürklein, "Humour, Please," 2019.

12 Waldheim, "The Landscape Architect as Camouflageur," 2010, unnumbered.

13 Barth, "Hell of Fun," 2020.

14 Like Petra Blaisse, Cormier's floor patterns display strong graphics, many taken from textile design patterns. Some are ornate and flowery as a Victorian wallpaper; others, geometric and classic, like tweed men's wear.

15 LILA, "Berczy Park, Toronto," 2021

16 Cormier worked with Janet Rosenberg + Associates Landscape Architects and Hariri Pontarini Architects on HTO Park.

17 For a description of the project, see Roche, "Lure of the Water's Edge," 2014.

18 LAM editors, " 2012 ASLA Professional Awards," 2012, 152.

19 Jost, "How Sweet," 2013.

20 Hutton, *Erratics*, 2010.

21 Cormier's own work has been exhibited in art museums. See *Les Peluches*, a large mosaic of over 3000 stuffed animals nailed to plywood backing.

22 It has been suggested that Cormier's photographic mediation of landscape observation harks back to the Claude glass, a small, tinted convex glass credited to the 17th century French landscape painter Claude Lorrain and used by 18th century tourist travelers to observe and draw landscapes. Waldheim, "The Landscape Architect as Camouflageur," 2010.

23 Steiner, *Creative Infidelities,* 2016, 20.

24 WebEx interview, April 23, 2021. Unless otherwise attributed, Rein-Cano quotations are from this conversation.

25 Richardson, "Topotek 1," 2008, 298.

26 Rein-Cano, "Where Do Things Go from Here?," 2016, 409.

27 Rein-Cano, "The Thoughts, Working Methods and Approaches of TOPOTEK," 2016, 217–19.

28 Rein-Cano, "The Thoughts," 2016, 218.

29 Steiner, *Creative Infidelities*, 50.

30 Ibid., 59.

31 Ibid.

32 Schröder, "Film AB! Roll It!," 2004, 15.

33 Valle, "Activated Surface," 2008, 53.

34 Schröder, "Thinking + Working," 2002, 15.

35　Rein-Cano, "Where Do Things Go?," 2016, 409. Also see Schröder, "Thinking + Working," 2002, 16; Schröder, "Instructions for Seeing," 2006, 338.

36　Steiner, *Superkilen*, 2013.

37　Steiner, *Superkilen,* 2013, 26, 28.

38　Ibid., 155.

39　Ibid., 26.

40　On the semantic possibilities of TOPOTEK 1's codified visual language, see Valle, "Activated Surface," 2008, 52.

41　Ibid., 44.

42　Hood, *Blues & Jazz*, 1993.

43　Explained during a WebEx interview with the author, May 18, 2021. Unless otherwise attributed, Hood quotations are from this conversation.

44　Hood, "Awakening," 2004, 79.

45　Hood, an architect, landscape architect, and artist, is a professor of landscape architecture at the University of California, Berkeley. He chaired the department (1998–2002) and was a fellow in landscape architecture at the American Academy in Rome.

46　Hood, "Ritual and Displacement in New Orleans," 2020, 134.

47　Green, "Black Landscapes Matter," 2020.

48　Hood, "Ritual and Displacement," 2020, 135.

49　For studies of Aldo Rossi's and Lars Lerup's drawings and paintings, see Zabala, "A Fat House for a Thin Man," 2021; Adjmi and Bertolotto, *Aldo Rossi: Drawings and Paintings*, 1993.

50　Hood, "Color Fields," 2008, 56–61, 59.

51　*LAM* editors, "Portfolios," 1993, 60.

52　Lawson, "The Street as Avenue for Community Expression," 2000.

53　Green, "Black Landscapes Matter," 2020.

54　Hood and Levy, *Urban Diaries*, 1997, 70.

55　Green, "Black Landscapes Matter," 2020.

56　Hood and Tada, *Black Landscapes Matter,* 2020.

57　Thompson, *Flash of the Spirit*, 1983.

58　Hood and Basnak, "Diverse Truths," 2015, 37.

59　Hood, "Ritual and Displacement," 2020, 152.

60　Hood Design Studio website, www.hooddesignstudio.com/iaam

61　Budds, "The Frank Lloyd Wright Project History Conveniently Forgot," 2017.

62　Hood, "Afterword," 2020, 178.

63　Hood, "Awakening," 2004, 82.

References

Claude Cormier

Barth, Brian. "Hell of Fun." *Landscape Architecture* 110, no. 4 (April 2020): 112–31. https://landscapearchitecturemagazine.org/current-issue/april-2020

Bürklein, Christiane. "Humour, Please." *Domus* 1034 (April 2019): 366–9.

HDM editors. "Claude Cormier + Associés: Interview with Claude Cormier." *Harvard Design Magazine* 36 (2013): 46–7.

Herrington, Susan. "Introduction." In *On Landscapes*, 1–17. London: Routledge (2008).

Hutton, Jane, curator. *Erratics: A Genealogy of Rock Landscape, Featuring the Work of Claude Cormier, Architects, Paysagistes*, exhibition catalogue. Harvard University Graduate School of Design, March 22–May 12, 2010.

Jost, Daniel. "How Sweet." *Landscape Architecture* 103, no. 1 (2013): 62–75. Accessed March 11, 2021. https://landscapearchitecturemagazine.org/2013/01/28/how-sweet

LAM editors, "2012 ASLA Professional Awards: Canada's Sugar Beach." *Landscape Architecture* 112, no. 11 (November 2012): 152.

Landezine International Landscape Award (LILA). "18 Shades of Gay, Montreal," July 2021. Accessed March 4, 2021. https://landezine-award.com/18-shades-of-gay-montreal

Landezine International Landscape Award (LILA). "Berczy Park, Toronto," July 2021. Accessed March 4, 2021. https://landezine-award.com/berczy-park-toronto

O'Connell, Kim. "Layers Revealed." *Landscape Architecture* 91, no. 9 (September 2001): 98–9.

Palavecino, Alejandro. "The Best Architecture and Design, La Rue en Rose, Pink Balls." *Azure* 209 (2011): 42.

Roche, James. "Lure of the Water's Edge." *Topos* 89 (2014): 30–5.

Treib, Marc, and Susan Herrington. *Serious Fun: The Landscapes of Claude Cormier*. Novato, CA: ORO Editions, 2021.

Waldheim, Charles. "The Landscape Architect as Camouflageur: Observing the Work of Claude Cormier." In *Erratics: A Genealogy of Rock Landscape*, exhibition catalogue. Harvard University Graduate School of Design, March 22–May 12, 2010.

TOPOTEK 1

Rein-Cano, Martin. "The Thoughts, Working Methods and Approaches of Topotek 1." In *Creative Infidelities: On the Landscape of Architecture of Topotek 1*, ed. by Barbara Steiner, 213–27. Berlin: Jovis, 2016.

Rein-Cano, Martin. "Where Do Things Go from Here?" In *Creative Infidelities: On the Landscape of Architecture of Topotek 1*, ed. by Barbara Steiner, 407–29. Berlin: Jovis, 2016.

Richardson, Tim. "Topotek 1." In Avant Gardeners: 50 Visionaries of the Contemporary Landscape, 298–313. London: Thames & Hudson, 2008.

Schröder, Thies. "Thinking + Working." In *Topotek 1, Thinking + Working*, ed. by Thies Schröder and Sandra Kalche, 14–17. Berlin: Aedes, 2002. Accessed April 3, 2021. https://www.topotek1.de/publications/thinkingworking

Schröder, Thies. "Instructions for Seeing." In *Topotek 1, Paradise Remix,* ed. by Kristin Feireiss, 334–40. Munich: Prestel Verlag, 2006.

Schröder, Thies. "Film AB! Roll It!" In *Schlosspark Wolfsburg, TOPOTEK 1*. Berlin: TOPOTEK 1, 2004. Accessed March 4, 2021. https://www.topotek1.de/publications/castle-park-wolfsburg-ii

Steiner, Barbara, ed. *Superkilen*. Stockholm: Arvinius + Orfeus, 2013.

Steiner, Barbara, ed. *Creative Infidelities: On the Landscape Architecture of Topotek 1*. Berlin: Jovis, 2016.

Valle, Pietro. "Activated Surface." In *Topotek 1 Reader*, ed. by Thilo Folkerts, 44–53. Melfi, Italy: Casa Editrice Libria, 2008.

Walter Hood

Adjmi, Morris, and Giovanni Bertolotto, eds. *Aldo Rossi: Drawings and Paintings*. New York: Princeton Architectural Press, 1993.

Budds, Diana. "The Frank Lloyd Wright Project History Conveniently Forgot." Fast Company, 11 July, 2017. Accessed April 12, 2021. https://www.fastcompany.com/90132505/the-frank-lloyd-wright-project-history-conveniently-forgot

Green, Jared. "Black Landscapes Matter." *The Dirt*, Interview with Walter Hood. Accessed June 24, 2020. https://dirt.asla.org/2020/06/24/interview-with-walter-hood-black-landscapes-matter

Hood, Walter. *Blues & Jazz: Landscape Improvisations*. Berkeley, CA: Poltroon Press, 1993.

Hood, Walter. "Awakening: Quilt Top Patterns in the Third Dimension." In *ROW: Trajectories Through the Shotgun House*, ed. by David Brown and William Williams, 78–89. Houston, TX: Rice University School of Architecture, 2004.

Hood, Walter. "Color Fields." In *Representing Landscape Architecture*, ed. by Marc Treib. London: Taylor & Francis, 2008.

Hood, Walter. "Afterword." In *Black Landscapes Matter,* ed. by Walter Hood and Grace Mitchell Tada, 173–8. Charlottesville: University of Virginia Press, 2020.

Hood, Walter. "Ritual and Displacement in New Orleans." In *Black Landscapes Matter,* ed. by Walter Hood and Grace Mitchell Tada, 134–52. Charlottesville: University of Virginia Press, 2020.

Hood, Walter, and Megan Basnak. "Diverse Truths: Unveiling the Hidden Layers of the Shadow Catcher Commemoration." In *Diversity and Design: Understanding Hidden Consequences*, ed. by Beth Tauke, Korydon Smith, and Charles Davis, 37–54. New York: Routledge, 2015.

Hood, Walter, and Leah Levy. *Urban Diaries*. Washington: Spacemaker Press, 1997.

Hood, Walter, and Grace Mitchell Tada, eds. *Black Landscapes Matter*. Charlottesville: University of Virginia Press, 2020.

Lawson, Laura. "The Street as Avenue for Community Expression: Courtland Avenue and Courtland Creek Park." arcCA 00.2, 2000. Accessed June 1, 2021. http://arccadigest.org/street-avenue-community-expression-courtland-avenue-courtland-creek-park

LAM editors. "Portfolios: Drawings of Landscape Architects." *Landscape Architecture* 83, no. 5 (1993): 60.

Thompson, Robert Farris. *Flash of the Spirit: African and Afro-American Art and Philosophy*. New York: Random House, 1983.

Zabala, José. 'A Fat House for a Thin Man,' Lars Lerup. *Quaderns*. Accessed June 5, 2021. http://quaderns.coac.net/en/2016/07/lerup

Postscript
Color Prospects

The function of color ultimately is not to present a distinct vision of the world but to prompt people to imagine another world for themselves and its full range of possibilities.

Elena Manferdini and Christina Griggs, "Color Corrections," 2020, 109

There is no single theory or approach in contemporary landscape color design, as in the cases of the preceding practices in Part III of the book. Color design is permissive; it can be democratic and inclusive or corporate and exclusive.[1] The vigorous color experiments that began in postmodern temporary landscape art installations in the 1980s, followed by garden festivals a decade later, inundated the broader landscape and public urban domain in the new millennium with colors previously considered vulgar or garish. The colors of the contemporary urban landscape are almost entirely new: completely synthetic or electrical, shiny, glowing, or flashing. Alongside this exuberant polychrome, one can also find quiet but no less powerful atmospheres of luminous softness, translucencies, and colorlessness.

Never a fixed idea, color is open to different interpretations now more than ever. It presents an exceptional opportunity for a range of voices—not only of designers—to engage with landscape—broadly interpreted—on their own terms.[2] Color is enlisted by civic rights groups in greater scale and boldness for political ends, thus changing the urban landscape. The rainbow colors of the LGBTQ community have moved from flags to urban surfaces such as pedestrian crossings, and on Pennsylvania Avenue last year, "Black Lives Matter" was painted in gigantic, bright letters that could be seen in low-orbit satellite imagery. Alternately, telecom and hi-tech companies emblazon their brand color in increasing scale for commercial ends. In Ghana, for instance, Vodafone paints its logos and brand colors on entire building façades.[3]

What does the future hold for landscape color design? As I have demonstrated in this book, the history of color in landscape architecture has been inextricably tied to three variables: (1) disciplinary traditions and ideas about nature and art, (2) the influences of related professions and cultural values, and (3) the media technology with which color is conceived, represented, and ultimately conveyed (whether through plants or built structures). These variables have been undergoing major changes. Boundaries between art, architecture, landscape design, and other design disciplines continue to blur, and designers increasingly mix techniques from different disciplines, developing a hybrid mode of practice. The long-held view among designers that nature stands in opposition to art or culture has continually been reframed: the idea of a benevolent nature is now being morphed into a deeper concern for the health of planet Earth that is directly impacted by people's behavior, bringing nature and culture together. These changes will free landscape designers to explore new material and color.

Contemporary landscape practices in the past two decades point to three future opportunities for landscape and urban colorism practices which I call Color Politics, Chromotherapy, and Mixed Reality Chroma.

Color Politics emphasizes the potential of color to change policy. As a recognizable emblem, color can dismantle hierarchies and stereotypes and engage cultural identities, including gender and race, as the works of Claude Cormier and Walter Hood have shown. The agency of landscape color to distinguish high, middle, and low class, used since Humphry Repton, has been gradually removed by Postmodernists, notably Martha Schwartz. The White hegemony on deciding what is good taste has been replaced by diverse taste agents. Strict and prescriptive chromatic narratives, such as landscape palette in modern landscape architecture, have become an expanded chromatic spectrum, allowing for a wider, more inclusive set of sensibilities. Color mixtures and palettes assume multiple social significances and political agency.

A prime example of Color Politics is Chicago architect and artist Amanda Williams, who has been harnessing color in the fight against racial inequalities. Operating in inner city neighborhoods, she uses the power of paint to force city officials to confront the invisible policies and forces of architecture and planning that misshaped these landscapes. Her Color(ed) Theory series (2014–16), done in the south side neighborhood of Englewood, was one of the 25 most significant works of postwar architecture selected by a group for architects, journalists, critics, and designers.[4] Williams' bold and often bright colors represent zoning maps and redlining the negative impacts of which have lasted for generations. At the same time, her color is a mnemonic device that carries cultural references specific to the Black experience. A house she painted turquoise, for instance, is named "Ultrasheen" after a hair conditioner, and a house she painted violet is named "Crown Royal Bag" after the whisky brand. Williams's palette speaks the language of difference, one that is meaningful to her own community, first and foremost.

The second practice, Chromotherapy, continues to explore the ability of color to remake neglected landscapes, invite social engagement, and forge place identity and attachment—as in the case of Hood's work and that of Martin Rein-Cano. During past interventions in run-down neighborhoods, designers opted for the power of cheap, yet impactful, paint to valorize space. Today, their temporary and permanent interventions in cities around the world use ever-larger, mostly monochromatic swathes of planting, walls, and pavements to try to uplift the neighborhood. Boa Mistura, the Spanish artist collective with roots in graffiti art, paint large-scale urban surfaces in projects, such as Guadalajara, Mexico (2018), to inject optimism and energy in disinvested neighborhoods. And, in City Lounge (2016–17), the architect Carlos Martinez and the visual artist Pipilotti Rist energize informal social interaction and created strong place identity with an all-consuming red. They threw a red rubber carpet over the ground and outdoor furniture in a revitalized commercial area of Bleicheli Quartier in St. Gallen,

Switzerland, thus turning public spaces into intimate domestic-like spaces—living room, dining room, entrance hall, and study.[5]

Mixed Reality Chroma, the third practice, continues to investigate color's ability to brand and reinvigorate public landscapes—akin to TOPOTEK 1's Superkilen and Schwartz's Mesa Arts center—in a hybrid real-virtual world. Color needs to keep up with shifting online consumer preferences and social media and, as such, to project the sensibilities of the time. The experiences people have in these mixed-reality public spaces have to be sufficiently good for them to want to snap photos and videos with their mobile devices and then transfer them to the internet—to Instagram, for instance—where place narratives instantly spread on social media and take on a new life. As computationally produced, color-filled designs increasingly end up on people's personal devices, the designs themselves are geared to compete for their attention, using strong colors and effects.[6]

Landscape and urban designers have to create compelling events and active play spaces that participate in both real and virtual worlds to draw children into the physical world, as they increasingly watch TV and play video games at home and like to share their activities with a group of friends who are part of their social networks, or even strangers on YouTube. Designers are developing strategies to integrate different elements from virtual worlds into physical space, such as screens that project and allow people to actively engage with them. For example, in their proposal WII-Playgrounds in Amsterdam the urban designers Helena Casanova and Jesús Hernández introduced a group of urban elements in public space that combine active video games controlled by body movements, with video screens that allow a wider audience to follow the games.[7] The new "hybrid reality" is attractive to children and, at the same time, activates urban public space with electronic images, sounds, and colors.

If there is a fourth direction in landscape color design, I believe it will come from solar system explorations and travels to Mars. Designs will draw from the colorful mosaic of natural and cultural systems at a grand earthly, even otherworldly, scale, from different time and light systems of other planetary landscapes whose images will livestream on our screens. As a result, landscape architects will use terms like real, super-real, and virtual as a means to reconceptualize new relationships with art, nature, technology, and each other. Future landscape design will invite us to reimagine and color the world in new sensibilities.[8]

Notes

[1] An excellent contemporary collection of color discourse and urban design practices is Doherty, "Urbanisms of Color," 2011.

[2] Manferdini and Griggs, "Color Corrections," 2020, 109.

[3] See Abbas and Osseo-Asare, "Color Coating/Coding in Ghana's Mobility Marketplace," 2011, 8.

[4] Soller and Snyder, "The 25 Most Significant Works of Postwar Architecture," 2021.

[5] See Casanova and Hernández, *Public Space Acupuncture*, 2014, 250–4.

[6] Printing space, another color space that applies to graphics and print media, is of minor importance in landscape architecture. New algorithms give digital images a greater range of more realistic color. It is becoming increasingly possible to compare, describe, and convert colors in different color spaces through standards issued by the International Commission on Illumination (CIE) for defining colors visible to humans based on the optical responses of our eyes.

[7] Casanova and Hernández, *Public Space Acupuncture*, 2014, 232–7.

[8] Manferdini and Griggs, "Color Corrections," 2020, 109.

References

Abbas, Yasmine, and D. K. Osseo-Asare. "Color Coating/Coding in Ghana's Mobility Marketplace." In *New Geographies 3: Urbanisms of Color*, ed. by Gareth Doherty, 7–11. Cambridge, MA: Harvard University Press, 2011.

Casanova, Helena, and Jesús Hernández. *Public Space Acupuncture: Strategies and Interventions for Activating City Life*. New York: Actar, 2014. https://issuu.com/actar/docs/public_space_acupuncture

Doherty, Gareth, ed. "Urbanisms of Color." In *New Geographies 3: Urbanisms of Color*. Cambridge, MA: Harvard University Press, 2011.

Manferdini, Elena, and Christina Griggs. "Color Corrections." *Log* 49 (Summer 2020): 105–9.

Soller, Kurt, and Michael Snyder. "The 25 Most Significant Works of Postwar Architecture." *New York Times,* August 2, 2021. https://www.nytimes.com/2021/08/02/t-magazine/significant-postwar-architecture.html?referringSource=articleShare

Index

Figures in *Italic* page numbering, tables and diagrams in **Bold** page numbering